THE U.S. NAVY SEAL / UNDERWATER DEMOLITION TEAM (UDT) HANDBOOK

1965

©2011 Periscope Film LLC
All rights Reserved
ISBN #978-1-937684-82-2
www.PeriscopeFilm.com

PROJECT EDITOR
T. Dunne, LTJG., USNR

DISCLAIMER:
This manual is sold for historic research and entertainment purposes only. It contains obsolete information about complex and potentially hazardous operations and techniques. It is not intended to be used as a present-day instructional reference or as part of an actual training program. No book can substitute for proper training by an authorized instructor.

This text has been digitally watermarked, and some attributes altered to prevent illegal duplication.

Originally printed in 1965.
This enhanced edition
©2011 Periscope Film LLC
All rights Reserved
ISBN #978-1-937684-94-5
www.PeriscopeFilm.com

"Let your plans be dark and as impenetrable as night, and when you move, fall like a thunderbolt."

- Sun Tzu, The Art of War

Table of CONTENTS

- 7 FORWARD
- 11 INTRODUCTION
- 12 HISTORY OF UDT

- 15 CHAPTER ONE BOATS
- 23 CHAPTER TWO COMMUNICATIONS
- 29 CHAPTER THREE DEMOLITIONS
- 55 CHAPTER FOUR DIVING
- 111 CHAPTER FIVE ELECTRONICS
- 125 CHAPTER SIX FIRST AID
- 131 CHAPTER SEVEN INTELLIGENCE
- 153 CHAPTER EIGHT MAP READING
- 159 CHAPTER NINE PARACHUTE OPERATIONS
- 171 CHAPTER TEN SURVIVAL
- 181 CHAPTER ELEVEN SWIMMER DELIVERY VEHICLES
- 189 CHAPTER TWELVE WEAPONS
- 199 CHAPTER THIRTEEN MISCELLANEOUS UDT OPERATIONS

- 216 APPENDIX I SELECTED WEIGHTS AND MEASUREMENTS
- APPENDIX II TECHNIQUES OF INSTRUCTING
- 217 APPENDIX III APPLICATION & QUALIFICATIONS FOR UDT
- 218 APPENDIX IV SEABAG CHECKLIST
- APPENDIX V WARBAG CHECKLIST
- APPENDIX VI UDT REQUALIFICATIONS
- 219 INDEX

RECORD OF CHANGES AND CORRECTIONS

Change No.	Date of item	Date of entry	Signature	Grade

The purposes of the UDT HANDBOOK are:

To provide, under one cover, a ready reference on matters of importance to members of Underwater Demolition Teams.

To provide information helpful to members of SEAL Teams.

To serve as a textbook for personnel undergoing Underwater Demomlition Team Training, in conjunction with the U. S. Navy Diving Manual (NavShips 250-583), Demolition Materials (NAVWEPS OP 2212), and supplementary handouts, as necessary.

To provide guidance for members of amphibious staffs responsible for the employment of UDTs, as well as any other persons interested in UDTs.

foreword

to the reader

This handbook has been designed to meet your needs (as outlined in the Foreword).

Since it covers so many topics, and since this is its first edition, it is bound to contain some inadequacies (and perhaps some inaccuracies).

Any suggestions concerning the improvement of this handbook will be welcomed. Use the form letter on the following page for this purpose. All suggestions will be considered when compiling the first revision to the handbook.

T. DUNNE
7 May 1965

Date

From:
To: UDT Handbook Representative

Subj: UDT Handbook; suggestions for improvement of

1. Following are my recommendations for improvement of the UDT Handbook:

--fold--

OFFICIAL BUSINESS

POSTAGE AND FEES PAID
NAVY DEPARTMENT

UDT HANDBOOK REPRESENTATIVE
c/o NAVAL OPERATIONS SUPPORT GROUP, PACIFIC
U.S. NAVAL AMPHIBIOUS BASE
SAN DIEGO, CALIFORNIA 92155

--fold--

introduction

From the earliest stages of preparation for an amphibious landing, numerous organizations are called upon to obtain intelligence information on the proposed landing area. However, during the final days and hours preceding the landing, two specialized organizations are called upon to perform amphibious reconnaissance and related tasks: Marine Reconnaissance Units and Underwater Demolition Teams. The following paragraphs outline the specific missions of these intelligence-gathering organizations.

<u>Marine Reconnaissance Units.</u> Marine Reconnaissance Units are divided into two types: the Force Reconnaissance Company ("Force Recon"). Both Force and Division Recons are tasked with reconnaissance of the landing area, and terminal helicopter guidance. However, Force Recon Teams are introduced clandestinely into the landing area prior to H-Hour, or prior to D-Day. Operating in four-man teams, they provide intelligence information directly to the Landing Force Commander. Division Recon, following Force Recon ashore, may be introduced before, or after H-Hour. Operating as platoons or companies, Division Recon gathers intelligence information for its own particular Division or smaller task organization, and relies extensively upon helicopters and light motor vehicles for mobility.

Force Recon personnel are trained as surface and SCUBA (self-contained Underwater Breathing Apparatus) swimmers, inflatable boat handlers, and parachutists. Division Recon personnel are trained as surface swimmers and inflatable boat handlers, and a limited number are trained as SCUBA swimmers.

As a rule, both Force and Division Recon personnel conduct reconnaissance landward from the water's edge.

<u>Underwater Demolition Teams.</u> Reconnaissance of, and clearance of the area from the 3 1/2 fathom curve to the High Water Mark, on a prospective landing beach, is the primary mission of UDT. "Clearance" could involve mines, or other man-made or natural obstacles. Additional primary tasks include channel location, marking and improvement; assault wave guidance; and the gathering of beach intelligence for the Task Force Commander. Additional capabilities include mine clearance to the 10 fathom curve; landing supply and recovery of agents and guerrillas; and harbor or river penetration for the purpose of demolition attacks against ships or harbor installations.

UDT personnel are qualified parachutists, SCUBA divers and rubber boat handlers. They are also trained in exiting helicopters at low altitude without parachutes, and cast and recovery from high speed small craft.

While UDT normally does not proceed landward from the High Water Mark, it does possess a limited capability for penetration into the Hinterland for the purpose of reconnaissance or demolition raids.

A UDT, composed of 15 officers and 100 men, is divided into four operating platoons and a headquarters platoon. A team is capable of operating either as an integral team or as detached elements. When not assigned to definite missions UDTs are administered directly by a Naval Operations Support Group (NOSG). The administrative organization of a UDT follows:

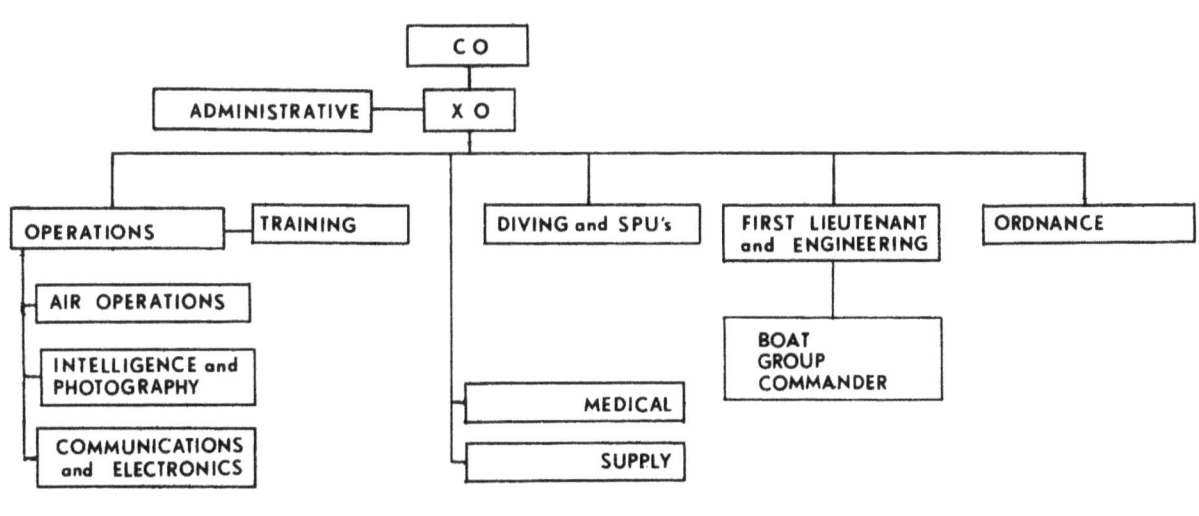

history

For centuries, men have discussed the possibility of using swimmers for purposes of war. In the early months of World War II, the possibility became a reality when Italian divers, piloting submersible "chariots", began to damage and sink allied Mediterranean shipping almost at will. In due time, English, Japanese, German and Russian navies began employing similar tactics.

On November 23, 1943, the United States Navy became painfully aware of the need for combat swimmers. On that day, during the amphibious invasion of the Japanese-held island of Tarawa, tragedy struck. A submerged reef caused the Marine-laden landing craft to stop far off shore, forcing their occupants to wade several hundred yards to the beach. To the heavily - laden invaders submerged depressions and holes became as lethal as enemy bullets. Hundreds drowned.

To provide better pre-assault hydrographic information, and to demolish beach obstacles, Navy Combat Demolition Units were formed.

The first Navy Combat Demolition Unit personnel were garnered from Navy Construction Battalions and Navy/Marine Scout and Raider Volunteers. All were in rugged physical condition and had previous swimming experience. They came together at Fort Pierce, Florida, in the early summer of 1943.

An intensive physical training program was devised, apparently based on the theory that a man is capable of about 10 times as much physical output as is usually thought.

Demolition work was emphasized and non-restricted. Methods were developed for demolishing the type obstacles expected at Normandy. Grueling night-time problems conducted in the snake and alligator infested swamps of Florida produced a specimen of man who was at home with mud, exhaustion, water, and hostile beings, human or otherwise.

The graduates of the school were organized into small 6 man Navy Combat Demolition Units, and a large number were sent to England to join the large invading force in the winter of 1944. No one there knew exactly what they were or what to do with them. Only after many weeks of being shipped around to various stations and being used merely for watches and guard duty were they finally able to settle down for training and invasion rehearsals. Additional men were picked up from other commands to swell the units, and though previously untrained, these men were fitted into the six man and one officer units.

These men were our original ancestors and no amount of honor bestowed upon them will be excessive; they will always have a place in the rank of history's gallants.

The story of the two American beaches at Normandy, Utah, and Omaha has been recorded in detail and is available in many sources.

Operations on Utah beach proceeded with ease, compared to Omaha Beach. The Navy Combat Demolition Units accompanied the assault infantry in the boats of the first wave.

The Navy Combat Demolition Unit men did not anticipate any swimming, for the clearance was to be conducted at low tide. They wore impregnated, hooded, canvas fire fighting suits, with field shoes and long stockings, also impregnated. A protective mask covered the bare part of the face; this garb was in anticipation of a spray of mustard gas.

The invasion force was wet and seasick after the two day delay on the rough channel. As they neared the beach, the preliminary bombardment was lifted on schedule, but the cloudy skies had made it impossible for planes accurately to hit the enemy strong points.

The Germans had reserves available at Omaha and immediately replaced losses at bombarded bunkers. As the boats neared the beach the enemy fire began to fall. Within minutes the water was littered with debris and wrecked craft, and many demolition units were wiped out altogether. An example of the discouraging losses in this H-hour period was the fact that out of some 20-30 amphibious tanks which were to give supporting fire, only four were seen in action. The Demolition Men proceeded nevertheless to set up charges at their assigned gap spots. There was no shelter on the wide sand field, and the men worked as though in a rainstorm; only instead of rain there was shrapnel. The disorganized and misplace infantry were seeking shelter behind some of the charged obstacles; they were tripping over the detonating cord lines laid out between obstacles. In four places however, they heeded the purple warning flares, and four

HISTORY

gateways to France were unveiled with tremendous triumphant explosions. The Navy Combat Demolition Unit losses at Utah were 30%, and at Omaha about 60-70%, giving an over-all average of 41% men lost in the assault.

The survivors of this great day were shipped to the Pacific to form the nucleus of the great force being formed. They had not utilized their swim training in Europe but were now to do so. The lessons of Normandy were applied to the amphibious problems of the Pacific Islands, and the basic tactics were developed that still are the basis for operational procedure today.

The concept of the 6-man Navy Combat Demolition Units was changed to embrace a structure of Underwater Demolition Teams, consisting of 100 men and 13 officers, two or three of which comprised a unit, and in turn, several of these units comprised squadrons.

Basic training was still conducted at Fort Pierce, Florida, followed by six weeks of advanced training at Maui, Hawaii, which became a staging area for advance operations.

The missions became standardized. There was usually a reconnaissance mission on the morning or evening of D-Day minus 4, followed by a demolition clearance on D-1, or on D-Day at dawn preceding H-Hour. Under support from the bombardment group's guns and the air support's bombs and strafing, the APD's (Attack Personnel Destroyers, Destroyer Escorts, converted to fast troop carriers), carrying 4 fast landing craft, would move in through the heavy ships to within several miles of the beach. There they would lower their boats with the teams aboard and withdraw. A seven man rubber boat would be slung along the port side of each LCPR. The LCPR's would speed in to a distance of 1000 yards from the beach, zigzagging, and showing no heads above the gunwales except that of the officer and coxswain. Each LCPR would then turn its starboard side to the beach and commence the splash run parallel to the beach. The swimmers would slip over into the rubber boats one by one and, when signalled, roll into the water on the seaward side of the LCPR. Any heavy equipment, such as marker buoys or demolition packs, would be thrown over with the swimmers. Thus a whole string of men would be dropped. At that range their tiny bobbing heads were unnoticeable from the beach.
On reconnaissance missions the swimmer would take soundings and record all underwater data for his own channel upon his plastic slate. When the swim to the shore had been completed, the swimmers would then swim back out to sea and form another line for pickup. The LCPR would then make its run as before, the men grabbing hold of the snare-loop held out by a man in the outrigged rubber boat, and being swung into the rubber boat by the momentum of the speeding boat.

On swimming into the beach on demolition missions, certain men on the flanks were assigned to carry rolls of detonating cord. This was exploding cord along which a detonation traveled at a speed of four thousand feet per second. They would secure the cord at one end of the beach and unroll it to the other end. Meanwhile the others would tie their packs to the obstacles and tie into small lengths of detonating cord by simple knots to the interconnecting main lines. Fuse pullers would tie long lengths of this cord to the main lines and drag them out to sea. To these they would attach already prepared fuse assemblies, waterproofed and floated. When the swimmers had withdrawn, the fuse pullers would pull the lighters upon signal from sea and then swim to sea for pickup. The lighter would light the time fuse; this would burn for the amount of minutes for which it was cut and would then ignite the small blasting cap at the end. The detonating cord taped next to the cap would be detonated in turn; the explosion would be transmitted into the beach and around to all the packs in a fraction of a second, thus detonating the entire field in one large shot.

The main story of UDT comes out of the Pacific operations which were all done in approximately this same manner. Highly developed methods made UDT an effective weapon, and from the Normandy operation until the end of the war, losses were only about 1%. 28 or 29 Teams were now in combat operations; Borneo, Peleliu, Saipan, Tinian, Guam, Lingayan and Leyte Gulfs, Iwo Jima, and finally, Okinawa. At the end of the war there were 34 teams in commission; about 3500 men in all.

The 34 teams were combined into 6 large teams for purposes of demobilization. The thousands of fins, coral shoes, and facemasks were stored in warehouses. The reservists went back home to their civilian occupations and lives; the others were sent to duties on ships and stations as their individual rates called for. Personnel for five standard teams were kept, with three teams in the Pacific Fleet and two in the Atlantic.

Korea called UDT into combat again. In September 1950, UDT took part in the big amphibious landing at Inchon - charting the harbor, fixing buoys on shallows and submerged rocks, occasionally engaging the enemy at close quarters on his own territory. Korea demanded innovations and improvisations for everybody. UDT responded by conducting many night demolition raids against enemy bridges, railway tunnels, and similar targets, in addition to the primary job of beach reconnaissance. UDT also proved invaluable as human minesweepers in the restricted waters of the Korean harbors and rivers. UDT men in a line abreast would swim through a channel attaching time-delay destructors to the mines as they found them.

Since Korea, the administrative organization of UDT's has changed considerably. At present there are four teams: UDT's 11 and 12 at Coronado, California; and UDT's 21 and 22 at Little Creek, Virginia.

UDT missions in recent years have included ice demolitions in the arctic and astronaut recovery in the Pacific. However, the primary UDT mission remains the same: To chart and clear enemy-held beaches in preparation for an amphibious landing.

16 IBS
17 IBS MOTOR
20 LANDING CRAFT

CHAPTER ONE
BOATS

IBS

The 7 person, CO2 inflatable boat (commonly referred as Inflatable Boat Small, "IBS") was designed and procured by the U.S. Navy as an emergency life-boat for seagoing vessels. Since its introduction and application into the Navy's Underwater Demolition Team it has been utilized for various surface uses. It can also be rigged with a parachute and dropped from an aircraft, or (with minor valve modifications) launched and recovered from the deck of a submerged submarine. The IBS can carry 7 men and 1000 lbs of equipment.

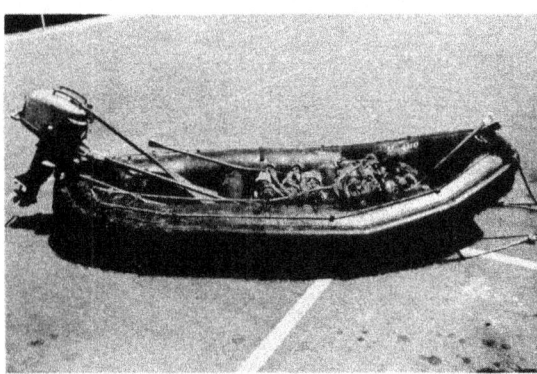

* SPECIFICATIONS

FEDERAL STOCK NUMBER: H-1940-294-2300
SIZE: APPROXIMATELY 12 FT. LONG, WITH OVERALL BEAM OF 6 FT.
WEIGHT COMPLETE: 289 LBS.
BOAT COMPONENTS: MAIN TUBES, CROSS TUBES AND SEAT, INFLATABLE FLOOR MAT, INFLATABLE SKEG, SPRAY TUBE, CARRYING HANDLES AND LIFELINES, TOWING BRIDLE, CO2 INFLATION SYSTEM, AND MOTOR MOUNT.
ACCESSORY EQUIPMENT: LARGE HAND AIR PUMP, SMALL HAND AIR PUMP, SEA ANCHOR, PADDLES, EMERGENCY SEALING CLAMP KIT, EMERGENCY REPAIR KIT, AND FIELD REPAIR KIT.
MANUAL: OPERATION AND MAINTENANCE MANUAL SUPPLIED WITH BOAT.

MAINTENANCE

The following Preventative Maintenance should be followed when using the IBS:

1. Never drag the boat. Head or hand carry method should be used.
2. Keep air valve threads lubricated with heavy grease.
3. NEVER tow or pull IBS using tie-up line on top of main tube. Use towing bridle ONLY for towing.
4. WASH complete IBS with fresh water after each usage. REMOVE floor mat upon washing. This will keep the rubber pliable. Powder with talcum or soapstone when boat dries.
5. Keep IBS in carrying case whenever possible.
6. While using boat for recreational dives, extreme care should be exercised with fishing equipment. NEVER place spiney lobsters in IBS unless protection for the rubber boat surface is provided.
7. When towing IBS behind LCSR or other high speed power boats, be sure to place reinforcement lines from the port and stbd side towing bridle "D" rings to the after "D" rings near motor mount. This will distribute the towing strain to four points rather than two points.
8. NEVER stow IBS in direct sunlight, and never stack over three high.

PATCHING

There are two methods for patching the IBS: The REMA Vulcanizing Method, and the Standard Patching Method, using the IBS patching repair material supplied with the boat. The REMA Vulcanizing method:

(1) Deflate IBS as needed for patching.
(2) Clean surface with hand roughing tool, grit #2 waterproof sandpaper, or wire brush.
(3) Wipe area to be patched clean with "Camel" liquid buffer, "Gross" rubber scrubber, methyl chloroform, or carbon tetrachloride.

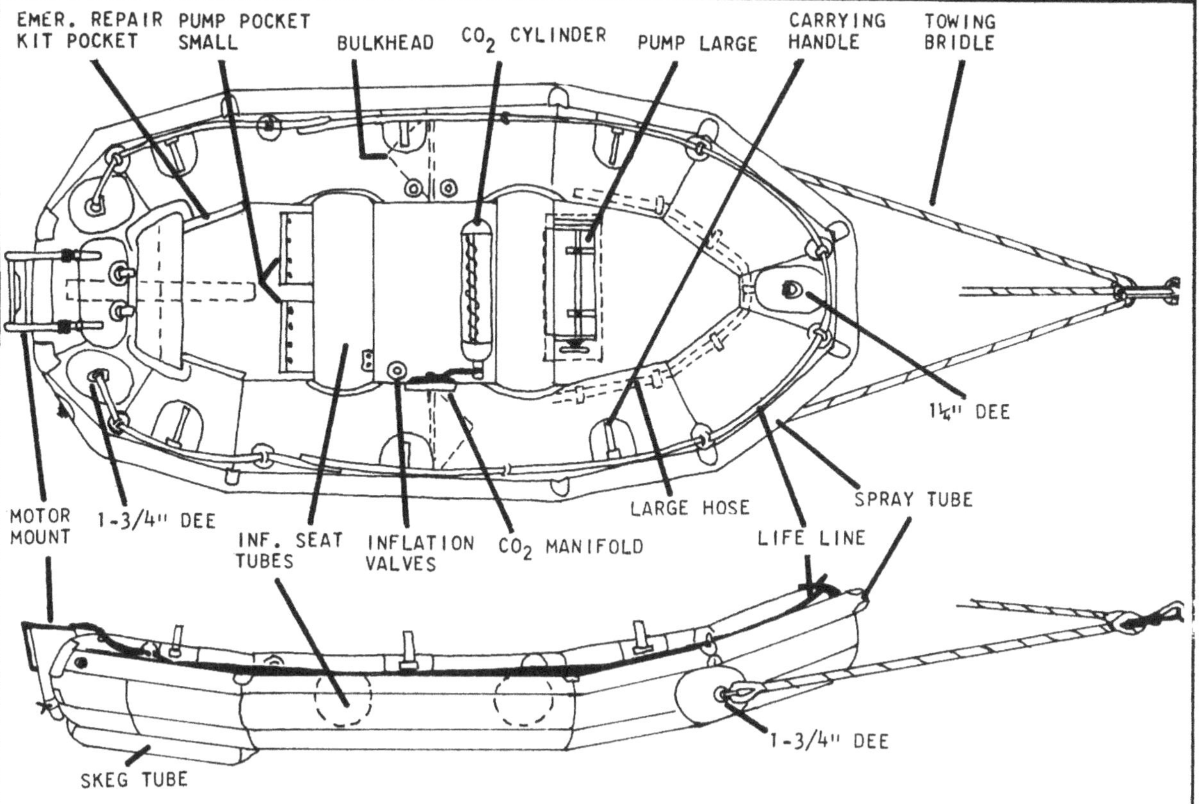

IBS, inflatable boat small

Labels: EMER. REPAIR KIT POCKET, PUMP POCKET SMALL, BULKHEAD, CO_2 CYLINDER, PUMP LARGE, CARRYING HANDLE, TOWING BRIDLE, 1¼" DEE, SPRAY TUBE, LIFE LINE, LARGE HOSE, CO_2 MANIFOLD, INFLATION VALVES, INF. SEAT TUBES, 1-3/4" DEE, MOTOR MOUNT, SKEG TUBE, 1-3/4" DEE

---

(4) Apply two coats of "REMA" cold vulcanizing fluid. Allow first coat to dry thoroughly before applying second coat.

(5) Remove protective cover on "REMA TIP TOP" vulcanizing patch and apply over prepared repair surface. NOTE: Apply this patch immediately as soon as the second coat of "REMA" cold vulcanizing fluid is dry. (As soon as the fluid is not tacky to the touch).

(6) Roll patch with repair roller until vulcanizing takes place.

(7) Allow to dry overnight before inflating IBS.

b. Standard Patching Method:
   (1), (2), (3) Same as "REMA" patching repairs above.
   (4) Cut and round off corners of "HOLLAND" back patch material. (This patch should overlap the tear or hole by two inches on all sides).
   (5) Apply three coats of neoprene cement, allowing each coat to dry thoroughly before applying next.
   (6) Remove white gauze cloth backing from "HOLLAND" back patch, and apply patch to repair area. This should be done approx.

five minutes (In shaded or covered area) after the third coat of neoprene cement has been applied.

(7) Roll with roller getting out all trapped air pockets. NOTE: If patching material does not adhere to the boat, remove patch and apply an additional coat of cement. Allow cement to dry approx. three minutes before applying patch.

(8) Apply weight to patch area and allow to dry overnight before inflating.

IBS OUTBOAD MOTOR

The outboard motor designed for use with the IBS is a 7.5 HP (at 4000 RPM), Manually started silent running motor. It is reliable only when cared for properly.

OPERATION

a. Starting
   (1) Install rip cord with clip on air inlet valve and exhaust valve.

(2) Open cover drain valve until enclosure is drained.
(3) Open front access door (to vent gasoline vapors and prevent explosion).
(4) Remove dummy fuel connector and install fuel hose from fuel tank.
(5) Depress pressurization button on fuel tank several times. Be sure gas filling cap is tight.
(6) Depress gasoline valve tickler.
(7) Pull out choke button if engine is cold.
(8) Set hand throttle to "start" position.
(9) Pull starting cord till engine starts and push choke button in.
(10) Replace forward access door.

b. Running
(1) Before using the motor on an IBS, be sure a securing line is attached between the engine and the boat.
(2) This engine is designed to withstand complete submersion in water for short periods of time (10 sec. approx.) if rip cord is pulled before submersion. The engine should start upon reinstallation, provided that seals are intact and have been properly maintained. Immediately after starting you should observe a stream of cooling water coming out a small hole between the cover drain and exhaust valve. Be SURE hole is clear. This motor should not be operated at low RPM's, due to special design features. It has a device to control minimum speed.
(3) Move gearshift lever only at lower engine speeds.

* SPECIFICATIONS

OPERATING RANGE - 3500 TO 4500 RPM
BORE - 2 1/8 X 1 3/4 STROKE
TYPE - 2 CYCLE ALTERNATE FIRING
PROPELLER - 8" DIA. X 8½" PITCH 2 BLADE
IGNITION - FLYWHEEL MAGNETO
FUEL TANK CAPACITY - 6 GALLONS (5 TO 6 HOURS)
WEIGHT (MOTOR: 75 POUNDS APPROXIMATE)
      (FUEL TANK - 10 POUNDS EMPTY)
FUEL TO OIL RATIO - ½ PINT PER GALLON OR ONE QUART PER FUEL TANK
FUEL TYPE - WHITE GAS PREFERRED OR REGULAR (NO ETHYL)
OIL TYPE - 30 GRADE AUTOMOTIVE, AVOID LOW PRICED (ML) OILS

MAINTENANCE

If possible, when securing engine, disconnect fuel hose while engine is running and allow the engine to consume all remaining fuel.

Run engine in fresh water after use, if possible.

Occasionally grease the two zert fittings located on end of shift lever shaft, and the starboard side of swivel bracket. Also, clean and oil all throttle shafts, pivots and linkages. Oil latches on rear door shaft, on air inlet valve and exhaust valve. Check oil level in lower unit by removing screw on port side, just above propeller, marked "FILL WITH HYDOID OIL (90W)" or "OIL LEVEL". Oil level should be filed to the screw hole. (NOTE: Removal of the lower screw will drain the lower unit. Occasionally this is desirable to check for an emulsion (water in oil). If an emulsion is detected, lower seal is defective and will require immediate replacement.

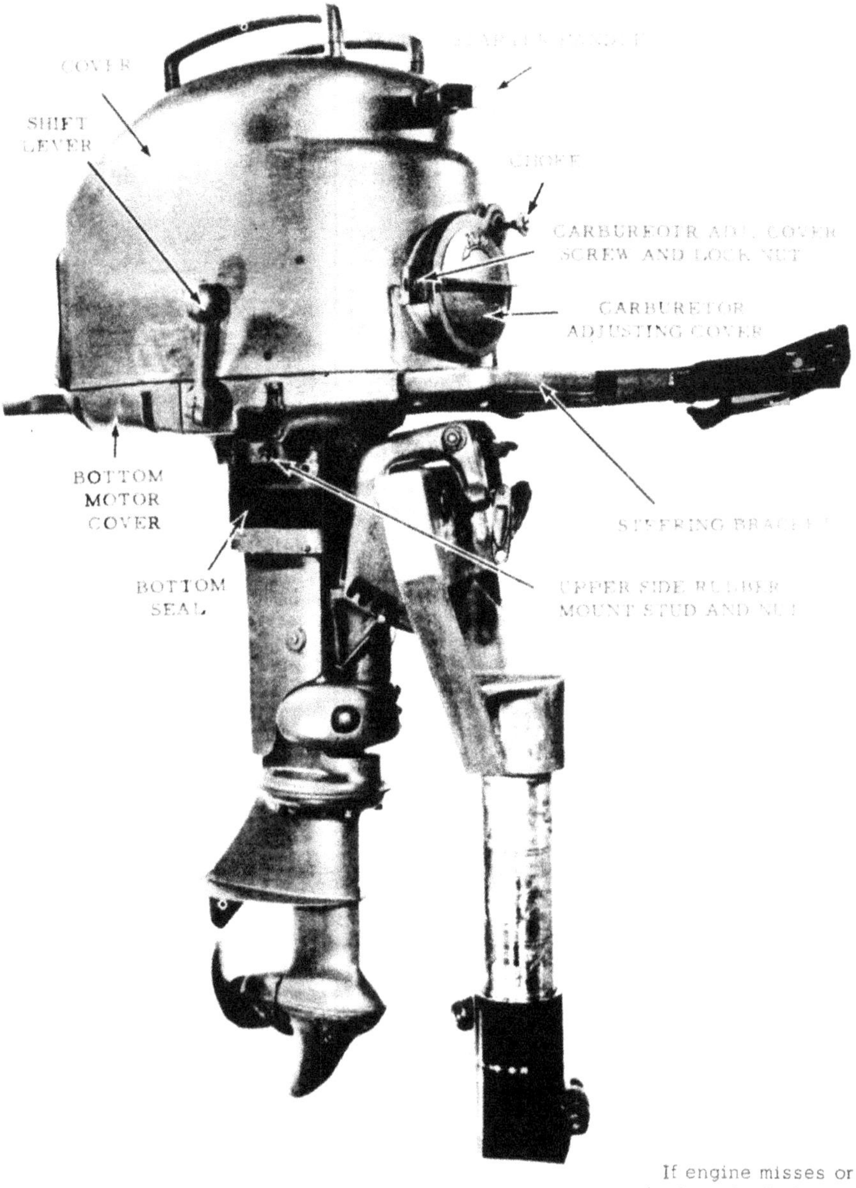

Labels on diagram:
- COVER
- SHIFT LEVER
- STARTER HANDLE (?)
- CHOKE
- CARBURETOR ADJ. COVER SCREW AND LOCK NUT
- CARBURETOR ADJUSTING COVER
- BOTTOM MOTOR COVER
- BOTTOM SEAL
- STEERING BRACKET
- UPPER SIDE RUBBER MOUNT STUD AND NUT

Always oil throttle linkage after saltwater use.

NEVER lay engine on port side, or fuel connection may be broken off. Set engine on rear handle.

For replacement of shear pin on propeller hub, remove rubber propeller cap, cotter pin and propeller. One-eighth inch brazing rod makes an acceptable shear pin. Do not use steel shear pins. Excessive engine damage will result if propeller fouls, with a steel shear pin.

By far the greatest damage sustained by outboards during UDT operations are: water in the gasoline, improper fuel-to-oil ratio and rough handling practices. Be especially cautious when using gasolines from drums on board ships. Such facilities are a prime source of water. Also, 9250 oil has a tendency to foul spark plugs when used in outboard engines.

If engine misses or has loss of power, check spark plugs for fouling, clean and regap to .030 in.

If carburetor setting is not correct, adjust it as follows: with engine running in forward gear position, turn large button needle jet on carburetor until maximim RPM is reached, with about 1/2 to 3/4 full throttle position. Turning counter clockwise enriches mixture and vice versa. The smaller upper needle jet is for low speed operation. Hand throttle must be in the slow position. Adjust low speed jet in the same manner as high speed jet. (NOTE: Special design features will prevent this model from running below 800 RPM's. As a result, proper adjustment of low speed jet is difficult).

All other troubles or adjustments will require the disassembly of the unit, and are beyond the scope of this Handbook. Refer to "Operation and Maintenance Handbook Model 287A-1959 287-501".

BOATS-1

SRS

SWIMMER RECOVERY SLED:
THIS SLED IS SIMILAR IN CONSTRUCTION TO THE IBS. IT HAS A SQUARE STERN WITH REMOVEABLE TRANSOM BOARD, AND IS MUCH FASTER OVER THE WATER THAN THE IBS (DUE TO ITS BOTTOM CONSTRUCTION). ITS BOTTOM IS FORMED BY AN INFLATABLE DECK MAT, RATHER THAN THE REMOVABLE DECK MAT OF THE IBS.

✲ SPECIFICATIONS

LCPR

THE LANDING CRAFT, PERSONNEL, RAMP (LCPR):
THE LCPR IS A V-BOTTOM WOOD FRAME LANDING CRAFT, WITH PLYWOOD SIDES AND A DOUBLE-PLANKED BOTTOM (PLYWOOD INNER, CARAVEL OUTER). ALTHOUGH THE LCPR WAS LAST BUILT IN 1945, IT IS STILL CONSIDERED THE "WORKHORSE" OF UDT. THE BOW RAMP MAKES THE CRAFT IDEAL FOR DIVING OPERATIONS, AND THE SPACIOUS INTERIOR ACCOMMODATES TWENTY DIVERS AND THEIR EQUIPMENT.

✲ SPECIFICATIONS

LENGTH: 36'
BEAM: 10' 9-½" (MAXIMUM)
DRAFT: 3' 6" (LOADED)
CAPACITY (INCLUDING CREW):
39 MEN (WITHOUT EQUIPMENT) OR 8,595 POUNDS OF EQUIPMENT
SPEED: UNLOADED: 15 KNOTS AT 2100 RPM LOADED: 10 KNOTS
HOISTING WEIGHT: 16,000 POUNDS
RANGE: 110 NAUTICAL MILES AT FULL POWER AND WITH FULL LOAD.
REFERENCE: NAVSHIPS 250-452 (BOATS OF THE U. S. NAVY)

LCPL MK-4

THE LANDING CRAFT, PERSONNEL, LAUNCH (LCPL) MK 4:
THE LCPL MK 4 IS A V-BOTTOM, STEEL-HULLED LANDING CRAFT USED BY UDT FOR ESSENTIALLY THE SAME TASKS AS THE LCPR. ALTHOUGH IT IS FASTER THAN THE LCPR, IT IS MORE DIFFICULT TO WORK FROM SINCE IT HAS NO BOW RAMP AND ONLY A SMALL COCKPIT.

✲ SPECIFICATIONS

LENGTH: 36'
BEAM: 11' 2-½" (MAXIMUM)
DRAFT: 3' 6" (LOADED)
CAPACITY (INCLUDING CREW): 20
POWER: ONE 300 HP TURBINE EXHAUST DIESEL ENGINE (MODEL 61217)
SPEED: 19 KNOTS (LOADED)
HOISTING WEIGHT: 18,000 POUNDS
RANGE: 140 NAUTICAL MILES AT FULL LOAD
REFERENCE: NAVSHIPS 250-452 (BOATS OF THE U. S. NAVY)

BOATS-1

LCPL MK-11

THE LANDING CRAFT, PERSONNEL, LAUNCH (LCPL) MK 11:
THIS MODIFICATION OF THE LCPL HAS A LOWER FREEBOARD AND MORE STOWAGE AREA THAN THE MK 4. HOWEVER, THE MK 11 IS NOT ADAPTED FOR LIFTING BY WHELIN DAVITS, AND THE HULL WILL NOT FIT IN STANDARD SHIPBOARD SKIDS. THE HULL OF THE MK 11 IS CONSTRUCTED OF LAMINATED FIBERGLASS AND PLASTIC, AND IS EASILY MAINTAINED.

* SPECIFICATIONS

LENGTH: 36' 1/8"
BEAM: 13' 1/2" (MAXIMUM)
DRAFT: 3' 11" (LOADED)
CAPACITY:
POWER: ONE 300 HP GRAY MARINE DIESEL ENGINE (6121T)
SPEED: 17 KNOTS (LOADED)
HOISTING WEIGHT: 18,500 POUNDS
RANGE: 173 NAUTICAL MILES AT CRUISING SPEED (17.3 KNOTS)
REFERENCE: NAVSHIPS 250-529-3 (INSPECTOR'S HANDBOOK FOR BOATS AND SMALL CRAFT)

LCSR

THE LANDING CRAFT, SWIMMER RECONNAISSANCE (LCSR)1
THIS CRAFT HAS BEEN DESIGNED ESPECIALLY FOR UDT, AND IS FULLY EQUIPPED FOR FULTON DROP AND PICKUP. ITS HULL IS SANDWICH-TYPE PLASTIC, FIBERGLASS AND FOAM LAMINATE. THE NOISE OF THIS CRAFT PRECLUDES ITS BEING USED CLOSE TO LAND IN COVERT OPERATIONS. IT IS EQUIPPED WITH RADAR, FATHOMETER, AND IFF EQUIPMENT.

* SPECIFICATIONS

LENGTH: 52' 4-1/2"
BEAM: 14' 9-1/4"
DRAFT: 5' 7"
CAPACITY: (SWIMMER CABIN) 20 SWIMMERS, FULLY EQUIPPED.
POWER: TWO 1000 HP GAS TURBINE ENGINES
SPEED: 34 KNOTS
HOISTING WEIGHT: 54,000 POUNDS
RANGE: 150 MILES
REFERENCE: BUSHIPS PLAN # LCSR 52-145-1, 847, 427-436

24 RADIO VOICE PROCEDURE

24 PHONETIC ALPHABET and NUMBER

25 PROWORDS and PROSIGNS

27 INTERNATIONAL MORSE CODE

27 SEMAPHORE

CHAPTER TWO
COMMUNICATIONS

RADIO VOICE PROCEDURE

DO

Assume the enemy is monitoring all radio transmissions.

THINK before you speak into a radio. Organize your thoughts and transmit them slowly and distinctly to facilitate accurate reception at the other end.

Keep messages brief and concise, getting across the complete thought you want to transmit to the receiving end.

Make sure that the receiving radio operator clearly understands your message before you secure transmission.

Know and make use of the phonetic alphabet when required by the text of the message or transmission.

Know and use only unit radio call signs.

If possible, write out all messages sent and received.

Know applicable authentication tables, and how to use them.

Send only as fast as you can receive.

DO NOT

Do not waste time by transmitting lengthy rambling messages.

Do not use personal names or unit designations.

Do not conduct unnecessary test counts, exchanges of readability, or other traffic that would tend to clutter up the net.

Do not link authorized call signs with actual unit designations.

Do not use profane language.

PHONETIC ALPHABET and NUMBERS

LETTER	PRO-WORD	PRONUNCIATION
A	ALFA	AL FAH
B	BRAVO	BRAH VOH
C	CHARLIE	CHAR LEE
D	DELTA	DELL TAH
E	ECHO	ECK OH
F	FOXTROT	FOKS TROT
G	GOLF	GOLF
H	HOTEL	HO TELL
I	INDIA	IN DEE AH
J	JULIETT	JEW LEE ETT
K	KILO	KEY LOH
L	LIMA	LEE MAH
M	MIKE	MIKE
N	NOVEMBER	NO VEM BER
O	OSCAR	OSS CAR
P	PAPA	PAH PAH
Q	QUEBEC	KEH BECK
R	ROMEO	ROW ME OH
S	SIERRA	SEE AIR RAH
T	TANGO	TANG GO
U	UNIFORM	YOU NEE FORM
V	VICTOR	VIK TAH
W	WHISKEY	WISS KEY
X	XRAY	ECKS RAY
Y	YANKEE	YANK KEY
Z	ZULU	ZOO LOO

NUMBERS	PRONUNCIATION
1	WUN
2	TOO
3	THUH-REE
4	FO-WER
5	FI-YIV
6	SIX
7	SEVEN
8	ATE
9	NINER
0	ZERO

PROWORDS and PROSIGNS

A "proword" is a word or small group of words which have been designated a standardized meaning. When both sender and receiver understand proword meanings, a radio voice message can be shortened considerably. A "prosign" is an abbreviation for a proword, used while sending morse code or semaphore in order to keep the messages as short as possible.

PROWORDS USED AT THE BEGINNING OF A MESSAGE

PROWORD	PROSIGN	MEANING
AUTHENTICATE		Used when beginning a message to determine if station called or calling is friendly or enemy.
I READ BACK		The following is my response to your instructions to read back.
MESSAGE FOLLOWS		A message which requires recording is about to follow.
SILENCE LIFTED		Resume normal transmission. (Silence can be lifted only by the station imposing it or by a higher authority. When an authentication system is in force, transmission lifting "listening" silence must be authenticated).
THIS IS	DE	This transmission is from the station whose designation immediately follows.
UNKNOWN STATION	AA	The identity of the station with whom I am attempting to establish communication is unknown.

PROWORDS USED DURING A MESSAGE

PROWORD	PROSIGN	MEANING
ALL AFTER	AA	The portion of the message to which I have reference is all that which follows _____.
ALL BEFORE	AB	The portion of the message to which I have reference is all that precedes _____.
CORRECTION	EEEEEE	An error has been made in this transmission. Transmission will continue with the last word correctly transmitted.
EXEMPT		The addressee designation immediately following are exempted from the collective call.
FIGURES		Numerals or numbers follow. (Optional)
GROUPS	GR	This message contains the number of groups indicated by the numeral following.
I SAY AGAIN		I am repeating transmission or portion indicated.
I SPELL		I shall spell the next word phonetically.
INFO	INFO	The addressee designations immediately following are addressed for information.
RELAY (TO)		Transmit this message to all addressees or to the address designations immediately following.
TIME		That which immediately follows is the time or date/time group of the message.
WORD TWICE		Transmit(ting) each phrase (or each code group) twice.
WORD AFTER	WA	
WORD BEFORE	WB	

25

PROWORDS USED AT THE END OF A MESSAGE

PROWORD	PROSIGN	MEANING
BREAK	BT	I hereby indicate the separation of the text from other portions of the message.
DISREGARD THIS TRANSMISSION		This transmission is in error. Disregard it. (This proword shall not be used to cancel any message that has been completely transmitted and for which receipt or acknowledgement has been received).
DO NOT ANSWER		Stations called are not to answer this call, receipt for this message, or otherwise to transmit in connection with this transmission. (When this proword is employed, the transmission shall be ended with the proword OUT).
	K	You may transmit now.
EXECUTE		Carry out the purport of the message or signal to which this applies. (To be used only with the executive method.)
EXECUTE TO FOLLOW		Action on the message or signal which follows is to be carried out upon receipt of the proword "EXECUTE." (To be used only with the executive method).
OUT	AR	This is the end of my transmission and no answer is required. (Since OVER and OUT have opposite meanings, they are never used together).
OVER	K	This is the end of my transmission and a response is necessary. Go ahead; transmit.
SILENCE		"Silence" spoken three times means "Cease Transmission immediately." Silence will be maintained until instructed to resume. Transmissions imposing "Listening" silence must be authenticated.
VERIFY	J	Verify entire message (or portion indicated) with the originator and send correct version. (To be used only at the discretion of or by the addressee to which the questioned message was directed.)
WAIT	AS	I must pause for a few seconds.
WAIT OUT	AS	I must pause longer than a few seconds.

PROWORDS USED WHEN REPLYING TO A MESSAGE

PROWORD	PROSIGN	MEANING
I VERIFY		That which follows has been verified at your request and is repeated. (To be used only as a reply to VERIFY).
READ BACK		Repeat this entire transmission back to me exactly as received.
ROGER	R	I have received your last transmission satisfactorily.
SAY AGAIN	IMI	Repeat all of your last transmission.
SPEAK SLOWER		Reduce speed of transmission.
THAT IS CORRECT		What you have transmitted is correct.
WILCO		I have received your message, understand it and will comply. (To be used only by the addressee. Since the meaning of the proword ROGER is included in that of WILCO, the two prowords are never used together).
WRONG		Your last transmission was incorrect. The correct version is _____ _____ _____.

PROWORDS USED IN MESSAGE FORMAT.

PROWORD	PROSIGN	MEANING
ORIGINATOR		The one who originates a message.
FROM	FM	The originator of this message is indicated by the address designation immediately following.
TO	TO	The addressee(s) whose designation(s) immediately follow are to take action on this message.
FLASH	ZZ	Precedence FLASH. (Reserved for initial enemy contact reports or special emergency operational combat traffic).
IMMEDIATE	OO	Precedence OPERATIONAL IMMEDIATE. (Reserved for important TACTICAL messages pertaining to the operation in progress).
PRIORITY	PP	Precedence PRIORITY. (Reserved for important messages which must have precedence over routine traffic).
ROUTINE	RR	Precedence ROUTINE. (Reserved for all types of message which are not of sufficient urgency to justify higher precedence, but must be delivered to the addressee without delay).
INTERROGATIVE	INT	Explain meaning of a word used in last transmission or do not understand last transmission, please explain.

international morse code

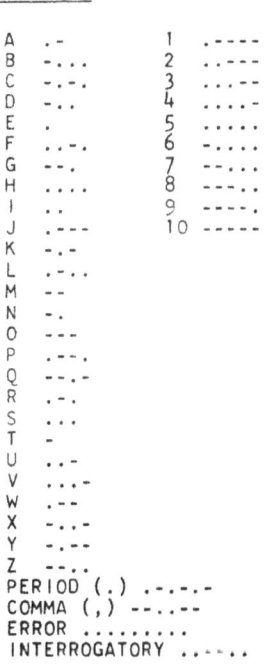

semaphore

30 SAFETY PROCAUTIONS

32 TYPES OF EXPLOSIVES

35 EXPLOSIVE MATERIALS

39 EXPLOSIVE PACKAGES

45 CHARGE ESTIMATION and PLACEMENT

48 CORAL BLASTING

50 COLD WEATHER DEMOLITION

50 ADVANCED DEMOLITIONS

52 IMPROVISED DEMOLITIONS

CHAPTER THREE
DEMOLITIONS

SAFETY PRECAUTIONS

Safety in handling explosives can be achieved only through a thorough knowledge of demolition materials and their hazards, the use of good judgement in conducting demolition exercises and proper application of appropriate safety precautions. This section is by no means a complete list of safety precautions. It lists only those precautions which are most pertinent to UDT demolition operations, and supplements those references listed at the end of the section.

GENERAL

Do not allow any instructions or any set rules to take the place of caution and thought in demolition exercises.

Review applicable safety precautions before each exercise.

Never divide responsibility for preparation, placement, and firing of explosives. One person should be responsible for supervision of the entire project, and should check the area and entire assembly prior to firing.

Do not use tools for any job other than that for which they were specifically designed.

Smoking will not be permitted at any time in the vicinity of explosives.

Ensure that the demolition area is clear of explosive hazards upon completion of the exercise.

STORAGE

Never store blasting caps, primers, detonators, boosters, or pyrotechnics with bulk explosives.

Do not leave exposed explosives unguarded.

Do not store or handle explosives in or near an occupied building.

Ensure that explosives are turned over frequently to avoid exudation.

If no permanent magazine is available, ensure that explosives are kept from the direct rays of the sun.

Allow no matches or spark producing articles in a magazine.

TRUCKING

Line the cargo portion with boards or canvas.

Display EXPLOSIVE sign on front, rear, and both sides of vehicle, or display a red flag 24" square marked with the word DANGER in white letters.

Cover the explosives with canvas.

Travel carefully over rough roads.

Whenever possible, avoid transporting caps and explosives in the same vehicle.

SHIPPING

The BRAVO flag shall be flown in the bow of all boats loaded with or transporting explosives.

All explosives will be securely stowed in wooden boxes on the main deck as far aft in the boat as possible.

All blasting caps and detonators will be stowed securely in a watertight, wood-lined, steel portable magazine as far forward in the boat as possible.

Care will be taken to stow all explosives in such a manner that they cannot move about.

All explosives shall be protected under a well-secured, fire-retardant tarpaulin.

FIRING

NON-ELECTRIC FIRING:

Use electric firing whenever possible.

Always carry caps in a cap box.

Do not blow into or introduce a wire, nail, or similar instrument into non-electric cap in an attempt to remove foreign matter.

Avoid kinks in safety fuse.

Always cut six inches off the end of safety fuse prior to use and ensure a square cut.

Always time no less than two feet of safety fuse prior to use.

If operational or training requirements necessitate using lengths of time fuse shorter than two feet, do not bend or mash the fuse or allow black powder to spill as this may speed up the burning rate.

Use dual firing systems whenever possible and especially if charges are buried or submerged.

In the event of misfire, observe full waiting time (FULL TIME OF FUSE PLUS 30 MINUTES).

ELECTRIC FIRING:

Never take shunt offleg wires until ready to connect to firing wire.

Take care not to pull leg wires out of caps.

The charge placement team or individual shall have in their possession all means of actuating the charge, i.e., HELL BOX HANDLE or HELL BOX.

Always follow complete check-out procedures for electrical firing.

 DEMO-3

Be aware of and take precautions for any electrical sources in the area (static, radio transmitters, thunderstorms, etc.).

Do not use any means other than a blasting galvanometer containing a silver chloride cell for testing electric circuits.

In the event of a misfire using plastic explosives, a full 30-minute waiting period shall be observed.

REFERENCES

NAVWEPS OP 3347 - U. S. Navy Ordnance Safety Precautions

OPNAVINST 8023.7 series - Rules and Regulations for Military Explosives and Hazardous Munitions

NAVWEPS OP 2212 - Demolition Materials

COMPHIBPACINST 8023.3 series - Military Explosives and Hazardous Munitions, Stowage Inst.

COMELEVENINST 8010.1 series - Ammunition Handling in the San Diego Area of ELEVENTH Naval District.

NAVWEPS OP 2239 - Driver's Handbook for Explosives and Dangerous Materials

USCG Publication CG 108 - Rules and Regulations for Military Explosives and Hazardous Munitions.

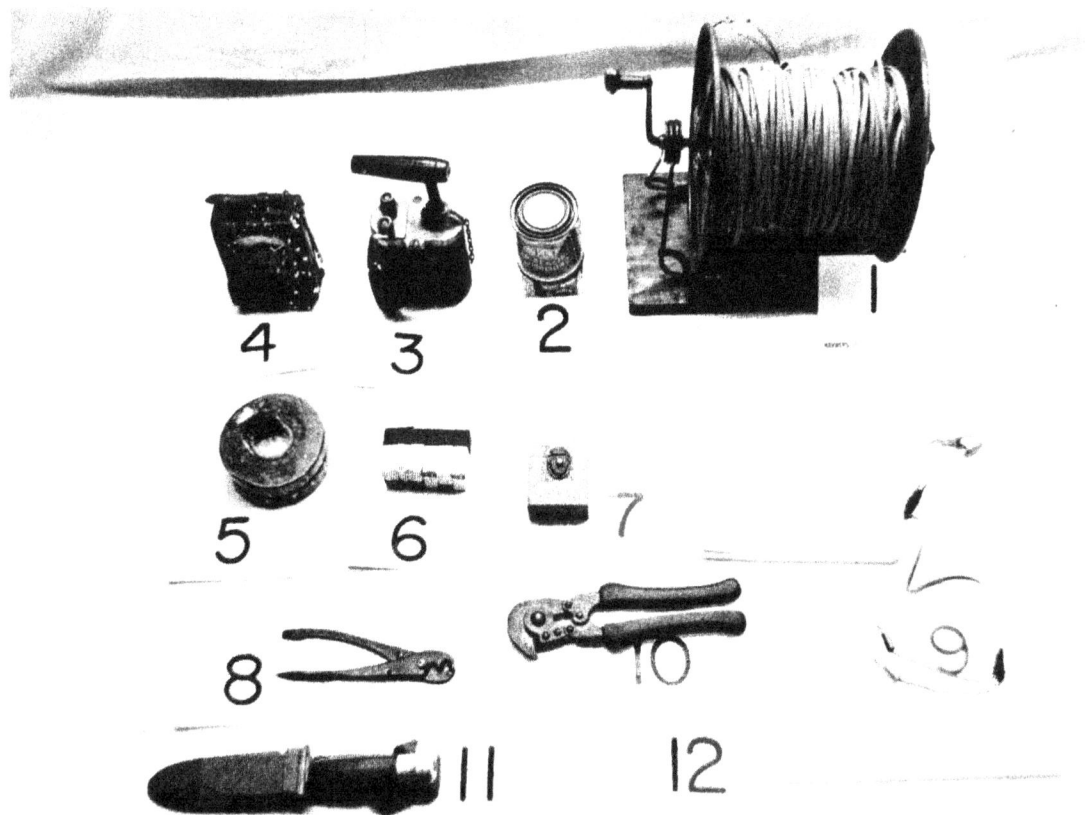

Demo Kit

1. FIRING WIRE REEL
2. CAP SEALING COMPOUND
3. 10 CAP "HELL BOX" OR BLASTING MACHINE
4. CIRCUIT TESTER (GALVANOMETER)
5. FRICTION TAPE
6. CONDOMS
7. CAP CONTAINER, (NON ELECTRIC)
8. BLASTING CAP CRIMPER, M2
9. FIRING LEADS
10. METAL PACKING BAND CUTTER
11. SHEATH KNIFE
12. RULER

DEMO-3
TYPES of EXPLOSIVES

80/20 AMATOL

COLOR: YELLOW TO DARK BROWN

COMPOSITION: A MIXTURE OF 80% AMMONIUM NITRATE AND 20% TNT.

DETONATION TEMPERATURE: 489°F (254°C).

LOADING: CAST, EXTRUDED, OR PRESSED DEPENDING ON THE CONCENTRATION OF AMMONIUM NITRATE.

MELTING POINT: DOES NOT MELT

RELATIVE EFFECT: 1.20

ROD: 14,8000 TO 21,300 FPS AT A DENSITY OF 1.54 GRAMS PER MILLILITER.

SENSITIVITY: LESS SENSITIVE THAN TNT, BUT IS READILY DETONATED BY OTHER HIGH EXPLOSIVES.

STABILITY: VERY HYGROSCOPIC; IS USUALLY PROTECTED BY A SEALING POUR OF TNT

STATE: CRYSTALLINE

TOXICITY: TNT IS ONLY TOXIC COMPONENT

USE: DEMOLITION KIT, BANGLORE TORPEDO, M1A1. ALSO USED AS SUBSTITUTE EXPLOSIVE IN 3" AND 155 MM SHELLS.

AMMONIUM NITRATE

COLOR: WHITE

COMPOSITION: MANUFACTRUED BY NEUTRALIZING AMMONIA WITH NITRIC ACID.

DETONATION TEMPERATURE: BOOSTER OR SPECIAL CAP REQUIRED.

LOADING: PRESSED OR CAST, DEPENDING ON COMPOSITION OF THE MIXTURE.

MELTING POINT: 338°F (170°C)

RELATIVE EFFECT: 0.42

ROD: 3,6000 TO 9,000 FPS

SENSITIVITY: INSENSITIVE TO IMPACT. DETONATED BY A CHARGE OF EXPLOSIVE. SENSITIVITY IS INCREASED BY THE ADDITION OF NON-EXPLOSIVE MATERIALS SUCH AS ROSIN, SULFUR, CHARCOAL, FLOUR, SUGAR AND OIL.

STABILITY: VERY STABLE; IGNITES AT 869°F (465°C). VERY SOLUBLE IN WATER.

STATE: CRYSTALLINE POWDER

TOXICITY: NOT TOXIC; DOES NOT CAUSE DERMATITIS.

USE: AMMONIUM NITRATE IS AN OXIDIZING AGENT. IT IS USED ALONE AS A CRATERING CHARGE AND IS ALSO USED AS THE EXPLOSIVE INGREDIENT OF MIXTURES USED IN BOMBS.

COMPOSITION B and B-2

COLOR: PALE YELLOW TO YELLOW OR BROWN.

COMPOSITION: COMPOSITION B REFERS SPECIFICALLY TO A MIXTURE OF 52.2% RDX, 40% TNT, 4.8% BEES WAX. COMPOSITION B-2 IS AN UNWAXED COMPOSITION OF 60% RDX AND 40% TNT. COMPOSITION B-2 IS THE MORE SENSITIVE OF THE TWO.

DETONATING TEMPERATURE: 491°F (255°C)

LOADING: A CAST EXPLOSIVE

MELTING POINT: COMPOSITION B-2; 178°F (81°C) COMPOSITION B SAME AS TNT

RELATIVE EFFECT: 1.35

ROD: 25,400 FPS AT A DENSITY OF 1.7 GRAMS PER MILLILITER.

SENSITIVITY: LESS SENSTIVE THAN TETRYL, BUT MORE SENSITIVE THAN TNT WAX HAS A SMALL BUT DISTINCT DESENSITIZING EFFECT.

STABILITY: IN STORAGE, GOOD NON-HYGROSCOPIC. WILL BURN WHEN UNCONFINED.

STATE: NON-PLASTIC SOLID

TOXICITY: A POISONOUS EXPLOSIVE THAT PRODUCES TOXIC EFFECTS PECULIAR TO ITS COMPONENTS.

USE: SHAPED CHARGES, MINES, TORPEDOES, AND LARGE CALIBER PROJECTILES

COMPOSITION C-3

COLOR: YELLOW TO BROWN

COMPOSITION: 77% RDX, 3% TETRYL, 4% TNT AND 16% PLASTICIZER CONTAINING NITROCOTTON.

DETONATING TEMPERATURE: 342°F (172°C)

LOADING: GENERALLY MANUFACTURED IN BLOCKS COVERED BY WAXED PAPER AND CARDBOARD.

MELTING POINT: DOES NOT HAVE DEFINITE MELTING POINT.

RELATIVE EFFECT: 1.26

ROD: 25,000 FPS AT A DENSITY OF 1.6 GRAMS PER MILLILITER.

SENSITIVITY: CONSIDERABLY LESS SENSITIVE THAN TNT

STABILITY: MAY EXUDE IN STORAGE AT ROOM TEMPERATURE, BUT DOES NOT LOSE SENSITIVITY TO INITIATION. MODERATELY HYGROSCOPIC. CATCHES FIRE EASILY AND BURNS WITH INTENSE FLAME. IF BURNED IN LARGE QUANTITIES, THE HEAT GENERATED DURING BURNING MAY MAKE IT EXPLODE.

STATE: A PLASTIC MATERIAL RESEMBLING PUTTY

TOXICITY: COMPOSITION C-3 IS POISONOUS AND CAUSES DERMATITIS. THE FUMES CAUSED BY ITS EXPLOSION ARE POISONOUS.

USE: MK-135, MK-137, DEMOLITION PACKS, AND M-3 DEMO BLOCKS.

COMPOSITION C-4

COLOR: WHITE
COMPOSITION: A MIXTURE CONTAINING 91% RDX, 2.1% POLYISOBULYTENE 5.3% DIETHYLHEXYL AND 1.6% MOTOR OIL.

DETONATION TEMP: 386.6°F (197°C)

LOADING: NORMALLY PREPARED IN 2½ POUND BLOCKS, AND WRAPPED IN WAXED PAPER OR PLASTIC.

MELTING POINT: DOES NOT HAVE DEFINITE MELTING POINT.

RELATIVE EFFECT: 1.35

ROD: 26,500 FPS AT A DENSITY OF 1.6 GRAMS PER MILLILITER

SENSITIVITY: SIMILAR TO TNT IN SENSITIVITY

STABILITY: IN STORAGE, GOOD NON-HYGROSCOPIC

STATE: PLASTIC MASS, RESEMBLING PUTTY

TOXICITY: NOT MARKEDLY TOXIC AND GENERALLY DOES NOT CAUSE DERMATITIS.

USE: M5A1 DEMO BLOCK.

HBX-1 and HBX-3

COLOR: SLATE GRAY

COMPOSITION:

	HBX-1	HBX-3
RDX	39.6%	31.0%
TNT	37.8%	29.0%
ALLUM POWDER	17.1%	35%
DESENSITIZER	1.5%	3.5%

DETONATING TEMP: 365° TO 500°F (185° TO 260°C)

LOADING: LOADED BY CASTING.

MELTING POINT: 178°F (81°C)

RELATIVE EFFECT: 1.48 IN AIR 1.68 UNDERWATER-HBX-3 IS 10-15% MORE EFFECTIVE THAN HBX-1 AS AN UNDERWATER EXPLOSIVE.

ROD: 24,3000 FPS AT A DENSITY OF 1.7 GRAMS PER MILLILITER.

SENSITIVITY: ABOUT THE SAME AS COMP. B. SLIGHTLY MORE THAN TNT

STABILITY: IN STORAGE, GOOD. AT TEMP. ABOVE 149°F (65°C), WAX DESENSITIZER WILL EXUDE. NON-HYGROSCOPIC AND NOT ADVERSELY AFFECTED BY MOISTURE.

STATE: SOLID MORTAR-LIKE SUBSTANCE.

TOXICITY: PRODUCES TOXIC EFFECTS PECULIAR TO ITS COMPONENTS. TNT IS THE ONLY SIGNIFICANTLY TOXIC COMPONENT.

REMARKS: USED PRIMARILY IN UNDERWATER ORDNANCE, (TORPEDOES, MINES, BOMBS, DEPTH CHARGES AND GENERAL DEMOLITION CHARGES, MK-133 MOD 2).

PENTOLITE

COLOR: WHITE, GRAY OR YELLOW

COMPOSITION: 50% TNT, 50% PETN, WAX IS SOMETIMES ADDED AS A DESENSITIZER

DETONATION TEMP: 374°F (190°C)

LOADING: MELT OR CAST LOADED

MELTING POINT: 169°F (76°C)

RELATIVE EFFECT: 1.26

ROD: 24,600 FPS AT A DENSITY OF 1.6 GRAMS PER MILLILITER

SENSITIVITY: LESS THAN PETN, APPROXIMATELY SAME AS TETRYL.

STABILITY: NOT AS STABLE AS TNT IN STORAGE. NON-HYGROSCOPIC

STATE: SOLID

TOXICITY: PRODUCES TOXIC EFFECTS PECULIAR TO ITS COMPONENTS

USE: CAST SHAPED CHARGES, GRENADES, ROCKETS, ANTI-TANK SHELLS.

PETN

COLOR: WHITE WHEN PURE, LIGHT GRAY WITH ADDITION OF WAX AND IMPURITIES.

COMPOSITION: PENTAERYTHRITOL TETRANITRATE (PETRIN)

DETONATION TEMP: 347°F (175°C)

LOADING: LOADING BY PRESSING

MELTING POINT: 286°F (141°C)

RELATIVE EFFECT: 1.45

ROD: 26,000 FPS AT A DENSITY OF 1.6 GRAMS PER MILLILITER. 21,000 FPS WHEN LOADED INTO DETONATING CORD.

SENSITIVITY: MOST SENSITIVE OF THE PRIMARY MILITARY EXPLOSIVES; HOWEVER, WHEN LOADED IN PRIMA CORD, PETN BECOMES INSENSITIVE TO HEAT,

SHOCK FRICTION AND MUST BE DETONATED BY BLASTING CAP.

STABILITY: IN STORAGE, GOOD. IT IS STORED WET WHEN IN BULK. NON-HYGROSCOPIC.

STATE: FINE CRYSTALLINE OR GRANULAR POWDER.

TOXICITY: SMALL DOSES EITHER ABSORBED THROUGH THE SKIN OR INHALED MAY CAUSE A DECREASE IN BLOOD PRESSURE; LARGER DOSES CAUSE DIFFICULTY IN BREATHING AND CONVULSIONS.

USE: IN DETONATING CORD, AND AS A BOOSTER AND DETONATOR IN BASE CHARGES.

RDX (CYCLONITE)

COLOR: WHITE

COMPOSITION: CYCLOTRIMETHYLENETRINITRAMINE

DETONATING TEMP: APPROXIMATELY 455°F (235°C)

LOADING: ALWAYS USED IN U.S. ORDNANCE WITH A DESENSITIZER. IN EXPLOSIVES SUCH AS HBX, THE RDX IS CAST WITH TNT.

MELTING POINT: 396°F (202°C)

RELATIVE EFFECT: 1.60

ROD: 27,000 FPS AT A DENSITY OF 1.6 GRAMS PER MILLILITER.

SENSITIVITY: SENSITIVITY LIE LIES ABOUT HALF-WAY BETWEEN TETRYL AND PETN. SENSITIVITY IS APPRECIABLY REDUCED BY ADDITION OF WAX.

STABILITY: IN STORAGE, VERY GOOD. NON-HYGROSCOPIC, AND NOT ADVERSELY AFFECTED BY MOISTURE.

STATE: CRYSTALLINE SOLID

TOXICITY: NOT MARKEDLY TOXIC, AND GENERALLY DOES NOT CAUSE DERMATITIS. IF INGESTED, HOWEVER, IT MAY AFFECT CENTRAL NERVOUS SYSTEM.

REMARKS: MOST POWERFUL OF ALL MILITARY EXPLOSIVES DEVELOPED BY BRITISH DURING WORLD WAR II. USED PRIMARILY AS A COMPONENT OF EXPLOSIVE MIXTURES.

TETRYL

COLOR: COLORLESS WHEN FRESH AND HIGHLY PURIFIED; TURNS YELLOW WHEN EXPOSED TO LIGHT. TURNS GRAY WHEN LOADED, DUE TO THE GRAPHITE WHICH IS USED AS A LUBRICANT IN TETRYL.

COMPOSITION: A DERIVATIVE OF METHYLANILINE, TETRALITE, TETRYLITE AND PYRONITE.

DETONATING TEMP: 453°F (234°C).

LOADING: MIXED WITH A LUBRICANT, SUCH AS GRAPHITE, STEARIC ACID, OR MAGNESIUM STEARATE WHILE PRESSED INTO PELLETS (CAN NOT BE CAST).

MELTING POINT: 266°F (130°C) MAXIMUM SAFE TEMPERATURE: 212°F.

RELATIVE EFFECT: 1.28

ROD: 24,600 FPS AT A DENSITY OF 1.6 GRAMS PER MILLILITER.

SENSITIVITY: SENSITIVITY IS INTERMEDIATE BETWEEN TNT AND PETN; IT WILL USUALLY DETONATE WHEN SUBJECTED TO BULLET IMPACT. MAY BE IGNITED BY SPARK, HOWEVER, IT DOES NOT DETONATE FROM THE SPIT OF A FUSE.

STABILITY: NO SERIOUS DECOMPOSITION WHEN STORED AT NORMAL TEMPERATURES. SLIGHTLY HYGROSCOPIC. BURNS READILY. FIRST MELTS, THEN DECOMPOSES AND EXPLODES WHEN HEATED.

STATE: FINELY DIVIDED CRYSTALLINE POWDER.

TOXICITY: CAUSES DERMATITIS, DISCOLORATION OF THE SKIN AND HAIR, IRRITATION OF THE UPPER RESPIRATORY TRACT, AND POSSIBLY SYSTEMIC POISONING.

USE: BASE CHARGE IN COMPOUND DETONATORS (CAPS), ALSO USED AS A BOOSTER.

TETRYTOL

COLOR: YELLOW

COMPOSITION: 70% TETRYL, 30% TNT

DETONATING TEMP: 345°F (179°C)

LOADING: CAST LOADER, DESIGNED TO OBTAIN A BOOSTER COMPARABLE TO TETRYL THAT COULD BE CAST.

MELTING POINT: 169°F (76°C)

RELATIVE EFFECT: 1.22

ROD: 23,900 FPS AT A DENSITY OF 1.6 GRAMS PER MILLILITER.

SENSITIVITY: LESS SENSITIVE TO SHOCK THAN TETRYL AND ONLY SLIGHTLY MORE SENSITIVE THAN TNT.

STABILITY: IN STORAGE, GOOD; SLIGHTLY LESS STABLE THAN TETRYL AT ELEVATED TEMPERATURES.

STATE: SOLID

TOXICITY: MAY CAUSE DERMATITIS. CONSIDERED A POISONOUS EXPLOSIVE.

USE: CHARGE DEMOLITION M-1 CHAIN TYPE, CAST SHAPE CHARGES, AS A BOOSTER IN CHEMICAL SHELLS.

TNT

COLOR: STRAW YELLOW TO YELLOWISH BROWN.

COMPOSITION: TRINITROTOLUENE.

DETONATING TEMP: 869°F (465°C)

LOADING: USUALLY CAST, BUT MAY BE PRESSED (TAMPED)

MELTING POINT: 176°F (80°C)

RELATIVE EFFECT: 1.00

ROD: 22,200 FPS AT A DENSITY OF 1.6 GRAMS PER MILLILITER.

SENSITIVITY: ONE OF THE MOST INSENSITIVE HIGH EXPLOSIVES; DISTINCTLY MORE SENSITIVE WHEN DECOMPOSED BY LIGHT.

STABILITY: IN STORAGE, VERY GOOD AT PRESCRIBED TEMPERATURES. HOWEVER, WHEN STORED AT ELEVATED TEMPERATURES, TNT MAY EXUDE AN OILY LIQUID WHICH IS INSENSITIVE ALONE, BUT WHICH WHEN MIXED WITH WOOD OR COTTON, FORMS A LOW EXPLOSIVE WHICH IS EASILY IGNITED.

STATE: A FLAKED, GRANULAR, OR CRYSTALLINE MATERIAL.

TOXICITY: HIGHLY POISONOUS. IS EASILY ABSORBED BY THE SKIN. TNT DUST AND FUMES ARE TOXIC WHEN INHALED. INGESTION MAY ALSO CAUSE POISONING. CAUSES LIVER DAMAGE AND JAUNDICE WITH FATAL RESULTS.

USE: 1 LB AND ½ LB TNT BLOCKS, MK 2 MOD 2 55 LB CHARGE MK 133 MOD 0, DEPTH CHARGES, MINES, AND ROCKETS.

EXPLOSIVE MATERIALS

Reinforced Primacord

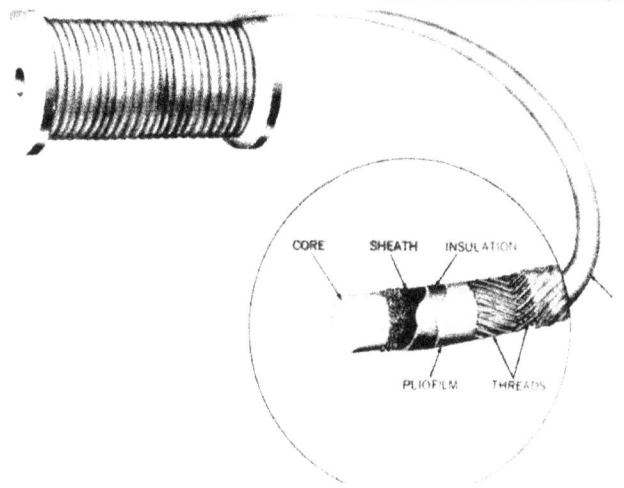

REINFORCED PRIMACORD CONSISTS OF A PETN CORE, PROCTECTED BY SIX LAYERS OF MATERIAL. THE NOMINAL OUTSIDE DIAMETER OF THE CORD IS 0.203". THE CORD WEIGHS 18 POUNDS PER 1,000 FEET AND HAS A TENSILE STRENGTH OF ABOUT 160 POUNDS. THE CORD EXPLODES WITH ENOUGH FORCE TO DETONATE ANY STANDARD MILITARY CHARGE TO WHICH IT IS PROPERLY CONNECTED. THE EXPLOSION TRAVEL AT APPROXIMATELY 21,000 FEET PER SECOND.

USE: DETONATING CORD EXPLODES THROUGHOUT ITS ENTIRE LENGTH, AND IT WILL DETONATE ANY ARRANGEMENT OF CHARGES PROPERLY CONNECTED TO IT. IT WILL FUNCTION AFTER 24 HOURS SUBMERSION, PROVIDED THE CUT ENDS HAVE BEEN PROTECTED BY WAX OR CAP SEALING COMPOUND DIP.

SAFETY: IN COLD WEATHER UNCOIL WITH CARE TO AVOID BREAKING POWDER TRAIN. ALL KINKS AND SHARP BENDS MUST BE STRAIGHTENED BEFORE FIRING. USE ONLY SQUARE KNOT OR HITCH WHEN TYING INTO TRUNK LINE.

✶ SPECIFICATIONS

DOD CODE: M456
FEDERAL STOCK NO: 1375-028-5168
METHOD OF PACKING: WOODEN BOX CONTAINING 8 CANS, EACH CAN CONTAINING 500 FEET OR A SPOOL. BOX IS 2.6'X 1.3'X 1.3'
TOTAL WEIGHT: 11.7 POUNDS

✶ SPECIFICATIONS

DOD CODE: M457
FEDERAL STOCK NO: 1375-310-2678
METHOD OF PACKING: PAPER BOX CONTAINING ONE SPOOL, 1000 FEET. THE BOX WEIGHS 35 LBS AND IS 1' X 1' X 1'.

Wirebound Primacord

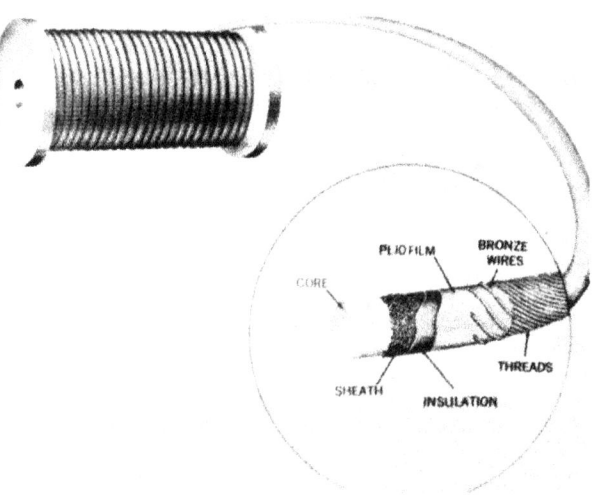

SAME AS REINFORCED PRIMACORD, EXCEPT THAT THE FOURTH PROTECTIVE LAYER IS A SPIRAL OF BRONZE WIRES REPLACING THE LAYER OF TEXTILE THREADS USED IN REINFORCED PRIMACORD. THE CORD WEIGHS 35 POUNDS PER 1,000 FEET AND HAS A TENSILE STRENGTH OF ABOUT 220 POUNDS. THE CORD CONTAINS SIX POUNDS OF PETN PER 1,000 FEET. THE RATE OF DETONATION IS 21,000 FPS.

USE: ROUGH USE, IN UNDERWATER AREAS AROUND SHARP ROCKS, CORAL, OR AREAS WHERE TIDE AND CURRENTS ARE STRONG.

SAFETY: SAME AS REINFORCED PRIMACORD.

DEMO-3

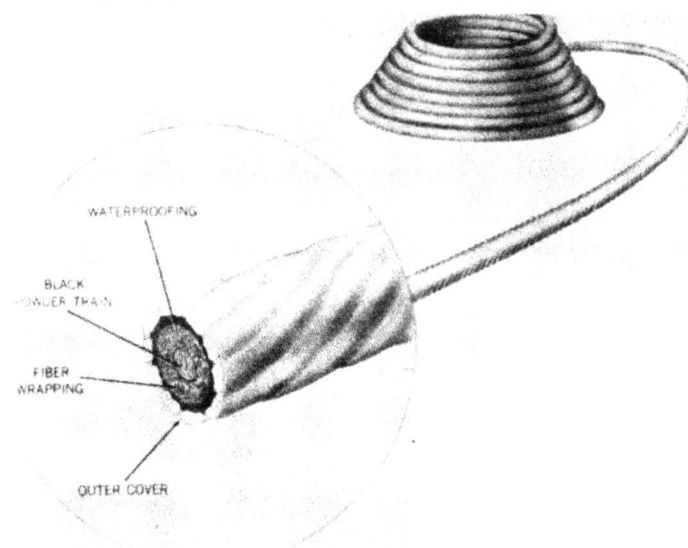

Safety Fuse

THE FUSE IS A FLEXIBLE CORD ABOUT ¼" IN DIAMETER. IT CONSISTS OF A BLACK POWDER CORE ENCASED IN A FIBER WRAPPING WHICH IS COVERED WITH A WATERPROOFING MATERIAL (ORANGE-COLORED WAX). SAFETY FUSE IS SHIPPED IN A PAPER PACKAGE CONTAINING TWO 50 FOOT LENGTHS OF COILED FUSE. EACH COIL OF FUSE BURNS AT A FAIRLY UNIFORM RATE, WHICH VARIES BETWEEN 36 AND 47 SECONDS PER FOOT.

USE: SAFETY FUSE PROVIDES A BURNING TIME DELAY BEFORE IGNITION OF A NON-ELECTRIC BLASTING CAP.

SAFETY: DO NOT RELY UPON VISUAL RECOGNITION OF THIS FUSE, AS MANY FOREIGN TIME-FUSES AND DETONATING CORDS RESEMBLE IT.

USE ONLY FUSE THAT HAS BEEN POSITIVELY IDENTIFIED. BEFORE USING, ALWAYS CUT AND TIME AT LEAST TWO FEET FROM THE ROLL TO BE USED. NO METHOD OF LIGHTING FUSE SHOULD BE USED THAT OBSCURES OR CONCEALS EVIDENCE THAT THE FUSE HAS BEEN LIGHTED. THE BURNING SPEED OF FUSE VARIES DUE TO DIFFERENCES IN TEMPERATURE, ALTITUDE, WEATHER, STORAGE CONDITIONS, CHARACTER OF TAMPING, AND MISHANDLING.

* SPECIFICATIONS

DOD CODE: M670
FEDERAL STOCK NO: 1375-028-5149
METHOD OF PACKING: SAFETY FUSE IS SHIPPED IN A WOODEN BOX 2.6' X 1.8' X 1.4'.
TOTAL WEIGHT: 162 POUNDS

FUSE LENGTH CALCULATION

BURN AND TIME A SIX FOOT LENGTH OF FUSE.

DIVIDE THAT TIME (IN SECONDS) BY SIX, TO DETERMINE THE BURNING RATE PER FOOT.

DIVIDE DESIRED TIME OF FUSE (IN SECONDS) BY THE BURNING RATE (IN SECONDS) TO ARRIVE AT LENGTH OF SAFETY FUSE IN FEET AND TENTHS.

NOTE: TO CONVERT .1 TO INCHES, MULTIPLY 12 BY .1.
EXAMPLE: TO OBTAIN A 10 MINUTE (600 SECOND) FUSE:

(1) BURN 6 FEET. TIME CONSUMED (E.G.) 270 SECONDS.

(2) DIVIDE 270 BY SIX TO OBTAIN THE AVERAGE BURNING RATE OF 45 SECONDS PER FOOT.

(3) DIVIDE 600 BY 45 ARRIVING AT A FUSE LENGTH OF 13.3' CONVERT .3' TO INCHES BY MULTIPLYING BY 12. ANSWER: 13', 3.6".

NOTE: THE CONDITIONS UNDER WHICH THE ACTUAL FUSE MAY BE BURNED AND THOSE UNDER WHICH THE TEST LENGTH ARE BURNED MAY DIFFER. THEREFORE, DO NOT EXPECT THE TIMING OF THE FUSE TO BE EXACT, BE SURE TO ALLOW FOR SAME.

Non-Electric Blasting Cap

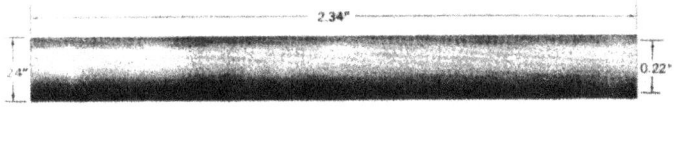

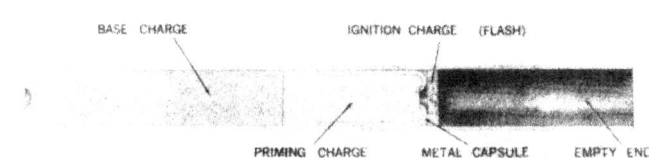

THE NON-ELECTRIC BLASTING CAP IS A CLEAR LACQUERED COPPER OR ALUMINUM TUBE CONTAINING THREE SMALL EXPLOSIVE CHARGES: IGNITION CHARGE, PRIMING CHARGE, AND BASE CHARGE. THE CHARGES WHICH ARE IN LAYERS, ONLY PARTIALLY FILL THE TUBE. THE REMAINING PORTION OF THE TUBE IS EMPTY, SO THAT THE BLASTING CAP CAN BE FITTED OVER AND CRIMPED TO TIME FUSE OR A COUPLING BASE. THE CAP CONTAINS 13.5 GRAINS OF PETN.

USE: PROVIDES THE DETONATING IMPULSE REQUIRED TO EXPLODE DEMOLITIONS.

SAFETY: SEE SECTION "A" OF THIS CHAPTER.

✱ SPECIFICATIONS

DOD CODE: M131
FEDERAL STOCK NO: 1375-028-5288
METHOD OF PACKING: NON-ELECTRIC BLASTING CAPS ARE PACKED IN A WOODEN BOX 1.33' X 1.33' X 0.75' THERE ARE 5,000 CAPS IN THE BOX, IN CARTONS OF 1,000 (EACH CARTON CONTAINS TEN BOXES OF 100 CAPS EACH).

Electric Blasting Cap

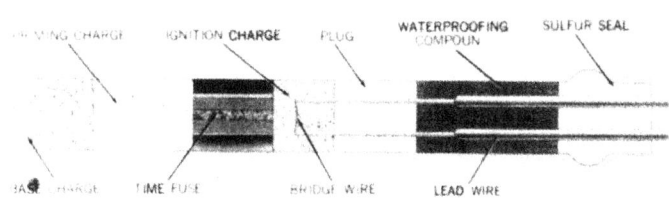

THE SPECIAL ELECTRIC BLASTING CAP CONSISTS OF A BASE CHARGE OF PETN (13.5 GRAINS), A PRIMING CHARGE, A BRIDGE WIRE, AND TWO 12 FOOT LEG WIRES.

THE CHARGES AND BRIDGE WIRE ARE ALL SEALED INTO END OF A COPPER OR ALUMINUM SHELL. WHEN CURRENT IS PASSED THROUGH THE LEG WIRES, THE BRIDGE WIRES, STRONGLY HEATED BY THE CURRENT, IGNITE THE PRIMING CHARGE, WHICH DETONATES THE BASE CHARGE. SPECIAL CAPS ARE THE ONLY ONES THAT WILL POSITIVELY DETONATE ALL PRESENT MILITARY EXPLOSIVES. BOXES CONTAINING THESE CAPS WILL BE MARKED "WILL DETONATE COMPOSITION C".

SAFETY: SECTION "A" OF THIS CHAPTER.

✱ SPECIFICATIONS

DOD CODE: M131
FEDERAL STOCK NO: 1375-028-5214
METHOD OF PACKING: ELECTRIC CAPS ARE SHIPPED IN A WOODEN BOX 1' X 1' X 0.9', WEIGHING 23 POUNDS AND CONTAINING 500 CAPS.

 DEMO-3

Delay Blasting Cap

SPECIAL DELAY BLASTING CAPS ARE THE SAME AS SPECIAL ELECTRIC CAPS, EXCEPT THAT A DELAY IS OBTAINED BY EMBEDDING THE BRIDGE WIRE IN A BURNING CHARGE INSTEAD OF AN EXPLOSIVE CHARGE, OR BY INSERTING A SHORT PIECE OF TIME FUSE BETWEEN THE BRIDGE WIRE AND PRIMING CHARGE. SPECIAL DELAY CAPS ARE ISSUED IN TEN DIFFERENT DELAY PERIODS.

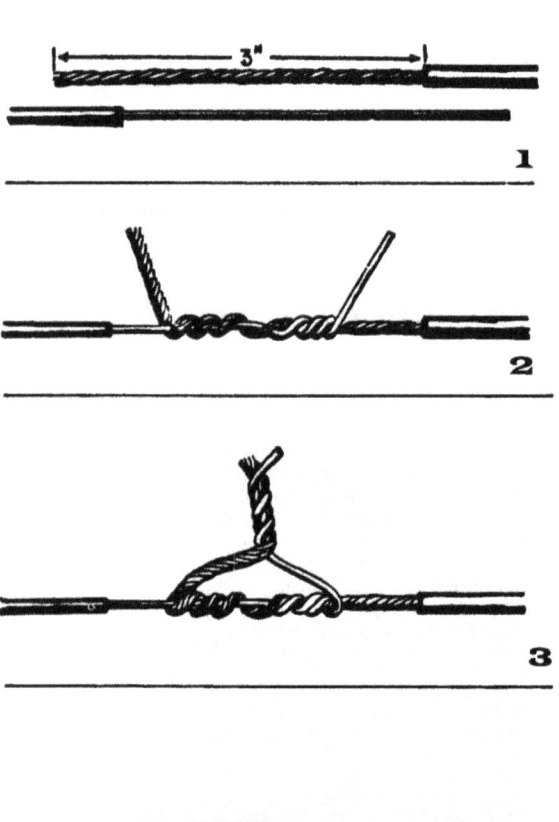

Western Union Splice

FOLLOWING ARE THE FOUR STEPS INVOLVED IN MAKING A UDT APPROVED WESTERN UNION SPLICE:

DEMO-3
EXPLOSIVE PACKAGES

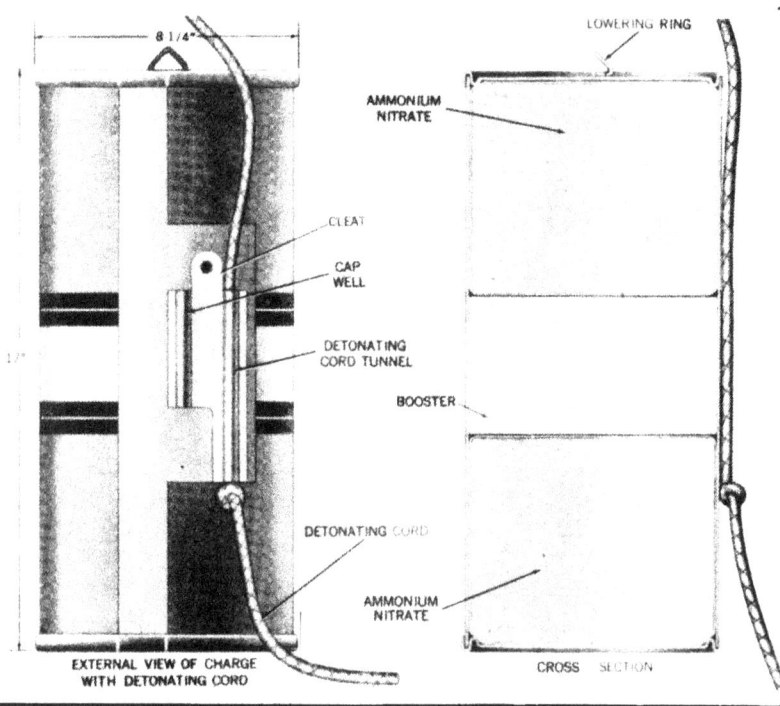

External view of charge with detonating cord / Cross section

Ammonium Nitrate

CONSISTS OF 40 POUNDS AMMONIUM NITRATE CHARGE IN A SEALED METAL CAN. CONTAINS A BOOSTER OF TNT TO ENSURE DETONATION. A LOWERING RING IS PROVIDED ON ONE END FOR ATTACHING A LINE WHEN LOWERING THE CHARGE IN A HOLE A CAP WELL (UNTHREADED) AND A DETONATING CORD TUNNEL ARE ATTACHED TO THE SIDE OF THE CONTAINER TO ACCOMMODATE EITHER AN ELECTRIC OR A NON-ELECTRIC CAP.

USE: POST ASSAULT DEMOLITION. USED PRINCIPALLY FOR EARTHMOVING. NOT SUITABLE AS A CUTTING CHARGE.

SAFETY: DO NOT PUNCTURE THE CONTAINER, AS AMMONIUM NITRATE READILY ABSORBS MOISTURE.

✱ SPECIFICATIONS

DOD CODE: M039
FEDERAL STOCK NO: 1375-028-5145
METHOD OF PACKING: ONE PER WOODEN BOX 1.67' X 0.82' X 0.80'.
TOTAL WEIGHT: 46 POUNDS

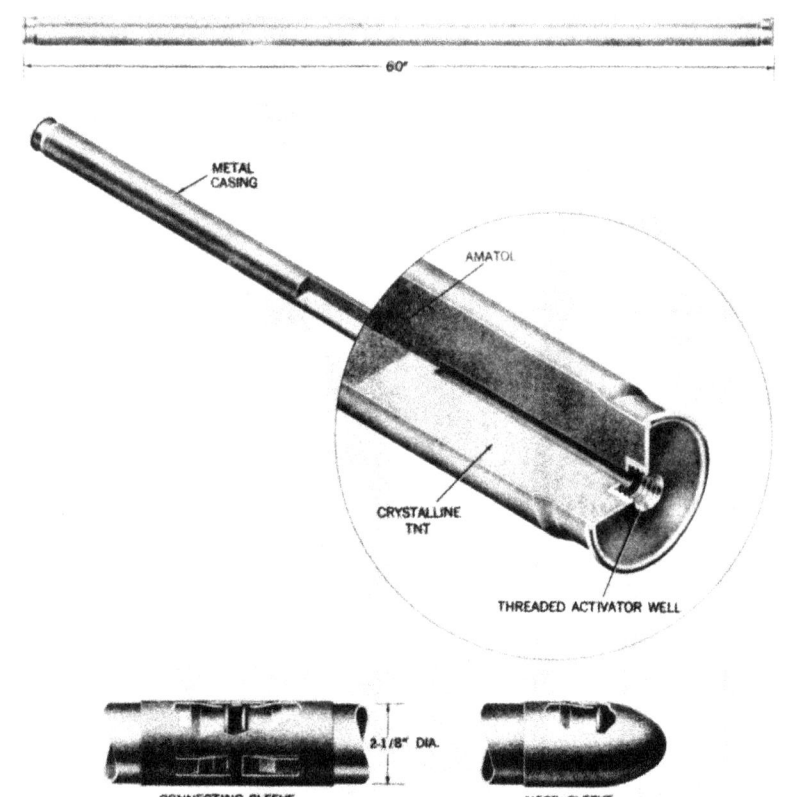

Bangalore

THE KIT CONSISTS OF 10 BANGALORE TORPEDOES PACKED IN A WOODEN BOX. EACH TORPEDO IS A FIVE FOOT OLIVE DRAB STEEL TUBE. IT CONTAINS ABOUT 9 POUNDS OF 80/20 AMATOL. EACH END OF THE TUBE IS FILLED WITH A BOOSTER CHARGE OF CRYSTALLINE TNT. BOTH ENDS HAVE A THREADED ACTIVATOR WELL TO PROVIDE MEANS OF PRIMING WITH A BLASTING CAP AND PRIMING ADAPTOR OR STANDARD DEMOLITION FIRING DEVICE. TORPEDOES CAN BE LINKED TOGETHER TO PROVIDE FOR A CHARGE OF ANY LENGTH DESIRED.

USE: TO CLEAR PATH THROUGH MINEFIELDS, BARBED WIRE OR OTHER LIGHTWEIGHT OBSTACLES. MAY ALSO BE USED UNDERWATER TO CLEAR SANDBARS OR DEAD CORAL.

SAFETY: PRIME ONLY WHEN LAST TORPEDO IS IN PLACE. BE SURE TO PUT PROTECTIVE NOSE CONE ON FIRST TORPEDO.

✱ SPECIFICATIONS

DOD CODE: M026
FEDERAL STOCK NO: 1375-028-5247
METHOD OF PACKING: TEN IN A WOODEN BOX 5.28' X 1.32' X 0.45'.
TOTAL WEIGHT: 168 POUNDS.

 **DEMO-3**

15 lb. Shaped Charge

THE 15 LB M2A3 SHAPED CHARGE CONSISTS OF APPROXIMATELY 11.5 POUNDS OF CAST 50/50 PENTOLITE, OR 9.4 POUNDS OF COMPOSITION B, WITH A 2.1 POUND 50/50 PENTOLITE BOOSTER. IT IS PACKED IN AN OLIVE DRAB, MOISTURE-RESISTANT, MOLDED FIBER CONTAINER. THE THREADED ACTIVATOR WELL AT THE TOP PERMITS PRIMING WITH A BLASTING CAP AND ADAPTOR, OR ANY STANDARD DEMOLITION FIRING DEVICE.

USE: THE M2A3 CHARGE IS USED TO BLAST A HOLE IN ARMOR PLATE OR CONCRETE, SO THAT A MORE POWERFUL EXPLOSIVE CAN BE PLACED IN THE HOLE.

SAFETY: PERSONNEL MUST TAKE COVER AT A DISTANCE OF NOT LESS THAN 100 YARDS, WHEN THE M2A3 IS DETONATED.

✱ SPECIFICATIONS

DOD CODE: M420
FEDERAL STOCK NO: 1375-529-7698
METHOD OF PACKING: TWO CHARGES IN A WOODEN BOX 1.1' X 0.9' X 1.7'.
TOTAL WEIGHT: 57.8 POUNDS

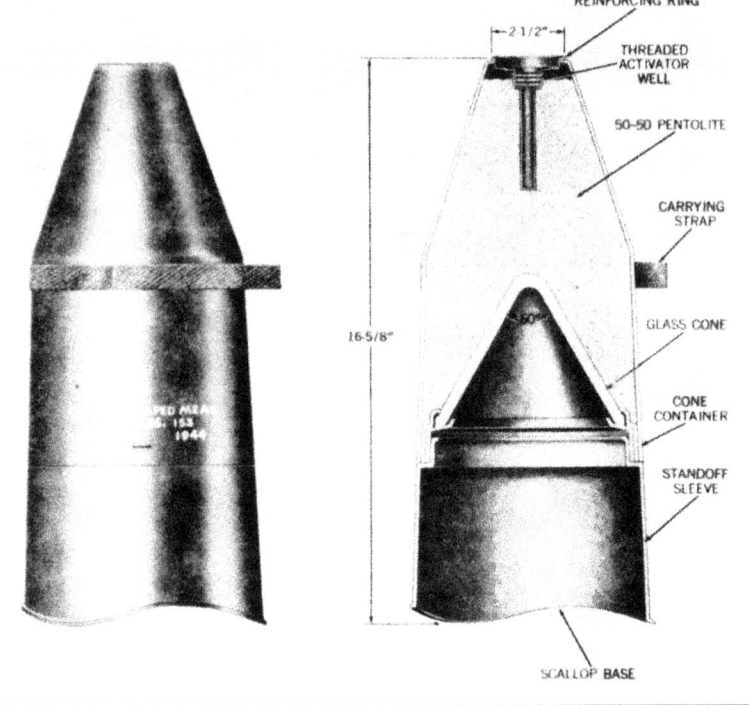

40 lb. Shaped Charge

DESCRIPTION: THE DEMOLITION CHARGE M3 CONSISTS OF APPROXIMATELY 30 POUNDS OF 50/50 PENTOLITE IN A SHEET METAL CASE. A DETACHABLE STEEL PEDESTAL PROVIDES A STANDOFF AND SUPPORT. THE THREADED ACTIVATOR WELL AT THE TOP OF THE CASE PERMITS PRIMING WITH A BLASTING CAP AND ADAPTOR, OR ANY STANDARD DEMOLITION FIRING DEVICE.

USE: USED AGAINST STEEL OR CONCRETE TO BLAST A HOLE INTO WHICH A MORE POWERFUL CHARGE CAN BE PLACED.

SAFETY: BEFORE DETONATION, PERSONNEL MUST TAKE COVER AND REMAIN AT A DISTANCE OF NOT LESS THAN 100 YARDS, BECAUSE THE METAL LEGS FLY FROM THE CHARGE WHEN DETONATED.

✱ SPECIFICATIONS

DOD CODE: M421
FEDERAL STOCK NO: 1375-028-5241
METHOD OF PACKING: ONE CHARGE IN A WOODEN BOX 1.8' X 0.9' X 1.2'.
TOTAL WEIGHT: 65 POUNDS

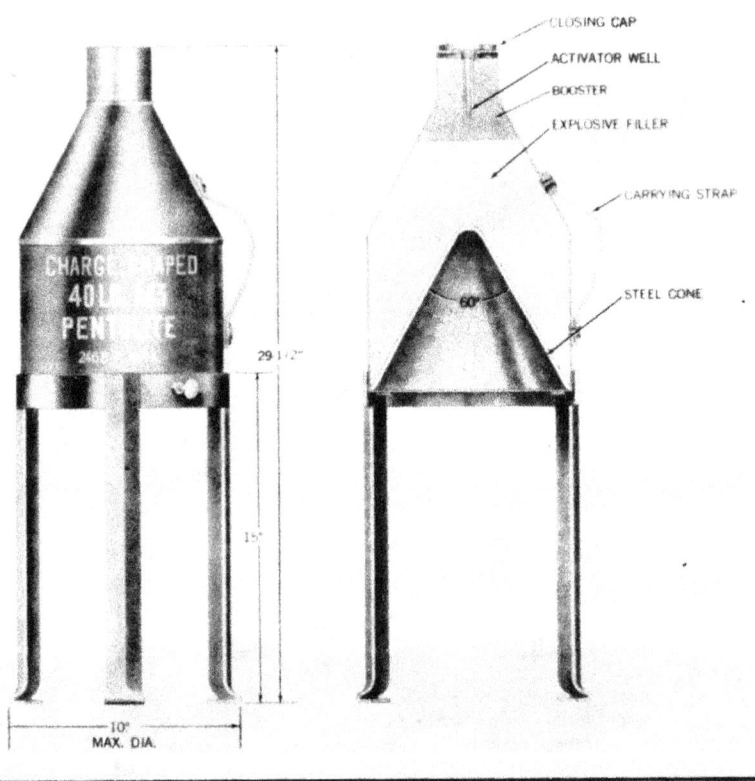

2.5 Pound Block

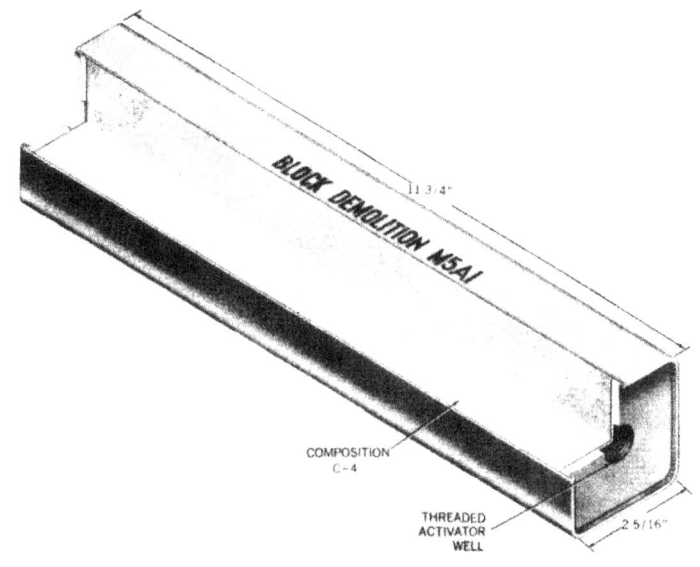

DESCRIPTION: 2.5 POUND BLOCK OF COMPOSITION C-4 PACKED INTO A RETANGULAR PLASTIC CONTAINER WHICH IS SEALED AT EACH END BY A PLASTIC PLATE. EACH END HAS A THREADED BLIND HOLE TO RECEIVE A BLASTING CAP WITH A PRIMING ADAPTOR.

USE: AS A GENERAL DEMOLITION CHARGE, INCLUDING UNDERWATER DEMOLITIONS. VERY EFFECTIVE AS A CUTTING OR BREACHING CHARGE.

SAFETY: DO NOT DETONATE IN CLOSED SPACES. C-4 PRODUCES POISONOUS GASES WHEN IT EXPLODES.

✵ SPECIFICATIONS

DOD CODE: M038
FEDERAL STOCK NO: 1375-529-7705
METHOD OF PACKING: TWENTY-FOUR CHARGES IN A WOODEN BOX 1.6' X 1.2' X 1.1'.
TOTAL WEIGHT: 75 POUNDS

Cable and Chain Cutter

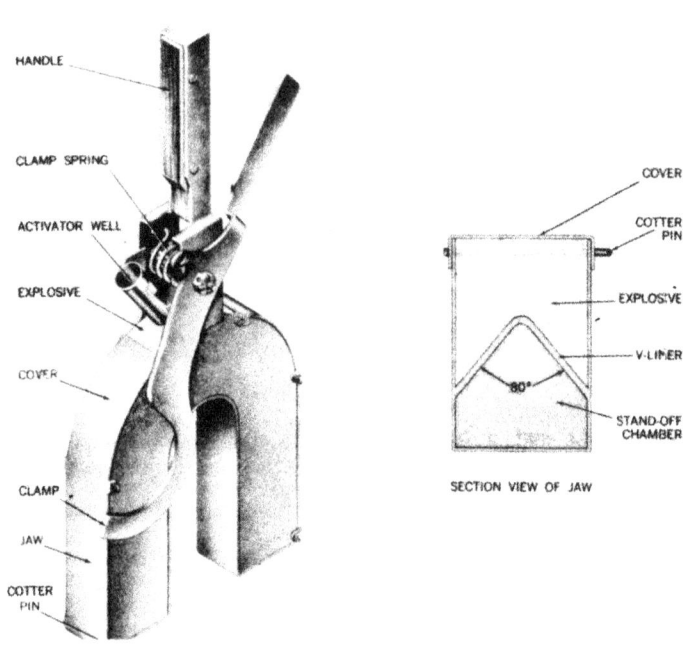

DESCRIPTION: THE CUTTER IS MADE OF CORROSION-RESISTANT SHEET STEEL. IT IS ISSUED WITHOUT EXPLOSIVE AND MUST BE LOADED IN THE FIELD WITH 1.25 POUNDS OF PLASTIC EXPLOSIVE. THE UNLOADED CUTTER WEIGHS ABOUT 2.5 POUNDS.

USE: TO CUT CABLE, CHAIN, OR ROD. CABLE UP TO TWO INCHES IN DIAMETER AND CHAIN UP TO 1.5 INCHES CAN BE CUT WITH THIS CUTTER. IT WILL WITHSTAND DEPTHS OF WATER UP TO 20 FEET.

SAFETY: NEVER FORCE A CAP INTO ACTIVATOR WELL. TAKE CARE NOT TO EXERT PRESSURE ON THE CAP WHEN TIGHTENING THE PRIMING ADAPTOR.

✵ SPECIFICATIONS

DOD CODE: X240
FEDERAL STOCK NO: 1375-093-0103
METHOD OF PACKING: TWENTY-FIVE IN A WOODEN BOX 4.67' X 1.6' X 0.9'.
TOTAL WEIGHT: 125 POUNDS

55 lb. Demolition Charge

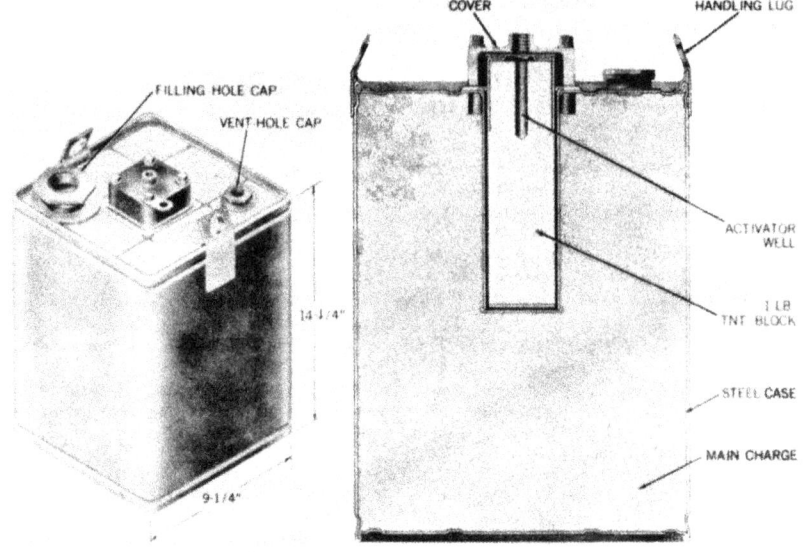

✶ SPECIFICATIONS

DOD CODE: M040
FEDERAL STOCK NO: 1375-038-5326
METHOD OF PACKING: ONE PER BOX 1' X 1' X 1.3'.
TOTAL WEIGHT: 61 POUNDS

Cable Cutter

DESCRIPTION: CONSISTS OF TWO MAIN SECTIONS: THE HOUSING AND THE CONTAINER. THE HOUSING IS MADE OF HARDWOOD OR PLASTIC WHICH IS DRILLED AND THREADED TO RECEIVE PRIMING ADAPTOR OR STANDARD FIRING DEVICE. THE CONTAINER IS MADE OF BRASS, AND HAS AN 80 DEGREE COPPER "V" LINER IN ITS LOWER END. THE CUTTER COMES LOADED WITH ¼ POUND COMPOSITION B; WITH A SMALL TETRYL BOOSTER IT WILL CUT ONE INCH DIAMETER STEEL CABLE UNDER 15 FEET OF WATER.
USE: CABLE CUTTING UP TO ONE INCH.
SAFETY: HANDLE CAREFULLY TO AVOID DAMAGE OR DEFORMATION OF CUTTER JAWS OR SPRING.

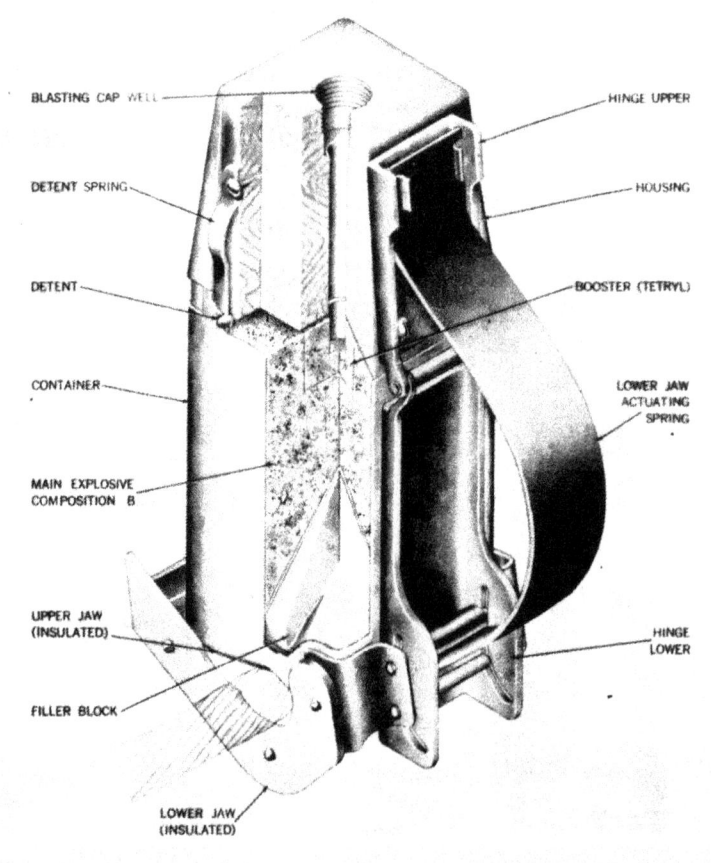

✶ SPECIFICATIONS

DOD CODE: X245
FEDERAL STOCK NO: 1375-6539-754
METHOD OF PACKING: TWENTY IN A WOODEN BOX 3' X 1.8' X 1'.0'
TOTAL WEIGHT: 37 POUNDS

Flexible Linear Demolition Charge

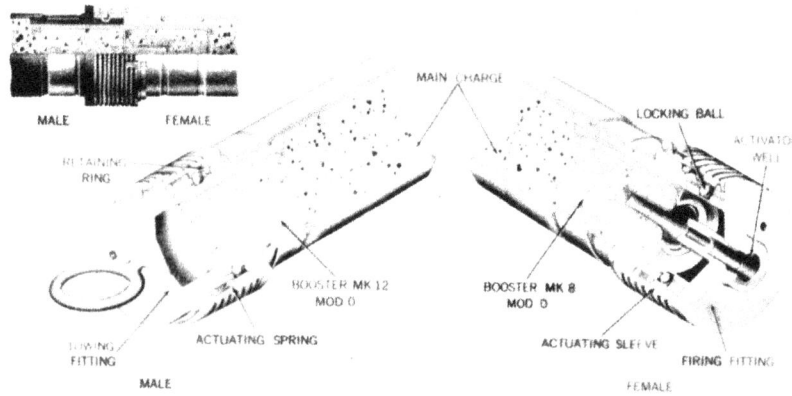

DESCRIPTION: THE MK 8 MOD 2 FLEXIBLE LINEAR TYPE DEMOLITION CHARGE CONSISTS OF A 25 FOOT LENGTH OF TWO INCH DIAMETER RUBBER HOSE, WITH A MAIN CHARGE OF 50 POUNDS OF 70/30 COMPOSITION A-3 AND ALUMINUM POWDER. THE CHARGE CONTAINS A MK 8 MOD 0 BOOSTER IN THE FEMALE END, AND A MK 12 MOD 0 BOOSTER IN THE MALE END. EACH BOOSTER CONTAINS 76 TO 79 GRAMS OF GRANULATED TNT. THE MK 8 MOD 0 BOOSTER CONTAINS AN ACTIVATOR WELL.

USE: CLEARING CHANNELS THROUGH SANDBARS AND CORAL REEFS. CAN ALSO BE LASHED TO OR WRAPPED AROUND IRREGULARLY SHAPED OBSTACLES.

SAFETY: HANDLE CAREFULLY TO PREVENT DAMAGE TO BOOSTERS, COUPLINGS, AND FITTINGS.

✶ SPECIFICATIONS

DOD CODE: M042
FEDERAL STOCK NO: 1375-6203-409
METHOD OF PACKING: THREE 25 FOOT LENGTHS IN A BUNDLE 25' X 0.4' X 0.4'.
TOTAL WEIGHT: 150 POUNDS

TNT Half-Pound Block

THE CHARGE CONSISTS OF A ½ POUND BLOCK OF COMPRESSED TNT ENCLOSED IN A YELLOW, WATER-RESISTANT FIBERBOARD CONTAINER HAVING METAL END CLOSURES. AN ACTIVATOR WELL, WHICH IS NOT THREADED, EXTENDS ABOUT 2 - 7/8 INCHES INTO ONE END OF THE BLOCK.

USE: MAIN CHARGE FOR A SMALL DEMOLITION OPERATION OR AS A BOOSTER CHARGE FOR A MAJOR DEMOLITION OPERATION MAY BE USED UNDERWATER.

SAFETY: SEE "TNT" SECTION. TAKE ADEQUATE COVER, METAL ENDS WILL FLY WHEN FIRED.

✶ SPECIFICATIONS

DOD CODE: M 031
FEDERAL STOCK NO: 1375-529-7706
METHOD OF PACKING: HALF-LB BLOCKS ARE PACKED IN WOODEN BOX 0.83' X 0.83', 100 TO A BOX
TOTAL WEIGHT: 63 POUNDS

One Pound Block

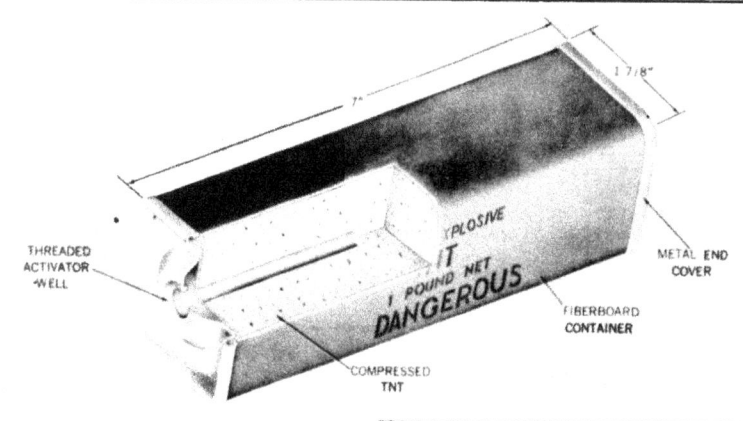

DESCRIPTION: THE ONE POUND TNT BLOCK CONSISTS OF TWO ½ POUND BLOCKS ENCLOSED IN AN OLIVE DRAB, WATER-RESISTANT, FIBERBOARD CONTAINER, WHICH HAS METAL END CLOSURES. ONE END IS PROVIDED WITH A THREADED ACTIVATOR WELL. THE FIBERBOARD CONTAINER CAN BE CUT TO PROVIDE TWO ½ POUND UNCOVERED BLOCKS, EACH WITH AN ACTIVATOR WELL.

USE: USED EITHER AS A MAIN CHARGE FOR SMALL DEMOLITION OPERATIONS, OR AS A BOOSTER CHARGE FOR A MAJOR DEMOLITION OPERATION. MAY BE USED UNDERWATER.

SAFETY: WHEN USING, TAKE ADEQUATE COVER, AS METAL ENDS FLY WHEN FIRED.

✶ SPECIFICATIONS

DOD CODE: M032
FEDERAL STOCK NO: 1375-529-7701
METHOD OF PACKING: POUND BLOCKS ARE PACKED IN A WOODEN BOX 1.67' X 0.83' X 0.83', 50 TO A BOX
TOTAL WEIGHT: 63 POUNDS

**DEMO-3**

Mk 133 Demolition Charge

DESCRIPTION: THE MK 133 MOD 0 DEMOLITION CHARGE ASSEMBLY CONSISTS OF A MK 2 MOD 0 HAVERSACK WITH AN EXPLOSIVE COMPONENT OF A MK 23 MOD 1 DEMOLITION CHAIN.

USE: GENERAL PURPOSE DEMOLITION, INCLUDING UNDERWATER OPERATIONS. THE ASSEMBLY CAN ALSO SERVE AS A SOURCE OF EIGHT INDIVIDUAL 2-½ POUND CHARGES.

✱ SPECIFICATIONS

DOD CODE.: M791
FEDERAL STOCK NO: 1375-093-0167
METHOD OF PACKING: TWO ASSEMBLIES ARE PACKED IN A WOODEN BOX 2.2' X 1.3' X 0.7'.
TOTAL WEIGHT: 65 POUNDS

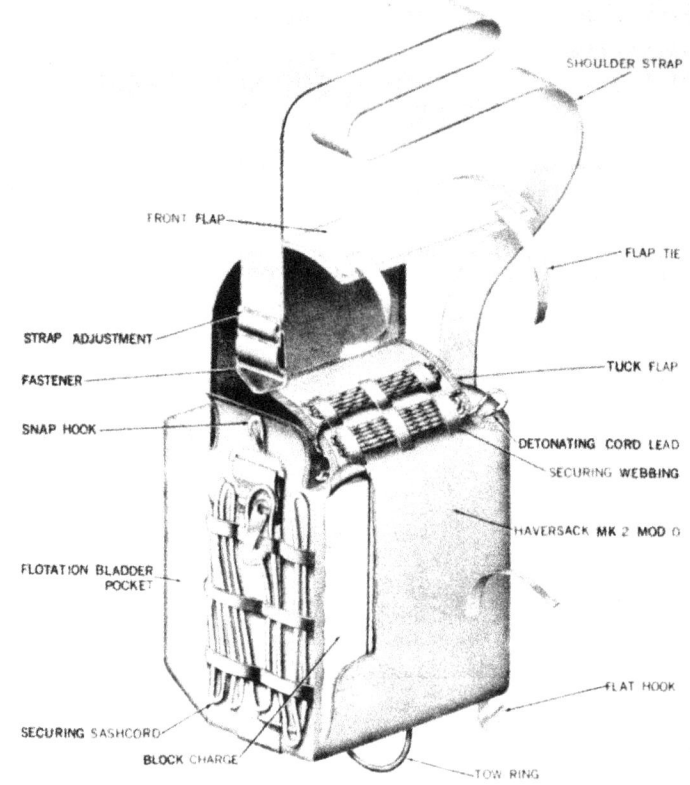

Mk 135 Demolition Charge

DESCRIPTION: THE MK 135 CONSISTS OF A HAVERSACK PACKED WITH 10 INDIVIDUAL MK 20 MOD 0 DEMOLITION CHARGES. THE MK 20 IS COMPOSED OF A TWO POUND BLOCK OF COMPOSITION C-3, CONTAINED IN A CANVAS BAG. THE BOOSTER AND EXPLOSIVE LEAD ARE MADE OF 11 FEET OF REINFORCED PRIMACORD. FIVE FEET OF DETONATING CORD ACT AS A BOOSTER, AND THE REMAINING SIX FEET EXTEND FROM THE BLOCK TO FORM AN EXPLOSIVE LEAD.

USE: GENERAL DEMOLITION OPERATIONS, INCLUDING UNDERWATER OPERATIONS.

SAFETY: PROTECT FROM HIGH TEMPERATURES AND SEVERE DROPS AND JOLTS. THE CHARGE PRODUCES POISONOUS GASES WHEN IT EXPLODES.

✱ SPECIFICATIONS

DOD CODE: M792
FEDERAL STOCK NO: 1375-093-0170
METHOD OF PACKING: TWO ASSEMBLIES ARE PACKED IN A WOODEN BOX 2.7' X 1.3' X 0.7'.
TOTAL WEIGHT: 67 POUNDS

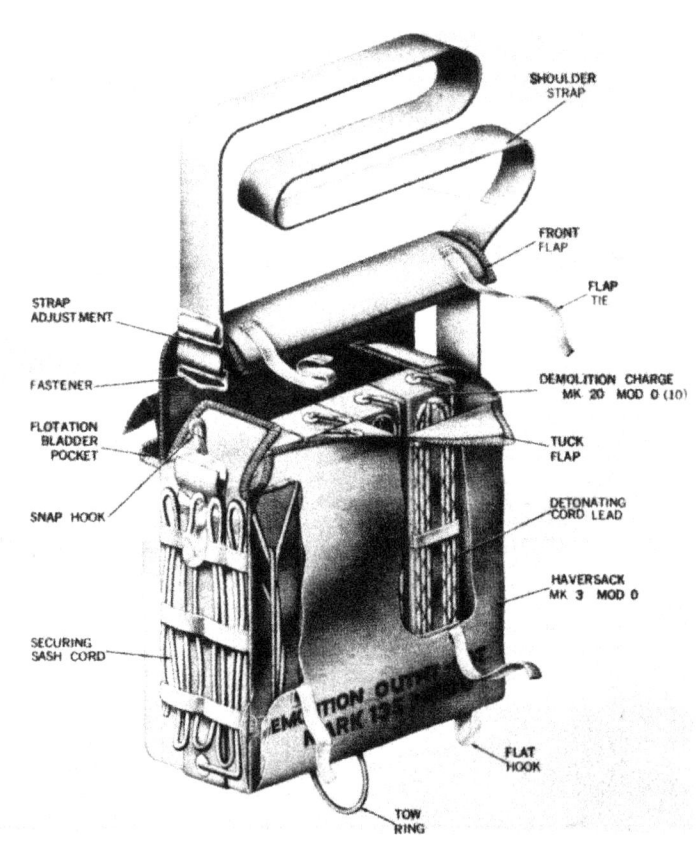

CHARGE ESTIMATION and PLACEMENT

Depending upon what type of explosive you are going to use, there are either one or two steps involved in determining exactly how much explosive you will need for a particular job:

(1) Apply the appropriate formula to determine the necessary amount of TNT.
(2) If using an explosive other than TNT, apply the appropriate relative effectiveness factor to your answer to determine the necessary amount of your particular explosive.

The next few paragraphs present the most commonly used formulas, and the final paragraph in this section shows how to use relative effectiveness.

CUTTING STRUCTURAL STEEL: Use the following formula to cut structural steel:
$$P = 3/8 \, A, \text{ where}$$
P = pounds of TNT necessary, and
A = the cross-sectional area to be cut (in square inches).

CUTTING TIMBER: Trees, as well as wooden posts, beams, etc., can be cut either with an untamped, external charge, or a tamped, internal charge. While the former can be placed much more easily and rapidly than the latter, an internal charge will produce the same results, with much less explosive. The formulas are as follows:

(1) Untamped, external charge:
$$P = \frac{D^2}{40}, \text{ where}$$
P = pounds of TNT required, and
D = diameter of the timber in inches
NOTE: For timber having diameters larger than 28 inches, increase P by 1/4. When diameter exceeds 36 inches, cutting with explosives is not reliable unless excessive amounts of explosives are used.

(2) Tamped, internal charge:
$$P = \frac{D^2}{250}, \text{ where}$$
P = pounds of TNT or plastic required, and
D = diameter, or least cross-sectional dimension at the point where the explosive was placed (in inches).

FELLING TREES TO CREATE AN OBSTACLE: The following formula applies when using an untamped, external charge to fell a tree but leave it attached to its stump:
$$P = \frac{D^2}{50}, \text{ where}$$
P = pounds of TNT required, and
D = diameter of the tree in inches.
NOTE: For trees having diameters greater than 24 inches, increase P by 1/4.

BREACHING WALLS: Use the following formula to breach walls of concrete, masonry, rock, or similar material:
$$P = R^3 K C, \text{ where}$$
P = pounds of TNT required
R = breaching radius, in feet
K = material factor
C = tamping factor
NOTES:
1. For breaching walls one foot in thickness and over, increase the total calculation by 50%.
2. For charges under 50 pounds, add 10%.

DEMOLISHING WALLS: To demolish a wall with external charges, calculate the breaching charge necessary, as explained in the above paragraph, and then determine the number of charges required by using the following formula:
$$N = \frac{W}{2R}, \text{ where}$$
N = number of charges
R = breaching radius in feet

PRESSURE CHARGE FOR BRIDGE STRINGERS: When using a tamped pressure charge on bridge stringers use the following formula to calculate the amount of explosive necessary:
$$P = 3H^2 - T, \text{ where}$$
P = pounds of tamped TNT required for each stringer.
H = height of stringer (including thickness of roadway) in feet, and
T = thickness of stringer in feet.
NOTE: Increase P by 1/3 if charge is untamped.

RELATIVE EFFECTIVENESS CONVERSION: If you know how much TNT is necessary for a job, and you want to find out how much of a substitute explosive is necessary to do the same job, use the following formula:
$$SP = \frac{PT}{RE}, \text{ where}$$
SP = pounds of substitute explosive
PT = pounds of TNT required
RE = relative effectiveness of substitute explosive
Following is a list of commonly used explosive, and their Relative Effectiveness:

AMATOL:	1.20
AMMONIUM NITRATE:	0.42
COMPOSITION A:	1.35
COMPOSITION B:	1.35
COMPOSITION C-3:	1.26
COMPOSITION C-4:	1.26
HBX-1:	1.48 in air
	1.68 in water
HBX-3:	1.48 in air
	1.90 in water
MILITARY DYNAMITE:	0.92
50/50 PENTOLITE:	1.26
TETRYTOL:	1.22
TNT:	1.00

DEMO-3

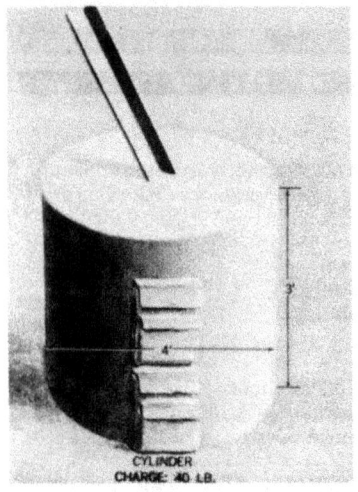
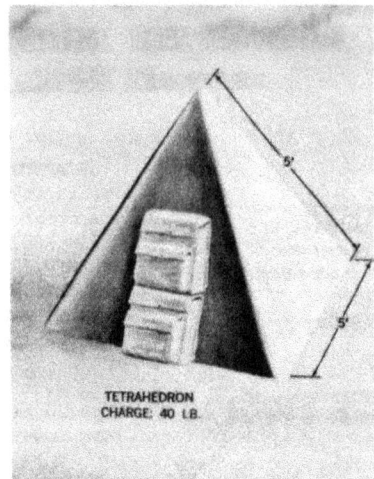

Charge Placement for Some Small Concrete Obstacles.

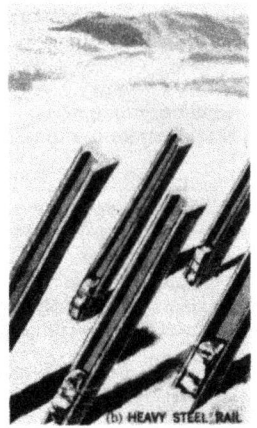
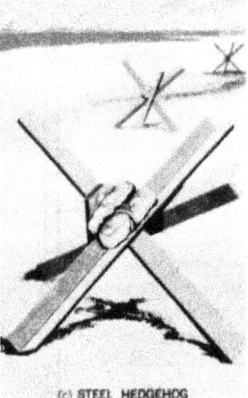

Placement of Charges Against Common Steel Obstacles.

Japanese Type of Scully.

American-Type Horned Scully With Charge Attached.

CHARGE PLACEMENT

DEMO-3

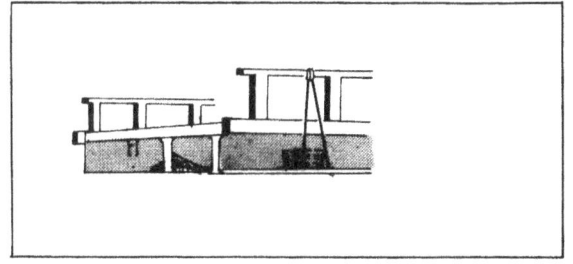
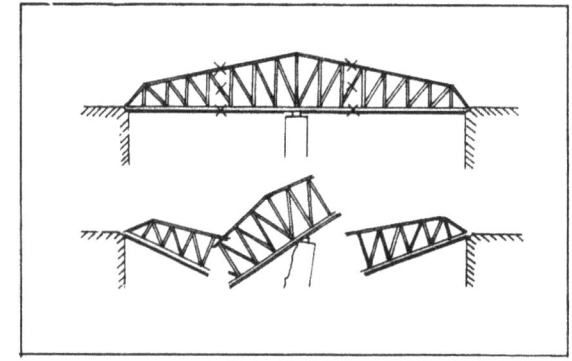
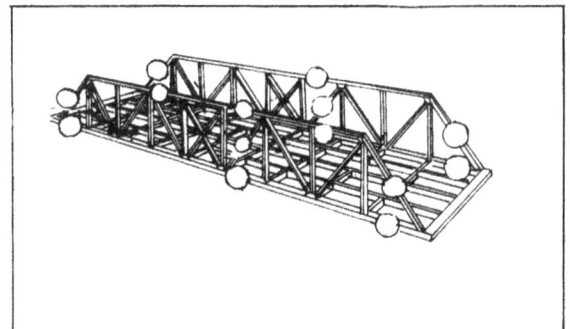
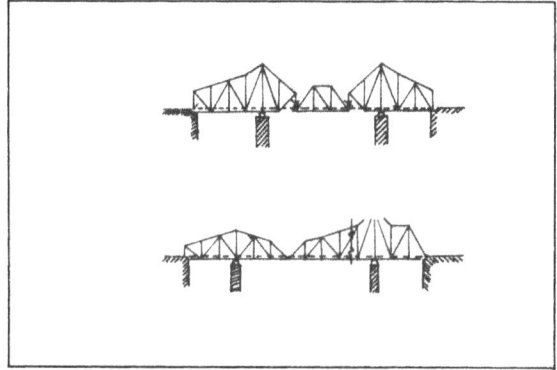
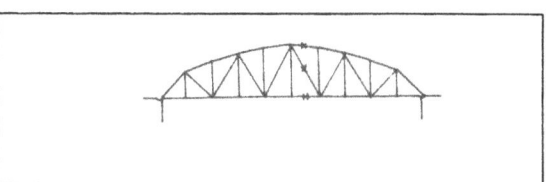

BRIDGE PLACEMENT

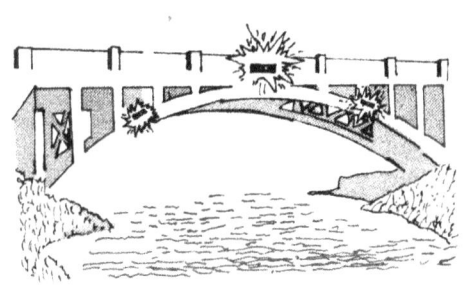
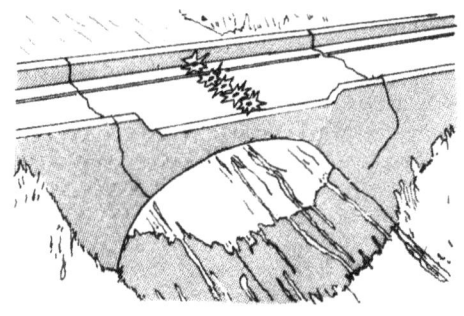

CORAL BLASTING

SELECTING TYPE OF EXPLOSIVE:
   Explosives with low detonation velocities, such as ammonium nitrate, are the best explosives to use against coral when powder points are not used. TNT, Tetrytol, and plastic explosive, however, have all been used with success. Powder points ordinarily are loaded with plastic explosive, Nitramon, or blasting gelatin.

PLACING CHARGE ON CORAL HEADS:
   In order to keep packs of demolition charges in position about either type of coral head, they should be saddled together by their haversack straps. Packs should be secured so that the detonating cord will be moved against the coral by wave action as little as possible. The sharp edges in coral growths can cut detonating cord as would a knife.
   If the detonating cord leads are not long enough to be tied together, additional detonating cord should be placed in one of the packs before it is placed in the water. A float should be connected to the detonating cord lead of this pack so that the pack can be identified.

MUSHROOM-TOP HEADS:
   The simplest method of clearing a mushroom shaped coral growth is to break the stem and let the head fall to the bottom. Let one pack of demolition charges hang down near the stem and place at least one pack on top of the head. Place the other packs about the edges of the head. This type of loading will crumble the whole head when it is exploded.

SOLID-CORAL HEADS:
   Place most of the packs on top of the head to force it down. Suspend a few packs around the side of the head.

PLACING CHARGES FOR CHANNEL BLASTING IN CORAL:
   Five types of explosive charges are commonly used to blast channels in coral growths. These are:
   (1) Explosive charges placed in powder points.
   (2) Bangalore torpedoes.
   (3) Explosive hose.
   (4) Explosive charges placed in a checkerboard pattern.
   (5) Explosive charges placed in a heavily loaded center pattern.

POWDER POINTS:
   Coral may be blasted with explosive charges dropped into powder points. They are used in place of drilled boreholes for coral, because coral particles clog a drill. Powder-point blasting requires less explosive per cubic foot of coral than any other type of blasting. Except during assault operations, it is usually the most practical type of coral channel blasting.

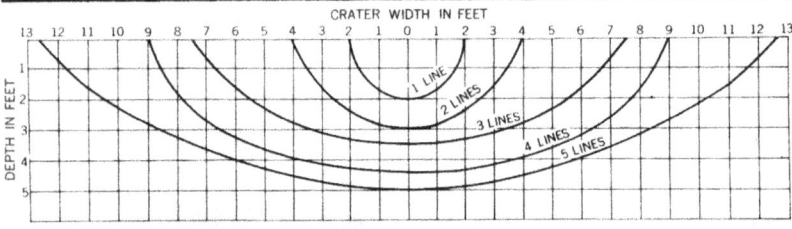

Comparative Depth and Width of Cuts Made in Coral by Bangalore Torpedoes.

BANGALORE TORPEDOES
   Bangalore torpedoes may be used, either singly or in bundles, to blast channels in coral. Bundles of torpedoes can be prepared in advance and either carried by hand or floated into position. A bundle of as many as nine lines of torpedoes can be carried by a column of men with ease if each man has only a 3 or 4 foot length to support.
   When a bundle is floated, it is lashed to light wood spreaders and enough buoyancy for a 9-line bundle. When a bundle is in position over the coral, it is cut loose from the float.

LINER-TYPE CHARGE:
   Linear-type charges may be used either singly or in bundles to blast channels in coral. When desired, several lengths may be connected to blast a long channel.

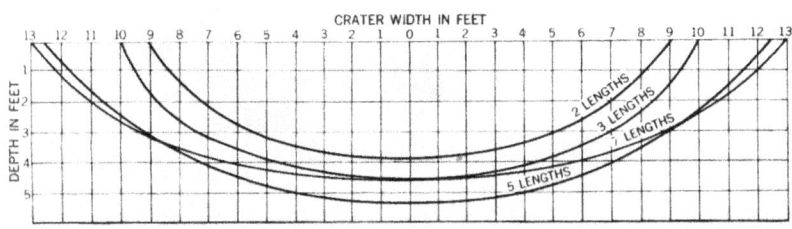

Comparative Depth and Width of Cuts Made in Coral by Demolition Charge Mk 8.

CHECKERBOARD PATTERN:

Checkerboard-pattern channel blasting is used to create a shallow channel of uniform depth. The charges are spaced uniformly about 3 or 4 feet apart. If the charges are pack charges, they are then tied together by their detonating cord leads into lines perpendicular to the beach. If the detonating cord leads are too short to be tied together, they can be tied to detonating cord trunk lines, which should be perpendicular to the beach. The surf does not move packs connected in lines perpendicular to the beach as much as it moves packs connected in lines parrallel to the beach.

CAUTION: Do not place packs in crevices that may be present. In most cases, a pack placed in a crevice tosses big coral boulders into the bottom of the channel.

HEAVILY LOADED CENTER PATTERN:

This pattern is used more often that the checkerboard pattern. It produces a channel with gently sloping sides about 30 feet wide, with a center that is about 4 feet deeper than the original floor. The charges are laid and tied in three lines perpendicular to the beach. The centerline charges are 3 feet apart; the charges in the two outer lines are 3 to 5 feet apart. Each outer line is about 10 feet from the centerline. If the charges are pack charges, they are connected to three detonating cord trunk lines with any number of jumpers between the lines.

DETERMINING AMOUNT OF EXPLOSIVE:

Underwater mushroom - top heads require about 5 pounds of TNT, or 4 pounds of either tetrytol or C-3, per cubic foot of coral. Underwater solid coral heads require more explosive than this. The illustrations show graphically the results obtained in test channel blasting with various standard demolition charges. The figures can be used as guides to the quantity of explosive needed when a channel is blasted.

A coral obstacle above water requires about three times as much untamped explosive as the same obstacle underwater. If the charge is well tamped, only about twice as much explosive is needed. If the charge is placed in a blockhole and thoroughly tamped, the same amount of explosive is used as underwater.

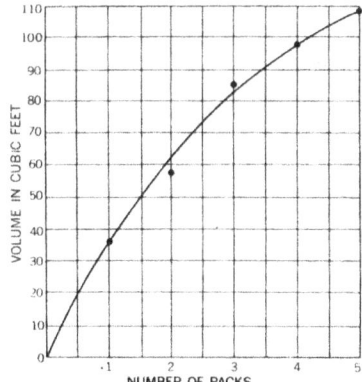

Comparative Volume of Coral Removed by 20-Pound Packs of Plastic Explosive.

COLD WEATHER DEMOLITION

EFFECTS OF COLD WEATHER ON EXPLOSIVES AND EXPLOSIVE MATERIALS:

Since extremely low temperatures cause changes in various articles, it is important to forsee these changes and handle them properly.

Explosives:

C-3: Becomes lumpy and difficult to mold at 30°F. Loses much of its plasticity after 48 hours at 15°F.

C-4 and TNT: Perform normally at low temperatures.

Primacord: Becomes brittle below 0°F.

Explosive Materials:

Electric Firing Cable: Rubber insulation becomes brittle, more easily cut, and more difficult to splice, at low temperatures.

Friction Tape: Loses its adhesive quality below 35°F. Back up tape with marlin or copper wire.

Fuse Lighter: The pin breaks and jams at low temperatures.

Galvanometer: Silver chloride cell may by rendered useless by extreme cold. Keep next to body.

Hell Box: May be rendered useless by extreme cold. Keep next to body.

Non-Electric Caps: Often misfire below 15°F.

Safety Fuse: Is rendered brittle by cold, and is easily broken. Measure fuse while it is warm, and keep it as warm as possible. Use electric firing whenever possible.

EFFECTS OF EXPLOSIVES ON ICE:

Although data on ice demolition is conflicting, the following information can be used for general guidelines when beginning an ice demolition task:

Surface blasting is relatively ineffective.

Under-ice blasting is eight times more effective than surface blasting, and it produces much less flying ice. To place packs under the ice, bore a hole in the ice, or work in from the edge of a floe. Place inflated floatation bladders in the packs to keep them against the under-side of the ice. After a shot, wait 30 to 60 minutes to allow fissures to form.

Following is a list of explosives and their effect on ice:

Bangalore Torpedoes: Relatively ineffective.

C-4 and TNT: Most effective.

Shaped Charges: Usually effective.

The M3 makes a hole 10' deep with 3' diameter at the surface and 8" diameter 3' down in Permafrost, and makes a usable hole up to 8' deep in winter ice.

The M2A3 makes a hole as deep as the M3, but with a diameter of only 5" at the top. A second shaped charge fired in the same hole is relatively ineffective.

CHANNEL BLASTING:

To make a channel 3' wide in ice 6' thick (or less):

Dig or blast holes 1-2' deep, 4' apart in the direction of and for the length of the desired channel.

Then place 2-1/2 pounds of C-4 or HBX in each hole, and detonate.

For a wider channel, make two lanes of explosives, 5' apart.

FREEING AN ICEBOUND SHIP:

First select the point of maximum pressure on the ship. From this point, move out 10' from the hull.

Then dig a hole 2-3' deep. Place 2-5 pounds of C-4 or TNT in the hole. Cover with canvas (to minimize danger from flying ice) and detonate.

ADVANCE DEMOLITIONS

Charges constructed employing advanced techniques generally produce more positive results, while using less explosives than required by conventional or standard formulas. Disadvantages of advanced technique charges are that they are usually require more time to construct, and once constructed they are usually more fragile than conventional charges. Following are rules of thumb for various charges and the targets they are designed to destroy.

SADDLE CHARGE: This charge can be used to cut mild steel cylindrical targets up to eight inches in diameter. Dimensions are as follows: The short base of the charge is equal to one-half the circumference of the target. Thickness of the charge is 1/3 block of C3 or C4 for targets up to six inches in diameter. Use one-half block thickness for targets from six to eight inches in diameter. Above Charge. Prime the charge from the apex of the triangle, and the target is cut at a point directly under the short base by cross-fracture. Neither the Saddle nor Diamond will produce reliable results against non-solid targets, such as gun barrels. These charges benefit from prepackaging or wrapping, providing that no more than one thickness of the wrapping material is between the charge and the target to be cut. Heavy wrapping paper or aluminum foil are excellent, and parachute cloth may be used if nothing else is available.

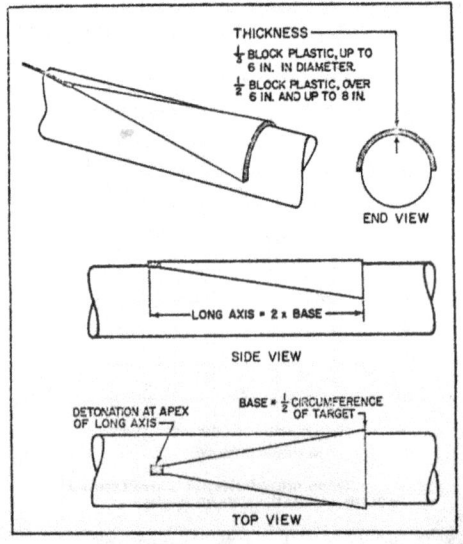

DIAMOND CHARGE: This charge can be used to cut hard or alloy steel cylindrical targets of any size that would conceivably be encountered. It has reliably been used, for instance, against a destroyer propeller shaft of 17 inch diameter. Demensions are as follows: The long axis of the Diamond charge should just touch on the far side. The short axis is equal to one-half the circumference. Thickness of the charge is 1/3 thickness of a block of C3 orC4. To prime the charge, both points of the short axis must be primed for simultaneous detonation. This can be accomplished electrically or by use of equal lengths of detonating cord, with a cap crimped on the end that is inserted into the charge. As detonation is initiated in each point of the Diamond and moves toward the center, the detonating waves meet at the exact center of the charge, are deflected downward, and cut the shaft cleanly at that point. The Diamond charge is more time-consuming to construct, and requires both more care and more materials to prime. Transferring the charge dimensions to a template of cardboard (or even cloth) permits relatively easy charge construction. (Working directly on the target is extremely difficult). The completed wrapped charge is then transferred to the target and taped or tied in place, ensuring that maximum close contact is achieved. The template technique should be used for both the Saddle and Diamond charges.

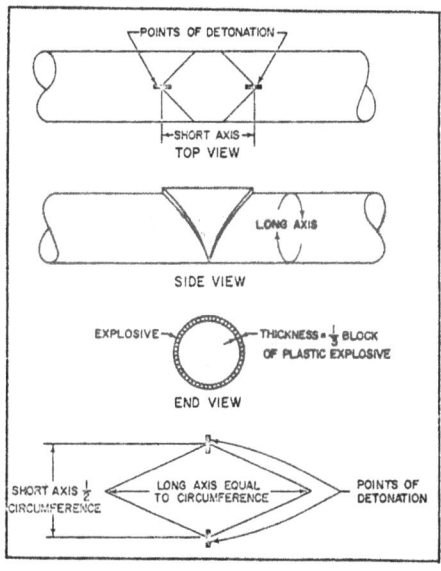

RIBBON CHARGE: To cut flat or non-cylindrical steel targets, the Ribbon charge produces excellent results at a considerable savings in explosive. Demensions are as follows: The thickness of the charge is equal to the thickness of the target to be cut. (NOTE: NEVER construct a charge less than 1/2" thick.) Width of the Ribbon is equal to twice the thickness of the target. Length of the charge is equal to the length of the desired cut. Prime from an end, and for relatively thin charges, build up the end to be primed. Build up corners if the charge is designed to cut a target such as an I-beam. Tamping is unnecessary with the Ribbon charge. A frame can be constructed out of stiff cardboard or plywood to give rigidity to the charge and to facilitate handling, carrying and emplacing it. The Ribbon charge is effective only against targets up to two inches thick, which effectively accounts for the great majority of flat steel targets likely to be encountered.

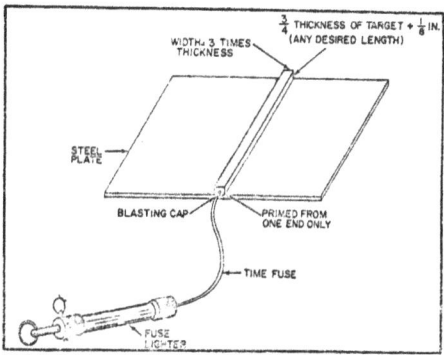

EAR-MUFF CHARGE: Within its limitations (which are quite restrictive) the Ear-Muff charge offers dramatic savings in explosives for destroying reinforced concrete targets. The rule of thumb for construction is as follows: For each foot of target thickness (up to a maximum of four feet) use one pound of C4; for fractions of a foot, go to the next higher pound. Divide the total amount of C4 exactly in half, placing one half of the charge on each side of the target, diametrically opposite each other. (This brings up one limitation; the requirement to have two sides of the target accessible). Prime the two charges to detonate exactly simultaneously, and the target will be destroyed as the shock waves meet in the center of the target and, in effect, cause it to virtually explode from within. This charge is effective and reliable only against targets that are approximately square, and not much more than four feet square.

IMPROVISED DEMOLITIONS

IMPROVISED TIME FUZE
    Boil equal parts of potassium chlorate and sugar in water. Dip cotton string in the solution, and let dry. Burning rate is approximately 60 seconds per inch.

IMPROVISED BLASTING CAP
Seal off one end of copper tubing or pipe. Pour in tetryl (finely ground)(A). Fix carbon or lead from a pencil between two wires (B) and insert into tubing. Seal off other end and detonate electrically.

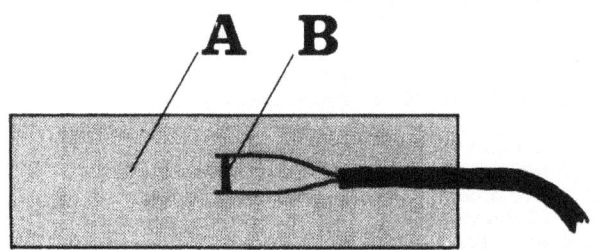

IMPROVISED BLACK POWDER
    Mix 3 parts charcoal powder, 10 parts sulphur and 25 parts perchlorate (potassium nitrate). Wet, and let stand. When almost dry, granulate by forcing through a piece of fly screen. Spread thinly and allow to dry.

IMPROVISED HIGH EXPLOSIVE
    Mix 3 parts potassium chlorate and 1 part granulated sugar. Confine in any container, and prime with time fuze.

IMPROVISED THERMITE
    (1) Combine 1 part aluminum powder, 3 parts potassium chlorate, and 1 part sugar or
    (2) Combine 1 part ferric oxide and 1 part aluminum powder.

IMPROVISED CRATERING CHARGE
       Materials: 25 lbs Amonimum Nitrate fertilizer in pellet form. 1 Quart any type motor oil.
       Procedure: Pour pellets in hole, add motor oil. Prime with a one-pound block TNT.

IMPROVISED SHAPED CHARGES
       Material: Plastic Explosive, and any cylindrical container.
       Procedure: Pack plastic explosive into container so that the cone is approximately as deep as 1/2 its diameter, and the standoff is approximately 1/2 its diameter.

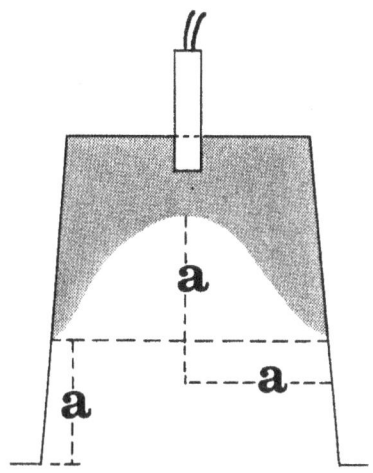

C-4 AND VASELINE
       Combined in the proper mixture, it can be made to stick to almost anything.

NOTES

- 56 THE DIVING OPERATION
- 57 DUTIES OF PERSONNEL ON A DIVE
- 61 OPEN CIRCUIT DIVING
- 66 CLOSED CIRCUIT DIVING
- 71 SEMICLOSED CIRCUIT DIVING
- 78 DIVING ACCESSORIES
- 85 EMERGENCY DIVING PROCEDURES
- 87 COMPRESSORS
- 94 UNDERWATER PHYSICS
- 96 UNDERWATER PHYSIOLOGY
- 99 DIVING DISEASES and INJURIES
- 105 DECOMPRESSION and RECOMPRESSION CHAMBER
- 109 THE RESUSCITATOR

CHAPTER FOUR
DIVING

The diving procedures and safety precautions outlined in this chapter are general in nature, and are not intended in any case to supercede specific instructions. Procedures and safety precautions are written with administrative dives in mind. It must be remembered that while training situations require strict adherence to safety precautions, the combat operation will, in most cases have to be "played by ear", with the general requirements kept as guidelines.

THE DIVING OPERATION

This section is designed to cover, in sequence, the standard procedures and safety precautions for an average dive.

GENERAL: Check bottle pressure before removing from diving locker. No dives will be made unless the minimum bottle pressure (any breathing medium) is 1500 psi for the first dive. All SCUBA tanks will be gauged and regulators tested immediately prior to use by the person swimming the equipment.

ENTERING, SWIMMING AND DIVING: No diver shall enter the water until he has been checked and been told to do so by the diving supervisor. Always enter the water feet first, holding onto the face mask. It is advisable to spit into the facemask and then wash it out to prevent fogging. Enter the water well away from any projections, exhausts, intakes, etc., and always remain on the surface for a few moments in order to accustom the body to the water. All SCUBA tanks will be put to use with the reserve valve (if available) up. Divers should surface immediately when the reserve valve is activated or when gas pressure drops below 200 psi, whichever occurs first.

Each man is responsible for checking his buddy both prior to and after entering the water for possession and proper operation of equipment. It is especially important to check for indications of leaks once in the water, and to carefully watch the buddy during descent for any malfunction. Buddies will maintain a close watch on each other at all times, and will never under any circumstances deliberately become separated.

Descend as slowly as possible to avoid squeezes; attempt to stay ahead of the pressure; and do not force the ears.

Always watch your buddy and be prepared to assist him or to wait for him. Never rush or force; do not hold the breath on the way down.

NEVER OVER-SWIM THE EQUIPMENT. This is particularly important in closed and semi-closed equipment, but can also be of importance in air SCUBA, especially if you are forcing your buddy to struggle to keep up.

On the bottom, do not separate from buddy. If you become separated, stop, look, listen, bang bottle with your knife to alert buddy, and immediately surface. If he is not already on the surface, bang the bottles again and inform the Diving Supervisor. Do not attempt to stay down and find a lost buddy.

Think calmly, think ahead, react in a calm manner. Never fight the surge or attempt to jerk away from kelp or other sea growth.

Know when your bottom time is up; surface then. Come up immediately upon activation of reserve. Do not attempt to skip breathe to increase duration. This forms bad habits which can be fatal with closed and semi-closed units.

Ascend slowly, maximum of 60' per minute. Follow your bubbles.

Breath normally at all times, especially when ascending. Relax and conserve air on the surface.

SURFACE IMMEDIATELY UPON ANY SENSATION OF MEDICAL SYMPTOMS OR SIGNS. NEVER TRY TO BE A HERO.

BUDDY SYSTEM AND LINES

Buddies are required, and buddy lines should be fastened to the wrist in such a manner that they can-

not slip off. Line signals for the buddy line should be known by all swimmers and are as follows:
- 1 tug: OK
- 2 tugs: STOP
- 3 tugs: SURFACE

No line signal should ever be ignored; i.e., an OK tug should be answered with the same tug if such is the case (it can be used for either question or answer), and the STOP and SURFACE signals must be followed immediately and without question.

DIVERS' SIGNALS

The standard diving signals as outlined in the U.S. Navy Diving Manual, section 3-13, shall be used as required. The most important ones, which should be emphasized in the briefing, are the closed fist "STOP" sign, the thumbs up "SURFACE" sign, and the pointing sign to indicate an area of difficulty (e.g., reserve, out of air, knife fouled, etc.,). The buddy line signals should always be stressed for use under conditions of poor visibility. They can also be used as "tap" signals.

The standard UDT distress signals must be used only in bonafide emergencies. These should be included in every briefing and are as follows:
(a) Lighting of the MK-13 flare.
(b) Yelling for help.
(c) Waving both arms over the head (or waving one arm if that is all that is free).
(d) A series of short blasts on the whistle.

Except in an emergency, use the hail signal: Stiff arm, palm toward boat (do not wave the arm). Never question a buddy's signal to surface (thumb up, three taps or tugs).

Any boat in the area shall immediately proceed to a diver giving the emergency signal; this signal shall always take precedence over the hail signal no matter how close the hailing personnel may be.

RETURNING FROM THE DIVE

The first step to be taken after divers leave the water is a thorough check of their condition by the corpsman/diving supervisor. Next is a check with the divers to determine any equipment malfunction. Any malfunction should be immediately recorded and reported to the Diving Locker upon return. Equipment should be washed, broken down, and returned immediately upon return to the diving locker. Breakdown procedures (as outlined in the sections on open, closed, and semi-closed circuit SCUBA) will be precisley followed.

DIVING RESPONSIBILITIES

DIVING DEPT

The Diving Department is responsible for ensuring that requested equipment is ready to go at the specified time if given sufficient prior notice. The department will check the equipment out to the individuals going on the dive and check it back in after it has been properly cleaned and broken down. The Diving Department is also responsible for training (initial training only; 6 month requals should be arranged by the platoons) and records of training, and is useful in providing information to the OIC as to his personnel's capabilities. The department is strictly administrative and will not plan or organize any operations.

O-in-C

The Officer in Charge may or may not be a Diving Supervisor, and even when qualified is not necessarily the supervisor on the dives he organizes. He should solicit the aid and knowledge of his diving supervisor in planning the dive. He has overall responsibility for the operation, must be at the scene at all times, and should not enter the water with the other swimmers. He may, however, make the initial dive to determine depth and other conditions. He should conduct the briefing and oversee the checkout and return of all equipment to be used. He is responsible for all post and pre-operational reports with the exception of the Diving Log.

The specific planning responsibilities of the OIC are as follows:

(a) Make provisions for boats through appropriate external channels or through the First Lieutenant if team boats are to be used.
(b) Notify the First Lieutenant of any additional rigging or equipment that may be required.
(c) Ensure that the Compressor watch, the chamber watch, and the UDT Senior Duty Officer are notified of the times and particulars of the operation.
(d) Ensure that adequate medical personnel and equipment, including the UDT Diving Barge for free ascent training, are provided.
(e) Notify cognizant commands if the operation is closer to a non-UDT recompression chamber.
(f) Arrange for land transportation through the CMAA and for communications equipment through the ET shop.
(g) Notify the Diving Locker of all diving equipment required.
(h) Assign personnel and ensure that they are informed as far in advance of the operation as possible.
(i) Prepare and present a full UDT briefing to all participating personnel, including representatives of the medical department, boat crews, and other supporting personnel.
(j) Ensure that minimum operational requirements for personnel and equipment as outlined above and specified in team regulations have been complied with.
(k) Ensure that U.S. Navy Diving Manual, Sections 1.7 and 3.7, current Fish and Game Laws, and Rules of the Road have been checked for compliance.
(l) Ensure that all equipment has been signed for, tested, and properly prepared.
(m) Assume overall responsibility for the operation's success and safety.

DIVING-4

HELPFUL HINTS: The Officer in Charge must ensure that the diving department has been informed sufficiently ahead of time to properly prepare the equipment; he must also be prepared to supply such help to the department as may be requested. The relation with the boatswain's locker will generally be the same as that with the diving department. In general, two days notice is desirable. In San Diego, Boat Support Unit ONE generally requires a minimum of three days notice for its boats. Chits are available and must be utilized for Boat Support Unit, although direct contact is advisable and in all cases the coxswain should be present at the briefing.

Prior notification must also be made to the medical department for arrangements for a corpsman (as required) and in order to have the chamber ready. It is also a good idea to check with the compressor watch or diving department to ensure that sufficient air is available. In the event that the UDT chamber/doctor is not available, the nearest chamber to the dive should have prior notification. Chamber locations in the area are:

USS NEREUS
USS SPERRY
Any ARS or ASR
Long Beach Naval Shipyard
Point Mugu
U. S. Naval Station Diving Barge (No Doctor available after 1600

Some of the overseas locations are:

Pearl Harbor Submarine Base Escape Tank (FPO) 96610
Yokosuka, Japan (Naval Ship Repair Facility)
Subic Bay, Philippines (Naval Ship Repair Facility)
Naha, Okinawa

In the San Diego area, in case of the absence of the UDT Medical Officer, the first locations to try by phone in case of an emergency are COMSUBRON FIVE or COMSUBRON THREE; channel requests through the Command Duty Officers.

Briefings must be held in all cases, no matter how thoroughly trained the personnel appear to be. All the information in the standard format should be covered, with special emphasis on the prevailing conditions and specifics of the operation.

Transportation for the operation can generally be provided at relatively short notice by the CMAA of the Team; however, if some special type of equipment (e.g., bus, crane, low boy) is required, Base Transportation must have a minimum of a day's notice; three or four days is preferable, for if the requested transportation has to be provided by them from other than their own vehicles, the cost is charged against the Team.

The Naval Operations Support Group, Pacific, Diving Barge, which must be utilized for free ascent training and should be available for decompression dives, is obtained through Boat Support Unit ONE.

In addition, in many cases arrangements must also be made for using the area desired for the dive (e.g., Pacific Reserve Fleet for sneak attacks, PHIBPAC for Strand, etc.). This should be done at least one week in advance.

DIVING SUPERVISOR

The Diving Supervisor is in full operational control of the dive. His responsibilities as outlined in Article 3.2.1 of the Diving Manual, and supplemented herein, are as follows:

The Diving Supervisor is the man in immediate charge of diving operations. He is either the Diving Officer or his specified representative.

The Diving Supervisor has complete authority and full responsibility in the conduct of operations. All divers are in turn responsible to him for carrying out their assigned missions as completely as possible according to the preliminary planning and briefing.

Under normal conditions the Diving Supervisor DOES NOT ENTER THE WATER; his usual post is on the surface. Whenever possible he has a full surface crew under his command and he does not have any of the routine duties of a tender or a timekeeper.

As a Diving Supervisor, observe the following:

(a) Plan the operation as completely as possible.
(b) Brief the divers as fully as possible.
(c) Take all proper precautions against forseeable contingencies.
(d) Supervise and direct all phases of the diving operations.
(e) When working with an optimum surface crew, do not enter personnally into any phase of the operation except to make the predive and postdive inspections, to give directions, or to handle an emergency.
(f) Aid the officer in charge of the operation in the planning phase and ensure that existing regulations are complied with.
(g) Conduct all necessary musters.
(h) Ensure that all divers have the required equipment with them before departing the staging area.
(i) Conduct initial and periodic radio checks with the command area and other stations on the net.
(j) Conduct pre-dive inspection of each diver (see Diving Supervisor's Check off list, P__); ensure that buddy pairs conduct mutual inspections and enter the water together; ensure that each diver fully understands his instructions before he enters the water.
(k) Fill out all applicable information on the rough diving log at the scene. Check with divers for equipment malfunction at the scene.
(l) Complete the smooth Diving Log within 24 hrs after completion of the dive.
(m) Supervise returning and cleaning of equipment; ensure that it is properly maintained and stored.
(n) Take complete charge during any diving emergency during the operation, and ensure that proper action is taken and reports made.
(o) Ensure that all safety precautions, Team Instructions, and other pertinent orders are followed.

Diving Supervisors are qualified only for the team in which they are serving; upon transfer they must be requalified in accordance with the new units instruc-

O-in-C CHECKLIST

ADMINISTRATION AND PLANNING

____ Have you notified all interested activities that diving operations are in progress?

____ Is the type of gear you have chosen to use adequate and safe for the job?

____ Is the recompression chamber ready for use or have you notified the nearest command having one that you may need it?

____ Have you made provision to obtain medical assistance in case of emergency?

____ Has a timekeeper been detailed and does he understand his duties and responsibilities?

____ Is a copy of the decompression tables available?

____ Have the divers been thoroughly briefed and understand what is to be accomplished and how?

____ Has a lead line or fathometer measurement of the depth of water been made?

____ If conducting a search, have you exhausted all other means before putting the divers down?

____ If diving on a ship, have you informed the duty engineer and received an acknowledgment?

____ If diving around the hull of a submarine, have you notified the duty officer not to operate bow planes, stern planes, vents, sound heads, or propellers?

PERSONNEL

____ Have you determined that all of the divers you intend to use have been examined and found to meet the physical standards for deep sea diving within the current calendar year?

____ Have all of your men been trained to use the equipment you have selected?

____ Do you have reason to suspect the physical condition of any of your men? Consider the following:

____ Do not dive a man if he is suffering from a cold, sinusitis, or ear trouble.

____ Do not dive a man who is fatigued from lack of sleep or previous physical or emotional strain.

____ Do not dive a man who shows evidence of alcoholic intoxication or its after-effects.

____ If you question the physical condition of any man, have him report to medical officer and be guided by his advice.

____ Have all the divers been qualified to the depth of the job?

____ Do not force or urge a man to dive if he honestly desires to be excused. If his reasons for wishing to be excused do not appear to be sufficient or appropriate, it is best to take administrative action.

EQUIPMENT

____ Has the equipment you intend to use been tested and adopted for Navy use?

____ Have you inspected the equipment to determine that it is in usable condition?

____ Do you have an adequate supply of compressed gas available?

SAFETY DURING DIVING OPERATIONS

____ Have all efforts been made to prevent the divers from becoming fouled on the bottom?

____ Have divers been instructed not to cut any lines until they have made certain of the purpose for which they are being used?

____ Is the diving boat moored in the most advantageous position to minimize effort by the divers to reach their work?

____ Are you displaying the proper signal? FOUR Flag.

____ If diving in international waters, either of the following hoists are correct:

"Underwater task" shapes--red ball. white diamond. red ball. spaced 6 feet apart.

International diving hoist: code pennant. Foxtrot-Charley-Zulu.

____ Has a standby diver been designated and is he ready to enter the water in a minimum of time?

____ If working inside a wreck, have you made arrangements for one diver to tend the lines of the diver working inside from the point of entry?

____ If using explosives, have you taken measures to prevent a charge being set off when a diver is in the water?

Use the full deep sea diving outfit when using electric power for underwater welding or cutting.

REMEMBER: In all cases the depth of the water and the condition of the diver (especially in regards to fatigue), rather than the amount of work to be done, shall determine the amount of time the diver is to spend on the bottom.

____ Have you made provisions for decompressing the divers should this be necessary?

tions. In addition, they are qualified only for the equipment in which they are already qualified, and may be required to take periodic requalification courses and tests.

STANDBY DIVER

A standby diver is required on all operations. He should be qualified in all types of equipment to be used on the dive. He will be completely dressed, checked out, and ready to go at all times on the scene. He usually will not have SCUBA on his back, but will always have it within quick and easy reach; he will always use open circuit equipment, preferably a light small rig. He will enter the water only in case of an actual emergency, as ordered by the Diving Supervisor. When standing by for a surface tended diver without a buddy, he should also have a tending line available for his own use as required.

CORPSMAN

A corpsman is required on all training dives and is advisable on all others. He should not enter the water, but should standby on the surface with his medical kit and resuscitator ready. If he is present, he should conduct a pre-dive and post-dive

DIVING-4

DIVING SUPERVISOR'S CHECKLIST

Before a swimmer enters the water, the diving supervisor will inspect him to ensure that:
(a) The diver is in possession of all required equipment.
(b) He has purged properly (if necessary).
(c) His physical and mental condition is suitable for diving.
(d) Lifejacket: Toggle operates smoothly, no holes in cartridge.
(e) Weight Belt: Quick release operative and in proper position (e.g., outside all other equipment; below waist valve on Emerson). Worn so as to fall freely when pulled. Sufficient weight for slightly negative buoyancy.
(f) Scuba: Worn properly, with quick releases when applicable. Breathing medium turned on. Proper purging procedure has been followed. All connections tight, all valves operating freely, reserve up, equipment in satisfactory operating condition.
(g) All equipment operating properly, knife readily available, buddy line and float attached as applicable.
(h) Diver thoroughly familiar with his duties, with UDT/SEAL distress signals, underwater signals as applicable, and specifically with regard to his operation.
(i) Diver using equipment in which he is qualified, familiar with depth/time limits.
(j) Diver leaves boat/pier only when told, properly logged out by timekeeper.

inspection of all divers to determine fitness to dive and effects of the operation. He should also have a supply of nose drops available.

DOCTOR

A diving medical officer is required for free ascent training and for some submarine operations. Check COMNAVOPSUPPGRUPACINST 03120.1 and COM SUBFLTONE 03120 series Instructions for requirements in submarine operations.

BOAT CREW

The standard boat crew, as required by the type craft. The boat crew should not dive, but the engineer may be used as necessary for a timekeeper or tender.

TIMEKEEPER

Whenever possible, the timekeeper should have no other duties during the dive. His primary job is to keep stopwatch time on all divers and inform the diving supervisor of any irregularities, as well as keeping him informed at all times of the status of the dive. The following is a list of his duties:
(a) Log time of starting descent.
(b) Know the probable diving depth and duration of the apparatus.
(c) Notify the supervisor when bottom time is up.
(d) Forsee decompression and warn the diving supervisor soon enough to make adequate arrangements.
(e) Provide the supervisor with assistance in figuring decompression schedule.
(f) Log times of starting ascent, decompression stops, and surfacing, when known.

The timekeeper should be an on-shore assistant to the supervisor when the operation requires departure from boats and egress on land.

TENDER

The tender is used to assist divers as necessary in dressing, leaving, and boarding the boat and to handle equipment used by the divers. He shall tend the lines of divers who require surface control. The tender is mandatory when a single diver is used. He is not necessarily diving qualified, but he must thoroughly know the diving line signals.

DIVERS

Divers must be qualified in the type equipment they are using in accordance with the pertinent team instructions (i.e., qualification from one unit does not necessarily mean blanket qualification from the others). They must be either in buddy pairs or surface line tended. The diver has the responsibility of carrying out the task assigned to him to the best of his ability, and he must exercise full judgement in doing so. He may use his own discretion in performing any phase of his mission, but must immediately obey a signal to surface. The diver is further responsible for thoroughly understanding the briefing and for ensuring the safety of his buddy to the best of his ability.

OPEN CIRCUIT

The open circuit is the least economical of all types of SCUBA, for only five percent of the available breathing media is utilized. Because of this, and because of the large amount of bubbles and noise emitted by the units, open circuit cannot be used for extended swims, where secrecy is necessary, or when working near acoustically activated demolitions. Their primary use in the teams is for training and searches. The depth limit is 130' due to the increasing effect of nitrogen narcosis beyond that depth. Normally, open circuit dives requiring decompression should not be conducted. When decompression dives are required, the UDT Diving Barge with its chamber should be on the scene, as available.

The open circuit SCUBA unit presently furnished by BUSHIPS and on the UDT Allowance List is regulator and cylinder assembly, low magnetic effects model FSN S4220-541-7397. This is a low magnetic effect model designed for EOD use with non-acoustic mines, and consequently all replacement parts are to be requisitioned only from Ship Parts Control Center, Mechanicsburg, Pennsylvania. Requests for parts must specify non-magnetic parts.

The unit is manufactured by U. S. Divers and utilizes their DA Aqua-Master regulator attached to twin 90 s. The bottles are constructed of spun aluminum and each has a nominal internal volume of 725 cubic in. When charged to 3000 psi, the assembly contains approximately 170 cubic feet of free air. Weight when charged is 90 pounds. Technical Manual 394-0065 provides repair and maintenance instructions and part numbers.

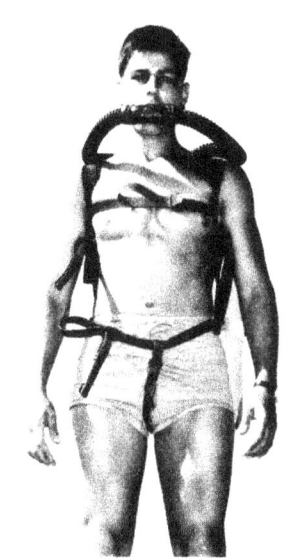

OPERATING PROCEDURES

The following is a list of routine procedures to be followed by each diver prior to leaving the lung locker. They are general in nature and should be used in conjunction with specific procedures outlined by the individual teams.
  (a) Gauge bottle (Minimum pressure: 1500 psi. Maximum: 3000 psi).
  (b) Check that all bottle straps are complete and that quick release "D" rings are present.
  (c) Check reserve valve for proper operation and charging: Activate it and return it to the ready position. This procedure ensures that if the bottle was charged with the reserve valve up it will now have a reserve charge. You should hear the air equalize.
  (d) Check regulator for leaks by installing it on bottle manifold, turning air on, blocking first inhalation then exhalation hoses to check for flapper valve leak. Turn off air; suck off pressure. If air is obtained after pressure is removed there is indication of

either a leak in the intake hose or a loose h.p. assembly.

When loading bottles on trucks, ensure that they are stood up against the cab, and that the manifolds are not banged in any way. Manifolds are constructed of brass and can be very easily damaged, especially on the reserve end.

When returning equipment, the following procedure will be used:

(1) Wash bottles and regulator thoroughly; ensure that hoses and mouthpiece are thoroughly rinsed off. Do not get water in the h.p. assembly or on the filter. This can be avoided by leaving the regulator on the bottle while washing it, by keeping a finger over the filter, or by replacing the dust cover. If the dust cover is used, ensure that its "O" ring is in place.

(2) Ensure that equipment is drip-dried before returning it to the locker.

The same procedure applies to the care and handling of single hose regulators. BUSHIPS has not approved the use of single hose regulators for general diving. Therefore, their use is restricted to hooka rigs, SDV operations, and other specialized work (e.g., astronaut rescue). Single hose regulators held by the teams vary in trade name, as none are obtained through supply channels.

Open circuit regulators are assigned to individuals for hygienic reasons, in accordance with BUMEDINST 6420.1 series. This Instruction also contains cleaning instructions. Regulators will generally be thoroughly overhauled yearly, and repaired as necessary. Maintenance on the bottles includes hydrostatic test (to 5000 psi) after five years of operation and every three years thereafter, and an annual internal inspection in accordance with BUSHIPS letter 9930.6 serial 638C-149 of 15 March 1963.

RULES OF OPEN CIRCUIT DIVING

(a) Never charge the apparatus with oxygen.
(b) Always charge the apparatus with clean air from a known source.
(c) Charge the cylinders to the full pressure rating.
(d) Gauge the cylinder pressure immediately before a dive.
(e) Do not dive without an adequate air reserve mechanism.

EMERGENCY PROCEDURES

LEAKY BOTTLE MANIFOLD: Best noticed by buddy on initial water check; surface if bad; if minor, permissible to use for short shallow dives when no decompression is required.

TAKING IN WATER: Leak in intake hose or exhaust valve not water-tight, allowing water to enter through side of mouth. Permissible to continue for short shallow dives if the amount is not sufficient to cause inhalation of the water.

HARD TO BREATHE: LP diaphram is not well set, or swimmer is inexperienced. Surface. This may also be an indication that the bottles are empty; activate reserve and surface.

IMPOSSIBLE TO EXHALE: Exhaust valve installed backwards, or flapper valve stuck shut. Exhale forcibly to try to unstick flapper valve; if impossible, exhale through nose, and surface. This may also indicate a restriction in the exhalation hose.

IMPOSSIBLE TO INHALE: Air not turned on, hose restriction in inhalation hose, inhalation valve in backwards. Surface.

cylinder valve assembly

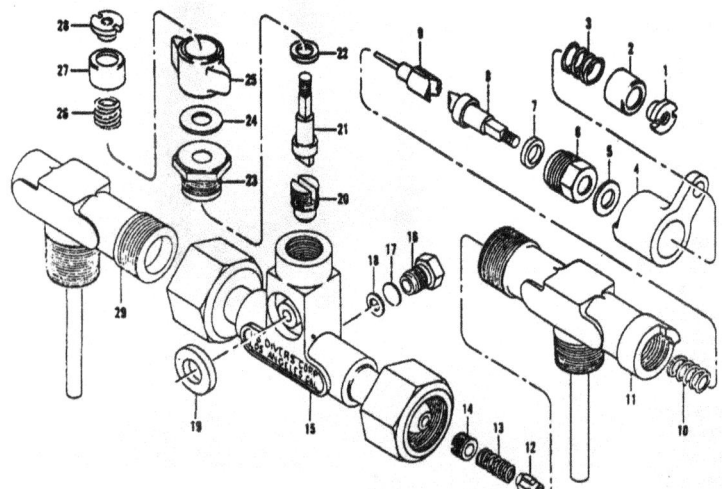

1. NUT
2. CAP
3. SPRING
4. SLIDE LEVER
5. WASHER
6. BONNET
7. WASHER
8. SIT STEM
9. PLUNGER AND PIN ASSEMBLY
10. SPRING
11. SCREW PLUG
12. FLOW CHECK
13. SPRING
14. SCREW PLUG
15. BODY
16. SAFETY PLUG
17. SAFETY DISC
18. SAFETY DISC WASHER
19. OUTLET WASHER
20. NIPPLE AND DISC ASSEMBLY
21. STEM
22. WASHER
23. BONNET
24. WASHER
25. VALVE HANDLE
26. SPRING
27. CAP
28. NUT
29. BODY

two hose regulator

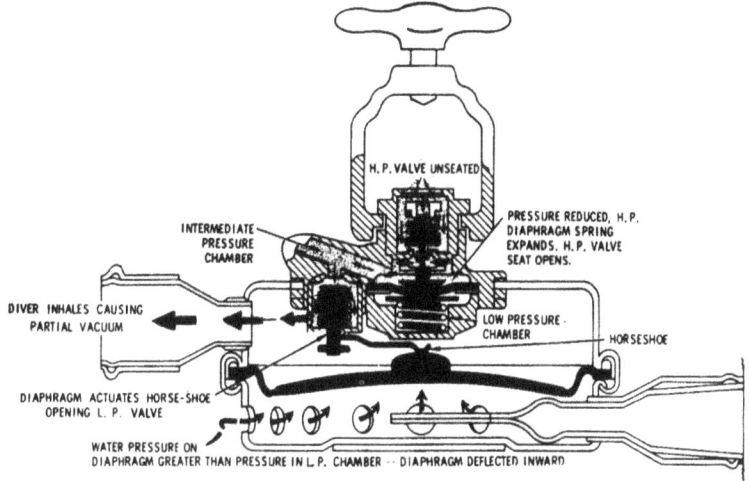

EXHAUSTION OF THE AIR SUPPLY

Running out of air is not a serious situation unless the air reserve mechanism has failed to function. Even in this case, the increase in breathing resistance prior to complete exhaustion of the air supply warns the diver.

When breathing resistance becomes noticeable, open the air reserve valve and start the ascent.

If opening the air reserve valve does not restore a normal breathing supply, surface immediately. During ascent the reduction in water pressure provides at least a small amount of additional air unless the failure is mechanical.

Continue to breathe normally throughout ascent, if possible. If not, exhale continuously throughout.

REGULATOR LEAKS AIR

Indicated by hissing even when not in use. HP leak or horseshoe damaged. Surface. Air leak from between regulator and manifold "O" ring worn or regulator not properly attached. Attempt to straighten regulator; surface if leak is bad.

---

notes

DIVER RESCUE PROCEDURES

The general procedure for open circuit is to get behind the victim, squeeze his lungs or gut to force him to exhale, straighten him out and start him to the surface. If this is difficult, drop his weights and actuate his lifejacket if necessary. If not already done, activate his lifejacket on the surface, then remove his mouthpiece and facemask, call for help, and if possible and necessary attempt to administer mouth to mouth resuscitation while waiting for the boat.

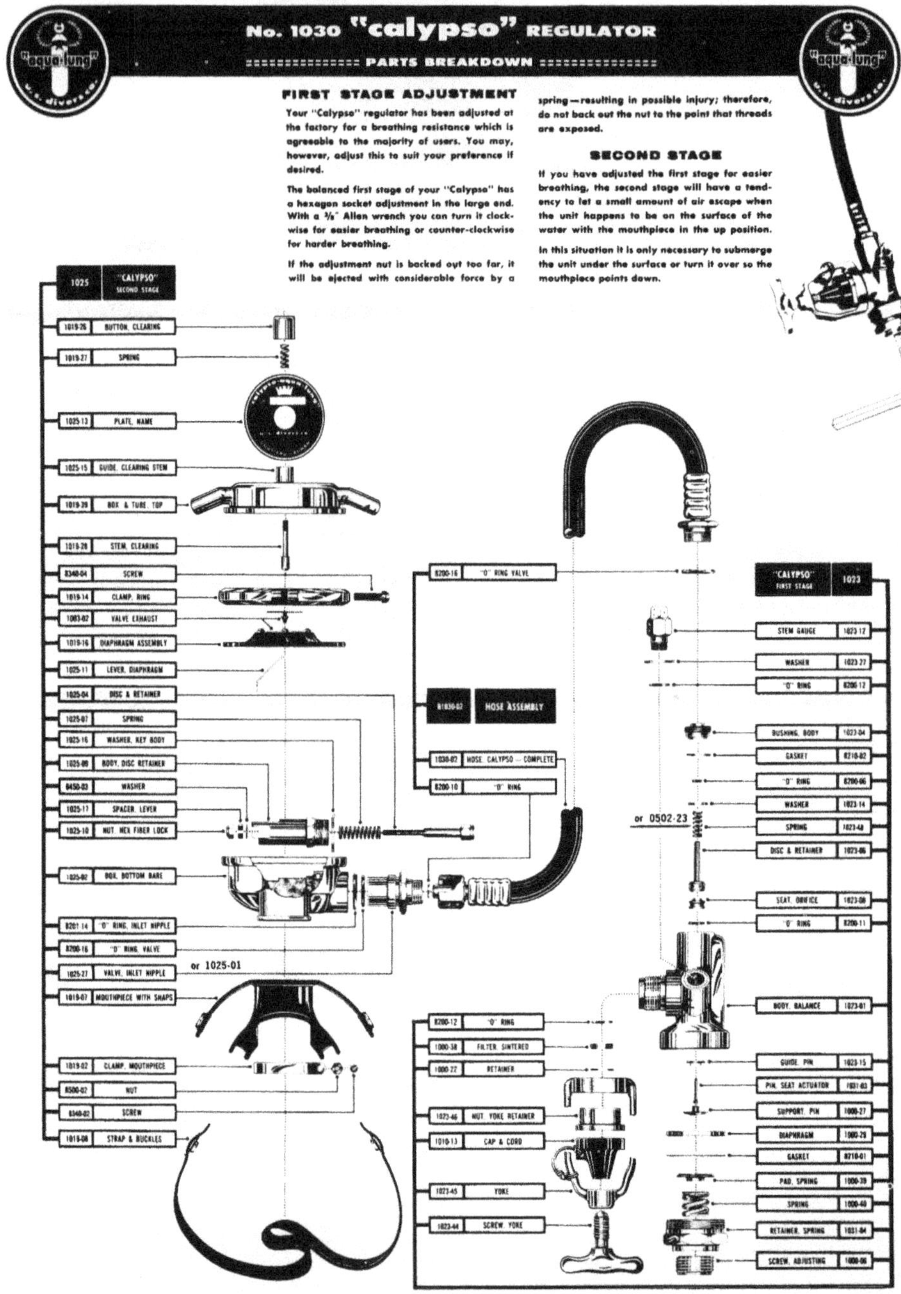

No. 1030 "calypso" REGULATOR
PARTS BREAKDOWN

FIRST STAGE ADJUSTMENT

Your "Calypso" regulator has been adjusted at the factory for a breathing resistance which is agreeable to the majority of users. You may, however, adjust this to suit your preference if desired.

The balanced first stage of your "Calypso" has a hexagon socket adjustment in the large end. With a 3/8" Allen wrench you can turn it clockwise for easier breathing or counter-clockwise for harder breathing.

If the adjustment nut is backed out too far, it will be ejected with considerable force by a spring—resulting in possible injury; therefore, do not back out the nut to the point that threads are exposed.

SECOND STAGE

If you have adjusted the first stage for easier breathing, the second stage will have a tendency to let a small amount of air escape when the unit happens to be on the surface of the water with the mouthpiece in the up position.

In this situation it is only necessary to submerge the unit under the surface or turn it over so the mouthpiece points down.

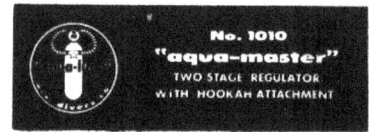

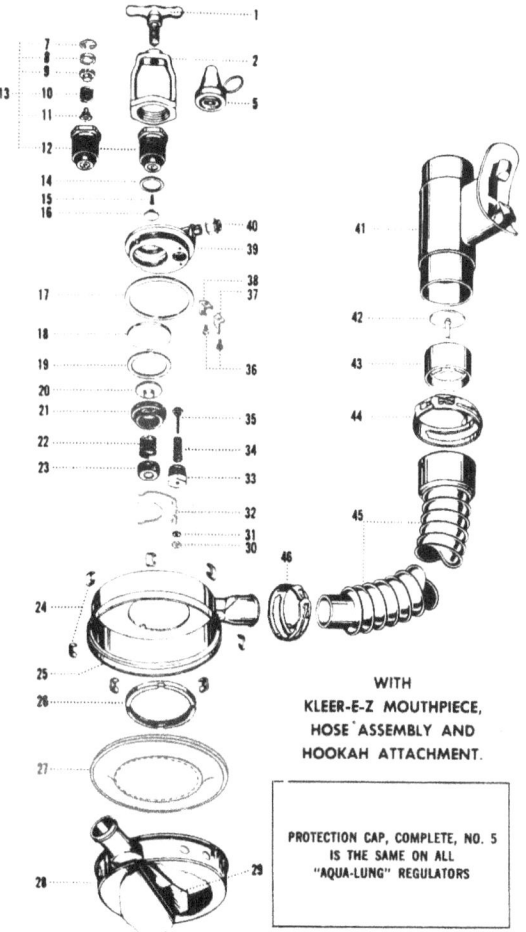

WITH
KLEER-E-Z MOUTHPIECE,
HOSE ASSEMBLY AND
HOOKAH ATTACHMENT.

PROTECTION CAP, COMPLETE, NO. 5
IS THE SAME ON ALL
"AQUA-LUNG" REGULATORS

PARTS BREAKDOWN NO. 1010		
Index	Stock No.	Description
1	1010-57	
	or	
	1000-03	Yoke Screw
2	1000-04	Yoke
5	1010-13	Protection Cap and Cord
7	1000-22	Circlip
8	1000-38	Filter Sintered
9	1000-23	Spring Block
10	1000-24	Spring
11	1000-33	Seat Assembly
12	1000-21	High Pressure Nozzle
13	1000-20	High Pressure Valve Complete
14	8210-03	
	or	
	1000-13	Gasket
15	1000-25	Pin
16	1000-27	Pin Support
17	1000-34	Gasket
18	1000-29	Diaphragm H.P.
19	8210-01	
	or	
	1000-16	Gasket
20	1000-39	Spring Pad
21	1000-05	Spring Retainer
22	1000-40	Spring
23	1000-06	Adjusting Screw
24	1000-15	Clip (7)
25	1000-28	Top Box Assembly
26	1000-14	Ring
27	1000-37	Diaphragm L.P. Neoprene
28	1000-30	Bottom Box
29	1010-18	Exhaling Valve
30	1004-09	Nut
31	8450-03	
	or	
	1003-19	Washer
32	1010-05	Horseshoe
33	1010-04	Seat Holder
34	1010-06	Spring
35	1010-07	Seat Holder and Disc Assembly
36	8340-03	Screw
37	1010-02	Lock Support R.
38	1010-02	Lock Support L.
39	1010-08	Body
40	1010-09	Cap for Hookah Outlet
41	1128-02	Mouthpiece Tee, Black
42	1108-02	Rubber Valve Disc
43	1108-03	Valve Disc Support
44	1123-07	Clamp 1-3/4", Black
45	1128-08	Neoprene Hose, Black
46	1123-06	Clamp 1-1/4", Black

65

CLOSED CIRCUIT

The primary advantages of closed circuit equipment are that it is quiet, can be utilized effectively on long, shallow swims, is hard to detect, is economical of gas, and is comfortable to wear. 100% of the gas media can be utilized and the gas consumption is dependent only on the work rate, not on depth. Disadvantages include depth limitations (oxygen becomes extremely toxic at two atmospheres); the delicacy of the equipment; the consequent length of time spent in training, preparation, and maintenance; and the reduced work rate necessitated by the possibility of rapid CO_2 buildup. The apparatus lends itself excellently to SDV and/or sneak attack operations.

EMERSON

The EMERSON Closed circuit Oxygen Breathing Apparatus, hereinafter referred to as the Emerson, was accepted by and phased into the U. S. Navy on or about June, 1963. It replaced the German made DRAEGER LT LUND II, which had in turn replaced the Italian made PIRELLI 901 and 701. The Emerson is a recirculating, closed circuit, selfcontained oxygen breathing apparatus. It has a 12.7 cubic foot (359.6 litre) standard oxygen cylinder which can be charged to 2000 psi, and a cylindrical canister which will hold approximately 6 pounds of baralyme. It has a useful duration of up to four hours at a moderate work rate (1 litre/minute). Other major components include the gas supply control unit (waist valve) which can be set to provide a constant flow of 0 to 3.5 litres/minute, a by-pass valve which permits 75 psi air to pass directly into the right breathing bag, two breathing bags (each with a 4 litre capacity) attached to a zippered vest with common sense fasteners, a regulator preset to 75 psi, and a mouthpiece assembly fitted with non-return valves and a 2-way (off/bag) valve. The completely assembled unit weighs about 35 pounds out of water (including baralyme), and is approximately neutrally buoyant underwater. The unit is carried under FSN 9L6505-053-2461, and is covered in Instruction Book NAVSHIPS 393-0656. The use of granular, as opposed to pellet, baralyme, is required by Naval Operations Support Group, Pacific, Instruction 9940.1.

REBREATHING CYCLE

The rebreathing cycle when the unit is in use is as follows: On inhaling, the diver receives gas directly from the right-hand breathing bag through the right-hand tubing and the one-way inhalation valve. On exhalation, exhaled gas (now containing carbon dioxide from the lungs) is prevented by the one-way inhalation valve from passing back into the right-hand breathing bag. Instead, it passes from the mouthpiece assembly through the one-way exhalation valve, and through the left-hand tube to the left-hand breathing bag. As it enters the left breathing valve, the exhaled gas displaces gas from the left breathing bag, causing flow into the absorption canister, where the carbon dioxide is removed. Gas within the canister, now free of carbon dioxide gas, is displaced into the right breathing bag where it is joined with the flow straight from the oxygen cylinder and remains until the next inhalation. This circuit-breathing system minimizes rebreathing of apparatus dead-space gas. There is also an over-pressure valve at the top of the canister which is set at 2-4 pounds over bottom pressure, in order to protect the breathing bags from being overextended during storage.

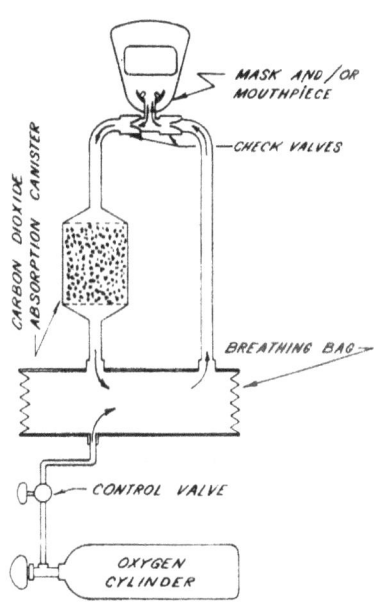

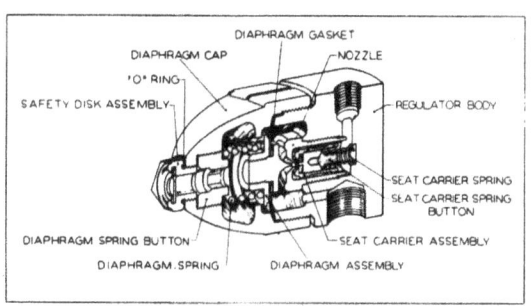

-3 Regulator (sectional view)

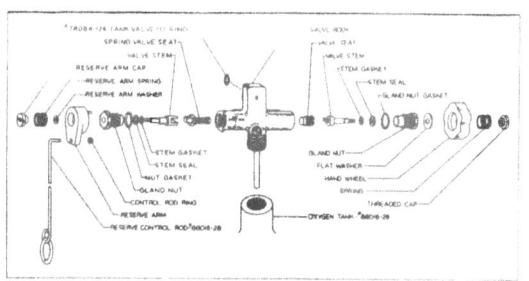

Cylinder and Constant-Reserve Valve (exploded view)

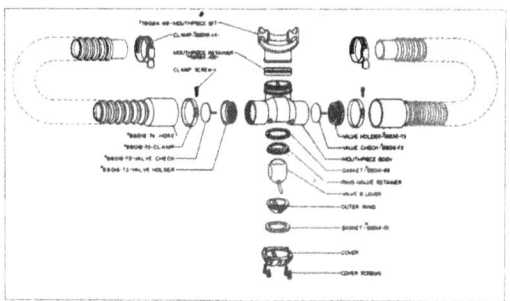

Mouthpiece and Breathing Valve (Exploded view)

CARE

The Emerson is a delicate unit requiring great care in handling and use, and fairly large amounts of maintenance. Some of the major problems encountered in the past are as follows:

The regulator is preset to 75 psi, but often varies from this amount. It was not primarily designed for use in a diving apparatus, and must be maintained watertight. For this reason, special care must be taken when washing the unit to ensure that no water is allowed to come in contact with the hp filter. In addition, there is no relief valve in the regulator, so that if an hp leak develops a hose will either burst or break away from its hansen fitting.

The one-way valves in the mouthpiece warp easily; for this reason they must be thoroughly cleaned after each dive and regularly inspected.

DIVING-4

The waist valve contains the by-pass and a metering valve which can be set by the operator from 0-3.0 l/min. The needle valve in this metering assembly is designed and set for the particular unit in which it is installed, so that these valves are not interchangable. This requires the user to be very wary about his meter setting. Malfunctions of the by-pass include sticking open, which can generally be corrected by working the handle, and sticking closed, which often indicates an hp leak.

The oxygen bottle has a Sportsway manifold without reserve; this was installed to replace the factory-installed unit which had a 1000 psi reserve which had burst in several cases.

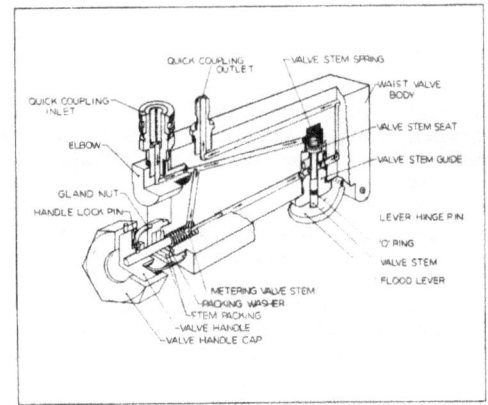

Waist Valve (sectional view)

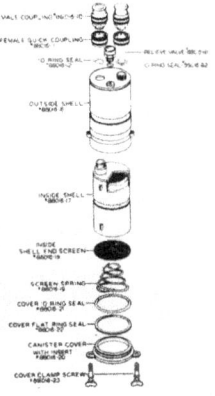

Canister Assembly (exploded view)

MAINTENANCE

CANISTER CLEANING: Periodically the inner canister should be removed from the outer shell for cleaning and inspection. To remove the inner canister, detach the exhalation quick-connect fitting and "O" ring from the canister and slide the inner shell out. When it has been cleaned, re-insert the canister into its outer shell, making sure it is properly aligned, and press firmly into place. (There are two corresponding markings on the outer shell and inner canister for easy alignment.)

LUBRICATION: No lubrication of metal parts of the apparatus should be necessary. If corrosion occurs on threaded areas of the fittings, clean them with a fine wire brush. Before re-assembly, take care to blow corrosion dust off with oil-free compressed air or oxygen.

On the "O" rings which effect seals on the fiberglass components, it is advisable to use a small amount of silicon lubricant (such as Dow Corning #4 compound).

BARALYME: Baralyme is the standard CO_2 absorbent prescribed for use in Closed and Semi-Closed Circuit diving equipment. In accordance with NAVOP SUPPGRUPACINST 9940.1, granular as opposed to pellet-type Baralyme will be used. Granular Baralyme is considered to have numerous advantages over the pellet-type, such as: longer canister time, greater absorbent qualities, and less dust. The proper nomenclature, source of supply, and FSN are as follows:

Barium Hydroxide-Lime, USP, Granular, 7 lbs (3.8 KG)
FSN 6505-053-2461
Source of Supply:
Defense Supply Agency
Defense Medical Supply Center
3rd Avenue and 29th Street
Brooklyn, New York 11232

DIVING-4

OPERATING INSTRUCTIONS

(a) Draw designated unit from rack; set on table; remove backpack cover.

(b) Thoroughly inspect unit for holes, tears, and other visual defects. Check breathing bags mouthpiece and hoses for water.

(c) Inspect mouthpiece and non-return valves.

(d) Assemble mouthpiece unit, ensuring that inhalation non-return valve is on RIGHT side; install on hoses.

(e) Check mouthpiece unit for easy breathing position; test for inhalation and exhalation leaks. Stretch hoses and inspect for pinholes and excessive cracks.

(f) Remove canister from unit.

(g) Fill canister with Baralyme, in the following manner:

(1) Hold canister firmly. (Preferably in a bulkhead mounted mechanical device.)

(2) Place inner canister screen in canister smooth-ring side down.

(3) Place plastic ring or other barrier in a position to prevent Baralyme from entering the space between the inner and outer canister shells.

(4) Pour granular Baralyme into the canister while holding the container approximately eight inches above canister opening. This allows any excess dust to escape.

(5) Tap the canister with the heel of the hand lightly after each two pounds of Baralyme has been added. This will settle the Baralyme in the canister. Fill to within one-fourth inch of top of inner canister shell.

(6) Leave bottom two inches of Baralyme in carton because of dust and discard.

(7) Remove barrier.

(h) Insert screen and spring combination, and replace the canister cover.

(i) Replace canister, ensuring tight bottom seal and snug fit in backpack.

(j) Gage oxygen bottle; USE O_2 GAUGE ONLY; MINIMUM PRESSURE 1500 psi.

(k) Insert bottle in unit; attach regulator.

(l) Test regulator pressure; limits 60 to 80 psi (regulator should be set to supply oxygen at 75 psi optimum).

(m) Attach all hoses and connections; close drain plugs and mouthpiece valve.

(n) Ensure "O" ring is in place on Hansen fitting connecting LP air hose to waist valve.

(o) Turn on O_2; inflate unit using by-pass.

(p) Inspect/listen for leaks; place rig in water and test for leaks; water test canister relief valve only as directed.

(q) Shut off O_2; release pressure from bags using mouthpiece valve; close mouthpiece valve to seal unit.

(r) Check all fittings and screws for tightness.

(s) Don unit; Buddy check; replace cover over backpack.

PURGING

Always Purge before entering the water in order to prevent Anoxia. Purging will be accomplished simultaneously by all swimmers, under the direction of the Diving Supervisor, and the following procedure will be adhered to:

Any time that the purge is broken, it is IMPERATIVE to start over again.

Turn on O_2; turn off metering valve; rinse and don face mask.

Turn mouthpiece valve to bag; breathe and dump all air/oxygen in apparatus.

Fill bag using by-pass; breathe and immediately dump.

Fill bag using by-pass; turn on metering valve; remain on O_2 gear for a minimum of two minutes before entering water; upon order of Diving Supervisor, go.

DEPTH TIME LIMITS

The safe diving limit for O_2 gear is 25'. The preferred depth is 15'. The normal depth-time limits are:

10' for 240 minutes
15' for 150 minutes
20' for 110 minutes
25' for 75 minutes

Limits for exceptional purposes, to be authorized by COMMANDING OFFICER ONLY, are:

30' for 45 minutes
35' for 25 minutes
40' for 10 minutes

RULES

The three basic diseases against which a Closed Circuit diver must protect himself are:

Anoxia
CO_2 buildup
O_2 poisoning

The following rules are designed to forestall one or more of these diseases:

(a) Never charge the apparatus with any gas except oxgyen.

(b) When swimming with closed circuit gear, wear sufficient weights, and always use a BUDDY LINE and a DEPTH GAUGE.

(c) Always use fresh absorbent in the canister.

(d) Ensure all check valves are working and all hose connections are secure.

(e) NEVER use oil.

(f) Wear standard UDT lifejacket OUTSIDE the rig in the following manner:

Yoke around neck, bib outside of breathing bags.
Straps under backpack and extending out through respective arm holes.
Straps fastened to "D" rings with quick releases.

(g) Always PURGE BEFORE entering water.

(h) DO NOT use controlled breathing.

(i) Swim at a moderate rate; approximately 1 knot.

(j) Ventilate unit (dump and fill) every 15

MINUTES.
(k) Follow depth/time limits precisely.
(l) Be aware at all times of possible symptoms or signs; surface IMMEDIATELY if ANY are noted.
(m) Maintain a good weight to buoyancy ratio.
(n) Always exhale on ascent; dump air as necessary to prevent over pressuring bags.
(o) Stay on bag for a short time on the surface in order to get your equilibrium.
(p) Always replace Baralyme after each swim, no matter how short the duration.
(q) Remember that fresh air is a cure for O_2 diseases; be confident of your ability and that of your buddy; if you are not, don't dive.

EMERGENCY PROCEDURES

The following are the emergency procedures to be used while swimming the Emerson:
MEDICAL EMERGENCIES: The primary treatment for the three basic O_2 divers' diseases is BREATHING FRESH AIR. Surface immediately upon noticing any symptoms or signs. Close mouthpiece valve BEFORE taking it out of mouth or removing mask. Signal the boat; do NOT attempt to continue the swim.
FLOODING: Clear mask by standard procedure; if bags flood, roll to left and blow; swim in slightly upright position and loosen straps to allow water to stay in bottom of bags; surface if it is impossible to breathe without taking on water.
GAS LINE RUPTURE: Surface slowly, utilizing gas in bag; have buddy investigate; if hose has just popped off, shut off O_2, replace, purge and continue, being sure to turn O_2 back on; if actual rupture occurs, shut off O_2 and secure.
STEADY O_2 FLOW: Attempt to work the by-pass valve, hit it; if it cannot be stopped, surface exhaling through nose.
REGULATOR MALFUNCTION: This is often indicated by a by-pass valve which cannot be activated and an increased flow through the metering valve; a ruptured hose will likely occur as well; surface.
OVERPRESSURE IN BAGS: Exhale through nose; allow O_2 to escape around corners of mouth.

EXHAUSTION OF GAS SUPPLY: Exhaustion of the gas supply is not a serious problem. The oxygen in the breathing system is usually enough for several minutes of light swimming. Simply swim to the surface and shift to air breathing.

EMERGENCY DITCHING
This is to be used ONLY if apparatus is severely damaged or caught on an obstruction where the buddy cannot free it, and it is impossible to surface with it on. The proper ditching procedure is as follows:
(1) Get rid of weights.
(2) Pull lifejacket quick releases; if it is necessary to remove it, hold it securely in the hand.
(3) Loosen Emerson side straps and unsip vest.
(4) Slip out of vest.
(5) Pull lifejacket toggle, holding bib against chest with one hand; extend other arm over head; blow and go.

DIVER RESCUE PROCEDURE
Should your buddy become unconscious or convulsive while submerged, the following procedure will be followed to bring him to the surface:
(a) Approach from the rear.
(b) Hold rescuee against your body with the left hand against his rib cage, right hand holding backpack
(c) Release HIS WEIGHTS; this should provide sufficient buoyancy.
(d) Swim toward the surface, squeezing his chest.
(e) On surface, or if necessary on the way up, inflate his LIFEJACKET.
(f) If necessary for additional buoyancy, inflate YOUR BAG. Ensure his buoyancy on the surface by inflating his lifejacket and bags.
(g) Close Valve on his mouthpiece; remove it.
(h) Remove his mask.
(i) Close his metering valve; check for breathing restrictions.
(j) Push him away to end of buddy line to test his buoyancy.
(k) If his buoyancy is adequate and there is NO CHANCE of losing him, come off diving status (ensure you close mouthpiece valve before removing it); light flare; call boats.
NOTE: Throughout the rescue, the rescuer must not do anything that would make himself unable to dive. He must never lose control of the rescuee. Finally, remember that fresh air is the primary treatment for O_2 diver's diseases.

POST-DIVE

(a) Secure the cylinder valve.
(b) Thoroughly rinse the outside of the apparatus with fresh water. This is best done by dipping the entire ASSEMBLED apparatus into a large can of fresh water, first making sure that the mouthpiece shut-off valve is closed and all gas delivery fittings are connected. This procedure will wash salt of the fittings.
(c) Alkali removal: If, during use, the breathing system has been flooded to the extent of wetting the carbon dioxide absorbent, wash the inside of the entire respiratory system, to remove alkali. Do not wash the gas delivery system if it is clean. Instead, disconnect the gas delivery tubes from the waist valve so that moisture will not reach it. If possible, dry all components before re-use.
If flooding results in entrance of water and alkali into the gas delivery system, corrosion and crystallization may in time obstruct passages in the waist valve. The waist valve should be separated from the regulator, and flushed copiously and repeatedly with fresh water. The waist valve and connecting tubing should be dry before re-assembly. The regulator can usually be cleared of dampness by discharging oil-free oxygen through it for one or two minutes at low pressure.

(d) Remove backpack cover; remove canister; empty Baralyme.

(e) Thoroughly wash canister, regulator, and backpack.

(f) Remove regulator from oxygen bottle, first ensuring that oxygen is off and pressure has been bled from regulator.

(g) Immediately dry and return oxygen bottle to rack.

(h) Blow canister and regulator dry; reassemble canister leaving bottom loose; reinstall canister in backpack; replace backpack cover.

(i) Disassemble mouthpiece assembly; thoroughly wash; place assembly in backpack cover and set clamps over canister hose connectors.

(j) Open drain plugs.

(k) Wash out breathing hoses.

(l) Allow unit to drain; return unit to its position on rack.

(m) If malfunction or damage has occurred, fill out tag provided and tie same to unit.

MARK VI

SEMI-CLOSED CIRCUIT

Dives were being made with various mixes on nitrogen and oxygen even before the discovery of the effects of nitrogen on the diver. In Germany at Gelsenkirchen a diving dress was being used in 1912; the breathing medium was 45% O_2 and 55% N_2. The following year the Draecjeriverk Company introduced a 60% O_2 and 40% N_2 mixture which was mixed automatically. During the Second World War, England's clearance divers used a self-contained mixed gas unit known as the CDBA. Many of the features of this unit were incorporated in the U.S. Navy unit developed by the Experimental Diving Unit, Washington, D.C. This unit, known as the MK V, was developed according to the requirements of the EOD units of the Navy. It was accepted in 1959, and field use showed many deficiencies. Another unit was built called the MK VI which included many of the changes and improvements recommended by the divers in the field. Although the unit was developed for EOD work, it is being issued to UDT's and used for sneak attacks. On initial use most UDT divers thought its exhaust bubbles would be detected easily. This proved otherwise and the percent of hits with MK VI was high. Future development calls for a bubble dispersing exhaust valve and the percent of detection should decrease. With the development of the SDV's and a longer bottom time requirement on the diver the future of the semi-closed unit in the UDT's appears secure.

DIVING-4

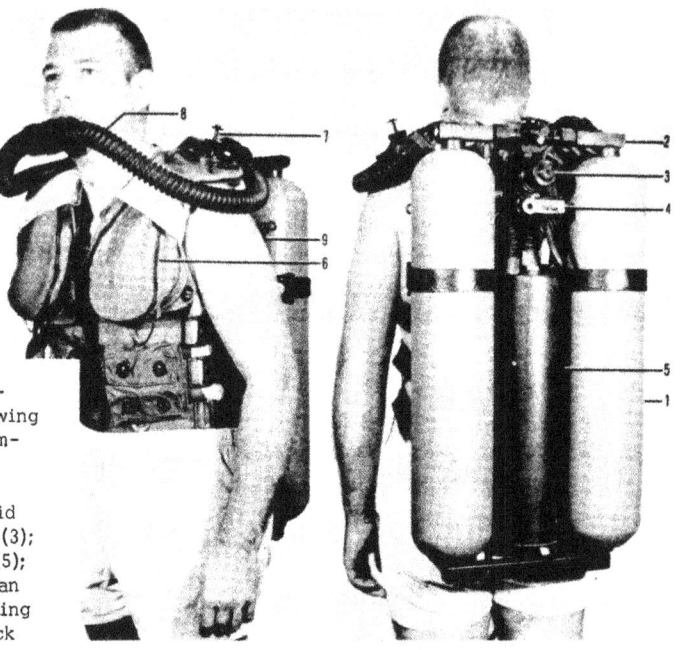

DESCRIPTION

The MK VI is a low-magnetic effects model which consists of the following parts; (see photograph) two high pressure spun aluminum cylinders (84 cubic feet at 3,000 pounds test pressure: 5,000 psi) (1); and a high pressure brass manifold valve assembly (2); a single stage, aneroid controlled, constant mass flow regulator assembly (3); a control block assembly (4); a canister assembly (5); a detachable breathing bag and vest assembly (6); an exhaust valve (7); mounted in the exhalation breathing bag; a mouthpiece "T" tube assembly (8); and a back plate (9).

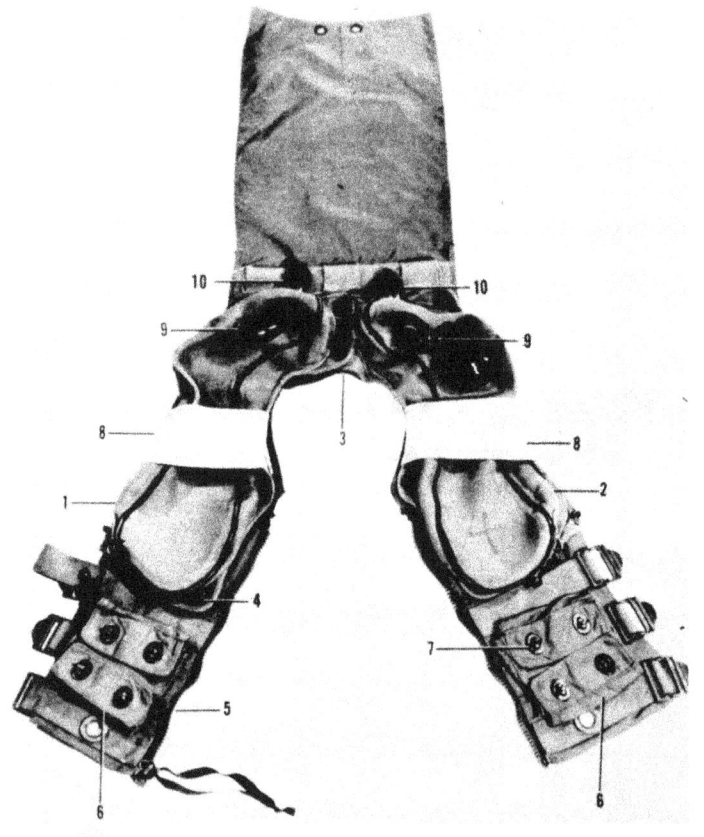

1. Inhalation Breathing Bag
2. Exhalation Breathing Bag
3. Vest
4. Fasteners
5. Zipper
6. Weight Pouch
7. Fasteners
8. Securing Bands
9. Connectors
10. Connectors

OPERATING INSTRUCTIONS

Following is the procedure for setting up a MK VI for a dive:
(a) Draw designated unit from rack; place on table
(b) Gauge bottles; MINIMUM PRESSURE 1500 PSI
(c) Remove spreader bar; remove canister; fill canister with Baralyme
(d) Check resister orifice for proper size
(e) Attach control block assembly and regulator to manifold yoke
(f) Attach by-pass rod
(g) Install canister
(h) Replace spreader bar
(i) Attach breathing bags and vest assembly to backplate.
(j) Check mouthpiece non-return valves; replace as necessary
(k) Assemble mouthpiece and attach hoses
(l) Connect canister hoses to breathing bags
(m) Close drain plugs
(n) Test and adjust regulator
   (1) Back off diaphragm on regulator
   (2) Turn on gas on manifold center yoke
   (3) Attach test hose and regulator to air inlet hose
   (4) Turn control block to ON position
   (5) Adjust regulator pressure as dive dictates (80, 140, or 180)
   (6) Turn control block to OFF position, detach regulator from test hose
   (7) Hit by-pass valve to test system pressure
   (8) Repeat steps c-f to ensure regulator pressure remains constant
(o) Test and adjust control block
   (1) With control block turned OFF and manifold valve ON, loosen jam nut and turn needle valve down until it GENTLY bottoms out
   (2) Connect test hose to flow meter
   (3) Turn control block to ON position
   (4) Back off needle valve and jam nut simultaneously until desired flow is reached (8, 12, or 21 l/min)
   (5) Tighten jam nut, observe flow meter reading for two minutes
   (6) Turn off control block
(p) Test Differential Pressure Gauge
   (1) Remove plug and cover from control block; attach DPG
   (2) Turn on control block, observe needle is in safe operating range
   (3) Turn control block to OFF, disconnect test hose
(q) Connect canister to control block at the air inlet block
(r) Test pressure relief valve
   (1) Remove drain plug on left bag and attach L. P. gauge
   (2) Turn on control block
   (3) Ensure that with pressure relief valve closed popoff is approximately 3/4 pound; with pressure relief valve open popoff is approximately 1/4 pound
   (4) Turn off control block, remove L.P. gauge and replace drain cap
(s) Pressurize unit, dip test to check for leaks

PROCEDURES

Observance of the following procedures is of the greatest importance during a dive with semi-closed SCUBA:
(a) After entering water, check that gas escapes from exhaust valve at the end of exhalation.
(b) When descending, supplement gas flow as necessary to prevent squeeze of the breathing bags. Keep bag about 2/3 full. Do not descend faster than the bag can inflate either automatically or manually.
(c) At working depth, adjust exhaust valve to provide for a comfortable breathing pressure without using the by-pass. At the end of any full exhalation the exhaust valve should discharge a small amount of gas.
(d) Work normally; avoid extreme exertion unless the flow was previously set for heavy work. Never attempt to swim if the gear was set for a non-swimming dive. Avoid fast descents or ascents for short distances. During an extremely long dive purge the breathing bag a minimum of once each hour.
(e) Keep a "mental eye" on the exhaust valve—it is by far the most reliable flow indicator. With irregular breathing the valve should operate at least every third or fourth breath; with normal breathing after each exhalation.
(f) Every few minutes exhale fully. If the exhaust valve does not function at the end of exhalation, the flow has stopped altogether. If it discharges a much smaller amount than on previous checks at the same depth, the flow has fallen off. Check the low flow warning device if available. Carry out emergency procedures for injector failure.
(g) Do not overstay duration time. Always take the proper precautions when the dive may involve decompression. Remember that the decompression for N_2-O_2 mixture diving is always specified in terms of the stops necessary for air to the equivalent air depth.
(h) During ascent, never exceed the rate specified in the tables. Prior to commencing ascent, flush the breathing bag by using the mixed gas by-pass. Use the following rules:
   (1) Take such a position that the exhaust valve is above the bag
   (2) Take several deep breaths and then exhale normally

DIVING-4

(3) Open the exhaust valve and let water pressure flatten the bag out
(4) Close the exhaust valve
(5) Open the by-pass and fill the bag to normal level. Do not leave this valve open long enough to exhaust any gas from the system.

(i) Commence the ascent and at 30' flush the breathing bag a second time. Then complete the ascent, including decompression as usual. Use the main injection system for the rest of the ascent. Flush the system immediately before leaving each decompression stop.

(j) Remember that equivalent air depths are figured on the basis of 1.3 l/m for non-swimming dives and 1.5 l/m for swimming dives.

DEPTH TIME LIMITS

Tables 3-3, 3-4 and 3-5 of the Diving Manual contain the depth time limits and minimum flow settings for mixed gas diving. The depth limits for the standard MK VI mixes are:

60/40 O_2N_2 Mix	80 feet
40/60 O_2N_2 Mix	140 feet
32.5/67.5 O_2N_2 Mix	180 feet

POST-DIVE

The following procedures are to be followed in disassembling the MK VI following a dive:
(a) Thoroughly flush unit with fresh water
(b) Secure manifold valve
(c) Pull by-pass to relieve pressure on regulator
(d) Back regulator off completely with T wrench
(e) Disconnect control block canister hose from canister
(f) Remove DPG
(g) Replace plug and cover on control block
(h) Remove regulator and control block assembly
(i) Disconnect canister hoses from bags
(j) Remove cylinder spreader bar and remove canister
(k) Replace cylinder spreader bar
(l) Dump and thoroughly flush canister
(m) Open breathing bag drain plugs
(n) Disconnect hoses from breathing bags and remove mouthpiece assembly
(o) Thoroughly flush hoses and mouthpiece assembly
(p) Ensure bottles have a MINIMUM PRESSURE of 150 psi. If not, notify diving locker personnel immediately.
(q) Dry and restow unit as directed

GENERAL

(a) Always charge the apparatus with a standard mixture.
(b) Always use fresh absorbent in the canister
(c) Carefully set the injector to the proper flow for the work anticipated
(d) Do not exceed the maximum depth specified for the mixture in use
(e) Be constantly alert for failure of the exhaust valve to bubble.

EMERGENCY DIVING PROCEDURES

FLOODING: Follow same procedure as for closed circuit for flooding of facemask or bags. For canister flooding: (indicated by failure of the breathing bag to inflate when by-pass is activated) surface.

NON-RETURN VALVE FAILURE: (indicated by CO_2 symptoms), surface.

REGULATOR PRESSURE DROPS: (Indicated by failure to obtain pop-off or movement of DPG needle out of safe zone) supplement reduced pressure by use of by-pass, and surface.

GAS FLOW RESTRICTED: Needle valve fails to deliver specified amount. (Same indications as regulator pressure drop). Hit by-pass, and surface.

ENTERING WATER WITHOUT CONTROL BLOCK TURNED ON: (Indicated by DPG showing bad reading and excessive use of by-pass): Corrected by turning it on.

EXHAUSTION OF GAS SUPPLY: Exhaustion of the gas supply requires immediate action to avoid oxygen deficiency. The exact procedure depends on the specific SCUBA and especially on availability of an emergency gas supply. Follow the procedure given in the instruction manual for the particular apparatus. After surfacing, shift immediately to air breathing.

FAILURE OF THE INJECTOR: If the injector fails, follow the technique for routine ascent, if the by-pass still works. Otherwise, follow the procedure for exhaustion of gas supply.

DIVER RESCUE PROCEDURES: The procedures for rescuing a diver who is wearing semi-closed SCUBA are the same as those for Closed-Circuit SCUBA (Page 70).

GAS SPLITTING and MIXING

It is possible for a diver to work with mixed gases merely by going to tables in the MK VI manual. It is much better, however for the diver to understand thoroughly the principles of mixed gas diving and the how and why specific mix and flow settings are determined.

The following paragraph explain how to solve the four problems encountered in gas mixing: determining what mix to use for a particular dive, adding O_2 to N_2, increasing the percentage of O_2 in a mix, and decreasing the percentage of O_2 in a mix.

PLANNING

Since various mixes can be used in a semi-closed SCUBA, it must be decided beforehand which is the best mixture for a particular dive. This is determined by the proposed depth of the dive. When this is known, the percentage of oxygen to be used, and the corresponding flow rate, can be calculated. With this information, it is easy to calculate what the following will be, during the dive: Bag level, Relative Oxygen Depth, Equivalent Air Depth, and Gas Supply Duration. All these factors must be considered when planning a mixed gas dive. The following paragraphs explain, step-by-step, how to calculate these factors:

1_____

Obtain the maximim depth of the area. You can do this by referring to a chart or if in the actual diving area, by using a sounding lead. Once this factor is known, second step follows.

2_____

Compute the maximum O_2 allowable for that depth. Remember you may not exceed a percent of O_2 greater than 2 atmospheres absolute. For our example we will assume we are making a dive at a depth of 66' on a 60/40 mix. It will be hard working dive, since we are swimming. Our second step is simply to see if the 60/40 mix is within the limits of the maximum O_2 allowable for 66'. The formula is:

$$\text{MAX } O_2 = \frac{66}{66+33} \quad \frac{66}{99} \quad .666 = 66.7\%$$

(numerator: THIS FIGURE REPRESENTS 2 ATMO-ABSOL; denominator: DEPTH + ATMOS — ADD DEPTH WATER TO 33 TO MAKE ABSOLUTE VALUE)

So we see that our 60/40 mix is within the maximum O_2 allowable limits.

3_____

Double check by determining the maximum depth to which we can take our selected mix. Our mix is 60/40. Use the $O_2\%$ of the supply mix, 60% O_2. This formula is:

$$\left(\frac{66}{O_2\% \text{ IN SUPPLY MIX}}\right) - 33 \quad \text{(WE SUBTRACT 33 TO HANGE ABSOLUTE TO GAUGE)}$$

SUBSTITUTING IN THE FORMULA

$$\left(\frac{66}{.60}\right) - 33 = 110 - 33 = 77'$$

(DO NOT FORGET TO SUBTRACT YOUR 33')

We see we can go to a depth of 77' with a mix of 60/40. Our depth of dive is only 66' so our mix satisfies the requirement, as to maximum depth. You can see if you forgot to subtract the 33' to convert absolute pressure to gauge, you would be exposing your divers to O_2 poisoning.

4_____

Compute the flow rate necessary to maintain the bag level at a minimum of 21% (or .21) O_2. Our formula is:

$$M = C\left(\frac{1.00-B}{S-B}\right)$$

C = CONSUMPTION RATE-TAKEN FROM DIVING MANUAL = 3 l/M FOR A SWIMMING DIVE
1.00 = A CONSTANT 100% EXPRESSED AS A DECIMAL
B = A CONSTANT ALWAYS .21 OR 21% MINIMUM $O_2\%$ IN BAG
S = % O_2 IN SUPPLY MIX IN THIS CASE 60%

SUBSTITUTING IN THE FORMULA

$$M = 3\left(\frac{1.00-.21}{.60-.21}\right) = 3\left(\frac{.79}{.39}\right) = \frac{2.37}{.39} = 6.1 \text{ l/M}$$

This is the required rate of flow to keep a bag level at a minimum of 21%.

5_____

Determine the actual percentage of oxygen in the Diver's Breathing Bag ("Bag Level"). In the example we have been using a flow setting of 6.1 l/m with a mix of 60/40. We are interested in this in order to see how long a diver can stay at a depth with regard to O_2 toxicity. We also want to know his bag level since it will effect his decompres-

sion time. You use the flow rate computed in the preious formula and for O_2 consumption use these consumption rates: (a) hard working 1.5 l/m (swimming), (b) non-swimming 1.3 l/m. This contains a safety factor to prevent O_2 poisoning. This is the formula to use:

$$B = \frac{MS-C}{M-C}$$

M = SURFACE FLOW RATE IN THIS PROBLEM 6.1
S = SUPPLY MIX IN THIS PROBLEM 60% = .60
C = CONSUMPTION RATE = 1.5 l/M

SUBSTITUTING IN THE FORMULA WE HAVE

$$B = \frac{(6.1 \times .60) - 1.5}{6.1 - 1.5} = \frac{2.16}{4.6} = .46956$$

Carry this out 5 places and round to 4, convert to percent, and you have 46.95% bag level. This is not an exact figure. It represents an average of the O_2 in your breathing bag. If you have just purged, your bag level may be almost the same as your supply, i.e., mix 60%. If you've been working hard and using your O_2, your bag level may be lower than 46.95%. This is an average predicted level based on variable factors.

6.

Determine the relative oxygen depth ("ROD"). This is the depth on the mix that corresponds to a relative depth of 100% O_2. We will need this factor in order to check our depth time limit on O_2. You will use the bag level computed in the preceding step. This is the formula:

$$ROD = [(\% O_2 \text{ IN BREATHING BAG}) \times (D+33)] - 33 =$$
$$(.4696 \times 99) - 33 = 46.49 - 33 = 13.49$$

For safety use the deepest depth, e.g., convert 13.49 to 14 feet. Consult you O_2 depth time limit table found in the MK VI Technical Manual or the Diving Manual, Page 125. This is one of the important limiting factors on the duration of dive.

7.

Determine the equivalent air depth ("EAD"). This is done in order to determine a decompression schedule. The EAD is the depth on the mix that corresponds to our depth figure as if we were breathing air. We will use the bag level computed in a previous step. This is the formula to use:

$$EAD = \frac{(1.00 - O_2\% \text{ IN BAG})(66+33)}{.79} - 33$$

$$EAD = \frac{(1.00 - .4696)(99)}{.79} - 33$$

$$EAD = \frac{.5304 \times 99}{.79} - 33 = \frac{52.50}{.79} - 33 =$$

$$66.46 - 33 = 33.46$$

EAD = 34'

Change to the deeper depth for safety. Now you see that at an actual depth of 66' we are at a EAD of only 34'. Look up in the standard decompression table and see what the diver's decompression is. This is another limiting factor in planning the dive.

8.

Compute the gas supply duration ("GSD"). We need to know a gas supply duration in order to plan our dive so we do not run out of gas at a decompression stop or on the bottom. We will use 600 psi as low pressure safety limit. This safety limit allows for by-passing, purging, and setting up the rig. We will use the liter flow previously computed for the problem. The formula is as follows:

$$T = \frac{(V)(P-S)}{(14.7)(F)}$$

T = TIME
V = TOTAL CYLINDER VOLUME (LITERS)
P = INITIAL CHARGING PRESSURE (PSI)
F = SURFACE FLOW RATE (l/M)

OUR CYLINDER VOLUME IS 12 LITERS.
OUR INITIAL CHARGING PRESSURE IS 2,000 PSI

S = 600 PSI
F = 6.1

SUBSTITUTE IN THE FORMULA

$$T = \frac{(12)(2000-600)}{(14.7)(6.1)} = \frac{(12)(1400)}{(14.7)(6.1)} =$$

$$\frac{(12)(\cancel{1400})^{95}}{\cancel{(14.7)}(6.1)} = \frac{1140}{6.1} = 186 \text{ MIN.}$$

186 minutes = gas supply duration. Now you have to consider the following factors: canister life, O_2 depth time limit, and the decompression required. The limiting factor will be the one that is shortest.

All the above information can be obtained by looking in the NAVSHIPS Manual 393-0653 p. 2-2. For depth time limits for O_2, refer to the Diving Manual.

MIXING OXYGEN INTO AN INERT GAS: Formula

FINAL PRESSURE = PRESSURE SPLIT CYLINDER
MIXED GAS   % OF INERT GAS
CYLINDER

EQUIPMENT: Cylinder of O_2, cylinder of N_2, mixing "T" with air N_2 fitting and air O_2 fitting.

EXAMPLE: You want to mix a gas with 32.5% O_2 and 67.5% N_2 - Substituting the values we know into our formula - 900 psi N_2, 2,000 psi O_2.

$$FOR \quad \frac{900}{.675} = 1333 \text{ PSI}$$

Now we see we must bleed O_2 into the bottle of N_2 until the pressure equals 1333 psi.

When mixing without a pump and non-return valves or cascading, you must ensure that the mixing cylinders have enough pressure to force the gas into the desired cylinder. For example, pressure required in O_2 cylinder to bleed into N_2 must be at least:

Original pressure of N_2: 900 psi
Final pressure of N_2O_2 mix: 1333
Difference in pressure: 433
Safety factor: 50
Required pressure O_2: 1816 psi

If the gas pressure is not high enough you can use booster pump, split the N_2 into another bottle, or bleed to atmosphere.

INCREASING THE O_2 PERCENTAGE OF A MIX
Formula:

$$F = \frac{(P)(1.00 - O_O)}{1.00 - O_f}$$

where,
F = Final cylinder pressure
P = Original cylinder pressure
O_o = Original O_2 percentage (decimal form)
O_f = Final O_2 percentage (decimal form)

EXAMPLE: We have a cylinder of 1000 psi with a mix of 32.5% O_2. We want to change to 60% O_2. All that is necessary is to substitute the known value in the formula.

$$F = \frac{(1000)(.675)}{1.00 - .60} = \frac{675}{.40} = 1687.5 \text{ PSI}$$

Round to 1688 psi. You will have to add 688 psi O_2 to make you mix 60/40.

Now let's see what pressure is required in our O_2 cylinder to mix by the cascade method:
1688 = final pressure
688 = difference in pressure
50 = safety factor
2426 = psi O_2 required in the cylinder used for charging.

DECREASING THE O_2 PERCENTAGE OF A MIX

This procedure consists of adding nitrogen to a mix in order to bring the O_2 percentage to the desired level.

Formula:

$$F = \frac{(P)(O_O)}{O_F}$$

The values are the same as the preceding formula. Our bottle of mix is P = 1000 psi
Original O_2 = O_o = 60%
Final O_2 = O_f = 40%

We desire to change our mix from 60% O_2 to 40% O_2. Substitute in the formula:

$$F = \frac{(1000)(.60)}{.40} = \frac{600}{.40} = 1500 \text{ PSI}$$

We need to add 500 psi of N_2 to our 1000 psi in the cylinders to make our final mix 40% with a pressure of 1500 psi.

DIVING ACCESSORIES

BUDDY LINE

The buddy line is a length of small stuff 6 to 10 feet in length. It is secured to each swimmer in a buddy pair in order to ensure contact between the swimmers. It is to be used during conditions of poor visibility, at night, during extremely deep dives and during training operations.

COMPASS

The MK 1 MOD 0 wrist compass is the compass utilized by the teams. It may be fastened on an attack board or worn on the wrist. Prior to using the attack board for a compass swim, ensure that the compass does not move freely on the board, the compass top does not rotate freely, and the fixed lubber's line is towards you on the board. In order to swim to a particular object, line the attack board up with the object by holding it steady and rotating the compass top putting the north arrow over N on the compass card. Swim to the target keeping "North over North". In order to swim a given compass course, turn the compass top until the desired course (inscribed on the side in 5° increments) is aligned with the lubber's line. Place North over North and swim to the target keeping the north arrow over N on the compass card.

When altering course, be sure to move the body and the attack board as a unit.

CORAL SHOES

Coral shoes are worn when it is necessary for the diver to operate in shallow water, around coral reefs or when crawling on a beach. They are designed to protect the feet and ankles when working around sharp objects. The shoes are constructed of a canvas upper attached to a rubber sole. Swim fins may be worn over the shoes, when necessary.

DEPTH GAUGE

The MK 1 MOD 0 Wrist Gauge is presently in use in the teams. It is marked in five foot increments from 1 to 200 feet and has a maximum safe diving depth of 300 feet. It is accurate to within one foot from 1 to 50 feet and within three feet from 50 to 200 feet. It is non-magnetic, corrosion and shock-resistant, and is reliable from 32° to 90° F.

Periodically, the diving department checks the calibration of the gauge in a recompression chamber or in water (by comparing depth indication with a sounding line). IMPORTANT - special stowage and handling instructions are promulgated in paragraph 18 (P___).

OPERATION: During descent water enters the water chamber thereby depressing the diaphragm. This in turn activates the gear movement causing the pointer to turn in a clockwise direction.

CARE AND MAINTENANCE: NEVER use the depth gauge unless the bezel guard and back cover are in place. Flush the gauge with fresh water after each use and replace the dial cover. Periodically, the diving department will remove the back cover plate to remove debris and sediment from the water. During this cleaning, care must be taken not to damage the diaphragm.

EXPOSURE SUIT

The exposure suit is used for cold water diving. The two types of exposure suits are the wet suit and the dry suit. The wet suit is the type most often used in UDT. The wet suit permits entry of water into the suit, where it is trapped and warmed by the body, thereby creating an insulating layer. The dry suit is designed to keep water out entirely, though generally a small amount seeps in. The dry suit is used while operating in extremely cold waters such as those found in the Arctic regions. Long underwear should be worn underneath to prevent suit squeeze. Both the wet and dry suits come in full length and shorty models. Long underwear may be used in lieu of the exposure suit, if the water temperature permits.

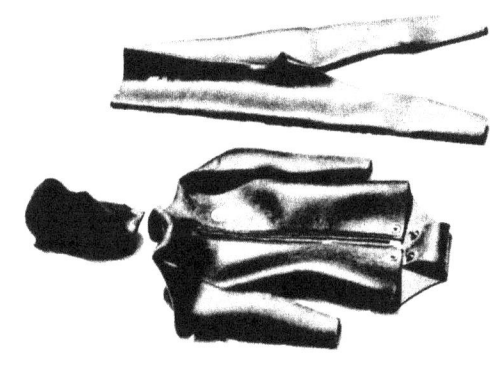

FACE MASK

The standard facemask in use at the present time in the teams is the eyes-nose mask. Facemask squeeze may be caused by too rapid descent with failure to equalize by letting air out the nose. Never wear goggles.

79

FINS

Swim fins are a most essential item for the team swimmer, as they will provide maximum thrust thru the water when used properly. The standard team fin fills the requirement for a relatively rigid fin with a large blade. Proper fit is essential, as a fin too large or too small may chafe and blister the feet, thereby incapacitating the swimmer unnecessarily. Booties are an additional item which tend to prevent fin burn and are highly recommended.

FLARE

The flare (MK 13, MOD 0, Signal Distress, Day and Night) is carried taped to the pistol belt or knife scabbard. One end of the flare contains the day signal, which is a heavy red smoke. The opposite end, which has raised beading around the edge, contains the night signal, which is a red light. The raised beading enables the diver to locate the night signal when unable to see. Both ends are activated by means of a pull ring. This signal flare is used as a distress signal or as an indicator of the commencement or end of the phases of an operation. After either end of the signal has been pulled, it should be held at arms length and the activated end pointed away from the diver, at an angle of about 45°. The diver's body should also be upwind of the signal. At night, the diver should not look directly at the light because it destroys night vision for several seconds.

The flare will work well after submergence to any standard diving depth. The user should, however, change flares at least every six months or 10 dives, whichever comes sooner. In the event the flare does not ignite immediately, waving it will cause ignition after a few seconds. The flare will not ignite if pulled underwater.

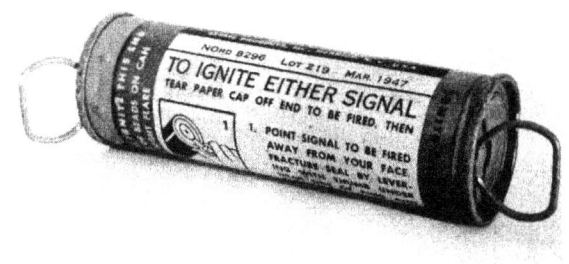

FLARE

Another flare which may be encountered is the standard Very Pistol. This can be submerged if kept in a watertight case. It comes with either a standard pistol or a small spring activated device. The red flare is the distress signal.

FLOAT

The float is a small buoyant plastic or glass container used during training evolutions to keep track of underwater swimmers. The buoy is attached to the center of a buddy line by a length of line which will permit the float to remain on the surface. During night operations a light is secured inside the float in order to facilitate location and progress of the swim pair.

KNIFE

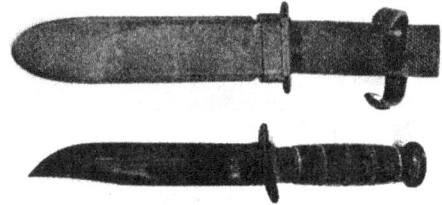

A standard sheath knife is required on all dives. Its primary use is to prevent entanglement. It is worn on a web belt or strapped to the leg and should be securely attached to prevent loss. At no time should it be worn attached to any releasable equipment (e.g., weight belt).
Either team - issued or commercially purchased stainless steel knives are satisfactory. A low magnetic effects knife is available for EOD operations, but should not be used for regular dives due both to its brittleness and its high cost.

LIFEJACKET

The lifejacket should be worn at all times when in the water. It should be worn under all releasable gear. It is provided with an oral inflation tube as well as the CO_2 cylinder; this tube should be utilized, rather than the cartridge, if possible. The lifejacket should be thoroughly rinsed the cartridge removed, and the inflation assembly and oral tube closely inspected for corrosion after each use.
In order to ensure the proper working and preservation of the lifejacket periodic preventive maintenance is necessary. In all maintenance jobs when disassembly and reassembly are necessary, proper step by step procedure is a must. The following is a

detailed disassembly and inspection, repair and reassembly of the lifejacket:

DISASSEMBLY AND INSPECTION

(1) Remove CO_2 bottle from CO_2 inflation assembly.
(2) Remove CO_2 inflation assembly securing nut with 9/16 box wrench.
(3) Remove rubber washer with scribe taking care not to tear it if possible.
(4) Remove CO_2 inflation assembly from inflation chuck.
(5) Using a drift punch, remove drift pin on which operation handle pivots. (Caution: Pin will only come out one way. Use drift on small end of pin).
(6) Remove the operation handle from the assembly.
(7) Remove the firing pin and spring from the channel in the inflation assembly, using a special punch.

Lifejacket is now disassembled. Inspect for corrosion, clogging, wear and broken parts.

Inflate lifejacket by means of oral inflation tube and water check for air leaks.

REPAIR AND REASSEMBLY

(1) Carefully clean all parts of CO_2 inflation assembly with steel wool or a wire brush using a solvent if necessary.
(2) Wire brush threads of inflation chuck on jacket.
(3) Wire brush threads of CO_2 cylinder (hand brush only. Do not put on a powered wheel brush).
(4) Repair any air leaks in jacket.
(5) Lubricate the following parts with waterproof grease:
  (a) Firing pin and spring
  (b) Firing pin channel
  (c) Operating handle
  (d) Operating handle slot
  (e) Base and threads of inflation chuck
  (f) CO_2 cylinder threads
  (g) Threads in top of CO_2 inflation assembly
(6) Replace firing pin and spring in firing pin channel.
(7) Replace operating handle, taking care to have the arm of operating handle on correct side of inflation assembly.
(8) Replace drift pin connecting operating handle to inflation assembly, taking care to insert pin properly.
(9) Check operation of firing pin and spring, by working operating handle, if pin or spring is faulty, replace with new part.
(10) Replace inflation assembly on inflation chuck.
(11) Replace rubber washer.
(12) Replace assembly securing nut. Tighten snugly with 9/16 box wrench.
(13) Insert specially adapted CO_2 bottle in the inflation assembly and inflate lifejacket with compressed air to test inflation device CO_2 passages.

If firing pin and spring operate properly and CO_2 passages in inflation assembly are clear, replace special CO_2 cylinder with a charged CO_2 cylinder.

CAUTION: Take high pressure precautions with CO_2 cylinders.

CAUTION: After reinserting charged CO_2 cylinder, do not pull operating handle except for the purpose for which the lifejacket was intended.

WEARING THE LIFEJACKET

There are three methods of wearing the lifejacket with a vest type SCUBA such as the Emerson and MK VI:

(1) The first is to wear it completely under the rig. This allows easy ditching and donning, but makes the toggle fairly hard to reach and will give strong pressure against the chest when inflated on the surface.
(2) The second method is to wear the straps under the rig, but the jacket outside, bringing the straps up above the zipper and out to attach to the "D" rings. This leaves the lifejacket outside and still provides for easy ditch/don, but tends to undo the zipper and allows the jacket, when inflated, to ride up about the face and head.
(3) The third method is to wear the jacket outside, the straps under the backpack but coming out through the arm holes and around the breathing bags to fasten into the "D" rings with a quick release. This method offers somewhat of a compromise in that the jacket is outside and easy to reach, is held in the proper position, and does not tend to undo the zipper. It does, however, slow down the ditch and don procedure.

The choice of method will be dictated either by Team directive or in the briefing by the Diving Supervisor. This problem will be alleviated with the advent of the underarm lifejacket.

LIGHTS

The primary light associated with Team dives is the single-cell marker light used in the float for night compass swim training. This light is not waterproof, and must be well protected.

Various commercial lights, both in standard flashlight configuration and in pistol configuration (e.g., Dacor Diving Light) are available, and are used as necessary for underwater work.

A third type of light, a strobe light, is used by some commands as a distress marker. This is generally about the size of a pack of cigarettes, is watertight at depths up to 150 feet, and emits a very bright blue-white flashing light. Battery life is generally eight to thirteen hours when activated. This light is easy to pick out in areas of complete darkness, but because of the short duration of the flash it is hard to pick out of other lights, particularly if the search must be omnidirectional.

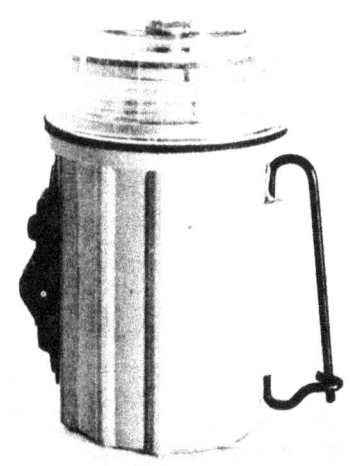

SLATE

The slate is composed of plexiglass 1/4 inch thick, three inches wide, and 10 inches long. Both surfaces are roughed up with fine sandpaper to give a frosted effect. This creates a surface which can be written upon with a pencil. A length of cord should be attached to the slate to permit attaching to the belt or hanging around the neck. The slate is used to record information during swimming and diving operations and is primarily used during hydrographic reconnaissances.

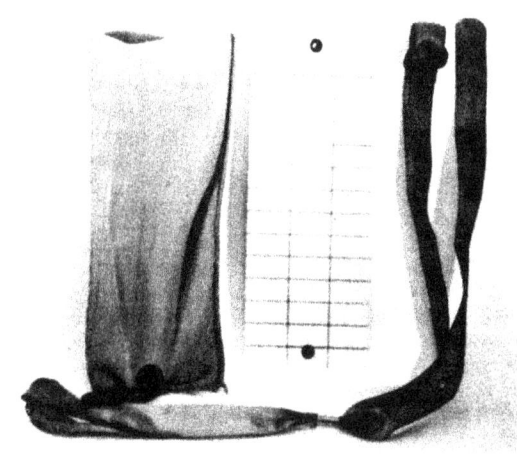

SNORKEL

The snorkel is strongly recommended on all dives requiring surface swimming or waiting on the surface for pickup, both to preserve gas and to ease the effort of swimming. The flexible hose type is sometimes easier to hold in the mouth, but has a tendency to flatten out and restrict breathing when swimming at any speed.

TENDER LINE

Required when one man is diving alone or when divers must penetrate under ice or any other substance which precludes free access to the surface.

WHISTLE

Is another valuable piece of safety equipment and when required should be worn on the lifejacket oral inflation tube.

WRISTWATCH

The wristwatch used in the team is waterproof and pressure proof. It is to be used for computing duration of water operations, for computing bottom time and decompression stops, and for controlling rates of descent and ascent. The Diving Supervisor and a member of each swim pair must have a watch for any diving evolutions.

STOWAGE AND HANDLING OF RADIOLOGICALLY HAZARDOUS EQUIPMENT

Due to the radioactive material used to illuminate the compass and depth gauge, certain stowage and handling requirements, as established by the Atomic Energy Commission, must be met. These instruments will be stowed in a lead-lined box constructed of CRES or stainless steel, which is located in the diving locker. They will be used only for operations and will be returned promptly upon completion thereof. The stowagebox will be secured in an area away from charging stations, scuba tanks, and regulator, and will be appropriately marked. The gauge and compass will be tested for decontamination each 6 months. The test will consist of both a wipe test and monitoring with appropriate radiac equipment. Only specifically designated personnel will work on these instruments and will do so only in designated areas. Upon completion of handling, thoroughly wash the hands. The seals are not to be broken but in the event that they should accidentally be broken, notify the Diving Officer. Never carry these instruments in pockets or place them face down against the skin. If individual contamination is suspected, collect and submit a 24 hour urine sample to the Navy Radiological Defense Laboratory for analysis. The Diving Officer is responsible for insuring that all team personnel are indoctrinated in the hazards and safety precautions pertaining to radiologically contaminated underwater equipment.

EMERGENCY DIVING PROCEDURES

Emergencies occasionally arise in the best planned and supervised scuba operations. Many of these emergencies are caused by failure to observe some safety precaution. Others are unforeseen or unavoidable. These emergencies can almost always be resolved if the diver, his buddy, his tender or the diving supervisor stops to think. Take a second to reason the situation through to a solution. Do not act immediately on what may prove to be a blind impulse brought on by panic.

Few situations in diving are so serious as to require instantaneous action. Remember your training. Do not panic.

Above all, never abandon the breathing apparatus under water unless you cannot ascend without doing so.

NOTE: This section is designed to cover general emergency procedures only. See the sections on open, closed, and semi-closed diving for procedures to be used with those types of scuba.

FLOODING OF A SEPARATE FACEMASK: Learn to dive without a facemask. Flooding of a separate facemask then is not a serious problem. To clear the facemask use the following procedure.
(1) Tilt the head backward.
(2) Hold the upper part of the facemask tight across the forehead.
(3) Exhale through the nose. Water will drain past the lower edge of the facemask.

During dive, exhale occasionally through the nose to clear the facemask of small amounts of water. This procedure will also prevent face squeeze by equalizing pressure inside the facemask.

FLOODING OF A FULL FACEMASK: Flooding of a full facemask is a serious problem, but every acceptable apparatus should have a means of overcoming it. The technique depends upon the type of apparatus used. The diver should be thoroughly trained in the method peculiar to the apparatus he is using.

FLOODING OF THE BREATHING BAGS: The seriousness of flooding of the breathing system depends on the type of scuba used. In general it is less of a problem in open-circuit scuba.

Be alert to the possibility that the cause of flooding (for example, a cut breathing tube) may prevent successful clearing of the system.

EMERGENCY ASCENT: Except in the most desperate situations, make an emergency ascent by swimming to the surface. The possibility of becoming entangled or of striking an obstruction makes it hazardous to use positive buoyancy for ascent. Swimming to the surface gives a better chance to avoid entanglement and to clear obstruction. In some situations a large object overhead may preclude anything but swimming.

An emergency situation can become so desperate that the need to surface outweighs the need for caution. If it becomes preferable to risk entanglement or injury rather than to remain on the bottom, inflate the lifejacket and ascend with the aid of its positive buoyancy. Bear in mind that the ascent will be very rapid. The danger of air embolism increases, and the possibility of serious injury upon striking an obstruction becomes very great.

Use free ascent only in order to resolve a life-or-death situation, and no other. Swim to the surface, and/or buddy-breathe whenever possible. If a free ascent becomes necessary, use the following procedures:

(a) Drop weight belt.
(b) Ditch gear if necessary.
(c) Look around and up.
(d) Pull lifejacket toggle, blow, then go. Remember that at depths below about 20' lifejacket will not appear to inflate; is is necessary to kick to get started.
(e) Keep hands over head, exhale continuously on the way up. If you feel comfortable, exhale sharply; you should need air all the way up.
(f) Upon reaching the surface, inflate the lifejacket. Decide whether to take off the breathing apparatus or to leave it on while swimming to safety. An open-ciruit scuba becomes very heavy when it breaks the surface. A closed-circuit scuba may hamper body motion. If the breathing apparatus interferes with swimming, remove the equipment and tow it to safety. A closed circuit scuba can provide additional buoyancy. If it is desirable to take advantage of this characteristic, inflate the breathing bag to the fullest extent that still allows comfortable breathing. If the breathing medium is not usable, close the bag cutoff valves and use the surface breather.

Before removing a facemask, consider the hazards of unfavorable surface conditions such as whitecaps and spray.

Even with closed and semi-closed circuit equipment there is generally a breath or two of air left in the bags, no matter what the emergency.

DIVER RESCUE PROCEDURES: The primary dangers in diver rescue are embolising the victum and losing both personnel. There are several procedures for rescue, and the specifics will be outlined in Team instructions. The most important thing to remember in all cases, however, is for the rescuer NEVER to come off diving status until he is absolutely sure that the victim is under control and will safely float by himself on the surface. The following paragraph outlines the

DIVING-4

proper rescue procedures for surface-tended divers. See the sections on open, closed, and semiclosed diving for rescue procedures to be used with those types of scuba.

(a) Insure that the line is secured around some part of the diver's body, and secured to itself under all of the diver's releasable equipment.
(b) When hauling in the diver, pull smoothly; do not jerk. Send standby diver down the victim's line if necessary to untangle it.
(c) Be alert for the distress signal; signal for O.K. check frequently and insure that the diver answers.

MEDICAL EMERGENCIES: See DIVERS DISEASES & INJURIES

In the event of medical emergency, the important thing is to surface immediately upon noticing any signs or symptoms, signal the boat, and do not attempt to continue the swim.

DIVING REGULATIONS

FISHING

If any is to be conducted on a dive, be sure to check the latest edition of the Fish and Game laws and thoroughly brief all personnel on them. Insure that proper measuring devices are carried. Remember that the game warden can come on board a Navy boat if he has reason to suspect that game is aboard. Also be sure to check the charts to determine if dive is going to be in Mexican waters; if so, a Mexican license must be obtained.

RECREATION

Team policies vary with regard to issue of equipment for recreation dives. The following is included for planning purposes:
Recreation dives should be organized and run in the same manner as any other dive and should follow Team Safety Precautions. In no case should civilians or members of any other organization be permitted to use Team controlled equipment.

SAFETY PRECAUTIONS

Careful observation of applicable safety precautions can prevent the majority of diving accidents. However, some diving operations (particularly tactical operations) do not allow personnel to observe all safety precautions without exception. The diving supervisor must decide which safety precautions to disregard in a given situation, and he must be able to justify his decision on a basis of absolute necessity. He must then make sure that all personnel affected by his decision:
  Realize the situation
  Remain constantly alert to the hazard
  Know the applicable emergency procedure
PERSONNEL: Except for trainees, only divers qualified in SCUBA should participate in self-contained diving operations.
  The diving supervisor should also be qualified in SCUBA.
  TECHNIQUES: Use the buddy system if at all possible, even for surface-tended dives. Use a buddy line in poor visibility.
  PREPARING FOR THE DIVE: Only SCUBA bottles designed specifically for the use and gas mixture for which they are to be used, will be used. An unfamiliar tank should be inspected for indication of proper hydrostatic testing.
  Load SCUBA rigs against front stake on truck or stand them up in boats; do not lay them down where they will be stepped on or where the manifolds can be damaged. (This is important not only with the delicate closed and semi-closed circuit equipment but also with open circuit; the non-magnetic manifolds in particular bend very easily and can be made to leak even by too strenuous manual operation).

DRESSING FOR THE DIVE
  Wear the minimum equipment.

  Wear other accessories as compatible with safety.

  Use quick-release methods of attaching all releasable equipment.

  Use a lanyard on a separate facemask.

  Use a lanyard on the knife.
MAKING THE DIVE
  Enter the water carefully.

  Carry out the surface check.

  Swim down or pull yourself headfirst down the

DIVING-4

descending line.

Extend hands ahead when swimming in poor visibility.

Avoid overexertion. At first sign of breathlessness, slow down. If possible, stop and rest.

Watch out for entanglement around wreckage, lines, and vegetation.

When in kelp move slowly and smoothly; never jerk.

Breathe normally during ascent. If out of air on the bottom, remember that you will generally be able to get a bite of air about every 30' on the way up. Don't exceed the rate of ascent specified in the decompression table applicable to the dive.

Never wear ear plugs.

Never wear nonequalizing goggles.

DECOMPRESSION
Avoid decompression dives.

Always follow standard procedures for decompression.

Decompress for maximum depth attained on multi-level dives.

Be prepared for cases of unplanned interrupted decompression.

OTHER CONSIDERATIONS
Learn to dive without a facemask.

Practice emergency procedures frequently to keep them ingrained.

Be forehanded. Before you dive, always mentally review the possible emergencies and their corrective action for the SCUBA in use. Line up a course of action for each emergency and keep it in mind. Be calm.

COMPRESSORS and ACCESSORIES

AIR COMPRESSORS

There are many compressors used throughout the services. Many are not suitable for scuba divers. A compressor is suitable for scuba divers only if the air which it produces is free from carbon monoxide, and is free from oil.

There are four sizes of portable compressors available for use to UDTs: 0.6, 4, 8, and 15 cf/m. The 0.6 and 4 cf/m units are light and easily handled, while the 8 and 15 are generally trailer-or skid-mounted. Both electric and gasoline powered units are available. In addition, charging lines with air filters attached are available for use for charging off of high pressure systems or submarines.

SAFETY

There are six general safety precautions to be observed when using an air compressor:

(1) The air intake for the compressor should be located so that air being drawn in will be clear of carbon-monoxide.
(2) Oil should be properly separated from the H.P. air before being stowed or used.
(3) The H.P. air should be filtered before being stowed or used.
(4) The H.P. air should have a carbon-monoxide and an oil content test before being used for diving, and should be checked periodically.

(5) The air that is to be compressed to high pressures should be taken from the outdoors, and away from any type of fumes that could possibly harm a scuba diver. After this air is compressed to high pressures, it should be run through a filter filled with some good filtering agents.

(6) Oil to be used in a high pressure air compressor should be of the right viscosity, and should be a high flash point oil.

The figure shown below will give you an idea of a good H.P. air system.

CHARGING PROCEDURES

Although charging facilities will differ from one command to another, the below listed procedure (which is used at the U. S. Naval School for Underwater Swimmers) is one that should be helpful to the student in charging scuba under any circumstances. Remember that in dealing with high pressure air, all

HIGH PRESSURE AIR SYSTEM

A - Air Intake
B - H.P. Air Compressor
C - Oil Separator (filled with Activated Alumina)
D - Air Filter (filled with felt Pads)
E - Stop Valve
F - Relief Valve
G - Pressure Gauge
H - Stop Valve
I - Relief Valve
J - Air Storage Banks
K - Stop Valve
L - Reducing Valve
M - Pressure Gauge
N - Relief Valve
O - Stop Valve
P - Bleeder Valve
Q - Pressure Gauge
R - Charging Manifold
S - Charging Coupling

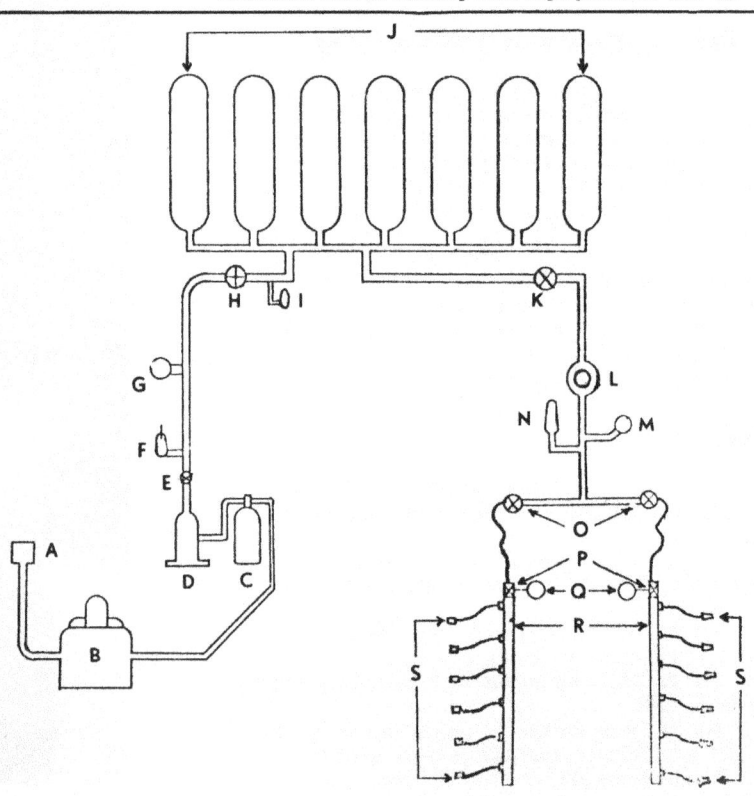

DIVING-4

possible safety precautions should be taken. Following is the procedure used when charging open circuit scuba:

(a) Connect charging lines to air cylinders to be charged. (If there are less cylinders to be charged than there are charging lines, connect loose charging line or lines to air cylinders that have been charged already).

(b) Place all reserve levers in down position.

(c) Close air bleeder valve on charging manifold.

(d) Open cylinder valves on air cylinders that are to be charged. (Do not open cylinder valves or valves on air cylinders that have been charged.)

(e) Open charging manifold stop valve slowly.

(f) Check for overheating of air cylinders (Maximum 130°F.) by putting hand on air cylinders.

(g) Air cylinders are normally considered charged when gauge pressure on manifold has reached 2150 lbs/sq. in.

(h) Close all cylinder valves.

(i) Mark all charged air cylinders with an "F" (Full) with chalk.

(j) Close charging manifold stop valve.

(k) Open charging manifold bleeder valve. Keep fingers clear of bleeder hole. If air being bled continues at a constant flow, close air bleeder valve and check that all cylinders valves are closed. Permit all air to bleed through bleeder before removing charging lines.

(l) Remove charging line from air cylinder.

OXYGEN TRANSFER PUMP

Two types of oxygen transfer pumps are available, manual and electric. The electrical units are not portable. With the oxygen transfer pumps, the primary precaution is keeping all the equipment free of petroleum based products to prevent explosions.

OPERATING INSTRUCTIONS ELECTRIC O$_2$

(a) Connect suction hose to supply cylinder.

(b) Connect discharge hose to bottle to be filled.

(c) Turn on cooling water.

(d) Open discharge and bypass valves on the control panel.

(e) Open the valve of the bottles' to be filled.

(f) Open the valve of the supply cylinder. Gas will flow between the two cylinders until the pressure is equalized. Cascade from all supply bottles if each bottle has its own pressure gauge.

(g) Start the compressor.

(h) Close the bypass valve. The compressor will now pump O$_2$ into the receiving bottle.

(i) When the desired pressure has been reached, stop the compressor or open the bypass valve.

(j) Close valves on supply cylinder and receiving bottle. If compressor is still running, close "discharge valve"

(k) Bleed lines through bleed valve or carefully crack open fittings on bottle.

(l) Disconnect flexible lines from bottle.

(m) If no more bottles are to be filled, stop compressor by pushing stop button and secure cooling water.

(n) Always check the oil level in sight glass and ensure that reservoir of distilled water is full. Do not pump supply bottles to a pressure less than 400 psi.

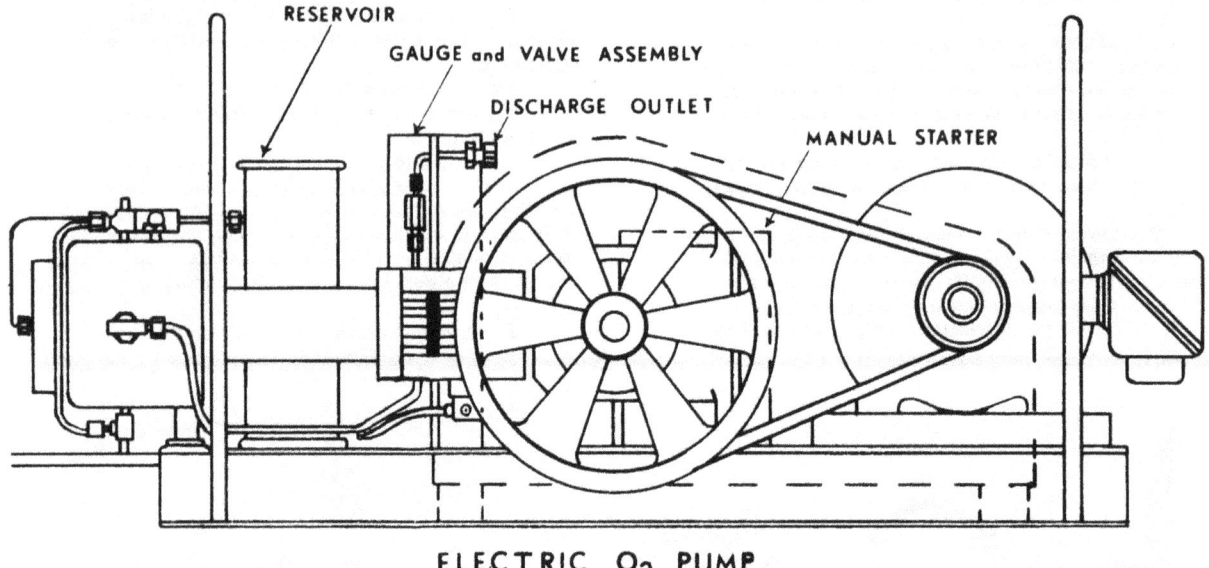

ELECTRIC O₂ PUMP

OPERATING INSTRUCTIONS
HAND OPERATED

All valves are to be operated slowly and carefully to prevent sudden expansion of the high pressure oxygen.

FILLING BOTTLES WITH OXYGEN: The maximum pressure to which bottles shall be filled with this pump is 2200 psi.

When first installing pump, flush system with oxygen as a precaution against impurities. This is done in the following manner:

(1) Attach supply cylinder to inlet manifold using long tube provided.
(2) Open valve on supply cylinder.
(3) Open bypass valve.
(4) Open outlet valve slightly and allow some oxygen to escape to open air.
(5) Close bypass valve, outlet valve, and valve on supply cylinder.

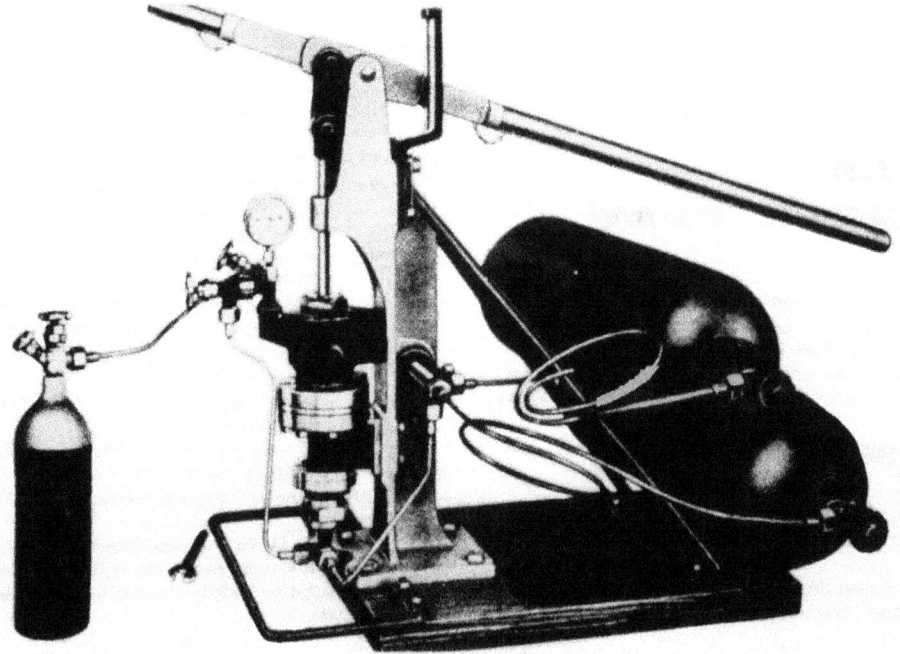

DIVING-4

USING ONE SUPPLY CYLINDER ONLY
(1) Connect bottle to be refilled to outlet manifold, using tube provided. Submerge bottle to neck in water, and keep water as cold as possible while charging. CAUTION: Place pump handle in upper position with piston at top of cylinder. Otherwise, handle may be suddenly lifted by gas pressure when Supply Cylinder Closing Valve is turned on.
(2) Open closing valve on the bottle to be refilled.
(3) Open outlet valve on pump.
(4) Open bypass valve then slowly open valve on supply cylinder.
(5) When pressure is equalized in system, close bypass valve and start pumping, moving handle up and down.
(6) Continue pumping until desired pressure is obtained.
(7) Close valve on refilled bottle.
(8) Close outlet valve on pump.
(9) Disconnect refilled bottle.

USING THREE SUPPLY CYLINDERS: With low, medium and high pressures, proceed as follows:
(1) Connect bottle to be refilled to outlet manifold, using tube provided. Submerge bottle to neck in water, and keep water as cold as possible while charging. CAUTION: Place pump handle in upper position with piston at top of cylinder. Otherwise, handle may be suddenly lifted by gas pressure when Supply Cylinder Closing Valve is turned on.
(2) Open closing valve on bottle to be refilled.
(3) Open outlet valve on pump.
(4) Open bypass valve then slowly open valve on supply cylinder.
(5) When pressure is equalized in system, close bypass valve and start pumping, moving handle up and down.
(6) Pump oxygen from low pressure supply cylinder, and continue pumping until the pressure in the refilled bottle is double that of the initial pressure of the low pressure supply cylinder. Close low pressure supply cylinder.
(7) Open valve on medium pressure supply cylinder. Pump oxygen from medium pressure supply cylinder, and continue pumping until the pressure in the refilled bottle is double the pressure obtained when pumping from the low pressure supply cylinder was discontinued. Close valve on medium pressure supply cylinder.
(8) Open valve on high pressure supply cylinder and continue pumping until desired pressure is obtained.
(9) Close valve on high pressure supply cylinder; close outlet valve; close valve on refilled bottle and disconnect refilled bottle.

TWO SUPPLY CYLINDERS: When high and low pressure is being used:
(1) Connect bottle to be refilled to outlet manifold, using tube provided. Submerge bottle to neck in water, and keep water as cold as possible while charging. CAUTION: Place pump handle in upper position with piston at top of cylinder. Otherwise, handle may be suddenly lifted by gas pressure when Supply Cylinder Closing Valve is turned on; except that pumping is continued on the low pressure supply cylinder until the pressure in the refilled cylinder is about 60 atmospheres.
(2) Open valve on high pressure supply cylinder and continue pumping until desired pressure is obtained.
(3) Close valve on high pressure supply cylinder; close outlet valve; close valve on refilled bottle and disconnect refilled bottle.

CARE OF PUMP AFTER REFILLING OF BOTTLES IS COMPLETED: After completion of refilling of bottles, close outlet valve on pump, open bypass valve and equalize pressure in discharge chamber and in supply cylinder. Close valve on supply cylinder, and leave bypass valve open. If gauge pressure falls, check for leaks. Pressure should be allowed to remain in system when pump is idle (usually 40 atm to 75 atm).

LUBRICATION

It is absolutely essential to keep the pump full of the lubricating liquid at all times so as to have the leather washers, valves and piston rod freely lubricated. Proper lubrication will ensure efficient operation of pump and reduce maintenance work to a minimum. The only lubricant to be used on or in the pump, or on any part with which oxygen comes in contact, is a glycerine in water solution consisting of eight parts of distilled water to one part of pure glycerine free from acid.

To fill the Pump with Lubrication Solution:
(1) Close bypass valve.
(2) Remove cylinder to be refilled and open outlet valve on pump.
(3) Disconnect tube from inlet of cylinder head.
(4) Use a supply cylinder connecting tube and attach one end to cylinder head and the free end place in a jar containing the lubricating solution.
(5) Remove plug located on side of compression chamber.
(6) Pump 2 to 10 strokes, depending upon amount of liquid in the pump, until the lubricant overflows at plug opening.
(7) Replace plug, and re-attach tube from manifold to inlet.
(8) Open bypass valve.
(9) Connect an oxygen supply cylinder to the pump and open cylinder valve slightly allowing a small volume of oxygen to flow through the pump to the air. Close valve on supply cylinder. This operation will blow out excess lubrication in the bypass tube and pump. The pump is now ready for use.

SAFETY

COMPRESSED GAS SAFETY PRECAUTIONS Team diving operations necessitate maintaining large amounts of compressed gases, both flammable and nonflammable, on board at all times. The diving officer is responsible for ensuring that these gases are safely handled and stored, and that all tanks, whether SCUBA or holding are properly handled, used, issued, and

maintained. Gases common to the teams are compressed air, oxygen, nitrogen, and three standard mixtures of N_2O_2. Electric, gasoline, and hand powered transfer pumps and compressors are utilized. BSTM and NAVAER 16-20-501 give a basic outline of procedures to be used in working with compressed gases. All compressed gases and gas cylinders should be handled in accordance with the general procedures and safety precautions outlined below. In addition, specific regulations will apply to particular gases and equipment. The following is an outline of procedures which should be followed:

OXYGEN. Gaseous oxygen is colorless, odorless, and slightly heavier than air. It is not flammable, but strongly supports and rapidly accelerates the combustion of all flammable materials.

(1) Keep all sparks, flames, and excess heat away from all oxygen and oxygen equipment. Keep all combustible materials away from possible contact with oxygen.

(2) Utilize only designated Aviator's Breathing Oxygen for any breathing medium.

(3) Never use any oil products, grease or fatty substance on or around any oxygen equipment. Handle oxygen and equipment in accordance with BUMEDINST 6270.1 series. Lubricate oxygen equipment only as specified in BUSHIPSINST 9230.15 series.

(4) Keep equipment clean at all times. Should any equipment come in contact with oil, or be contaminated by dirt which may contain oil, clean in the following manner: (IAW BUSHIPSINST 9380.12 series.)

(a) Dip in benzine or benzol and allow to dry.
(b) Steam thoroughly.
(c) Dip in boiling water to remove any possible traces of oil that may be in the steam.

(5) Utilize only copper, monel, or copper-nickel in transfer lines, gauges and other equipment used with oxygen.

(6) Don't use oxygen as a substitute for compressed air. Don't use to blow out pipe lines, dust clothing or working areas, or for head pressure in a tank of any kind.

(7) Never break connections without first bleeding the pressure.

(8) Keep oxygen and its equipment as near normal room temperature as possible (70° - 90° F.). Heat caused by friction of rapidly flowing oxygen or sudden compression is just as dangerous as sparks.

(9) Never use oxygen with equipment other than that specifically designed for its use; never use it in equipment that has been used with any other gas or material. Never use any gas except oxygen in equipment designed for oxygen.

(10) Never permit oxygen to enter a regulator suddenly. Open it slowly, with the face of any gauge away from the body.

(11) Never attempt to repair equipment unless properly qualified, and never use leaky or defective equipment.

(12) Permissible fire fighting agents are water, CO_2, and inert gas. The use of carbon tetrachloride, mechanical foam, soda and acid, and methylbromide, are prohibited.

NITROGEN. Nitrogen is an inert gas, slightly lighter than air. It does not form flammable or explosive mixtures with oxygen or air, and it will not support either combustion or respiration.

(1) Utilize only Nitrogen designated "dry" and "water pump" as part of a breathing medium.

(2) Work with nitrogen only in well ventilated areas.

(3) Lubricate nitrogen systems only in accordance BUSHIPSINST 9230.15 series.

(4) Never allow oil, grease, or fatty substances to contaminate nitrogen which may be used in conjunction with oxygen.

NITROGEN-OXYGEN MIXTURES. Standard diving mixtures of 60/40, 40/60 and 62.5/37.5 are available through Navy supply systems. These mixtures are not flammable, but will readily support combustion due to their high percentage of oxygen.

(1) Handle all standard N_2O_2 mixtures in accordance with the instructions for oxygen listed above.

(2) All gas mixtures will be thoroughly analyzed prior to use.

(3) If pre-mixed gases are not available, gases will be mixed into a standard H.P.I.C.C. gas cylinder only. Order of preference of cylinders into which gas can be mixed is as follows:

(a) Mixed gas cylinder of same mixture as gas desired.
(b) Mixed gas cylinder of different mix than gas desired.
(c) Oxygen cylinder
(d) Nitrogen cylinder

(4) If cylinders of type (b), (c), or (d) are utilized for gas mixing, cylinders shall be plainly marked in paint prior to returning them to the supply facility.

HELIUM. Helium is an inert gas, and will not support combustion.

(1) Grade C helium (97.5% pure, oil-free but possibly containing water vapor) only shall be used.

(2) Standard helium-oxygen mixtures shall be utilized when available.

(3) Helium and helium-oxygen mixtures shall be handled in accordance with paragraphs above, substituting helium for nitrogen.

COMPRESSED AIR. Compressed air is not flammable, but will support combustion.

(1) Only compressed air from an oil and carbon monoxide-free source shall be used. In general, air obtained from other than the compressors located at Team areas shall be filtered for both particulate and gaseous waste prior to use.

(2) High pressure air will not be utilized to dust clothing or work areas; it is mechanically dangerous.

COMPRESSED GAS CYLINDER SAFETY PRECAUTIONS
Handling and Storage Precautions:

(1) All cylinders shall be obtained through the Navy standard supply system whenever possible. Cylinders not properly painted, stamped and showing evidence of proper hydrostatic testing shall not be accepted.

(2) All cylinders shall be painted in accordance with Military Standard MIL-STD-101.

(3) Handle all cylinders with care, especially

cylinder containing flammable or explosive gases. Do not allow them to be bumped, dropped, or otherwise mishandled.

(4) The cylinder valve outlet cap and the cylinder valve protecting cap shall be in place when cylinders are being handled; every precaution shall be taken to avoid hitting the discharge valves during handling operations.

(5) When loading or transferring, cylinders shall be secured in a cradle, suitable platform, or rack. Electromagnets shall never be used.

(6) Cylinders shall never be used as rollers or as supports.

(7) Cylinders shall never be allowed to have more pressure in them than specified. Cylinders shall never be allowed to drain completely and valves shall not be left open, as this will permit them to be contaminated. Empty ones shall be so marked.

(8) Care will be taken to ensure that cylinders are maintained at approximate room temperature. Maximum temperature will never exceed 130°F. In case of freezing of valves, warm, not boiling, water will be used to free them.

(9) Flammable materials, especially grease and oil, shall be kept well away from the storage area.

(10) Cylinders will be stored in a vertical position, valve up.

(11) Protect cylinders from objects that might produce cuts or abrasions in the surface of the metal.

(12) Keep storage areas well ventilated.

(13) Do not refill cylinders unless such action is specifically approved by the Bureau concerned; never fill any cylinder with any gas other than that for which it was intended, except as prescribed in paragraph above, and in U.S. Navy Diving Manual.

(14) Do not remove or change any markings on cylinders except to designate contamination or malfunction, in which case notation will be made with white paint.

(15) Never force connections, tamper with safety devices, cross threads, or hammer and strike valve wheels on cylinders.

(16) Do not use regulators, manifolds, pressure gauges, analyzers, and related equipment which are provided for a particular gas on cylinders containing different gases.

(17) Do not repair or alter cylinders or valves except when authorized by the Bureau. When testing for leaks, use soapy water and keep the area clear of all sources of possible ignition and contamination.

(18) Never discharge cylinder into any device or equipment wherein the gas will be entrapped and create pressure, unless the cylinder is equipped with a pressure regulator set to control the pressure.

(19) Lubricate cylinders, valves, and other equipment only in accordance with appropriate instructions.

TESTING COMPRESSED GAS CYLINDERS

All cylinders are required to have periodic hydrostatic tests and inspections. No full cylinders which are past due for tests will be accepted from any supply source; no SCUBA bottles past due will be filled for any reason.

QUINQUENNIAL TESTING: BSTM Article 23.26 points out ICC requirements for quinquennial testing of "practically all cylinders". Compressed Gas Ass'n Inc. Pamphlet C-1 of 1959 requires five year inspections of steel cylinders, and CGA, Inc. Pamphlet C-6 of 1956 recommends annual inspections and hydrostatic testing of all steel SCUBA bottles.

ALUMINUM SCUBA BOTTLES: In accordance with BUSHIPSNOTE 9940 series aluminum bottles must be hydrostatically tested at 5000 psi every three years and after any repair work. These bottles must have an annual internal inspection in accordance with BUSHIPSINST 9930.6 series.

It shall be the direct responsibility of the Diving Officers to ensure that the required tests and inspections are preformed. This will include quinquennial hydro of all steel SCUBA, and tri-annual hydro of all aluminum SCUBA and annual internal inspection of all aluminum SCUBA.

MAXIMUM CHARGING PRESSURES

All bottles are stamped with ICC approved service pressures. These working pressures shall not be exceeded except as listed herein. Bottles shall be tested to the marked test pressure.

In accordance with BUSHIPS letter 9941 serial 636-72 of 28 April 1964, aluminum SCUBA bottles (open circuit) may presently be charged to their standard working pressure of 3000 psi.

In accordance with NAVAER 16-20-50, Section B.24., "...until further orders from the Interstate Commerce Commission, I.C.C. - 3A cylinders may be charged with compressed gases, other than liquified dissolved gases, to a pressure 10 percent in excess of their marked service pressure." Decision to implement this regulation will in each case rest with the Diving Officer, and shall be based upon operational necessity.

ISSUE OF NAVY-OWNED CYLINDERS

In accordance with BSTM, Art. 23.47, and NAVAER 16-20-501, Section B.10, Navy owned cylinders shall not be leased or transferred to private parties or other government agencies, including the Marine Corps, without the specific permission of GSSO, except in cases where an emergency is deemed to exist and such action is approved by the Commanding Officer. A detailed report is required in all cases. Such report shall contain an explanation, all markings on the cylinders, and shall be forwarded to GSSO, along with the details of transaction.

DIVING-4

UNDERWATER PHYSICS

To understand diving and its effect on the human body, it is necessary to know something about the physics of diving. Physics is the science dealing with the properties of matter and the way matter behaves under different conditions. All matter exists in one of three states: Solids, which have definite volume and shape; liquids, which have definite volume but conform to the shape of their containers; and Gases, which have neither a definite volume nor shape. Any specific kind of matter may exist in more than one state depending on the temperature and pressure. In diving we are primarily interested in liquids and gases. Compared with gases, liquids are considered incompressible. Gases have no definite shape or volume and can be compressed. All gases have weight and occupy space.

GASES

AIR: The composition of air is a mixture (not a chemical compound) which can be broken down into the following proportions:

	% BY VOLUME
NITROGEN	79.02
OXYGEN	20.29
CO_2	.04
Rare Gases(Argon,Neon,Traces of Radon, H, etc.)	.65

CARBON DIOXIDE: (CO_2) Carbon Dioxide is a colorless, odorless, tasteless gas when encountered in small quantities. It has a noticeable acidic taste and odor when in high concentrations. This gas can be harmful to the diver.

CARBON MONOXIDE: (CO) Carbon monoxide is a colorless, odorless, tasteless, very poisonous gas. If contained in a diver's air supply, serious consequences will usually result.

HELIUM: (He) At deep diving depths helium gains importance, for its intoxicating effects under pressure are very much less than those of nitrogen. Helium is a colorless, odorless, tasteless inert gas.

HYDROGEN: (H) Hydrogen is a colorless, odorless, tasteless gas. It is not used for diving by the U.S. Navy because it is explosive when mixed with certain concentrations of oxygen. Hydrogen is less dense than helium and therefore has potential value for very deep and prolonged dives.

NITROGEN: (N_2) Nitrogen is a colorless, odorless, tasteless inert gas that comprises approximately 79.02% by volume of the air which we breathe. It is incapable of supporting life or combustion. Under high pressure nitrogen has an intoxicating effect, and the diver becomes susceptible to Nitrogen Narcosis at deep depths breathing air.

OXYGEN: (O_2) Oxygen is a colorless, odorless, tasteless inert gas that forms approximately 20.29% by volume of the air which we breathe. Oxygen alone is capable of supporting life; however, it becomes toxic when high concentrations are breathed under high pressures, causing oxygen poisoning ("Oxygen Toxicity"). Oxygen readily supports combustion, however Oxygen itself will not burn.

PRESSURE

Pressure is a force applied to some surface or area, and is commonly expressed in pounds per square inch (psi). All gases are a collection of small particles called molecules that are in constant motion. If we increase the temperature, this motion becomes faster. If we decrease the temperature, the motion becomes slower. If we continue to decrease the temperature, the motion becomes slower and slower to a point where the molecules adhere to each other and the gas turns into a liquid. Further decreasing of temperature will result in a solid as the molecules "freeze together". This motion of the molecules of gas causes pressure, as each tiny molecule collides with other molecules and with the sides of its container while moving about. There are several different "types" of pressure:

ATMOSPHERIC PRESSURE is the result of the weight of the atmosphere, or the weight of the air around us producing a force on the surface of the earth in all directions. The miles of air above a square inch of surface area at sea level weighs 14.7 pounds. The term "one atmosphere" is used to denote a pressure of 14.7 psi.

GAUGE PRESSURE indicates the difference between the pressure being measured and the surrounding atmospheric pressure. When we say the pressure in a gas cylinder is 1000 psi we mean that the pressure is 1000 psi above atmospheric pressure. We indicate gauge pressure as "psig" ("pounds per square inch, gauge").

ABSOLUTE PRESSURE is the true or total pressure being exerted. It is gauge pressure plus one atmosphere of pressure. Absolute pressure is commonly expressed at "psia" ("pounds per square inch, absolute").

BAROMETRIC PRESSURE is the exact pressure of the atmosphere at any given time or place. It is measured by an instrument known as a Barometer. Barometric pressure changes with altitude, air temperature, the amount of water vapor in the atmosphere, and the movement of masses of air.

LIQUID PRESSURE: The pressure produced by a liquid is the direct result of its weight. A heavy liquid will naturally produce more pressure than a lighter one(sea water at 64 lbs/cu ft. is heavier than fresh water which weighs 62.4 lbs/cu ft). The pressure exerted by water is directly proportional to its depth. At any depth the pressure on one square foot of surface column of water over it. At a depth of 33

DIVING-4

feet in seawater, one can think of this as a stack of thirty-three 1 foot cubes of water, each weighing 64 pounds. The total weight would then be 64 x 33 or 2,112 pounds acting on one square foot of the bottom. To find out what the pressure is in pounds per square inch we must divide by 144, since there are 144 square inches in one square foot of surface area. Dividing 2,112 by 144 then, we arrive at 14.7 psi. This is the pressure exerted by seawater at 33 feet. The air above the water exerts another 14.7 pounds per square inch as we have already discovered.

The absolute total pressure at 33 feet, therefore is 29.4 psia. Each additional 33 feet of depth will add an atmosphere (14.7 lbs) of pressure per square inch. The absolute pressure exerted on a submerged body is the pressure of the water plus atmospheric pressure. Each foot of depth increases the pressure by 1/33 of 14.7 psi or 0.445 psi. Multiplying the depth in feet by 0.445 psi gives the water pressure at that depth in psi. Adding 14.7 gives the absolute pressure at any depth.

GAS LAWS

In diving we work with gases (usually air) under pressure. In order to do this, we must know how to measure gas pressure and gas volume (the space in which any gas is enclosed) and, in addition, learn how to figure out what happens when either one of these, or the temperature, changes. A number of important scientists, over the years, have discovered certain very basic facts about the behavior of gases in different situations, and these fundamental facts have come to be called the "Gas Laws", with the name of the discoverer attached to each one.

BOYLE'S LAW

Boyle discovered that increasing the pressure on a flexible container of gas (such as taking an inflated balloon down underwater to, say, 33 feet) caused the volume of the gas to decrease; not only that, but the amount that the volume was reduced was exactly proportional to (in balance with) the amount the pressure was increased, provided there was no change in the temperature of the gas. The reverse situation (i.e., decreasing the pressure with resulting increase in volume) works in the same way. This kind of pressure/volume relationship is called an "inverse relationship" and can be likened to a seesaw - when one side goes up, the other must always go down. Now, when a certain volume of gas is compressed (made smaller) by increasing the pressure on it, all those molecules, of which the gas is made, cannot do anything but get jammed closer together - in other words, that gas gets denser. Therefore, it can be seen that the denseness, more often called the "density", of a gas is another thing that varies with changes in pressure. Only in this case, it isn't an "inverse" (seesaw) relationship but what we call a "direct relationship", which is just a short way of saying that when the one thing increases, the other increases also. Putting the above findings into as few words as possible "BOYLE'S LAW" can be stated as follows: <u>If the temperature is kept constant (unchanged), the volume of a gas will vary (change) inversely with the pressure, while the density will vary directly with the pressure.</u>

CHARLES' LAW

Charles discovered that if you heat a certain volume of gas in a rigid container (so it cannot expand), then the pressure of the gas in that container goes up (like a pressure cooker). Naturally, the opposite happens when you cool the gas down. "CHARLES' LAW", then, states that: <u>If the volume of a gas is kept constant, the pressure of the gas will vary directly with the temperature.</u>

DALTON'S LAW

What happens to the pressures when you mix two or more gases together? DALTON discovered that the total pressure of the mix could be found by adding the pressures of each of the individual gases together. He called the pressure of any single gas in a mixture the "partial pressure" of that particular gas, since it only contributed a part of the pressure of the whole mix. Often we know the total pressure of a gas mixture, and want to find out what the partial pressure of some one of the individual gases in it is. To do this, we have to know what the percentage of that particular gas is in the mix. For example, we may want to know what the partial pressure of oxygen (O_2) is in the air-filled balloon (or a diver's lungs) which has been taken down to 33 feet in the sea. We learned earlier that for each 33 feet increase in depth of seawater there results an increased pressure of exactly 14.7 psi. Therefore at a depth of 33 feet the total pressure in the balloon must be 29.4 psia (14.7 from the atmosphere and 14.7 from the 33 feet). We know that air contains very close to 20% oxygen.

Since 20% of 29.4 psia is 5.88 psia, that is the partial pressure of O_2 in that air-filled balloon at that depth. Now we can better understand DALTON'S LAW which states that: <u>The total pressure exerted by a mixture of gases is the sum of the pressure that would be exerted by each of the gases if it alone were present and occupied the total volume.</u>

HENRY'S LAW

A certain amount of any gas in contact with a liquid (such as air at the surface of the sea) will dissolve in that liquid. HENERY discovered that the amount of any particular gas which will be dissolved in a liquid depends upon the partial pressure of that gas. "HENRY'S LAW" therefore states: <u>At any given temperature, the amount of a gas which will dissolve in a liquid is directly proportional to the partial pressure of that gas.</u>

DIVING-4

APPLICATION

In order to make practical use of all the facts outlined above we need to learn how to make certain calculations. But before we can go on to that, there are a few inconveniences that we must learn to put up with whenever we do figuring involving gases on gas laws:

Whenever you do any calculations involving pressure, you must always use absolute pressure (see page).

Whenever you use temperature in gas calculations, you must use absolute temperature; this means that if you are using the Fahrenheit scale, you must add $460°$ to your temperature readings; and if the centigrade scale is used, $273°$ must be added to that reading. To understand why this is necessary you should read two short paragraphs in the U.S. Navy Diving Manual 1.10.13 (8) and 1.2.4 (2).

Whenever you do any calculations, involving gases, or anything else, you must use the same units throughout the problem. What this means is that you cannot use both Fahrenheit and Centigrade, or inches and centimeters, or pounds per square inch and atmospheres together in the same problem. If the facts and figures that you are given are not in the same units, you must convert them to the same type of units before you can start solving the problem.

"GENERAL GAS LAW"

Keeping the above in mind, we can now make a practical application of BOYLE'S and CHARLES' LAWS. By combining them and putting them in the form of an equation, we can "plug in" known values and solve for unknown values. This is called the GENERAL GAS LAW and is written as follows:

$$\frac{P_1 V_1}{T_1} = \frac{P_2 V_2}{T_2}$$

Where; P_1 is the initial pressure (absolute) you start with
V_1 is the initial volume you start with
T_1 is the initial temperature (absolute) you start with
P_2 is the final pressure (absolute) you end up with
V_2 is the final volume you end up with
T_2 is the final temperature you end up with

In many problems, the temperature change will be none, or negligible, so that T_1 and T_2 will be the same and therefore cancel out of the above equation, leaving $P_1 V_1 = P_2 V_2$. Section 1.2.4(20) in the U.S. Navy Diving Manual gives some good examples of some problems that can easily be solved using the GENERAL GAS LAW equation.

UNDERWATER PHYSIOLOGY

The science of physiology is concerned with the functions and processes of the human body. The following paragraphs present an explanation of how the body works. An understanding of basic physiology is necessary before diving diseases and injuries can be understood.

METABOLISM

The process of oxidizing food is called metabolism. Every cell in the body maintains its life, grows, and carries out its particular function from chemical reactions that take place inside it. The chemical reactions can be compared to a flameless burning, or "oxidation", the purpose of which is to produce energy. Food is "burned", as fuel, in the presence of oxygen, and the result is energy, water, waste products, and carbon dioxide. This total process is called metabolism.

RESPIRATION

Accepting the fact of "metabolism" we should examine two aspects of this process: One how the food we eat is taken to the cells where it is "burned" in the presence of oxygen; and two, how the oxygen travels to the cells to support that "burning". We will concern ourselves only with how the oxygen arrives at the cells, for this phenomenon is particularly important to us in diving. The process of breathing and the exchange of gases in the lungs is sometimes called external respiration. The use, production, and exchange of gases that take place inside the tissues is referred to as internal respiration.

CIRCULATORY

The circulatory system includes the heart, the blood, the lungs, the arteries and veins. The heart is the muscular pump which propels the blood through the system. The arteries are the vessels which carry the blood to the cells from the heart. The veins are the vessels which return blood from the cells to the heart.

Although it forms one continuous system of tubes with the same blood flowing throughout, the circulatory system actually consists of two circuits. The Pulmonary circuit serves the lungs and its capillaries. The Systemic circuit serves the tissues of the body and its capillaries. Blood first passes through one circuit and then the other.

THE HEART

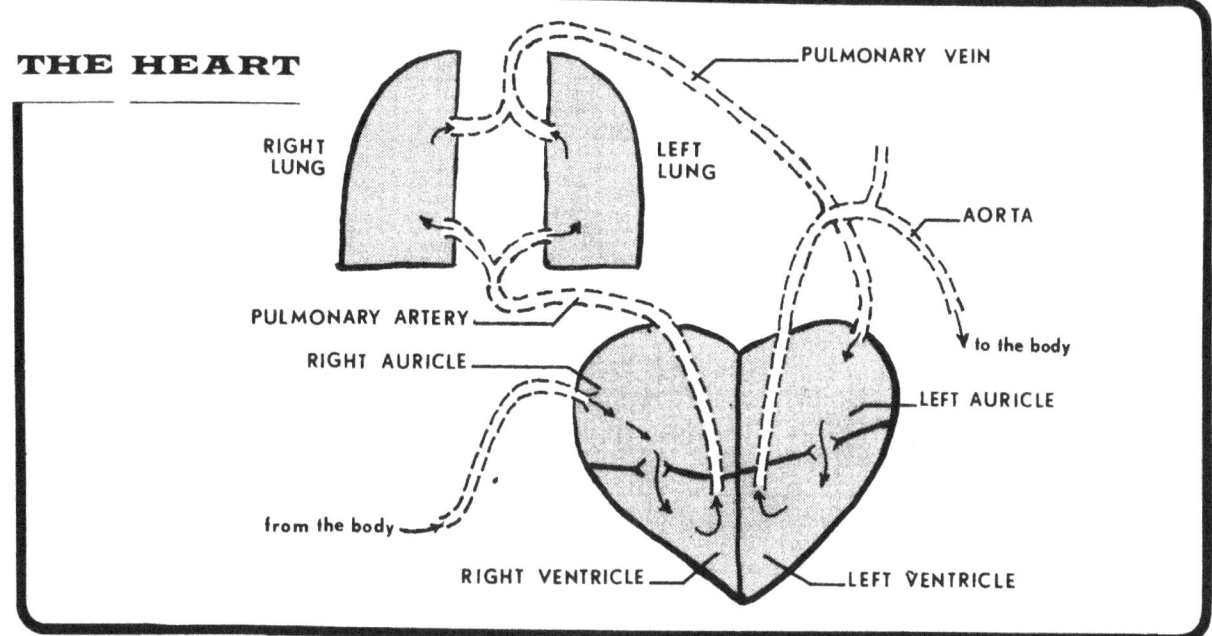

THE PATH OF A DROP OF BLOOD: A drop of blood leaving a capillary in a biceps muscle has lost most of its oxygen in a process of metabolism, and is loaded with carbon dioxide. It flows through small capillaries until it reaches a main vein. The main vein carries it to the right auricle. It passes through a one-way valve, (tricuspid), into the right ventricle. From the right ventricle it passes through another one-way valve into the pulmonary artery which leads from the heart to the lungs. Here it comes into contact with air. By diffusion, it loses its excess carbon dioxide and takes up a fresh load of oxygen. The drop of blood returns to the heart and enters the left auricle and then the left ventricle. Next it is pumped through the one-way aortic valve into the main artery (the aorta) of the systemic circuit. It then follows one of the main arteries to a tissue capillary where it again gives up its oxygen and takes up carbon dioxide.

HEART

The heart is a hollow organ almost entirely made up of muscle tissue to provide the pumping action. It is about the size of a closed fist and is located in the center of the chest cavity between the right and left lungs almost directly beneath the breast bone. The heart is divided lengthwise into two halves. The left half is the pump for the systemic circuit. The right half is the pump for the pulmonary circuit. Each half is divided into an upper chamber and a lower chamber. The upper chambers are called "auricles" and the lower chambers are called the "ventricles".

BLOOD

How does the blood carry the vital oxygen to the cells of the body? Oxygen is carried by the red blood cells of the blood. Red blood cells are extremely small (about 300 million in a drop of blood), and contain Hemoglobin. Hemoglobin is a complicated chemical compound that soaks up oxygen like a sponge soaks up water. When hemoglobin has a full load of oxygen, its color is bright red. As it loses oxygen it becomes increasingly bluish in color. Whether it gains or loses oxygen is related to the "partial pressure" of oxygen to which it is exposed. The amount of an individual gas which will move through a permeable membrane (body tissues) depends upon the partial pressure of the gas on both sides of the membrane. If the partial pressure is higher on one side, the gas will tend to move to the other side until the partial pressures are equalized. Because the cells are using oxygen, the partial pressure of oxygen in the tissues is lower than that of the partial pressure of oxygen in the hemoglobin (about 98%). The hemoglobin therefore gives up its oxygen to the tissue capillaries.

LUNGS

The lungs can be thought of as two elastic bags containing millions of little air sacs called alveoli. These air sacs are all connected to air passages which branch and rebranch like the twigs of a tree. Air that enters the main airways of the lung gains access to the entire surface of all the alveoli. Each alveoli is lined with a thin membrane and surrounded by a mass network of very small blood vessels. The lung membranes, then, have air on one side and blood on the other. Diffusion of gases takes place freely in either direction.

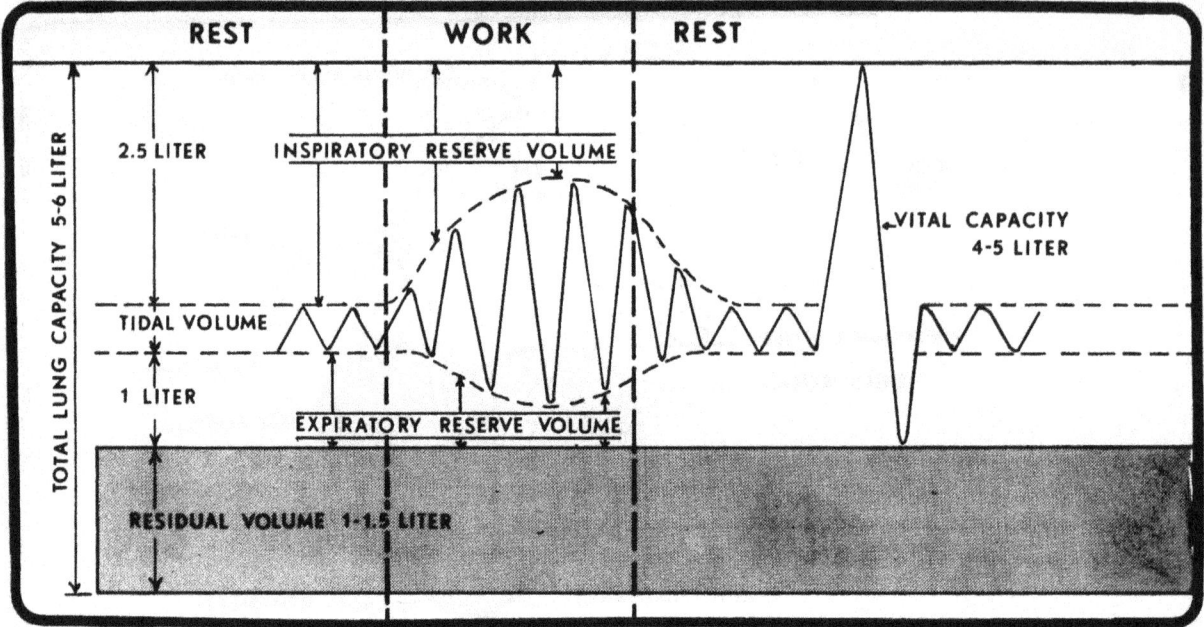

LUNG CAPACITY: The limits on the lungs' gas holding ability are of prime importance in diving. The following definitions and diagram are designed to explain the ability of the lungs to hold gas:

RESPIRATORY CYCLE: One complete breath.

RESPIRATORY RATE: The number of respiratory cycles that take place in one minute. A normal adult has a respiratory rate of between 10 to 20 "breaths" per minute.

TOTAL LUNG CAPACITY: The total volume of air that the lungs can hold when filled to capacity. It is normally between five and six liters.

VITAL CAPACITY: The greatest amount of air that can be moved in or out of the lungs in a single breath. It is normally between four and five liters.

TIDAL VOLUME: The volume of air moved in and out during a single normal respiratory cycle. At rest it is about 1/2 a liter. This can increase greatly with exercise, fear, or excitement.

RESIDUAL VOLUME: The amount of air that remains in the lungs even after the most forceful expiration. It normally is between 1 to 1 - 1/2 liters. It is impossible to rid the lungs of this residual volume.

RESPIRATORY QUANTITIES: The amount of work a man is doing is the main thing that determines respiratory quantities. A man of average size at complete rest consumes about 0.25 liters of oxygen each minute. Standing requires about 0.50 liters per minute. A moderate work rate may require up to 2.0 liters per minute. An oxygen consumption rate of 3 liters per minute represents exhausting work for the average man, but a man in excellent condition can consume as much as 4 liters per minute for a short time (10 - 15 minutes). The number of "oxygen molecules" a diver's body consumes per minute is not influenced by depth although the "volume" he breathes in and out is affected by depth. A diver working hard enough to consume 2 liters of oxygen per minute at the surface (1 atmosphere, absolute) would only consume 1 liter of oxygen per minute at 33 feet (2 atmospheres, absolute); but the number of molecules "used" would remain the same, since the density of the O_2 at 33 feet would be twice the density at the surface.

THE ROLE OF CARBON DIOXIDE IN RESPIRATION: For every liter of oxygen consumed, a man will normally produce close to a liter of carbon dioxide. However, the total amount of air moved in and out of the lungs in a minute is slightly over 20 times the "oxygen consumption" and air is approximately 20% oxygen, we could say that 4 times (20% x 20) as much oxygen is moved in and out of the lungs than is "consumed". The expired air in any one minute contains roughly 5 percent less oxygen and 5 percent more carbon dioxide than inspired air. In other words if we breath in (inhale) air containing approximately 0% CO_2, 20% oxygen and 80% nitrogen, we breath out (exhale) a gas that has 5% CO_2, 15% oxygen and still 80% nitrogen.

HYPERVENTILATION AND BREATH HOLDING: Hyperventilation consists of "blowing off" (reducing the percentage of) CO_2 just prior to a dive, by filling the lungs and exhaling rapidly, several times. It prolongs breath-holding ability, because it lowers the partial pressure of CO_2 in the body. This allows a longer period of time to elapse before the body's CO_2 builds back up sufficiently to warn the brain's respiratory center to "breathe". Meanwhile, of course, the body's partial pressure of O_2 is dropping, and sometimes reaches a dangerously low level (causing anoxia) before the person gets the urge to breathe.

DIVING-4

Hyperventilation should never be continued to the point of dizziness, and the "hyperventilated" diver should surface as soon as he notices a definite urge to resume breathing.

If a man hyperventilates and dives to a considerable depth, he will be able to hold his breath comfortably for quite some time. For he has not only "blown off" CO_2, but he has increased the partial pressure of O_2 in his lungs (by descending). However, when he ascends, the partial pressure of O_2 will drop sharply, and he may experience a severe increase in the desire to breathe. Anoxia and unconsciousness may result. Excessive breath-holding has caused heart disturbances and death.

DIVING DISEASES and INJURIES

After considering the complexity of human bodily structure and metabolism, and the tremendous pressure changes incurred immediately upon entering below the surface of a body of water, it becomes obvious that radical changes must take place within the human body when it is submerged. If these changes are not properly controlled by the diver, injury or death will occur. Most diving diseases and injuries may be attributed either to direct effects of pressure (causing mechanical damage sustained during descent or ascent), to indirect effects of pressure (involving solution and dissolution of gases in the body tissues), or to breathing an improper gas or gas mixture (Anoxia, CO_2 poisoning, and Carbon Monoxide poisoning). Drowning and convulsions can be the result of many factors.

The injuries sustained as a direct result of pressure may be divided into two groups. Those sustained during descent ("squeeze"), and those sustained during ascent (air embolism, mediastinal emphysema, subcutaneous emphysema, pneumothorax, stomach and/or intestinal pains).

DESCENT PROBLEMS (SQUEEZE)

Squeeze (sometimes called "Barotrauma") occurs when the water pressure to which a diver is exposed becomes greater than the air pressure in a closed air space either on the diver's skin (facemask, rubber suit) or inside the diver (sinuses, lungs, etc.). As a result, a relative vacuum occurs within the space. Nature attempts to equalize this unbalance of pressure by allowing air at the increased pressure to pass into the space. If, for any reason, the air passage is blocked (by skin, mucus, swelling, etc.), fluid, blood, and finally tissue are squeezed (sucked) into it, to fill the vacuum. Although many types of squeeze can occur, they are all caused in this same manner, and can be prevented by following the same rules. First, avoid diving if the air passages to the bodily cavities are not clear (during a head or chest cold, for example). Second, while descending prevent any vacuum from forming, by allowing pressurized air to enter into the closed spaces. Third, if a squeeze does begin, (signaled by pain) decrease the vacuum by ascending. Following are the common types of squeeze:

EXTERNAL EAR

During descent, air trapped at surface atmospheric pressure in the external ear canal (see diagram of ear structures) by a rubber suit hood or ear plug, forms a relative vacuum in the external canal, outside the eardrum. This causes blood and tissue fluids to be squeezed (sucked) from the canal walls and eardrum into the external canal. The flexible eardrum will, naturally, bulge outward into the external canal (causing intense pain) and may rupture.

CAUSE: Sealing of the external ear canal with rubber suit or earplugs.

SYMPTOMS: Pain in ears on descent even though able to "pop ears". If eardrum ruptures: Sudden stopping of pain, and as cold water enters inner ear: possible dizziness, nausea, vomiting or vertigo. Stability returns in approximately one minute, as the intruding water is warmed by body heat. Upon surfacing: Possible bleeding from ear and/or spitting up blood.

TREATMENT: While submerged: If dizziness or vertigo set in, causing a loss of sense of direction, relax and wait for a minute. Do not try to ascend, since what appears to be "UP" may really be "DOWN". When stability returns, ascend.

Upon Surfacing: Report to medical officer or corpsman immediately. Do not put medication or any objects in ear. Usual prescription: Without rupture of eardrum: avoid pressure until redness of eardrum and canal disappears, and ears can be cleared readily. With ruptured eardrum: avoid pressure until eardrum heals (approximately two weeks); 3-4 days of regular use of nose drops with head positioned to pool the drops at the back of the throat near the eustachian tube openings; this allows drainage from the middle ear.

PREVENTION: Never use ear plugs. When diving with a hood, cut a hole in the hood over the ear area, or line the ear area of the hood with porous material. Be sure to admit air to the ear while descending.

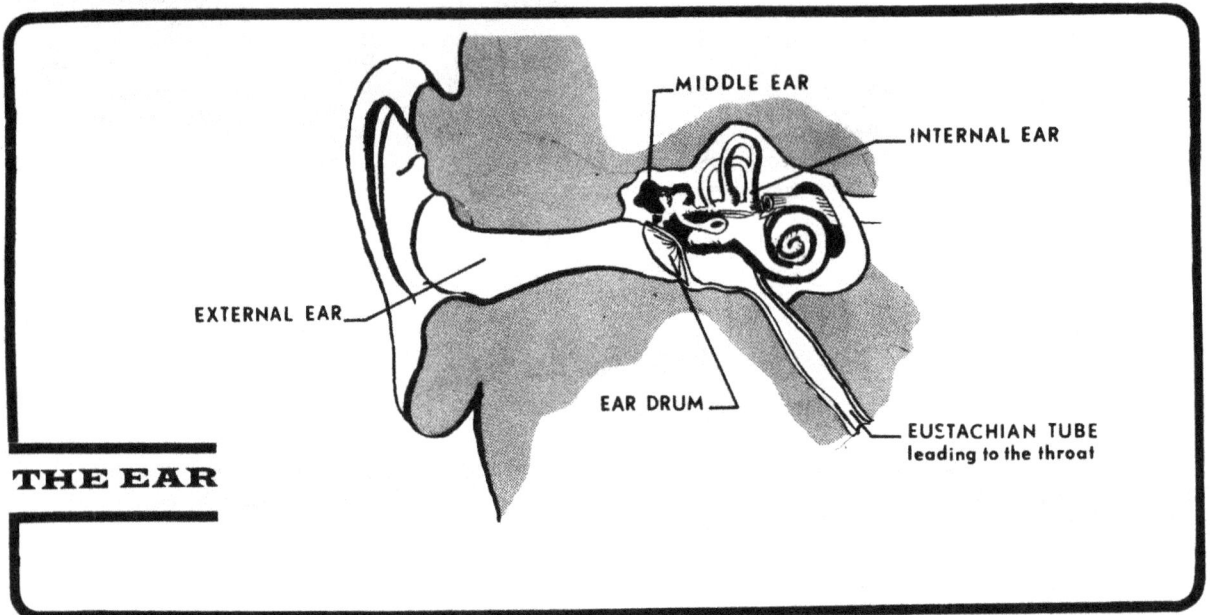

THE EAR

EAR

This is the most common form of squeeze experienced by divers. During descent a blocked eustachian tube (see diagram) keeps air from passing from the throat into the middle ear in order to counter (balance) increasing water pressure on the outside of the eardrum. The resulting relative vacuum in the middle ear squeezes (sucks) blood and tissue fluids into it from the surrounding surfaces, and if the vacuum becomes extreme, the eardrum is ruptured (this time inward). (Rarely, the reverse of this process happen when pressure builds up in the middle ear during ascent).

CAUSE: Diving with a eustachian tube blocked by mucus or swelling or failing to "pop ears" during descent.

SYMPTOMS: Pain in ear during descent with inability to "pop ears" properly. Other symptoms are the same as those of ear squeeze in the external canal.

TREATMENT: Same as for ear squeeze in external canal.

PREVENTION: Descend slowly enough to be able to "pop ears" properly (by swallowing, yawning, moving jaw, or blowing gently against closed nostrils). Do not dive with a head cold, or whenever unable to "pop ears". Use nose drops, spray, or inhaler, to clear eustachian tubes if it is necessary to dive while they are congested. Do not "force" ears. If ears will not "pop", ascend until they will. If continued attempts to "pop ears" fail, discontinue the dive.

FACE

During descent, a vacuum is formed in the diver's face mask, squeezing blood and tissue fluids out of the eyes and facial skin. In extreme cases, the eyeballs may be severely damaged by hemorrhages in and around them.

CAUSE: Wearing goggles (which cannot be equalized during descent), or failure to equalize facemask during descent.

SYMPTOMS: Sometimes, there are no warning symptoms of face squeeze. At other times, there is pain and a sensation of suction on the face. The victim of face squeeze will have a swollen and bruised looking face, blood shot and/or bleeding eyes.

TREATMENT: Apply cold packs to bruised or bleeding areas. Give sedatives and pain relieving drugs if required. NOTE: If the victim of face squeeze was wearing a full facemask, observe for signs of lung squeeze.

PREVENTION: Don't dive with goggles which only cover the eyes and not the nose while descending. Equalize the pressure within your facemask by exhaling through your nose periodically. With a full facemask and closed or semi-closed circuit SCUBA, activate the bypass valve while descending (NOTE: Be sure that the gas is turned on and that the bypass valve functions properly before descending). Never use excessive weight to cause yourself to descend rapidly.

LUNG

During descent, if a diver does not add air or gas to his lungs, the increasing outside water pressure will compress the diver's chest causing the gas volume within the lungs to become smaller and smaller. If this volume is compressed down to the lungs' residual volume (1-1.5 liters), the chest walls cannot be compressed further. A relative vacuum develops in the remaining lung air space and the delicate alveolar membranes, throughout the lungs, are ruptured by the squeeze, causing blood and tissue fluids to fill the vacuum within the

many alveoli. Holding breath, or failing to replenish breathing bags while descending, can cause lung squeeze.

CAUSE: While skin diving, descending too deep. While SCUBA diving, holding breath during descent or failing to replenish breathing bags during descent.

SYMPTOMS: Sensation of chest compression during descent and chest pain sometimes accompany lung squeeze. Upon surfacing, the victim experiences difficulty in breathing. Bleeding from nose and/or mouth, and bloody, frothy spit are also common. Suffocation can occur in severe cases.

TREATMENT: Bring the victim ashore, lay him down with his head lower than his feet, and try to clear blood from his mouth. If resuscitator is not available, administer mouth-to-mouth resuscitation if victim is not breathing. Administer positive pressure oxygen if breathing is labored. As soon as possible, contact a medical officer. (Most cases should be hospitalized, at least for observation). Prevent and treat shock.

PREVENTION: Do not skin dive to a point where the air present in your lungs on the surface (about 5-6 liters) will be compressed to a volume smaller than your lungs' residual volume (about 1-1.5 liters). This makes about 90-100 feet the maximum safe skin diving depth for the average person. When SCUBA diving, never hold your breath during descent, and utilize the bypass valve on closed or semi-closed SCUBA to ensure adequate gas volume in the breathing bags. Be sure that SCUBA cylinders are turned on and that bypass valve works properly before descending. Never use excessive weights to cause yourself to descend rapidly.

NOTE: Lung Squeeze may occasionally develop if a diver must strain his lungs in order to inhale against great resistance over a period of time.

SUIT

During descent, air filled wrinkles in a dry suit become compressed, and squeeze (suck) the skin into the wrinkles. This causes the appearance of welts or bruises on the skin.

CAUSE: Failure to wear flannel or other porous material between skin and dry suit, or failure to evacuate air from suit while submerging.

SYMPTOMS: Pinching sensation in the affected area. Blotched, welted skin.

TREATMENT: Put ice pack on affected skin. Generally not a serious condition.

PREVENTION: When wearing a dry suit, wear long underwear underneath to keep the rubber from direct contact with your skin. Smooth out the surface of a dry suit as much as possible before diving. Evacuate as much air as possible from suit by holding arms above head (out of water) and opening one wrist cuff and then the other while body is submerging.

TOOTH SQUEEZE: Air pocket trapped under a tooth-filling or in the pulp of an infected tooth forms a pocket of relative vacuum upon descent, causing irritation of nerves and resulting pain in the tooth. Not common.

CAUSE: Faulty tooth filling, or infected tooth.

SYMPTOMS: Pain in tooth upon descending.

TREATMENT: If symptoms appear, ascend for relief. Have dentist check the affected tooth.

PREVENTION: Proper care and maintenance of teeth.

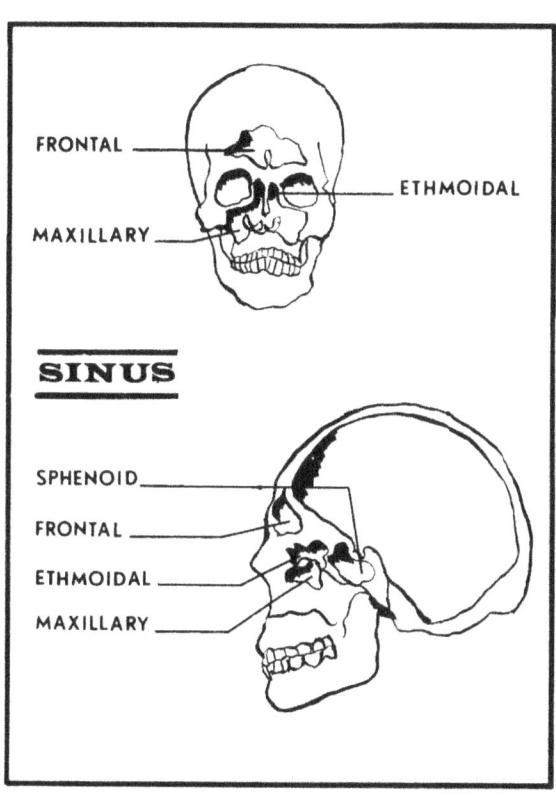

SINUS

During descent, a relative vacuum can be formed in the sinus cavities in the same manner that was described for the middle ear, causing blood and tissue fluids to be squeezed into the cavities from the mucous membrane lining the sinus walls.

CAUSE: Mucus (caused by a cold or other infection) in the openings (called "Ostia") between the nose and the sinuses will seal off the sinuses, causing squeeze to occur during descent.

SYMPTOMS: Increasing pain in forehead above the eyes and in the face (below the eyes) during descent. Upon surfacing, a victim of sinus squeeze may experience tenderness in the sinus area, and a discharge of blood and mucus from the nose.

TREATMENT: Immediately upon suffering a sinus squeeze, come to the surface. Use nose drops, spray or inhaler to promote drainage. See a medical officer, and return to him promptly in case of pain, pus drainage, or other signs of possible infection. Avoid diving until sinuses clear.

PREVENTION: Avoid diving with a head cold, or any kind of sinus infection. Use nose drops, spray, or inhaler for mild sinus congestion. Don't force the sinuses; discontinue the dive promptly if sinus pain develops.

ASCENT PROBLEMS

A panic stricken or unconscious diver, or one whose throat is clogged with water, mucus or vomit, will tend to hold his breath as he approaches the surface. Since the gas within his lungs expands as he ascends, it is obvious that, if he does not exhale while ascending, the gas will increase to such a volume that it finally ruptures his alveoli in an attempt to escape. Depending upon where the gas goes as it bursts through the alveolar walls, one or more of the following injuries will occur:

AIR EMBOLISM (AE)

Gas bubbles bursting through the alveolar walls leak into the pulmonary veins returning to the heart and are then pumped into the arteries going to the brain, causing blockage of same, anoxia of the blocked brain tissue, and death of that tissue if blockage is not relieved in 5-7 minutes.

CAUSE: Holding breath during ascent. (Sometimes because of throat muscle spasms caused by fright). Another cause could be entrapped pockets of air in the lungs, due to anatomical defects, disease, or a local obstruction, which restrict the flow of air from the lungs. (The pockets very occasionally can be caused by such diseases as pneumonia, asthma, bronchitis, or an ordinary "chest cold".) They are more apt to be caused by congenital anatomical defects or lung tuberculosis.

SYMPTOMS: Tightness and/or pain in chest during ascent. Collapse and unconsciousness on surfacing or within minutes thereafter. Bloody froth around mouth (may not occur). Bleeding from nose and mouth (may not occur). Loss of balance, visual disturbances, lack of coordination of body movements. Rigidity or numbness of extremities. Speech thick and mushy, paralysis, nausea, or any one combination of the above. Tightness in chest is not always noticeable but other symptoms usually start occurring within 2-3 minutes after ascent. Untreated severe AE will cause death.

TREATMENT: Recompress in recompression chamber to 165 feet as soon as first symptoms appear. Descend as rapidly as possible (disregard normal descent rates of 25'/min.). Bring out on Table 3 or 4. If no chamber is available, place the patient on a board and rock him (head up then head down) in seasaw fashion to break up the bubbles.

PREVENTION: With SCUBA: Breathe normally and continually during ascent. When executing a free ascent: Exhale continuously during ascent. In all cases, avoid diving with a chest cold.

OTHERS

PNEUMOTHORAX: Same cause as AE, except that air leaks in between the lungs and the chest wall, collapsing the lung and in extreme cases displacing the heart, causing shock. May accompany AE, or occur separately.
CAUSE: Same as for AE.
SYMPTOMS: Sensation of shortness of breath; rapid, shallow breathing; sharp chest pain made worse by deep breathing; blueness of skin, lips, or fingernails. A mild case may have no symptoms or only mild discomfort in one side of the chest or the other.
TREATMENT: Unless AE is present also, do not recompress. If breathing is markedly difficult, a medical officer can remove the trapped air by means of a needle or chest tube with applied suction. Emergency procedure: Give oxygen if shortness of breath, cyanosis, or signs of shock or collapse present. Get patient to doctor or medical facility as rapidly as possible.
PREVENTION: Same as for AE.

MEDIASTINAL EMPHYSEMA (VERY UNCOMMON): Same cause as AE except that air leaks into the tissues about the heart and trachea (windpipe). Mediastinal Emphysema may accompany AE, or occur separately:
CAUSE: Same as AE.
SYMPTOMS: Pain under the breast bone; (in extreme cases) shortness of breath or faintness (due to interference with circulation); blueness of skin, lips, or fingernails.
TREATMENT: Recompress (on Table 3 or 4) only if AE is present also, or if breathing or circulation is markedly impaired.
PREVENTION: Same as for AE.

SUBCUTANEOUS EMPHYSEMA (VERY UNCOMMON) Same cause as AE, except that air leaks into the tissues just under the skin (usually in the neck area). May accompany AE, or occur separately.
CAUSE: Same as for AE.
SYMPTOMS: Swelling (accompanied by a feeling of fullness) in the neck, change in the sound of the voice, crackling sensation when the skin is moved slightly, difficulty in breathing or swallowing.
TREATMENT: Recompress (Table 3 or 4) only if AE is present also, or if breathing or circulation is markedly impaired.
PREVENTION: Same as for AE.

STOMACH AND/OR INTESTINAL PAINS: Sometimes, gas present in the stomach and/or intestines during a dive will cause pain as it expands during ascent. Damage to internal organs may rarely result if it is not eliminated. Sometimes a somersault or other change of body position will help the diver to evacuate the gas.

DECOMPRESSION SICKNESS

("BENDS", "CAISSON'S, "COMPRESSED AIR ILLNESS"): During descent, a diver's body is subjected to increasing pressure. Compressed air enters the lungs, is forced into solution in the blood, and is carried to all tissues of the body. The deeper the dive, or the longer the dive, the more gas that is absorbed into the body tissues. During ascent, pressure is decreased on the body. The dissolved gas is transported from the tissues via the bloodstream to the lungs where it can come out of solution through the alveoli into the expired air and is expelled. However, if the diver ascends too rapidly, the air comes out of solution within the tissues and joints in the form of bubbles. These bubbles put pressure on the nerves and other structures and interfere with proper function of blood circulation, causing pain, paralysis, asphyxia, or (if bubbles are large and numerous enough) death.

CAUSE: Not obeying the diving tables, especially on repetitive dives within a 12 hour period. Diving when sick, after alcohol consumption, when overly fatigued, or when overweight.

SYMPTOMS: (Depending upon where the bubbles have formed).
If in blood or tissues: Tingling, burning, itching, numb or blotched skin; pain in joints.
If in brain: Dizziness, ringing ears, paralysis, blindness, convulsions, unconsciousness.
If in spine: Paralysis, loss of feeling.
If in lungs: Difficulty in breathing, choking.
Unusual fatigue, and death sometimes occur.

TREATMENT: Recompression in a recompression chamber according to the treatment tables.

PREVENTION: Don't dive when "hung over", or generally run-down. Avoid decompression dives whenever possible. Plan dives and use correct decompression tables if required. Use Repetitive Dive Tables if more than one dive is to be made in 12 hour period. Dive by the Tables. Report early symptoms (slight itch or pain) immediately. "HALDANE'S RULE" states that gas bubbles cannot ordinarily form in human tissues until the body is subjected to, and then released from, a pressure greater than 2 atmospheres absolute.

NITROGEN NARCOSIS

While the exact mechanism for the cause of "NITROGEN NARCOSIS: is unknown, indications are that excessive partial pressure of nitrogen produces an anesthetic, or intoxicating effect especially when combined with any CO_2 buildup. (Air is usually well tolerated at depths up to 100 feet). Beyond 100 feet, its intoxicating effect increases rapidly. Many people experience considerable narcosis beyond 150 feet. Nearly everyone experiences severe narcosis beyond 200 feet when breathing compressed air.

CAUSE: Exceeding safe depths with air or mixed gas.

SYMPTOMS: Similar to those of alcohol intoxication: Slowdown of mental activity; fixation of ideas; difficulty in concentrating, thinking, remembering; feeling of well-being; lack of care for own safety; difficulty in accomplishing simple jobs; near-unconsciousness.

TREATMENT: Effects disappear rapidly with ascent to shallower depths.

PREVENTION: Be aware of the cause and symptoms of Nitrogen Narcosis when diving. Know and obey the depth limits for the breathing medium being used. (Navy safe diving limit when breathing air is 130'.)

OXYGEN POISONING

While the actual mechanism of O_2 poisoning is unkown, it is suspected that the phenomenon is caused when high pressure oxygen disturbs the enzyme systems of cell metabolism.

CAUSE: Some people are unusually sensitive to 100% oxygen, even at atmospheric pressure. Such persons should not dive at all. However, 100% oxygen is not significantly toxic to the average person when breathed at depths less than 33 feet for short periods of time. The oxygen in air (20%) becomes dangerously toxic at 280 feet. If carbon dioxide build up occurs in the diver's body (such as from over-exertion) or in the diver's breathing medium, the danger of serious oxygen toxicity increases markedly.

SYMPTOMS: When warning symptoms of Oxygen Poisoning occur, they consist of muscular twitching (often in the lips or face), nausea, dizziness, disturbed hearing or vision (tunnel vision is common), a feeling of increased breathing resistance, inability to take a full breath, anxiety, confusion, fatigue, clumsiness. The following symptoms may attack the diver without warning or will occur if the above warning symptoms are not heeded: Convulsions (usually causing drowning and/or air embolism), loss of consciousness, rigidity, death.

TREATMENT: As soon as symptoms of O_2 poisoning begin, lower the partial pressure of oxygen by ascending. Rest, hyperventilate, and, if possible, surface and breathe air.

PREVENTION: When using closed or semi-closed SCUBA, ensure that the CO^2 absorbent is in proper condition, strictly observe the depth limits for the gas being breathed, and heed abnormal symptoms. While using closed-circuit SCUBA, avoid excessive exertion. Never charge open circuit SCUBA with oxygen.

ANOXIA

This disease occurs whenever tissue cells fail to receive or utilize enough oxygen to maintain their life and normal function. Brain cells are most susceptible to anoxia.

CAUSE: The most obvious cause of anoxia is the stoppage of a diver's air supply. A more insidious attack of anoxia occurs when the partial pressure of oxygen in a breathing medium falls below 2.35 psi

(16% O_2 at sea level). This can happen, for instance, in an improperly purged closed-circuit SCUBA. If there is nitrogen in the breathing bag, the diver will begin breathing pure nitrogen as soon as his O_2 supply is exhausted. Since his exhaled CO_2 is constantly absorbed by the Baralyme, he will receive no warning indicating a need to breathe. Euphoria, loss of control, followed by unconsciousness, will result. There are several other ways in which a diver can be subjected to a breathing medium of less than 2.35 psi of oxygen: Breathing gas from any type of SCUBA which has been charged from an unreliable source; breathing gas from a semi-closed SCUBA with a too-low setting, or one in which the flow has accidentally been reduced or stopped; or breathing in any space containing trapped air, as in a submerged wreck.

SYMPTOMS: The usual effects of anoxia, like those of alcohol, are quite pleasant, and by the time they are noticed, the will to take action is usually gone. Because of its sneaky nature, anoxia is one of the diver's most serious hazards. Symptoms of anoxia include: A decreased ability to concentrate, impairment of muscular control, feeling of giddiness, increase in pulse and respiration rates, and fainting. A victim of anoxia will often have blue lips and/or fingernails. He frequently trembles and has muscle tremors and often exhibits jerky movements and occasional rigidity. The latter may be confused with convulsions, but they are not true convulsions.

TREATMENT: Allow the patient to breathe fresh air, and, if possible, administer oxygen. Administer artificial respiration if breathing has stopped.

PREVENTION: With closed-circuit SCUBA, purge properly before diving and after any surfacing during the dive where air was breathed or the mouthpiece removed. With semi-closed circuit SCUBA, maintain and prepare gear properly, use the proper gas mix for the dive, be watchful for any sign of flow reduction or other malfunction during a dive, and make surfacing. Breathe air from approved sources only.

CARBON DIOXIDE POISONING

Carbon dioxide buildup can occur in one of two basic ways: Excessive CO^2 production in the body with failure to eliminate the excess through the lungs; or presence of a significant amount of CO_2 in the diver's breathing mixture. When present in sufficient quantity, CO_2 becomes a poison, affecting mainly the brain. The normal response of the body to an increase in CO_2 is to increase the respiratory rate and speed of blood circulation in order to get rid of ("blow off") the excess CO_2. However, if the overload is too great, symptoms of CO_2 poisoning will soon appear.

CAUSES: Breathing impure gas, failure of CO_2 absorbent in closed or semi-closed SCUBA (caused by poor quality, damp, overused, powdered or "channeled" absorbent), overexertion, or holding breath to conserve air while diving.

SYMPTOMS: As measured at the surface:
2% CO_2: Increased breathing rate (usually not noticed).
5% CO_2: Noticeable increase in breathing rate, shortness of breath, discomfort, panting, headache, dizziness, nausea, weakness, loss of ability to think clearly, drowsiness. NOTE that these last two symptoms are symptoms of anoxia also.
10% CO_2: Unconsciousness.
15% CO_2: Muscular spasms, rigidity, permanent brain damage, and death. However these are much less likely than with anoxia, and complete recovery usually occurs if fresh air is delivered to the victim.

After-effects upon recovery: Headache, nausea, dizziness.

TREATMENT: Stop, rest, and breathe deeply at onset of first symptoms. If at all possible, surface and breathe fresh air. Administering O_2 will hasten the recovery of an unconscious victim.

PREVENTION: Sift and load CO_2 absorbent properly. Never over-breathe CO_2 absorbent. Ensure that no water leaks into absorbent canister. Refrain from overexertion and controlled breathing ("skip breathing"). Breathe air from approved sources only. When using closed-circuit SCUBA, purge before ascending to the surface if possible. This will get rid of any excess CO_2 in the breathing bag, which might expand to dangerous proportions upon ascent. It is very important to remember that 2% CO_2 in the breathing mixture (as measured at the surface) will act exactly as if it were 4% when the diver goes down to the 33 feet, 6% at 66 feet, 8% at 99 feet, etc. This is due to the increased partial pressure though the true percent remains the same.

SHALLOW WATER BLACKOUT

Increased CO_2 percentage in a diver's body causes unconsciousness without warning.

CAUSES: "Skip-breathing", overexertion, "Over-breathing" the regulator, or "driving yourself to the limit" while breathholding, instead of obeying the urge to surface. Excessive dead air space in SCUBA or high breathing resistance in a regulator can also be causes.

SYMPTOMS: Sudden unconsciousness, increased pulse and blood pressure.

TREATMENT: Give fresh air or O_2.

PREVENTION: Proper maintenance of regulator, "relaxed" diving.

CARBON MONOXIDE POISONING

Takes place when more than 0.002% CO is present in the breathing medium. The CO combines with the hemoglobin in the blood, displacing the oxygen which the hemoglobin usually carries to the tissues. Anoxia of the tissues results, even though the lungs themselves are able to supply adequate oxygen to sustain life.

CAUSES: An air compressor containing flushing or lubricating oil will produce compressed air containing carbon monoxide. A compressor being used in an enclosed space, or with its air intake close to its exhaust, will also produce compressed air with dangerous amounts of CO.

SYMPTOMS: Frequently a victim of carbon monoxide poisoning will become unconscious without warning. Occasionally, the following warning symp-

toms will occur: tightness across forehead, pounding at the temples, headache, nausea, vomiting, weakness, dizziness, confusion, and other mental changes similar to anoxia. In severe cases, breathing will stop. Abnormally red lips, fingernails, and (sometime) skin are signs of CO poisoning.

TREATMENT: Expose the victim to fresh air or (if available) oxygen. Recompress, beginning with O_2 for 30 minutes at 60 feet, or air at 100 feet.

PREVENTION: Proper maintenance and operation of compressors. Ensure that the exhaust from an air compressor is downwind, and as far as possible, from the intake. Test compressed air periodically for CO.

DROWNING

(STOPPAGE OF BREATHING): Start artificial respiration immediately. Delay only to stop serious bleeding.

POSITION: Place victim on his back, and clear mouth and throat of gum, false teeth, tongue, vomit. Hold victim's jaw in "jutting out" position with one hand. Close nostrils with other hand. Place your mouth over his, making a good seal, keep his head tilted back.

INFLATION: Breathe into victim with smooth, steady action, until definite expansion of chest is noted, but do not exert too much pressure. If he does not inflate readily, airway is obstructed.

DEFLATION: Remove mouth and allow victim to exhale. If he fails to do so, apply gentle pressure on chest. Check for obstruction. (Operator inhales during this phase).

When able to do so: Loosen victim's clothing (collar, belt, etc.). Keep him warm. Check pulse and combat shock. If he begins to revive, time your movements to assist. Shift to a mechanical resuscitator if one becomes available. If he does not revive, continue artificial respiration for four (4) hours, or until victim is pronounced dead by a Medical Officer.

CONVULSIONS

While convulsions can be caused by many factors, the mechanism is the same: The brain sends out disorganized volleys of nerve impulses to the muscles. Muscles contract violently and sometimes the entire body stiffens. The brain soon (usually within five minutes of onset) fatigues, and the patient becomes unconscious and limp. This post convulsion sleep lasts from 15 minutes to an hour or more, and then the patient becomes restless and finally awakens. He will feel tired, sore, possibly have a headache, and remember nothing of the convulsions or unconsciousness. Breathing sometimes stops during stiff phase, but resumes spontaneously after convulsion.

Despite its alarming appearance, convulsion itself is usually not more than a strenuous muscular workout for the victim. Sometimes, however, the tongue will be chewed and (rarely) a bone will fracture under the excessive muscular strain.

TREATMENT: Insert anything except a metal object (or fingers) between teeth to protect patient's tongue. During convulsion try to maintain clear airway by holding lower jaw forward. After convulsion turn the patient on his side and position head and jaw for clear airway. Try to prevent injuries, but do not restrain movements. If in recompression chamber, do not ascend rapidly. (Air Embolism could result.) Do not leave an unconscious victim alone or unattended.

GENERAL

Stoppage of breathing and/or shock may accompany any diving disease or injury. Watch for and treat as necessary. Many decompression sickness and air embolism symptoms are the same. If any doubt exists, treat as air embolism, immediately.

Recompression can seldom do harm. Failure to recompress can cause needless death or permanent damage. As long as patient is alive, try to get him to a chamber. Emergency recompression in the water: This can seldom be recommended for an unconscious, injured, or sick man, if any other course of action is possible.

40' for 1/4 of 10' stop
30' for 1/3 of 10' stop
20' for 1/2 of 10' stop
10' for 1-1/2 of 10' stop

Send for a Diving Medical Officer immediately, in all cases of injury to a diver.

When in doubt (especially when a diver is unconscious), recompress.

Ignorance and poor physical condition are a diver's worst enemies. Dive often. Keep in top physical shape. Do not allow yourself to become overweight.

DECOMPRESSION and the RECOMPRESSION CHAMBER

DECOMPRESSION

Decompression may become necessary in any dive where the breathing medium contains a high percentage of inert gas. Normally the diving supervisor plans the dives to avoid decompression entirely. Where decompression is unavoidable, he must provide adequately for handling it.

In General, the arrangements and techniques for decompression are the same for any type of SCUBA although the decompression table may differ from the Standard Air Decompression Table. If the Decompression requires a shift from one gas to another (as it does for helium-oxygen diving), the technique be-

comes more complex. The diving supervisor then has an even greater responsibility than usual to make adequate provisions for decompresion.

The bulk of self-contained diving involves open circuit SCUBA charged with air. The following discussion applies primarily to air decompression for open-circuit SCUBA dives on air. For dives with other types of SCUBA or other breathing media, modify the procedures as necessary to make them compatible with the proper decompression table.

ARRANGEMENTS: Routine procedures for a SCUBA dive simplify handling decompression when the need arises. If possible, make the following provisions a routine for any self-contained diving operation. Give the timekeeper primary control of the ascent. Require divers to obey ascent and decompression signals without question. Provide communication with the diver. Any simple set of depth and time signals is satisfactory. A slate on a line is adequate. Require divers to check routinely before passing 20 feet to learn what decompression they must take. If they need deeper stops, be sure to signal well in advance. When the need for decompression becomes certain, the diving supervisor must make adequate provisions to handle the situation. Provide decompression depth markers. A weighted line with knots every 10 feet is adequate. Weight the line heavily enough to keep it completely vertical in a strong current. In large swells or high waves place the surface marker 5 feet below the surface. On a rolling vessel set it 10 feet under the surface. Require the diver to hold the line just below the proper marker in any comfortable position where the lower part of his body is not above the marker.

Provide an auxiliary air supply at the first decompression stop. Any adequate selfcontained or surface-supplied apparatus is satisfactory. Do not force the diver to surface for an additional air supply in the middle of his decompression.

TECHNIQUES: There are four techniques for decompression in selfcontained diving. They are:
(1) Surface supply: An air hose can supply air for a mask or demand regulator. The diver shifts to the surface supply at the first decompression stop and uses it for the entire decompression.
(2) Second scuba: A standby apparatus lowered to the first stop can also supply air for the decompression.
(3) Surface decompression: An adequate pressure chamber can provide surface decompression which may replace some or all of the required water decompression.
(4) Original scuba: If decompression requirements are slight, the original scuba may provide all of the decompression. If no other technique is available, the original apparatus must provide as much of the decompression as possible.

DECOMPRESSION TABLES: The situation may require the diver to use any combination of the techniques listed. Regardless of which technique the diver uses, apply the following rules in determining what decompression to give him.

For an air dive use the proper decompression table. Use the Standard Air Decompression Table when breathing air throughout (original scuba, second scuba, surface supply, or recompression chamber without oxygen). Use the Oxygen Surface Decompression Table when oxygen is available in the recompression chamber. For a nitrogen-oxygen dive find the proper equivalent air depth and use that depth to enter the proper decompression table. Use the Standard Air Decompression Table when breathing mixture (or air) throughout the decompression. Use Oxygen Surface Decompression table when oxygen is available in the recompression chamber. For other gas mixtures use the appropriate decompression table.

INTERRUPTED DECOMPRESSION: The diver may have to surface before getting his full decompression. This situation is much more likely in self-contained diving than it is in surface-supplied diving. The diver may complete his decompression by returning to the water or by entering a recompression chamber. In either case use the applicable procedure for interrupted decompression.

SURFACE DECOMPRESSION: Surface decompression is a valuable procedure in self-contained diving. It reduces the exposure to low water temperatures, and it eliminates the air supply problem for water decompression. When a chamber is available right at the scene of operations, use surface decompression as a routine measure where feasible.

RECOMPRESSION CHAMBER

The chamber is a two-lock chamber having a maximum working pressure of 200 psi. In addition there is a small medical lock to permit the passage of small articles to the attendants.

In order to charge the chamber to its maximum working pressure of 200 psi, 6800 cubic feet of air at atmospheric pressure is required. In general, to properly ventilate the chamber there should be a complete change of air at least every ten (10) minutes or as calculated from U.S. Navy Diving Manual depending upon the number of personnel being treated. This requires 580 cubic feet per minute. A large capacity compressor of ample size for standby or emergency service will be required. The air supply must be purified and as cool and as dry as possible. The chamber piping is so arranged that the flow of air can be controlled from either inside or outside the chamber. In each lock of the chamber there are three couplings that lead to a three outlet manifold for the connection of inhalators to the oxygen or oxygen-helium banks.

An inter-communication system makes contact between locks and the outside of the chamber possible.

The pressure in the chamber is read from caisson gauges, in pounds per square inch with coresponding foot graduations.

 DIVING-4

PRECAUTIONS

(1) The chamber is equipped with electric pressure-proof lights and inter-communications system.

(2) In securing the door, only a moderate amount of pressure is needed on the hatch dogs. With increase in pressure the seal becomes tighter. The dogs should be loosened before reducing the pressure. This is very important in the newer chamber where connecting rods extending from the crank are used.

(3) The danger of explosive fires is always present and increases with the use of compressed air at higher pressures or with the introduction of oxygen. In both cases the oxygen concentration is increased and the following precautions will be taken:

    (a) All wood decking, benches, shelving etc., will be removed and replaced with metal or other fire resistant materials.
    (b) Matresses if used will be covered with fire resistant material. All blankets or clothing will be clean and free from oil or grease.
    (c) Inflammable liquids will not be allowed in the chamber. If inflammable vapors are suspected to be present the chamber will be thoroughly ventilated.
    (d) Only fire-retardant paint will be used.
    (e) No open flames, matches, cigarette lighters, lighted cigarettes, pipes, etc., will be taken into the chamber.
    (f) While breathing oxygen, the chamber will be ventilated at least every fifteen (15) minutes for a period of (3) three minutes, or as calculated in accordance with the USN Diving Manual depending upon the number of persons being treated.
    (g) Water and sand buckets will be on hand within the chamber.

CHECK LIST

<u>CHECK LIST FOR PROPER LINE-UP OF CHAMBER PRIOR TO USE</u>

(1) Check 200 psi air cut into manifold.
(2) Check one valve supply (red) valves shut.

(3) Check 2 valve supply (red) valves open on outside and shut on inside.

(4) Check one valve exhaust (yellow) valves shut.

(5) Check 2 valve exhaust (yellow) valves open on outside and shut on inside.

(6) Turn on and test communications.

(7) Turn on lights.

(8) Check valves on medical lock shut (inside and outside) and doors of medical lock shut and dogged.

(9) Check pressure in O_2 manifold - two bottles on the line and at least one bottle at 1800 psi in reserves.

(10) Set regulators on O_2 manifold at 100 psi and check valves on O_2 manifold inside chamber open.

OPERATIONS

Air is supplied to the chamber by a four (4) stage; thirty cubic (30) foot high pressure compressor located in room 71, Building 600 of the Underwater Demolition Team area.

<u>DESCENT</u>

(1) Personnel concerned enter chamber and shut and dog inner door.

(2) Inside tender open two way supply valve and make descent at proper rate (25 ft/min). Outside tender time descent by stopwatch.

(3) On reaching bottom, outside tender assume control and ventilate.

<u>ASCENT</u>

(1) Inside tender undog inner door.

(2) Outside tender control rate of ascent, timing ascent by means of stopwatch. Proper rate is 60 feet per minute.

(3) Operation of chamber for O_2 tolerance and pressure tests is the same as for treatment of diving injuries, save that the outer door is shut as in the former cases.

OPERATION OF MEDICAL LOCK

(1) Line up (both doors shut and dogged at surface and both valves shut).

(2) Lock in

  (a) Open outside valve - then open outer door.

  (b) Place material to be locked into Medical Lock, shut and dog outer door, shut outside valve, and then undog inner door.

  (c) Open valve on inside to equalize pressures in Medical lock and inner chamber.

  (d) When pressures are equalized, inner door of Medical lock may be opened and material removed.

(3) Lock out

  (a) Place material to be locked out in Medical lock and shut and loosely dog inner door.

  (b) Open valve on outside to bleed off pressure in Medical Lock.

  (c) When pressure in Medical lock equals atmospheric pressure (not before) undog and open outer door.

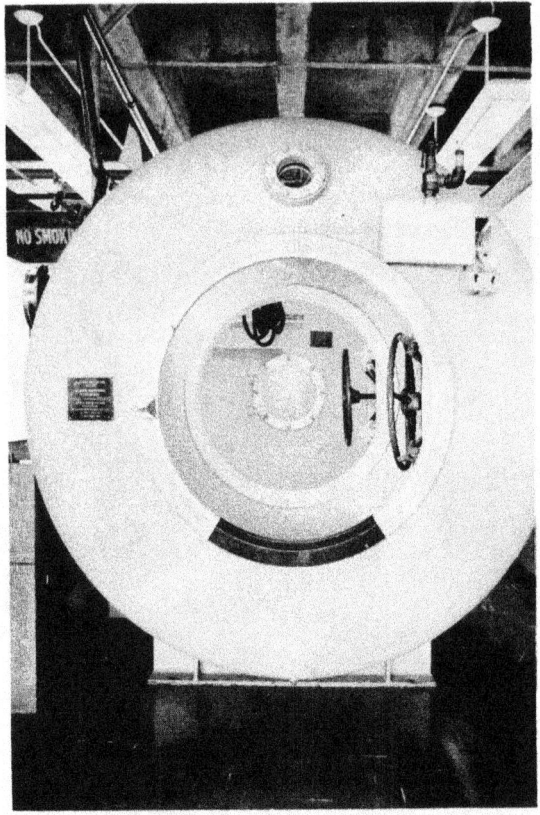

OPERATION OF OUTER LOCK

(1) Lineup: Manifold line-up is same as for large chamber - 2 valve supply and exhaust valves open on outside, shut on inside; one valve supply and exhaust shut. Shut and dog outer door. Undog inner door.

(2) Descent

  (a) Pressures in outer lock may be equalized by inside tender or outside tender, depending on circumstances. Air supply valves for outer lock are located in inner chamber, in outer lock, and outside the chamber.

  (b) When pressure in both chambers are equalized, open inner door and transfer personnel.

(3) Ascent

  (a) Undog outer door.

  (b) Inner door is shut and lightly dogged.

  (c) Ascent is made at proper rate controlled by outside tender.

GENERAL NOTES

It is essential that outside tender ventilate chamber at proper intervals. The outside tender is responsible for timing of all phases of chamber operations. Two stop watches shall be used to time chamber operations. One shall indicate total time elapsed since start of descent. The second shall be used to time individual phases of operation, such as ascent, or stops at various depths. The outside tender is responsible for maintenance of the Rough Diving Log.

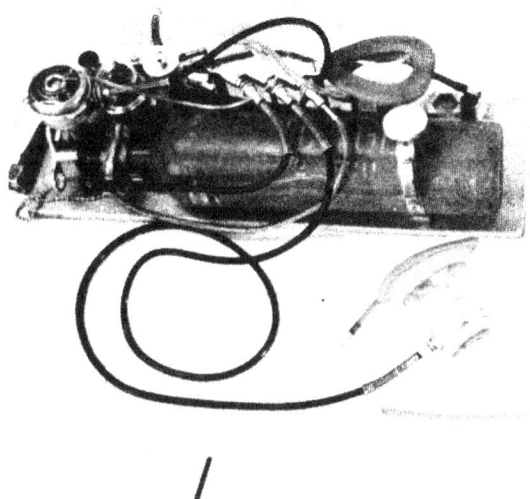

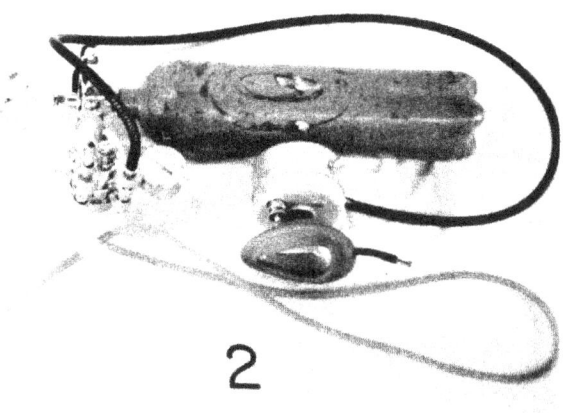

THE RESUSCITATOR

General: Whenever breathing fails, start artificial respiration immediately by some effective means, such as mouth-to-mouth. Do not wait for a mechanical resuscitator before starting, as the time lost could mean the difference between life and death. When a mechanical resuscitator becomes available and ready for use, switch to mechanical resuscitation and continue until the patient is breathing on his own, or until all hope of recovery is lost.

As a rule, place the patient on his back, with his chin lifted and neck extended. Turn head to one side so that fluids, if any, can drain from the corner of the mouth. Sweep a finger through the mouth to remove any obstruction. (A folded blanket or the like placed under the shoulder blades may help, by allowing the head to fall back and the windpipe to straighten.) Do not give stimulants, but keep the patient warm.

The EMERSON Resuscitator: The Emerson Resuscitator is the type used by the UDT's and is in general use throughout the Navy. It can be used as a resuscitator (if the patient is not breathing at all), an inhalator (if the patient is breathing, even though irregularly) or as an aspirator (if the throat is clogged and the airway is obstructed).

RESUSCITATION

(1) Turn on oxygen by one or more full turns of the cylinder valve.

(2) Plug in the resuscitator by pressing the end of the resuscitator hose into the receptacle on the regulator. Make sure that the inhalator valve of the resuscitator is adjusted to "resuscitate".

(3) Apply the mask (inflated) over the nose and mouth of the patient (wide end over the chin), and hold it firmly, making an airtight seal. Listen for the rhythmic cycling of the resuscitator. If working properly, each cycle will occur at about the same rate as normal breathing, indicating that the apparatus is carrying on respiration for the patient. Rapid click-

DIVING-4

ing means an obstruction from poor head and neck position, something blocking the throat, or very sticky lungs. Irregular clicking indicates the patient is starting to breathe on his own, and should be put on inhalation.

INHALATION

(1) Turn on the oxygen and plug in the hose as for resuscitation.

(2) Turn the inhalator valve on the mechanism to "inhalate".

(3) Apply the face mask (a tight fit is not necessary). The rhythmic cycling will not be heard. Watch the patient closely, and if the patient again becomes unable to breathe for himself, switch to "resuscitate".

ASPIRATION

(1) Plug in the aspirator the same way as the resuscitator. If necessary, unplug the resuscitator first.

(2) Insert the catheter (small rubber tube) carefully into the patient's throat, and rotate it gently with the finger tips, so that it can pick up fluids or froth at the back of the tongue. Fluid will be seen entering the collecting jar.

(3) If the catheter becomes clogged, remove it from the patient's mouth and blow it clear, by placing a finger over the outlet of the venturi.

(4) Do not let the collecting jar become tipped or overfilled.

(5) Return the patient to Resuscitation as quick as possible.

Pressure Selection: The usual pressures for resuscitation are +13 and -11mm. Hg. (millimeters of mercury). The selector knob on the side of the mechanism should be in this position at all times, unless the high pressure range is actually being used. If the high pressure range (27mm. Hg.) is needed to move more air into the lungs (nerve gases, for instance, make the lungs sticky and would justify the higher pressure range); turn the selector knob counter-clockwise (as marked). A manual over-ride button on the back of the mechanism provides an even higher positive pressure, (35mm. Hg.), which may be required in nerve gas casualties to overcome the stickiness of their lungs.

notes

112 AN/PRC - 6 RADIO

113 AN/PRC - 8,9, and 10 RADIOS

116 URC - 17 and URC - 17A RADIOS

118 AN/PQC - 1 (UTEL)

121 AN/PQC - 1B (HAND HELD SONAR)

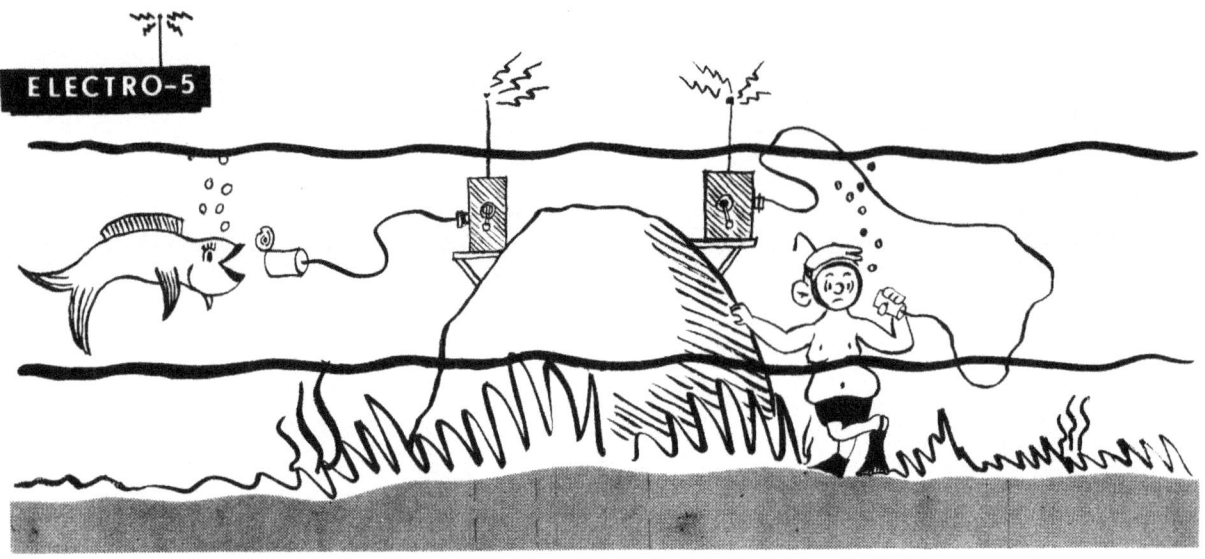

CHAPTER FIVE
ELECTRONICS

AN/PRC-6 RADIO

The radio set AN/PRC-6 is a small size, low power, battery operated, radio receiver and transmitter designed for communication over short distances. It is highly portable and is intended primarily as a handy-talkie for foot combat troops. No special skill is required to operate it.

The set is self-contained. All operating components necessary for reception and transmission are contained in a two-piece cast magnesium case. The set may be held in the left or right hand when operating.

The AN/PRC-6 has three controls:

(1) The EXT-OFF-INT switch (EXT to talk and receive with a handset, OFF to secure the set, and INT for self-contained operation).

(2) The volume control knob (to control the volume of the signal being received).

(3) The Push-to-talk button (to energize the transmitter).

OPERATING INSTRUCTIONS

Installing the Battery: To install the battery, open the case by releasing the four lever-type latches. After releasing the four latches, separate the two portions of the case. Place the battery in the equipment case with the rounded sides up. Insert the cable plug into the receptacle in the top of the battery. (If necessary, straighten any bent pins on the plug before inserting it). When properly aligned, the plug and the receptacle will mate without excessive force. Close the case by placing the catches on the latches under the restraining hooks, and pushing the latch so that it pulls the sections of the case together.

Installing the Antenna: To install the antenna, disengage the end of the antenna by pulling away from the case the portion wrapped around the bottom end of the radio. When the end of the antenna is free and protrudes from the end of the case, pull the whole antenna out from under the last two latches. Do not un-

✱ SPECIFICATIONS

WEIGHT (WITH BATTERY): APPROXIMATELY 6.5 POUNDS
FREQUENCY RANGE: 47.0 TO 55.4 MC
CHANNELS: 43 (A SPECIFIC CRYSTAL IS AVAILABLE FOR EACH CHANNEL)
POWER: BA-270/U BATTERY (CONSISTING OF THREE BATTERIES IN ONE CONTAINER, SHARING A COMMON PLUG. THE THREE BATTERIES SUPPLY +1.25V, -45V, AND +90V). UNDER NORMAL CONDITIONS (RECEIVING TEN TIMES AS OFTEN AS TRANSMITTING) BATTERY LIFE IS APPROXIMATELY 20 OPERATING HOURS.

fasten the lanyard. Screw the antenna into the threaded bushing in the center of the plastic antenna insulator. Make sure that the antenna is securely seated, but not more than hand-tight.

Energizing the Radio: To turn the radio on, place the EXT-OFF-INT switch in the INT position. A hissing or rushing sound should be heard in the earphone indicating that the equipment is now functioning as a receiver. If the sound is not heard, turn the volume control fully clockwise. If the background noise is still not audible, bring the equipment to the ET shop.

Transmitting: To transmit, push the push-to-talk switch, wait for the hiss to stop, and then talk distinctly and in a normal tone. Release the switch immediately after completion of the conversation. Intermittent operation results in a longer battery operating life. Turn the radio OFF for short intervals whenever possible.

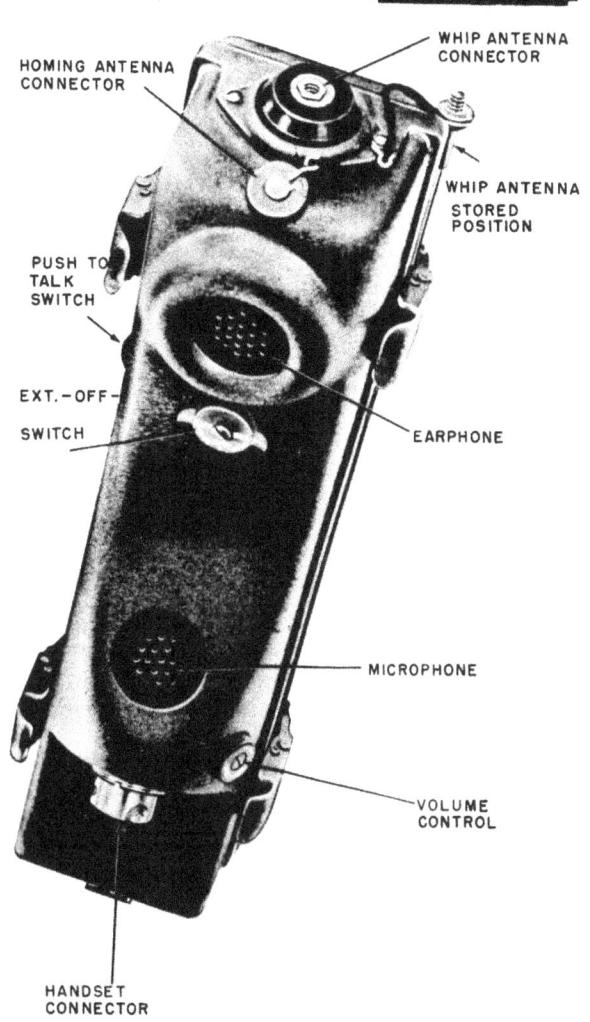

MAINTENANCE

To clean the Radio: Use #0000 sandpaper to remove corrosion from parts. Then, clean electrical contacts with a cloth moistened with trichloroethane, and wipe with a dry cloth. Finally, blow out moisture and dust with dry compressed air (see note below).

Battery: If the battery is bulging or leaking chemicals, remove it immediately and replace it with a new one. If chemicals leaking from the battery have corroded wires of the chassis, notify an ET.

If salt water gets into the radio, rinse it with fresh water as soon as possible and blow it dry with dry compressed air.

AN/PRC-8, 9 and 10 RADIOS

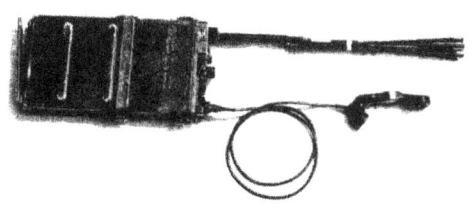

Radio Sets AN/PRC - 8, 9, and 10 are three portable, FM (frequency-modulated) radio sets intended to provide voice communications for UDT operations. The sets can be operated from aircraft, ships, land vehicles, ground installations, or while being carried by the operator. Provision is also made for homing use, remote operation, and unattended relay operation, using two sets.

There are twelve controls on the radios. Following is an outline of the controls and their function:

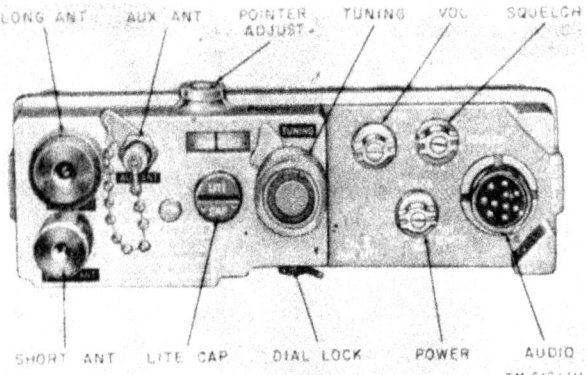

* SPECIFICATIONS

WEIGHT (WITH BATTERY): 26 POUNDS
CASE: FABRICATED MAGNESIUM WITH CAST-ALUMINUM CONTROL PANEL.
FREQUENCY RANGE:
  AN/PRC-8   20.0 TO 27.9 MC
  AN/PRC-9   27.0 TO 38.9 MC
  AN/PRC-10   38.0 TO 54.9 MC
OUTPUT: 0.9 TO 1.2 WATTS.
RANGE: 3 TO 12 MILES (DEPENDING UPON LOCATION AND ANTENNA USED)
ANTENNA: TWO TYPES OF ANTENNA MAY BE USED:
AT-272/PRC 36" SEMI-RIGID STEEL TAPE, DEMOUNTABLE.
AT-271/PRC 10 FEET, SEVEN SECTION WHIP
POWER: BA-279/U BATTERY (VOLTAGES: 1.5, 6, 67.5, AND 135). BATTERY LIFE: 20 TO 30 HOURS, DEPENDING UPON TRANSMISSION TIME, AGE, TEMPERATURE, ENVIRONMENT, ETC. BATTERY WEIGHT: 8 POUNDS

OPERATING INSTRUCTIONS

Install the Battery:
  Stand the radio set on a bench or on the ground with the control panel up. Make sure that the POWER switch is at OFF. Release the lower clamps (one on each side of the case) by pushing the topmost part of the clamp downward and outward at the same time.
  Lift the receiver-transmitter off the battery case and set it down, with the battery plug on the bottom facing the operator. Set the battery on the same surface so that the battery-pack jack is on the side on which the receiver-transmitter plug falls naturally. Hold the pull ring to the rear of the plug and insert the plug in the battery-pack jack, being careful to locate the key on the plug properly. Move the pull ring to the cable side of the plug and slide the battery against the bottom of the receiver-transmitter.
  Being careful to exclude foreign matter, slide the battery case over the battery until it seats against the receiver-transmitter. Fasten the catches by hooking the catch loops in the battery case hooks. Push the catches upward and toward the receiver-transmitter case until they snap against the sides. The battery installation is now complete.
  WARNING: Remove the battery when the equipment is not to be used for periods of one week or more.

Attach the Antenna:
  AT-272/PRC: Use this antenna when maximum range is not required. Screw the threaded end of the short antenna into the jack marked SHORT ANT. If necessary, bend the base of the antenna so that main portion of the antenna will be vertical.
  AT-271/PRC: Use this antenna when maximum range is required and a semipermanent installation is not feasible. Screw the antenna spring section into the LONG ANT. jack on the panel. Extend the long antenna by holding the base section (the heaviest section), and carefully whipping it outward. If all the sections of the antenna are not secure, repeat the

CONTROL	FUNCTION
AUDIO	A 10-prong receptacle providing external connections for the handset, remote control, or relay cables.
AUX ANT	Bayonet type jack to connect coaxial line from the homing or auxiliary antennas (not supplied) to the radio set.
DIAL LOCK	Locks TUNING control so operating frequency cannot be changed accidentally.
LITE CAP	Cap holding dial lamp in place. Permits rapid change of dial lamp without removing receiver-transmitter from case.
LONG ANT	Screw-type jack to mount and connect the long antenna to the radio set.
POINTER ADJUST	Varies position on pointer on TUNING dial to provide accurate dial frequency calibration.
POWER SWITCH	In ON position, connect receiver transmitter to power source. In REMOTE position, connect receiver-transmitter to power source, through the AUDIO receptacle and Control Group AN/GRA-6. In CAL & DIAL LITE position, connect receiver-transmitter source (spring-returned to ON when released).
PUSH TO TALK BUTTON	When pressed, puts radio set in transmit condition.
SHORT ANT	Screw type jack to mount and connect the short antenna to the radio set.
SQUELCH	Sets the signal level below which noise is cut off when no signal is being received. Switch S2 stops squelch operation when the knob is in the OFF position.
TUNING	Tunes receiver and transmitter to desired frequency.
VOL	Adjusts the loudness of signals heard in the handset earphone.

above procedure or insert the sections individually by hand. After extending the antenna, screw it into the spring section already installed.

Connect the Hand Set:

Insert the plug on the handset cable into the AUDIO jack on the panel. Apply light pressure and turn the plug until it drops in the guides. Push and turn in a clockwise direction as far as it will go.

Tune Radio:
(1) Set volume control to 10.
(2) Turn squelch control off.
(3) Turn power switch to "CAL & DIAL LITE".
(4) Unlock dial lock, turning counter-clockwise.
(5) Adjust tuning control to whole MC nearest desired operating frequency.
(6) Pick up zero beat.
(7) Move dial pointer with pointer adjuster until zero beat comes in most clearly.
(8) Lock tuning control with dial lock.
(9) Turn power switch off.

For Pack Operation:

Place Radio Set in Carrying Harness (Figure): Spread out the harness with the stenciled side down, the wide straps to the right, and the three narrow straps untwisted. Place the radio set in the harness on its back with the panel toward the wide straps. Adjust the position so that the middle narrow strap will come just below the battery case clamps. Fasten the narrow straps by feeding the loose end, from below, through the buckle slot close to the center, and then through the slot away from the center. The strap should enter the buckle from below and leave the buckle from below, making an untwisted fastening and returning over itself. The assembly now is ready to be fastened to the suspenders.

Attach Carrying Harness to Web Belt: Clip the suspenders to a web belt (not supplied) and adjust them to fit comfortably. The single clip ends go to the rear and the double clip ends go to the front. On the front, clip the two center clips to the web belt nd and adjust the suspenders to fit. Remove the assembled suspenders and web belt and fasten the wide harness straps through the loop slides, one on each suspender, so that the radio set carries well up on the back of the operator. Cloth guides on each suspender permit folding up the excess length of the wide straps. Clip the remaining clips to the rings on each side of the bottom strap of the harness. Put on the completed assembly and adjust for maximum comfort. The radio set is now ready for pack operation.

To light off the Radio:
(1) Turn squelch control off.
(2) Turn volume control fully clockwise.
(3) Turn power switch on.

To Transmit and Receive:
(1) Allow 10 seconds for radio to warm up.
(2) If no signals are received, considerable background noise will be heard. Turn squelch control clockwise until background noise disappears. If turned beyond this point, weak signals are lost. Squelch adjustment varies with the condition of the battery.
(3) Press button to transmit-release button at end of each transmission.

To secure Radio:
(1) Turn power off.
(2) Disconnect handset.
(3) Disconnect antenna.
(4) Remove battery, if set is not to be used for a week or longer.

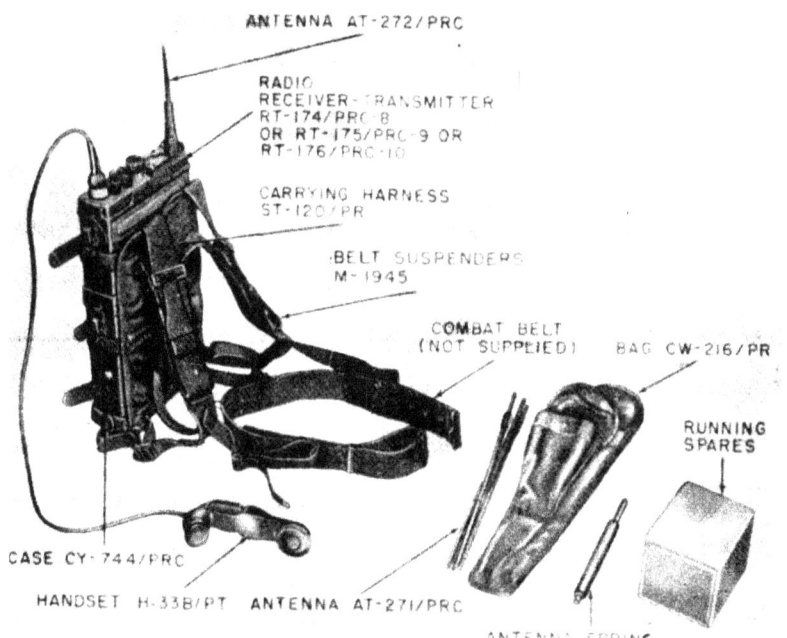

MAINTENANCE

Battery: The condition of the battery can be checked by observing the position of the squelch control. The further clockwise the control must be turned for proper squelch control, the weaker the battery.

Cleaning: Clean corrosion from jacks and plugs, clean case with brush or air (30psi), and damp cloth. Clean name plates and tuning dial windows.

Inspection: After each use, inspect the radio:

Inspect controls for binding, scraping, excessive looseness, misalignment, and positive action.

Inspect cables and hook-up wire for cuts, breaks, fraying, deterioration, kinks, strains, and mildew.

Check antennas for bends, corrosion, loose fit, and damaged insulators.

Lubrication: The dial-drive mechanism is the only assembly requiring lubrication. Lubricate every three months with light grease.

URC-17 and URC-17A RADIOS

The URC-17 and URC-17A Radios are FM (frequency modulated) radios mounted in UDT boats, for communications with ships, other boats, or shore facilities. The radio's receiver/transmitter unit is referred to as the RT-67/GRC. The separate power supplies are described below.

OPERATING INSTRUCTIONS

Preliminary Check: Before lighting off the radio or power supply, conduct a preliminary check:
(1) Check all cable and antenna connectors to ensure that they are tight and in proper places.
(2) Check all fuses to ensure that they are good and are screwed down tightly.
(3) Ensure that meter on transmitter unit is placed in R.F. position.

Lighting Off: The power unit should be lit off prior to the receiver/transmitter unit. The proper lighting-off procedure is as follows:

✱ SPECIFICATIONS

FREQUENCY RANGE: 27.0 TO 38.9 MC (VARIABLE)
POWER SUPPLY:
   URC-17: SEPARATE 24 VOLT DC UNIT (PP-112/GR)
   URC-17A: SEPARATE 12 VOLT DC UNIT (PP-109/GR)

(1) Power Unit
   (a) Place "Transmitter Power" switch to the "High" position. (Place in "low" for transmission of less than three miles.)
   (b) Place "Off - Receive - Transmit and Receive" switch to the "Transmit and Receive" position.
(2) Receiver/Transmitter Unit
   (a) Turn "Ring - On - Off Dial Light" switch to on.
   (b) Turn squelch "OFF".
   (c) Turn Volume to 1/2 full volume.

ELECTRO-5

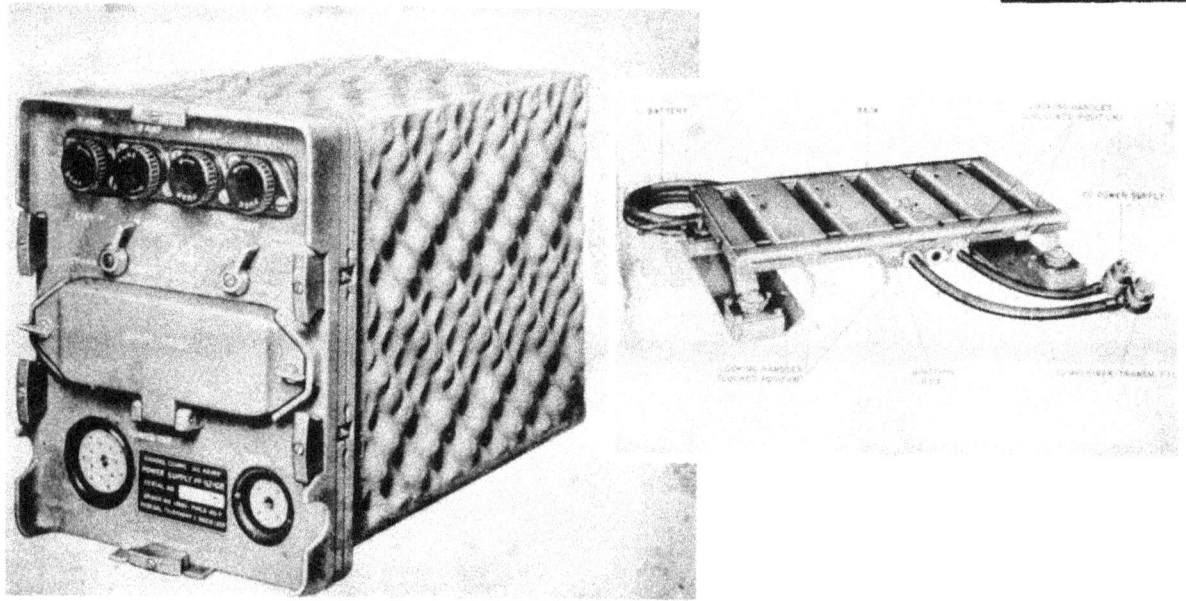

(d) Increase Squelch control until rushing noise in handset barely stops. (IMPORTANT Do not increase squelch past this point.)

Transmitting: Be sure to wait until incoming calls are completed before transmitting. To transmit press thumb button on handset. IMPORTANT: Wait approximately three to four seconds after pressing thumb button before starting your message. When you have completed your transmission, release thumb button and listen for answer or further messages.

Securing:
   (1) Power Unit: Place "Off - Receiver - Transmit and Receive" switch in OFF position.
   (2) Receiver/Transmitter Unit: Place "Ring - On - Off Dial Light" switch to OFF position.

CHANGING FREQUENCY: There are two steps involved in changing the frequency of the URC - 17A:

Set "MCS" control on receiver/transmitter, to nearest whole megacycle desired.

Adjust "Tenth MCS" control.

To "free-wheel", or continuous tune, turn "Tenth MCS" control full counter-clockwise. Then set up desired frequency.

For step-tuning turn "Tenth MCS" control full clockwise, and then back to desired frequency.

TROUBLESHOOTING: Troubleshooting and equipment maintenance are best performed by qualified Electronics Technicians. However, in the event that a URC - 17 or 17A is inoperative, and there is no ET on hand, the following troubleshooting may be conducted:

Basic Check:
   (1) Conduct the "Lighting Off" procedures
   (2) If the radio still does not operate at this time, determine whether the basic 12V or 24V DC power is being properly supplied to the power unit:
      (a) Clean all connectors and plugs with a stiff wire brush to remove rust or corrsion.
      (b) Check to ensure that all connectors and plugs are in their proper receptacles and are secure.
   (3) Ensure that all fuzes are not burned out and that they are securely tightened.

Secondary Check:
   (1) Open the receiver-transmitter unit and check for burned or broken tubes or parts, or for loose or disconnected wires.
   (2) Open the Power Supply Unit and check for burned or broken tubes or parts, or for loose or disconnected wires.

Tube Filament Check: Use the meter selector switch on the face of the receiver-transmitter unit for this check:
   (1) Turn the set on and place selector switch in the 90 volt position. The meter should read center scale deflection. If it does not, check the tubes and vibrators in power supply.
   (2) Turn the selector switch to positions 11 through 7 and press the push-to-talk button on the handset. The meter should read center scale deflection.
   (3)* Turn the selector switch to positions 6 through 2, and press push-to-talk button on the handset. The meter should read center scale deflection.

IMPORTANT: Use the below table for tube checks with meter readings. Readings are normal at approximately center scale deflection.

117

ELECTRO-5

METER SELECTOR SWITCH POSITION	ZERO READING	TOO LOW BUT NOT Z READ.	TOO HIGH BUT NOT FULL SCALE READING	FULL SCALE READING
2	V-7	V-7	V-9	V-9
3	V-8	V-8	V-10	V-10
4	V-6			V-5
5	V-106	V-106		V-104
6	V-105			
7	V-116, 114		V-113, V-3	V-3
8	V-4		V-2	V-2
9	V-102			V-107, V-103
10	V-108, 110		V-112	V-111, V-112
11	V-115		V-109, V-101	V-109, V-101

AN/PQC-1 (UTEL)

The UTEL is a device designed to allow a swimmer to communicate with a submarine, a surface craft, or another swimmer. While using UTEL submerged, a swimmer can receive voice transmissions, but if he is to transmit voice, he must be wearing a full facemask with a microphone ("lung microphone") imbedded in it. However, he can transmit voice while on the surface without a lung microphone (by means of a surface microphone).

In any event, he can always transmit and receive a homing tone, whether submerged or on the surface. This homing tone can be used either as a vector (to allow a submarine or another swimmer to find the user), or as a means of positive communications (if a code has been previously agreed upon).

There are four major components to the UTEL: Receiver-Transmitter, Microphone (Lung or Surface), Headset, and transducers. The transducer output pattern is in the form of a directional beam approximately 100° in width. To make use of its directional response, the transducer must be pointed as a flashlight, directly at the other station. To be used omnidirectionally the transducer is pointed at the ocean floor. The equipment will detect ship noises in the frequency range of 8.3 and 12.0 KC with a limited degree of bearing accuracy.

OPERATING INSTRUCTIONS

There are several stops involved in preparing UTEL for operation. They follow, in order:

Open the case: To do this, remove the hold-down nut located in the center of the panel by turning counter-clockwise. A 5/8 inch socket wrench should be used for this purpose. Remove the flat washer located beneath the hold-down nut. Raise the sealing clamp clear of the panel stud (be careful to avoid thread damage to the stud) and at the same time rotate the function switch from its center position to permit its clearing the switch locking mechanism. The sealing clamp may now be lifted free of the unit as far as the cable connectors will permit. CAUTION:

* SPECIFICATIONS

WEIGHT (IN CARRYING CASE): 23 POUNDS, 2 OZ.
SIZE (IN CARRYING CASE): 825.3 CUBIC IN.
TYPE EMISSION:
  VOICE: AMPLITUDE MODULATED (AM), SINGLE SIDEBAND, USING UPPER SIDE BAND.
  TONE: CONSTANT AMPLITUDE CONSTANT FREQUENCY SOUND WAVE.
FREQUENCY RANGE:
  VOICE: TRANSMISSION AND RECEPTION 8.3 TO 12 KC.
  TONE: TRANSMISSION: 9.2 KC.
MAXIMUM OPERATING DEPTH: 200 FEET
RANGES (UNDER NORMAL SONAR CONDITIONS):
  SWIMMER TO SWIMMER (DIRECTIONAL) 2,000 YARDS
  SWIMMER TO SWIMMER (OMNIDIRECTIONAL) 500 YARDS
  SWIMMER TO SMALL CRAFT (BOAT PHONE AN/WQC-1) 3,000 TO 4,000 YARDS
  SWIMMER TO SUBMERGED SUBMARINE (JT RECEIVER WITH TELEPHONE ADAPTER AND AN/UQC TRANSMITTER) 10,000 YARDS
POWER SUPPLY:
  2 "A" BATTERIES (BA-1328/U MERCURY CELL)
  1 B & C BATTERY PACK (BA-361/U BATTERY PACK)
WHEN STARTING WITH FRESH NEW BATTERIES, THE EQUIPMENT SHOULD OPERATE FOR SIX HOURS (THIS IS BASED ON A RATIO OF LISTENING FOUR TIMES AS LONG AS TRANSMITTING).
  REFERENCE: NAVSHIPS 92882

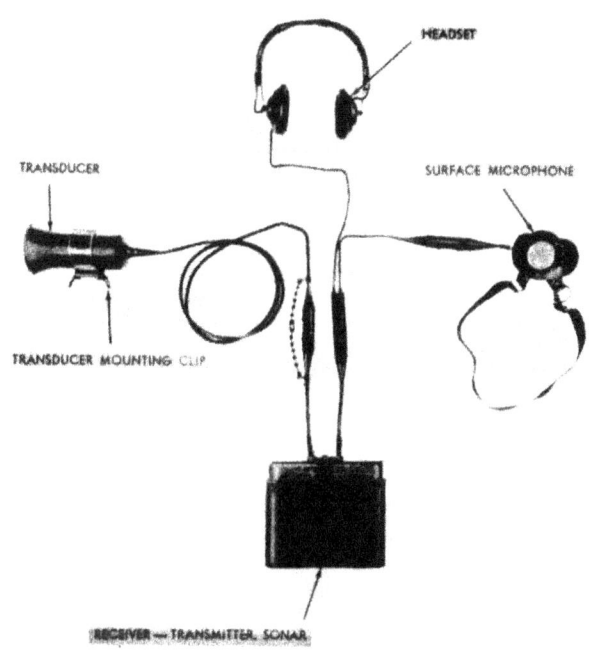

battery pack socket. Position the battery pack in its chassis compartment directly against the cover plate support bracket, withdrawing excess battery cable to the opposite side of the cover plate support bracket. Replace the cover plate, being certain that the battery pack and plug-in units lie within the outer lips of the cover plate.

Seal the case: Insert the electronics assembly in the case liner and replace the two retaining screws. Before rolling the rubber boot back into place, make a thorough examination of the rubber boot lip and the corresponding panel groove for the presence of any foreign matter. Both surfaces must be scrupulously clean. A soft-bristled brush or chamois is recomended for this purpose. The sealing clamp may then be replaced, observing the same precautions previously outlined.

The hold-down nut should be firmly tightened with a socket wrench. No excess leverage should be applied to the wrench, since excessive tightening of the hold-down nut may result in serious mechanical injury to the unit.

Before placing the receiver-transmitter into service for the first time, it is important to check the tightness of the two cable entrance packing gland nut, using a suitable flat wrench, as repeated mechanical shock and vibration during shipment could conceivably cause some loosening. The packing gland nuts should be tightened to approximately the same degree as the hold-down nut. Here again excessive tightening is unnecessary and in extreme cases may damage the cable jacket within the packing gland assembly due to excess pressure developed by the packing gland. NOTE: The panel packing gland nuts are not necessarily tightened flush against the surface of the cable gland bodies.

Install the Transducer: To do this, allow the cable to hang free for a moment to remove any twists or kinks. To ensure a satisfactory water seal, the engaging surfaces of the cable connectors must be clean and free of foreign matter. The transducer cable connector is inserted into the two contact transducer entry cable connector extending from the receiver-transmitter unit and the two connectors pushed tightly together. The periphery of each cable connector contains a small rubber protuberance to assist in aligning the pins and receptacles of the mating connectors. The cable connectors are separated by simply grasping the connector bodies and pulling apart.

Install the Headset: The headset cable assembly terminates in a three contact connector which mates to the corresponding three contact audio entry cable connector extending from the receiver-transmitter unit. Connection is made observing the same precaution outlined under Transducer Installation.

Install the Surface Microphone: The Surface microphone should be checked for tightness of water seal assemblies prior to initial use. The cable packing gland nut must be tightened to produce adequate pressure on the packing gland grommet. The mouthpiece to housing seal should be maximum hand-tight

Do not attempt to withdraw the cable connectors through the sealing clamp holes.

Next, roll the rubber boot down approximately 1 1/2 inches, and use a screwdriver to remove the two retaining screws on the sides of the plastic case liner. Then slide the electronics assembly out of the case liner. As a precautionary measure, be certain that the panel power switch is in the OFF position while installing batteries.

Install batteries: "A" Batteries: Remove the "A" battery connector plate by unscrewing the retaining screw. Insert two "A" batteries negative (-) end first, into the holes provided, being certain that they are firmly seated against the stationary contacts located in the opposite side of the chassis. IMPORTANT NOTE: Polarity must be observed. The negative ends of the batteries (center post) are inserted first. The batteries are of the mercury type. Unlike LE CLANCHE type, the outside battery case is positive. The positive terminals of the batteries are marked with a plus (+) sign and must be positioned at the opened end of the "A" battery retainer.

The connector plate may now be fastened firmly in place to ensure good electrical contact. Do not overtighten the retaining screw.

B AND C Battery Pack: Remove the two screws located on the rear of the rubber cushioned cover plate and remove the cover plate. Hold the unit in such a way as to avoid placing unnecessary strain on the contact pins of the plug-in units. Remove the protective tape from the "B and C" battery pack connector socket and insert the battery connector plug fully into the in a clockwise direction. The microphone should be handled carefully to avoid injury to the rubber disc sealing the mouthpiece aperture. The microphone cable connector mates with two contact connectors extending from the headset cable assembly, and the connection is made in the same manner as that recommended for the transducer installation.

Install the Lung Microphone: The lung microphone should be installed by inserting the grommet in the hole in the faceplate. Insert the threaded metal housing of the lung microphone through the hole in the grommet and tighten nut snugly, taking care not to apply too much pressure on the grommet or the glass will be damaged. Lock the nut with the set screw. The lung microphone may be used with any full facemask type of SCUBA of either the open or closed circuit type. Remove the face plate from the SCUBA and replace it with that of the lung microphone.

Don equipment: The equipment has been designed for installations as outlined in the following paragraphs, but it incorporates sufficient flexibility to permit deviation when desired to suit the comfort of the individual operators:

For swimmers: Don the web belt, and, by means of the mounting clips, mount the receiver-transmitter unit on the belt, at your right hip. Mount the transducer on the left side of the belt, rotated to point in the direction required to produce the desired beam pattern (see operation). Suspend the surface microphone from your neck by its strap. Finally adjust the headset to fit comfortably on your head, with the cable extending down to your right.

For surface users: The equipment may be operated from small craft using the same installation as specified for surface swimmers with the exception of the transducer. For operation from small craft the transducer is detached from the transducer mounting clip and either held in the water or suspended by its cable according to the desired beam pattern. For operation from larger ships whose freeboard will not permit submersion of the transducer, the transducer extension cable CX-3915/PQC-1 may be used. The mechanical locking devices on transducer extension cable should be secured to the transducer cable to prevent possible loss of the transducer.

For use with Full Facemask: The equipment may be used with a diving mask and is installed in the same manner as specified for surfaced swimmers with the exception of the microphone. Here the lung microphone is substituted for the surface microphone and is installed

PRE-DIVE CHECK

Visual Check: Check rubber enclosures and cables to ensure that there are no cuts or breaks that might cause leakage when the equipment is submerged
Operational Check: The operation of the equipment should be checked in an area of low ambient noise level before the swimmer enters the water. The following procedure is recommended:
(1) Receive - turn the equipment ON, scratch the transducer face, and listen for a rasping noise in the headset.
(2) Transmit (Voice) - turn the equipment ON, hold the function switch firmly in XMIT position, and talk into the microphone. The transducer should emit 8 to 11 KC unintelligible squeal.
(3) Homing Tone - turn the equipment ON, and hold the function switch firmly in HT position. The transducer should emit a steady 9.2 KC tone.
(4) A further check may be made by testing the equipment operation with a known good UTEL. Place the two UTEL'S with their transducers about three inches apart in the air and communicate from one to the other.

OPERATIONS

After the batteries have been installed and the components properly connected, the equipment is placed in operation by means of the ON-OFF switch. Selection of the type of operation is made by the function switch. The three functions controlled by this switch are homing tone, receive, and transmit; the corresponding switch positions are marked HR, R and XMIT, respectively. The function switch is spring loaded to return to its center position; thus the equipment functions normally as a receiver. To operate the equipment as a transmitter proceed as follows:

To transmit homing tone: Hold the function switch securely in the counter-clockwise (HT) position. With the function switch in the HT position, the equipment transmits a steady high-pitched tone for use in signalling or as a navigational beacon. Release the function switch immediately following completion of transmission.

To receive: The set will receive transmissions whenever the function switch is in the R position.

To transmit voice: Hold the function switch securely in the clockwise (XMIT) position; talk into the microphone. When speaking into the microphone (Lung or Surface), allow lips to touch the microphone aperture lightly. Do not push the microphone tightly against mouth, as this will distort speech intelligibility. Following completion of transmission, release the function switch immediately.

If prolonged transmission of voice or homing tone is required, a switch lock mechanism is provided, which, when engaged, will retain the function switch in either XMIT or HT position. To engage the switch lock, it is necessary to turn the function switch fully to the desired position and then raise the switch lock tab, which extends over the edge of the sealing clamp, until the switch locks into position. The function switch is released by holding the switch handle firmly in the position in which it has been locked, meanwhile pressing the switch lock tab down toward the panel, after which the function switch may be released. Releasing the function switch by depressing the switch lock tab without holding back on the function switch

handle will cause unnecessary wear on the rubber switch handle cover, which in time may jeopardize the effectiveness of the water seal.

The drain on the batteries when in the XMIT or HT positions far exceeds the drain when in the R position. For maximum battery life, avoid prolonged transmission except when necessary.

In order to conserve batteries, keep power switch off when equipment is not in use.

MAINTENANCE

Immediately after use, the equipment should be cleaned, dried, and returned to the transit case.

For extended period of storage, (one week or longer) the batteries should be removed from the receiver-transmitter unit and stored separately.

PROBLEMS

Underwater communication is affected by the following factors which may cause a reduction in maximum ranges or in quality of speech reproduction:

Reverberation: In underwater communication, reverberation can be discerned as a hollow sound such as produced by talking into an empty barrel or an empty auditorium. Over long ranges, one or more distinct echoes can sometimes be heard. Reverberation will most often be found in shallow water, near the coast, or in the vicinity of sharp temperature variations. The effect can be traced to multiple paths of transmission of a signal in water, such as the direct path signal plus signals which are reflectef from the surface and the bottom.

Noise: Since the equipment receives omnidirectionally to a certain extent, it will pick up any locally produced noise. If the level of any local noise is greater than that of an incoming signal, voice communication will not be reliable. Most of the noise in the water will be created by the screws and wakes of moving ships in the immediate vicinity. A secondary source of noise from nearby ships can be traced to auxiliaries and to overboard discharge.

Thermal Conditions: The obtainable range of the equipment will be considerably affected by variations in water temperature. Passage of the sonar beam through severe temperature gradients will cause bending of the sonar beam resulting in loss in range. Constant water temperature with varying depth will normally produce best results in sonar communication.

Topography, Etc: The presence of coral reefs, or rocks, as well as the general condition of the ocean bottom may cause appreciable reduction in the quality of voice transmission due to reflected echoes. Large masses such as reefs, if lying in the path of communication, may form an obstacle sufficient to seriously hamper the effectiveness of the equipment.

Scattering: When a sound wave reaches a region abundant in foreign matter, such as sea-weed, mud, or animal life, it encounters many small reflecting surfaces. Multiple reflections and refractions result, absorption losses increase, and efficient transmission to points beyond this region is made extremely difficult.

Corrective Measures: The effects of the limitations outlined above can generally be minimized to some extent by careful attention to the proper method of telephone procedure. The surface microphone should be held with the lips just touching the front of the microphone aperture. The operator should keep the mouthpiece substantially in a vertical position and talk in a loud clear voice without shouting. Regardless of the type of microphone used, it is important to speak slowly, pausing momentarily after each word. The operator should emphasize all terminal consonants such as "T" and "G" and emphasize with a distinct hiss all sibilants such as "S", "C", and "Z". When the situation permits, the operator should make every effort to position the transducer as accurately as possible to obtain optimum directional effectiveness.

AN/PQS-1B (HAND HELD SONAR)

The detecting - ranging set AN/PQS-1B is a completely self-contained hand held sonar. The set has two modes of operation: "ACTIVE" and "LISTEN". Either mode can be selected at any time by the operator, by rotating the mode selector switch. In the "ACTIVE" mode, the set transmits a sound pulse which reflects from objects in the water and returns to the sonar. The sonar detects these returning echoes and indicates to the operator the range, bearing, and (to some extent) the types of object reflecting the sound.

RANGE is indicated by a combination of the pitch of the tone and the position of the Range Switch.

The Range Switch has four positions: "OFF", "20", "60", and "120". The "OFF" position turns the equipment completely off. The numbers indicate the maximum range (in yards) at which the sonar will detect a target, at that setting. The minimum range at which the sonar will detect a target at that setting is the next lower possible setting of the Range Switch. For example, with the range switch on the "60" yard position, the operator will hear echoes from objects between 60 yards and 20 yards from the set. The pitch of the echo indicates where the object is between these two ranges. (A high pitch echo indicates that the object is near the outer limits of the range select-

ed whole a lower pitch indicates that the object is nearer the lower limits of the range selected.)

BEARING is indicated by the direction in which the sonar is pointed at the time the echo returns. A magnetic compass is provided to assist the operator in this phase of operation.

IDENTIFICATION of the object returning the echo echo can be determined to some extent by interpretation of the echo. For example, seaweed produces a fuzzy echo, while a moored mine produces a rather clear echo.

Efficient use of the set in the ACTIVE mode of operation requires considerable training, since accuracy depends greatly upon the evaluation of the echoes by the operator.

In the LISTEN mode of the operation, the sound transmitter section of the sonar is turned off. The receiver section of the sonar continues to operate and receives sound waves at frequencies of between 30 and 40 thousand cycles (KC) per second. This sound, which is of too high frequency to be heard by the unaided human ear, is normally emmitted from a beacon or marker which has been placed in the water nearby. There is no way to determine the range to a beacon. Only the bearing can be determined. Various types of marker beacons are used by UDT. The model 606 marker beacon manufactured by Burnett Electronic Lab., San Diego, is one of the most popular. This beacon transmits sound at 37 KC and has been picked up with the AN/PQS-1B at ranges up to 2000 yards.

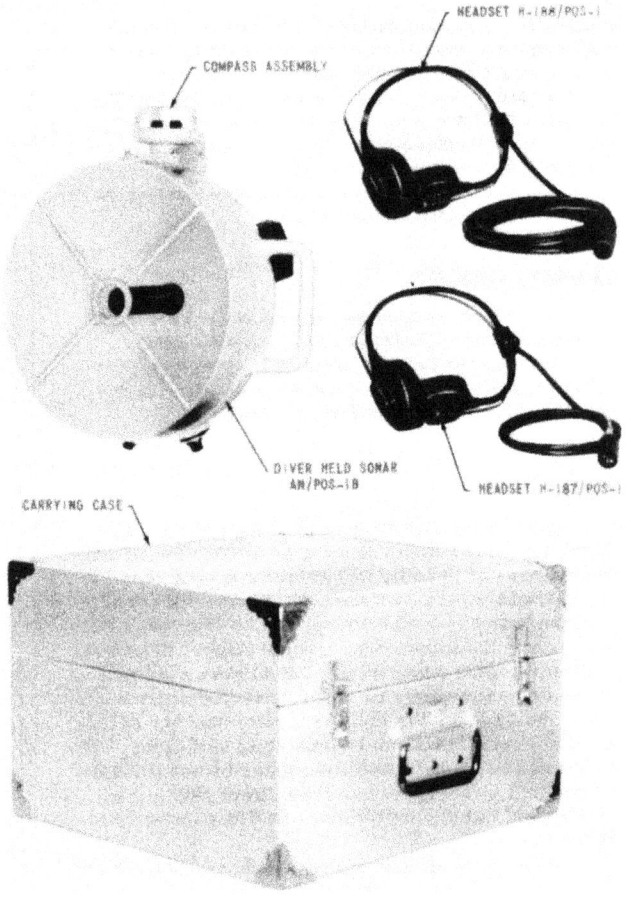

PREPARATION

INSTALL BATTERIES

(1) Place the unit reflector down on a flat surface and loosen the wing securing nut until hemisphere is free of the conical reflector assembly.

(2) Gently lift the hemisphere clear of the reflector assembly.

(3) Remove the battery retainer cover and insert the batteries, BA-30, in accordance with the diagram.

(4) Insert the BA-58 batteries in the receptacle on the battery box.

(5) Secure the battery box cover in place.

(6) Coat the quad ring with an appropriate silicone grease compound, per MIL-I-8660.

(7) Place the hemisphere back into position on the reflector housing, being sure the guide pin (7) is aligned with its mating hole.

(8) Before tightening the wing securing nut, be sure that all quad rings are properly seated and lubricated and that the sealing surfaces are not obstructed in any way.

(9) Tighten wing securing nut, sealing the reflector and hemisphere together.

(10) To install compass illumination battery remove the four screws which secure the switch assembly to the compass housing.

(11) Install the compass illumination battery with the center electrode facing out, in the cavity in the base of the compass assembly.

(12) Re-install the compass illumination switch assembly making certain that the switch contacts are not distorted and will make proper contact.

CONDUCT PRE-OPERATIONAL TEST:

(1) Connect either pair of headsets to the headset receptacle at the base of the equipment.

(2) Position the operator's RANGE-YDS control to the 20 yd. position.

(3) Place the ACTIVE-LISTEN switch in the ACTIVE position.

(4) Holding the equipment by the guide handles direct the reflector towards a flat (preferably metallic) vertical surface approximately 15 feet distant.

(5) If the equipment is operating normally and is a accurately pointed at the reflecting surface an echo tone will be heard in the headset. If no echo tone is heard, return the set to the ET shop for repair.

OPERATING INSTRUCTIONS

ACTIVE MODE

(1) Check all seals and the wing securing nut for tightness.

(2) Install headsets to connectors.

(3) Set ACTIVE-LISTEN switch in ACTIVE position (fully counter-clockwise).

(4) Submerge equipment below surface.

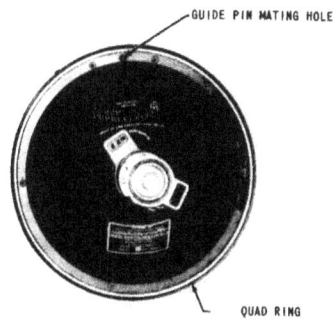
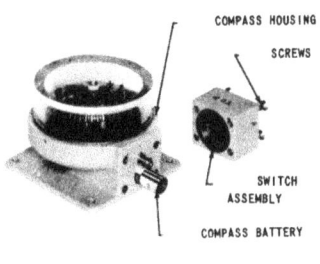
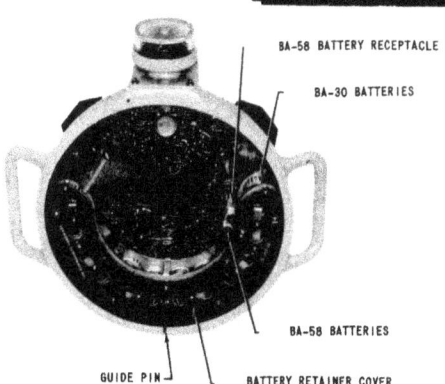

(5) Set RANGE-YDS switch at 20 yards.
(6) Adjust INCREASE-GAIN control for audible background.
(7) Set RANGE-YDS position at 120 yards position.
(8) Direct the beam towards a suitable producing object (best results are obtained with metallic surface reflections). Adjust GAIN control for comfortable listening level.
(9) Swim toward the target noting the decrease in pitch of the search tone.
(10) When the tone approaches its lowest pitch (approximately 250 cps) switch the RANGE switch to the 60 yard position and note that the pitch of the search tone increases (approximately 2500 cps).
(11) Follow the procedure in (9) above and switch to 20 yard position when tone reaches lowest pitch. Further swimming will take the diver directly to the target.

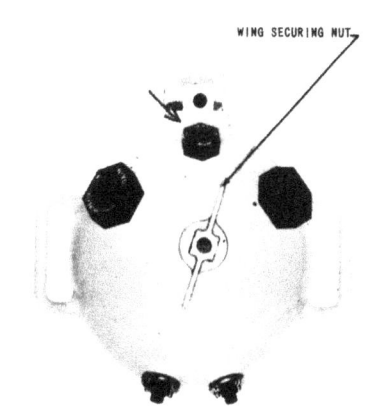

LISTEN MODE
(1) Insure that air operating marker beacon transmitter is in the operational area.
(2) Place RANGE-YDS switch in the 120 yard range position.
(3) Place GAIN control in maximum clockwise (highest volume) position.
(4) Place mode selector switch in LISTEN position.
(5) Take up a steady position, and, holding the set level, conduct a slow 360 degree search of the area from your position, constantly rotating the mode selector switch between the maximum clockwise position and the ACTIVE position. (Note: be careful not to turn the switch so far as to place the set in the ACTIVE MODE).
(6) When you hear the beacon signal, adjust the GAIN control until a comfortable listening level is reached.
(7) Determine the direction from which the beacon is heard most clearly. Swim in that direction, and adjust the GAIN control as necessary for comfort and clarity, as you approach the beacon.

MAINTENANCE

After each use, flush the equipment with clean, fresh water and allow it to dry thoroughly before storing it.

If the set is inoperative, install new batteries. If, after a battery change, it is still inoperative, check the battery contacts to insure that they are clear and are making positive contact. Check the contact springs on the two BA-58 penlight batteries. They often tend to exert too little pressure on the batteries, after the set has been assembled. If this seems to be the problem, exert slight pressure on these contact springs before installing the batteries, being careful not to exert too much pressure.

If the set needs any servicing other than a battery change or headset replacement, only a qualified person is allowed to service it.

✱ SPECIFICATIONS - UTEL

```
WEIGHT:   IN AIR 22 POUNDS
          SUBMERGED - ½ POUND (POSITIVE BUOY-
          ANCY)
FREQUENCY RANGE:
          ACTIVE: 50 TO 90 KC (IN CONE 9°
                  WIDE)
          LISTEN: 30 TO 40 KC
OPERATING TEMPERATURE RANGE:  32°F TO 122°F
MAXIMUM OPERATING DEPTH:  200 FEET
POWER SUPPLY:
          12 BA-30 FLASHLIGHT BATTERIES
          2 BA-58 PENLIGHT BATTERIES
THE SET SHOULD OPERATE FOR 50 HOURS WITHOUT
A CHANGE OF BATTERIES.
REFERENCES: NAVSHIPS 94422
```

notes

THESE PLACES ARE BAD FOR RADIO

VALLEYS — HIGH TENSION LINES — OVERHEAD STEEL BRIDGES — UNDERPASSES

BUT - THESE ARE GOOD

ON LEVEL GROUND — SLIGHT RISE — HIGH HILL

126 THE FOUR LIFE - SAVER STEPS

127 ARTIFICIAL RESPIRATION

127 CARE OF SPECIFIC INJURIES

130 GENERAL INFORMATION

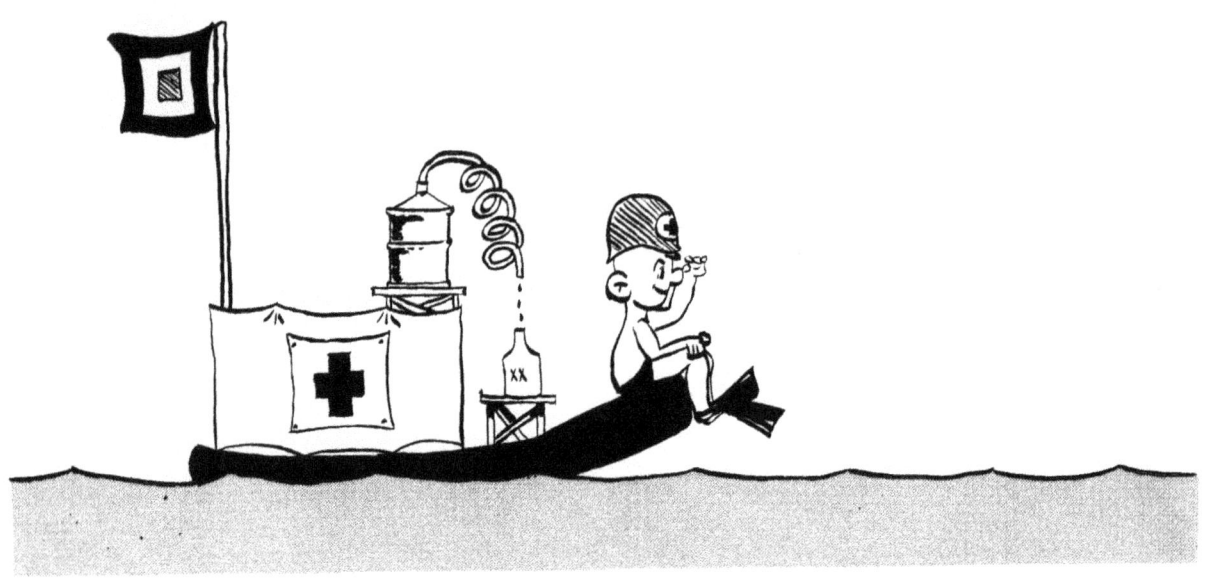

CHAPTER
FIRST AID

The four life-saver steps for the treatment of all injuries and wounds are:

STOP THE BLEEDING

Apply pressure directly to bleeding point with casualty's own first aid dressing at pressure point between wound and heart (see figure). Elevate wounded part if pressure does not stop bleeding (caution: splint suspected fractures before elevating). If pressure and elevation do not stop bleeding, or if blood is spurting from wound, apply tourniquet between wound and heart. Tighten tourniquet just enough to stop bleeding; bind stick used to tighten tourniquet to limb to keep tourniquet from unwinding. A tourniquet should be loosened only by competent medical personnel, if present. Leave tourniquet exposed if casualty has not been clearly marked to indicate that a tourniquet has been applied.

CLEAR THE AIRWAY

Position casualty in chin up position with head tilted back. Clear the mouth and throat of foreign matter. If casualty is having trouble breathing, start mouth-to-mouth resuscitation immediately.

PROTECT THE WOUND

Do not try to clean wound. Cover it with casualty's own first aid dressing. Wrap tails of dressing around it to exert even pressure over entire surface and cover edges to keep out dirt.

PREVENT OR TREAT SHOCK

Shock is a condition of great weakness of the body and can result in death. Any injury, either with or without bleeding, can cause shock. A person in shock may tremble and appear nervous, may be thirsty, may become very pale, have cold, clammy skin, and pass out. Shock may not appear for some time after an injury. Treat for shock before it occurs. Make comfortable, loosen belt and clothing, handle gently. Position with head and shoulders about 18" lower than rest of body in order that blood may flow to brain (unless there is a head or chest injury); splint fractures before moving! Keep warm by wrapping with blankets, poncho, etc., placed under as well as over casualty. If unconscious, place on side or belly with head turned slightly to one side. If conscious and no belly wound, replace lost fluid by giving either water (to which contents of a salt and soda pack have been added) or coffee, tea, cocoa, soup or plain water. No alcohol - it is not a stimulant. If victim has been diving, consider possible need for immediate recompression.

ARTIFICIAL RESPIRATION

The mouth-to-mouth method permits more air to enter the casualty's lungs than any other known manual method. It is done in the following manner:

Place casualty on back immediately. Do not waste time moving to a better place. Loosen clothing.

Quickly clear mouth and throat. Remove mucus, food and other obstructions.

Tilt head back as far as possible. The head should be in a "chin-up" or "sniff" position, and the neck stretched.

Grasp jaw by placing thumb into corner of mouth. Lift lower jaw and draw forward. Do not hold or depress tongue.

Pinch nose shut (or seal mouth). Prevent air leakage.

Open your mouth wide, take a deep breath, and blow forcefully (except for babies) into mouth or nose until you see chest rise. For babies, cover both mouth and nose with your mouth. Blow with small puffs of air from your cheeks.

Quickly remove your mouth when chest rises. Listen for exhalation. Lift jaw higher if casualty makes snoring or gurgling sounds.

Repeat last two steps 12 to 14 times per minute with an adult (and up to 20 times with a child). Continue until casualty begins to breathe normally.

CARE of SPECIFIC INJURIES

ABDOMINAL

Cover wound and protruding intestines with moist, sterile dressings, and keep the dressing moist. Do not try to replace intestines or bind dressing over protruding intestines firmly. Give nothing to eat or drink. Treat for shock before it occurs (casualty on side; with head and shoulders lower than rest of body). Evacuate casualties with a belly wound, at the highest priority.

BROKEN BACK

Suspect in any back injury, especially if casualty has no feeling in legs or cannot move legs. The sharp fragments of broken bone can cut or damage the spinal cord, and cause permanent paralysis.

DO: Place a low roll, such as a bath towel or clothing, under middle of the back to arch and support it. If the casualty must be moved, lift him onto litter or board without bending his spine. (It is best to have at least four men for this job.) If casualty is in face-down position, carry him face down on a blanket; keep body alignment straight and natural at all times, and keep air passages free. Caution casualty not to move.

DO NOT: Move casualty unless absolutely necessary, raise head (even for drink of water), twist neck or back, or carry in blanket face up.

BROKEN NECK

Extremely dangerous! Bone fragments may cut spinal cord just as in case of broken back. Keep casualty's head straight and still, with neck slightly arched. Caution him not to move. Moving him may cause his death. Place rolled bath towel or roll of clothing about same bulk as bath towel under neck for support and padding. (Roll should be thick enough only to arch neck slightly). Raise shoulders in order to place roll under neck - do not bend neck or head forward. Do not twist or raise head. Place roll so that when casualty is lying flat, the back of his head touches the ground. To keep head motionless after roll is in place, put a large padded rock or pack at each side of head. If man must be moved, get help. One person should support head and keep it straight, while others lift casualty. Transport on hard litter or board. Never turn over a casualty with broken neck! If a casualty is found with neck in abnormal position, do not try to straighten head and neck; immobilize head in position found.

BURNS

Minor burns (no blistering or charring) of small skin areas should be covered with first aid packet or other dry sterile dressing. If no dressing is available, leave the burn uncovered.

Severe burn (blistered or charred, or covers large area of body): infection and shock must be prevented. Cover burned area with dry, sterile dressing. Do not touch burn with anything other than sterile dressing. In the case of mass casualties, when sufficient sterile dressings are not available, cover with clean sheets, T-shirts, etc. Pad the sterile dressings sufficiently to keep from breaking the blisters. Only as last resort leave uncovered. Do not: pull clothes over burned areas, try to remove pieces of cloth sticking to skin, try to clean burned area, break burn blisters, or put grease, vaseline or ointment on burn.

In chemical burns, flush with large quantities of water, and avoid strong "neutralizers".

Prevent shock by placing head and shoulders lower than rest of body and by replacing body fluids and salt. If casualty is conscious, is not vomiting, and has no belly wound, give small amounts of cool or cold water to which salt or salt and soda have been added. (Add contents of 1 packet of Sodium Chloride-Sodium Bicarbonate Mixture from first aid pouch to one canteenful (1 quart) of water, if available. If not, dissolve four salt tablets or 1/2 tea-spoonful of loose salt plus two Sodium Bicarbonate tablets or 1/4 tea-spoonful of Baking soda in one quart of water). Give a few sips every few minutes; increase amount until 1/3 canteen cupful is drunk every hour. If casualty vomits or acts as if he might, do not give any more of this solution. Do not use warm water (warm salt water can cause vomiting).

CHEST

The chest wound itself may not be as dangerous as the air which may enter through it into the chest cavity and collapse the lungs. Seal wound and make airtight by covering it directly with the plastic or metal-foil side of the first aid dressing wrapper. Apply regular dressing over foil or plastic. Use additional bandaging material if necessary (poncho, shelter-half, etc.) to create enough pressure over dressing to make wound airtight. Casualty may be most comfortable in sitting position; if not, have him lie on injured side. Do not place in shock position.

CONVULSIONS: (See Diving Diseases and Injuries (Page   ))

FEET

Prevention of foot trouble is best first aid for the feet! Keep clean, dry thoroughly between toes, use issued foot powder twice daily and change socks daily. Do not cut a callus or corn. Keep toenails clean and short and cut straight across. If blister develops wash it and surrounding area with soap and water; sterilize a needle by heating it in a flame; open the blister by sticking it at the lower edge with needle that has been sterilized by heating in flame.

A trench foot (or immersion foot) is a serious condition which can require amputation of the feet. It results from a combination of cold weather and wet socks and boots. It occurs at temperatures above freezingg (can occur at temperatures as high as 50°F.). It can be prevented. Avoid standing in water, snow or mud. Whenever possible, exercise feet and legs and move toes and ankles about in boots. Massage feet for several minutes each day. Clean and dry feet thoroughly and put on dry socks at least once daily. (Carry an extra pair of socks and dry them by carrying inside shirt). Do not wear tight boots, socks or laces.

FROSTBITE

Frostbite is actual freezing of a part of the body (usually the face, hands or feet). There may be no pain. A frostbitten part of the body becomes grayish or white and loses feeling. Use a buddy system to keep watching one another's face for signs. Frostbite occurs quickly in cold weather, especially if wind is blowing. Prevent by wearing warm, loose clothing and by keeping dry. Don't overheat and perspire in cold climates; wear fewer clothes when exercising to avoid overheating and forming perspiration which will freeze later on. Dry or change wet clothing at once. Treat frostbite by removing any clothing (boots, gloves, socks) which fits closely over site of injury; thaw frozen part rapidly by putting it in warm water, by placing it next to a warm part of your own or someone else's body, or by exposure to warm air. Do not rewarm by such measures as walking, massage, exposure to open fire, cold water soaks or rubbing with snow. Wrap the casualty in blankets and give him warm drinks. After the affected part has thawed, wrap it loosely in dry, sterile dressings. If feet or legs are frostbitten do not let casualty walk. Evacuate him on litter to a medical facility. If hand or arm is frostbitten, put arm in sling.

FOREIGN OBJECTS

FOREIGN BODY IN EAR, NOSE OR THROAT: Never probe for foreign object in ear or nose. An insect in the ear may be removed by attracting with a flashlight, or by drowning with water poured into ear. Do not attempt to flush a foreign object out of the ear with water, if it will swell when wet. Remove a foreign object from the nose by blowing. Coughing will frequently dislodge a foreign object from the throat. If this fails, strike a sharp blow between the victims shoulderblades. As a final solution, if the object can be reached, try to remove it with the fingers; but be careful. Do not push it deeper down the throat!

FOREIGN BODY IN THE EYE: Do not rub eye. Tears will frequently flush out particle. If not, pull eyelid up or down, or attempt to remove with moist, clean corner of hankerchief. If unsuccessful, or if the foreign body is made of glass or metal, blindfold both eyes and evacuate patient to medical installation.

FRACTURES

Signs of broken bone: tenderness over injury with pain on movement; inability to move injured part; unnatural shape; swelling and discoloration of skin. All these signs may or may not be present with fractures. If not sure, give casualty benefit of doubt and treat as a fracture. Handle with care! Prevent shock and further injury. Broken ends of bone can cut nerves, blood vessels, etc. Do not move unless necessary. If casualty must be moved, splint fracture first; "splint them where they lie." If there is a wound, apply dressing as for any other wound. If there is bleeding, it must be stopped. If tourniquet is necessary, do not place over site of fracture. If time permits, improvise splints (sticks, blankets, poncho, etc.); if weapon is used, unload it first; pad splint well with soft material to prevent pressure and rubbing; splint should extend from above joint above fracture to below joint below fracture; bind splints securely at several points but not tight enough to interfere with blood flow (check pulse).

HEAD

Suspect head wound if casualty is or has been unconscious, has blood or other fluid

FIRST AID-6

escaping from nose or ears, has slow pulse or headache, is vomiting, if pupils are unequal or react slowly to light, or if victim has had convulsion or is breathing very slowly. Do not give morphine, and do not place in shock position (head lower than rest of body).

If conscious, evacuate on litter with head raised about 45°; if unconscious, remove false teeth and other objects from mouth and place on side or belly with head turned to one side to prevent choking on blood or vomitus.

HEART

Strike a vigorous blow, or a series of blows, with the fist against the victim's chest. If the heart does not begin to beat, place victim on his back; place one hand on top of the other with the heel of the lower hand resting on the victim's breastbone. Press vigorously (depress breastbone two inches). Repeat at rate of once per second.

HEAT

Can be prevented by commonsense, refraining from overactivity in hot climates, by taking salt tablets or extra salt with food, and by drinking enough water (as much as three gallons a day when working hard in high temperatures) to replace the salt and water lost in sweat.

HEAT CRAMPS: Are cramps of the muscles of the legs, arms, or belly; cramping is the first sign of heat cramps. They occur when a person has sweat a lot and has not taken extra salt to replace the salt lost in his sweat. He may also vomit and be very weak. Give him large amounts of salt water (see Heat Exhaustion, below).

HEAT EXHAUSTION: Casualty may have headache, become dizzy, faint, weak, and pale. He is sweating and his skin is moist and cool. This occurs when person has sweated a lot and has not taken extra salt and water to replace the salt and water lost in his sweat. Lay casualty down in shaded or other cool area, remove outer clothing, elevate feet ("when the face is pale, raise the tail"), and give him cool salt water to drink if he is conscious. (Dissolve two crushed salt tablets or 1/4 teaspoonful of table salt in a canteen (one quart) of cool water. He should drink three to five canteens in 12 hours.

HEAT STROKE: Very serious and may be fatal. Casualty stops sweating (this is a warning, and should be watched for). The face is extremely red, and skin is dry and hot. Body temperature becomes very high. Casualty may have headache, become dizzy, delirious and unconscious. Lower the body temperature as quickly as possible. Carry to shade, elevate head ("when face is red, raise the head"), remove clothing, and immerse in cold water bath containing ice, if possible, until normal body temperature returns. If ice is not available, use the coldest water available. Keep entire body wet by pouring water over him and cool him by continuously fanning his wet body. Get to medical aid! Continue cooling of casualty's body during evacuation to medical facility. Even after victim's body temperature has returned to normal, keep him under observation for several days, for possible rapid rise of temperature.

JAW

Remove broken teeth, pieces of bone and false teeth, from mouth and throat. Bind dressing in place to protect wound. If jaw is broken, support by additional dressing placed under jaw and tied on top of head. Do not cover mouth (so that vomitus and other fluids can escape). If unconscious, place on side or belly with head lower than rest of body and turned slightly to one side.

SNAKE BITES

Treat all snake bites as poisonous. Keep bitten person quiet, and do not let him walk or run; kill snake if possible and keep it so that it can be identified and proper antivenom serum given. Make casualty as comfortable as possible (preferably in sitting position); immediately immobilize bitten limb in a position below level of heart. Improvise tourniquet (hankerchief, strip of cloth, etc.) and place it between bite and heart, about two to four inches above bite, or ahead of redness or swelling. Tighten tourniquet enough to stop flow in superficial blood vessels (the veins will stand out prominently under the skin), but not tight enough to stop the pulse. As rapidly as possible, make a cut across the bite in the shap of the letter "H" about 1/4 inch deep and 1/2 inch long, sufficient to create a good blood flow. Suck out blood and venom. Apply cold pack to bite and to entire bitten limb; treat victim for shock. If swelling occurs, release tourniquet and reapply it further up arm or leg ahead of the swelling. Send someone to summon assistance. If litter or vehicle is available, transport casualty to nearest medical treatment facility at once. Should casualty stop breathing, start artificial respiration at once.

See Heat Stroke.

UNCONSCIOUSNESS

If you can determine cause (bleeding, heatstroke, head injuries, etc.) give first aid. It is often impossible to determine cause. If casualty has merely fainted, he will regain consciousness in a few minutes. Take off equipment, loosen clothing. Do not pour liquids into mouth of an unconscious person - if you do you may choke him. Remove false teeth, chewing gum or other objects which might choke him, from mouth or throat. If individual is

about to faint while sitting up, lower head between knees so that blood may flow to head; hold him so that he does not fall and injure himself. (If victim has been diving, recompress and treat for air embolism.)

general information

In anything but the most minor injuries, send for medical help, or get victim to hospital or dispensary. If another person is present, send him for medical assistance at once.

Do not move victim unless absolutely necessary. If victim must be moved, use stretcher (or improvise one). Transfer him to it with as little movement as possible. Use special precautions with possible back or neck injuries.

Use morphine with caution and only in case of severe pain. Use only if pain cannot be relieved by simple measures such as keeping casualty quiet, splinting injured are or leg, or carefully changing position. If syrette contains 30 mg. (1/2 grain) of morphine, give only one-half of the syrette. If it contains 16 mg. (1/4 grain) give contents of whole syrette.

Do not use morphine within four hours of previous injection or when casualty is unconscious, has a head injury, a fractured neck, is breathing with difficulty, is in shock, has chest wounds, or has severe abdominal pain with no visible wound.

notes

- 132 RECONNAISSANCE TECHNIQUES
- 139 PHOTOGRAPHY
- 141 CHART MAKING
- 146 BEACH REPORTS
- 148 TERMINOLOGY
- 151 TIDE and CURRENT TABLES

CHAPTER SEVEN
INTELLIGENCE

RECONNAISSANCE TECHNIQUES

MARKING THE SWIMMER'S SLATE:
    Each swimmer should mark off his slate prior to a recon so that all he has to do is "fill in the blanks" while he is in the water. Following are the different markings used for various recons:

DAY COMBAT

front

PAIR #			NAMES:	
DEPTH (FT)	DIST (IN)	DIST (OUT)		COMMENTS
1				
2				
3				
4				
5				
6				
7				
8				
9				
10				
11				
12				
13				
14				
15				
16				

back

CURRENT
OUTSIDE SURF ZONE: DIR___ VEL___ KT
INSIDE SURF ZONE: DIR___ VEL___ KT

SURF
TYPE: ___% SPILL ___% PLUNG ___% SURGE
ANGLE: ___° FROM___
AV HT:___ FT MAX HT_____ FT
PERIOD:_____ SEC
LINES IN SURF ZONE_____
WIDTH OF SURF ZONE_____

BOTTOM COMPOSITION
1 FATH_____
2 FATH_____
3 FATH_____

BEACH
COMPOSITION_____
SHAPE_____
GRADIENT 1:_____
OBSTACLES_____
EXITS_____
MISC_____

PERPENDICULAR ADMIN, IBS & SUBMERGED   PARALLEL ADMIN & NIGHT COMBAT

PAIR #	NAMES:								
DIST (YDS)	LANE		LANE		LANE		LANE		
	D	INFO	D	INFO	D	INFO	D	INFO	
25									
50									
75									
100									
125									
150									
175									
200									
225									
250									
275									
300									

SWIMMER NO: YARD MARKER:				NAMES:
LN	DEPTH	LN	DEPTH	COMMENTS
1		13		
2		14		
3		15		
4		16		
5		17		
6		18		
7		19		
8		20		
9		21		
10		22		
11		23		
12		24		

post-recon questionaire

When time permits, the following questionnaire should be filled out by each swimmer pair immediately after a combat recon. This allows the swimmers to submit more detailed information, and gives the cartographer more legible writing from which to work.

POST-RECONNAISSANCE QUESTIONNAIRE

SWIMMER PAIR NO._____   DATE_____

NAMES_____

1. CONDITION OF SEA FROM DROP POINT TO SURF LINE: CALM (LESS THAN 1 FT._____) SMOOTH (1-2 FT)_____ SLIGHT (2 - 3 FT)_____ MODERATE (3-5 FT)_____ ROUGH (5 FT- AND UP)_____.

2. CURRENT OUTSIDE BREAKER LINE: DIRECTION_____ VELOCITY_____ IN KNOTS.

3. DISTANCE FROM 1ST BREAKER LINE TO HWM_____YARDS.

4. TYPE OF BREAKERS: SPILLING_____ MIXED_____ PLUNGING_____ NONE_____

5. AVERAGE HEIGHT OF BREAKERS_____FT.

6. MAXIMUM HEIGHT OF BREAKERS_____FT.

7. PERIOD IN MINUTES BETWEEN SERIES OF HIGH BREAKERS_____.

8. NUMBER OF LINES OF BREAKERS:_____

9. DISTANCE FROM HWM TO BREAKER LINES: 1____ 2_____ 3____ 4_____YARDS.

10. TIME INTERVAL BETWEEN BREAKERS:_____SEC.

11. BREAKER ANGLE WITH RESPECT TO BEACH: QUARTERING_____ PARALLEL_____.

12. CURRENT INSIDE BREAKER LINE: DIRECTION_____ VELOCITY_____ KNOTS_____.
13. TYPE OF BOTTOM AT ONE FATHOM CURVE:_____.
14. RIP TIDES PRESENT: YES_____ NO_____.
15. SAND BARS PRESENT: YES_____ NO_____.
16. COMPOSITION OF BEACH: A. SAND_____ SHELLS_____ PEBBLES_____ LAVA_____ ROCK_____
                          B. VERY FINE_____ FINE_____ MEDIUM_____ LARGE_____
17. SHAPE OF BEACH: STRAIGHT_____ CURVED_____ CUSPED_____ OTHER_____.
18. TRAFFICABILITY: HOW DEEP IMPRESSION DID YOU MAKE IN SAND._____ (SPECIFY HOW IMPRESSION MADE_____.)
19. OBSTACLES, UNDERWATER (DESCRIBE NUMBER, TYPE, SIZE, LOCATION, DEPTH OF WATER OVER AND ESTIMATE AMOUNT OF EXPLOSIVE REQUIRED TO DEMOLISH):
    A. NATURAL -
    B. MAN-MADE -
20. OBSTACLES, ON BEACH (DESCRIBE TYPE AND NUMBER, SIZE, LOCATION, AND ESTIMATE AMOUNT OF EXPLOSIVE TO DEMOLISH):
    A. NATURAL -
    B. MAN-MADE -
21. INTELLIGENCE DATA:
    A. WAS THERE ANY INDICATION OF ENEMY ACTIVITY ON BEACH - YES____ NO____.
    B. TRACKS ON BEACH - YES____ NO____ TYPE_____.
    C. GUN IMPLACEMENTS - YES____ NO____ TYPE_____.
    D. PERSONNEL: SENTRIES: YES____ NO____ TYPE_____.
    E. TANKS: YES____ NO____
    F. OTHER COMMENTS_____.
22. EXITS FROM BEACH: A. PERSONNEL_____ B. VEHICLES_____.
23. DOES THE AREA APPEAR TO BE MIND: YES_____ NO_____.
24. SOUNDING AND DISTANCE FROM HWM:
    IN-SOUNDING   DISTANCE   OUT-SOUNDING   DISTANCE
    _____   _____   _____   _____
    _____   _____   _____   _____
    _____   _____   _____   _____
    _____   _____   _____   _____
25. DRAW BEACH PROFILE AS BEACH LOOKED TO YOU WITH APPROXIMATE LOCATION OF PROMINENT LANDMARKS.

DAY COMBAT RECON

This type of recon can be conducted more rapidly, and with less exposure of swimmers to enemy shorefire than any other type of recon. However, of all the different types of recon, it provides the least accurate information. The day combat recon is scheduled so that the delivery craft drops the swimmers as soon as it becomes light enough to identify the beach. In this way, the swimmers are in to the beach and back out again before the average man's working day has begun.

PERSONNEL: OIC, Pickup man, Cartographer, two swimmers for every 25 yards to be reconned.

EQUIPMENT: Appropriate cast and recovery and cartography equipment, and one slate, leadline, and pencil per swimmer (often, one member of a swimmer pair will lose equipment during the launch).

PROCEDURE: The swimmer pairs are dropped in the water 25 yards apart in a line parallel to and 500 yards from the water's edge. One pair, usually the pair on Right Flank, is designated Guide Pair and all

other pairs maintain a 25 yard interval from each other during the reconnaissance using the Guide Pair as a reference point. The move toward the beach commences upon signal from the Guide Pair. (The Guide Pair may use a compass to assist in swimming a predetermined course in to and out from the beach, or may guide upon a designated object on the flank.) The leadline man in each pair lets his leadline out to the required depth (usually 21 feet). When it touches the bottom, he notifies his buddy (the recorder) who estimates the distance to the High Water Line and records this on his slate. The pair continues this process all the way in to the beach, sounding and diving to the bottom at the 18, 15, 12, 9, 6, 5, 4, 3, 2, and 1 foot soundings. At the water's edge all pairs shift left 12-1/2 yards. During this time, the recorder in each pair records the beach gradient, as well as any other significant foreshore, backshore or hinterland features in his area. When the shift left has been completed, all pairs swim back out to sea taking soundings as before and still guiding on the Guide Pair. On command from the Guide, the swimmers form a line parallel to the beach, with each man 25 yards apart for the pickup. To do this, one man from the Center Pair remains stationary and all others swim towards the flanks. If another method of pickup is to be used, the pickup line formation will be changed accordingly. (See UDT operations for methods of delivery and recovery).

KEY POINTS

1. One pair is designated beforehand to take a SUROB rather than take soundings during the reconnaissance.

2. If the reconnaissance is to be accurate, it is imperative that each pair maintain proper interval from the next pair, and that all pairs follow the Guide throughout the reconnaissance.

3. When making a dive during a combat reconnaissance, care must be taken not to splash water. To accomplish this, the diver forcefully brings his arms up from his sides, palms upward, to thrust himself straight down. When he is several feet below the surface, he executes a jacknife dive and commences his underwater swim.

4. Swimmers should be careful to protect themselves as much as possible from detection from the beach. The actions to beware of are: Allowing the sun to reflect off the face mask holding the line or slate above water when sounding or recording proceeding into too shallow water, and raising the body out of the water when close to the beach.

NIGHT COMBAT RECON

GENERAL: This recon is second in stealth only to the submerged recon. However, personnel must undergo intensive training before they will be able to accomplish it properly.

PERSONNEL: OIC, Pacer, Beach Defense Perimeter, and one swimmer for each 25 yards of beach to be reconned.

EQUIPMENT: A minimum of three waterproof multicolored directional flashlights with a waterproof compass secured on each. (One flashlight is used as a backup in the event that either of the other two fail).

PROCEDURE: The OIC and Pacer, equipped with the flashlights described above, swim in to the beach, scout the area, and determine the starting point of the reconnaissance (considering the Littoral Current). The OIC points his flashlight (but does not shine it) down the length of beach to be reconned and reads his Base Line Bearing off the compass mounted on top of his flashlight. He then calculates the Right Angle Bearing (RAB) (The bearing at right angles to the Base Line Bearing), sets his compass on the RAB, and instructs the pacer to do the same. They double-check to make sure that their flashlights are aligned together.

The pacer then proceeds to the water's edge at the starting point and shines his (orange) out to sea on the RAB. He flashes his light if the reconnaissance is to proceed to the left flank, but shines a steady beam if the reconnaissance is to proceed towards the right flank.

The OIC proceeds several yards landward of the pacer and shines his light (orange) out to sea on the RAB. He assures that he is on proper range by holding the flashlight between his palms, his fingers pointing in the same direction as the light beam. He then moves laterally until, with his compass on the RAB, his fingers are pointing directly at the pacer.

When the reconnaissance personnel at sea sight the range lights, they swim in, on range, at 25 yard intervals along a marked flutterboard line. If a beach Defense Perimeter is to be used, they swim ahead of the #1 swimmer in to the beach. When the #1 swimmer reaches the water's edge, both the OIC and the pacer flash their lights (green) for several seconds and then turn them off. The pacer rapidly paces off 25 yards at the water's edge, turns his light to sea on the RAB, and turns it on (orange). The OIC aligns himself landward of the pacer as before and turns on his light (orange). When the swimmers swim on to the range, OIC and pacer flash their lights, (green) secure them, and proceed down the beach to set up the next lane as before.

The last lane can be indicated by flashing the lights red when the swimmers come on range. At this time, the swimmers take their last sounding and proceed to sea, maintaining their interval along the flutterboard line. The Pacer, OIC, and Beach Defense Perimeter follow the #1 swimmer to sea, in that order.

KEY POINTS

The OIC and Pacer must be careful not ot shine their lights in any direction other than seaward, or to allow their lights to shine on their hands, on swimmers in the water, or on other objects.

All hands, especially the OIC and the Pacer, must practice the reconnaissance thoroughly beforehand and be completely familiar with the meaning of all light signals.

All swimmers must maintain their hold on the flutterboard line throughout the reconnaissance.

All compasses must be securely fastened to the

flashlights, and exactly aligned, before the reconnaissance begins.

PARALLEL ADMIN RECON

GENERAL: The Parallel administrative recon can be conducted faster (and can consequently cover a larger amount of beach) than any other admininstrative recon. However, its disadvantage lies in the fact that a narrow sandbar (less than 25 yards wide) will be missed if it happens to come between two swimmers in a condition of poor visibility. Therefore, it is a good idea in poor visibility, for each swimmer periodically to measure the depth of water a few yards landward and seaward of his bunting marker when swimming between lanes. Other disadvantages include the necessity of keeping the same personnel in the surf zone throughout the recon and the large number of swimmers needed for a shallow gradient beach. Any kelp in the area will snag on the line, often necessitating the assignment of one or more swimmers to disentangle it. Finally, it is quite difficult to maintain a straight line of swimmers when the surf is high or the littoral current is strong. With highly trained swimmers, it is possible to conduct this type of recon without the assistance of a line to sea. This would alleviate the many problems caused by kelp, but would not be feasible in conditions of high surf.

PERSONNEL: OIC, Cartographer, two range pole men, two lane marker men, one swimmer for every 25 yards to be reconned, seaward of the water's edge.

EQUIPMENT: One flutterboard with line marked every 25 yards, long enough to cover the distance seaward of the water's edge to be reconned; two range poles of different height, each with a different colored flag; one 25 yard distance line (lightweight cable makes the best distance line); two lensatic compasses; pencil and paper for the Cartographer; slate and leadline for each swimmer.

SETTING UP THE BEACH

The OIC determines which flank of the beach will be used as a starting point. (If there is a Littoral Current, this will be the flank up-stream of the current.) The Cartographer marks Point #1, which is the beach flank. Then, using his lensatic compass, he determines the bearing from Point #1 to an object on the opposite flank of the beach. This is called the Base Line Bearing (BLB). He directs one of the lane marker men to place a marker (a large rock, piece of driftwood, etc.) at Point #2 (a point 25 yards (by distance line) towards the opposite flank on the BLB from Point #1). The Cartographer then calculates the Right Angle Bearing (RAB), which is the bearing pointing seaward 90° from the BLB. He directs one of the lane marker men to mark Point #3 (a point several yards landward of #1, on the reciprocal of the RAB) and Point #4 (by moving along the BLB from Point #3 until Point #2 lies along the RAB). Lane one is now marked by points #1 and #3 and lane two by points #2 and #4.

One lane marker man now proceeds down the beach (along the BLB marked by points #1 and #2) towards the opposite flank, placing a marker every 25 yards, as measured by the distance line (which he drags along with him). The other lane marker man follows him down the beach (along the BLB marked by points #3 and #4), and places a marker on a point which is on that range and (with the help of his lensatic compass) on the RAB landward of every marker already placed. The landward man also inscribes the lane number in the sand, next to each marker he leaves. Both land marker men continue this procedure until they reach the opposite flank.

THE RECONNAISSANCE

As soon as the lane marker men begin moving down the beach to mark the lanes, the range pole men set up their poles on points #1 and #3. Then the man who will be the outboard swimmer attaches the bitter end of the flutterboard to his web belt or lifejacket oral inflation tube and swims to sea on the range marked by the range poles. As each 25 yard bunting marker comes by, a swimmer grasps the line at the bunting and proceeds to sea on range. The man who will be the inboard swimmer tends the flutterboard.

When the outboard swimmer's leadline indicates a depth of 21 feet, the word is passed shoreward. When the after range pole man gets this word, he waves his range pole flag. Both range pole men then move rapidly to lane two where they set up their range poles at points #2 and #4. When the swimmers see the after range pole flag wave, they measure their depths with their leadlines, mark same on their slates, and proceed to the next lane as marked by the range pole men. When the swimmers are on range, the after range pole man again waves his flag and the swimmers measure and mark as before. The procedure is repeated until the final lane is reached. When the swimmers come on range both range pole men wave their flags, the swimmers take their final reading, and the reconnaissance is secured.

THE CARTOGRAPHER

The Cartographer's duty is to set up the beach as described above. Once the recon begins, he walks down the beach drawing a sketch of the foreshore, backshore and hinterland. He refers to the lane number in the sand next to each after range marker to align the information which he is gathering during the recon with the hydrographic information he will get later from the swimmers. He utilizes pacing, distance judging, and his lensatic compass in recording beach information as the recon proceeds.

In particular, his duties include:
Determining the range and bearing from the starting point to the reference point. (The reference point is specified by OIC with recommendation of Cartographer).

Determining the distance to HWL from Base Line (HWL to be considered the most landward line of debris).

Determining the size of BERM, placement of exits and other manmade from WL inland.

Obtaining a SUROB (this duty is usually designated to another person).

Designating, in conjunction with OIC, the photographs to be taken.

As the swimmers come out of the water after the recon, the Cartographer debriefs each one and records all information on his rough chart.

The Cartographer's final responsibility is to make the smooth chart of the recon.

KEY POINTS

During an administrative parallel recon, especially when there is a strong Littoral Current, the swimmers must make every effort to stay on range with the range poles and to maintain their hold on the flutterboard line. Also, as in all reconnaissances, it is important that each swimmer dive to the bottom frequently to better obtain information on bottom characteristics.

PERPENDICULAR ADMIN RECON

GENERAL: The perpendicular administrative recon provides the most accurate and complete information of any UDT recon. A further advantage of this type of recon is that it can be conducted by as few as two swimmers (although greater numbers of men will do it in less time). If just two swimmers are conducting the recon, they must fix the range poles firmly in the sand, and then bury the bitter end of the flutterboard line near the forward range pole by means of a "DEADMAN".

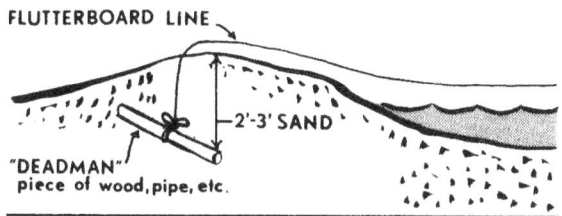

The disadvantage of the perpendicular recon is that it requires more time and equipment to accomplish than a parallel recon conducted with an equal number of men.

PERSONNEL: OIC, Cartographer, as many swimmers as are available, two lane marker men, and one range pole man for each set of range poles to be used (two range poles are needed for every three swimmer pairs).

EQUIPMENT: Same as for parallel recon, except that each three swimmer pairs require two range poles and a flutterboard. Also, one pair of binoculars is desirable for use by each range pole man.

PROCEDURE: The beach is set up in the same manner as for a parallel recon. However, range markers are placed every 75 yards rather than every 25 yards.

The actual recon is done in sections 50 yards wide. Each section is done in the following manner: One man from the Guide Pair gives the flutterboard to the range pole man, ties the bitter end of the line to his web belt, and stands at the water's edge, on range with the range poles. Two swimmers then line up at the water's edge, one 25 yards to the left, and the other 25 yards to the right of the flutterboard pair. On signal from the Guide Pair, all swimmers swim seaward. The Guide Pair stays on range with the range poles, and the other two swimmers maintain a distance of 25 yards from them.

When the first 25 yard bunting marker comes up, the range pole man waves the forward range pole and all pairs sound. All hands continue swimming seaward, repeating this process until the 21 foot curve is reached. At this time, the Guide Pair signals the range pole man (who is watching the swimmers with binoculars). The range pole man moves the bitter end of the flutterboard line and the range poles 75 yards down the beach to the next range marker. There he sets up the range poles and holds the flutterboard. The swimmers swim parallel to the beach until the Guide Pair is on a new range. Then, on command of the Guide Pair, they swim landward marking the depths as before. At the water's edge, the swimmers emerge move 75 yards down the beach. Repeat the whole process. This is continued until the area to be reconned has been completed.

THE CARTOGRAPHER

The Cartographer's duties on the perpendicular recon are the same as those for a parallel recon.

IBS RECON

GENERAL: The IBS recon is slower and less accurate and requires more personnel than a swimmer recon. However, it allows a recon to be completed without putting anyone in the water and therefore is useful in polluted, radioactive, or otherwise dangerous waters.

PROCEDURE: The IBS recon is run in the same manner as the perpendicular swimmer recon, except that a manned IBS is used on each lane rather than swimmers, and a heavy (about seven pound) leadline is used rather than the standard swimmer leadline. See the sketch below on preparing an IBS crew for a recon.

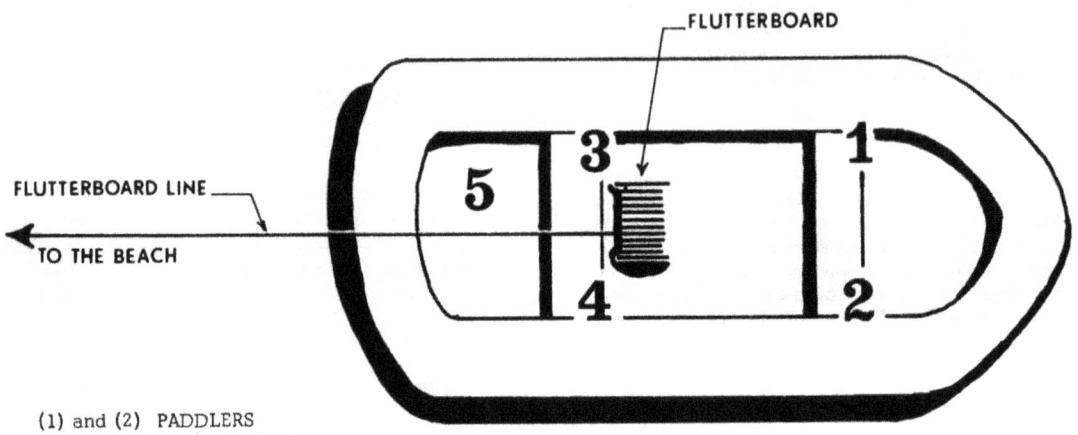

(1) and (2) PADDLERS
(3) LEADSMAN/RECORDER
(4) FLUTTERBOARD TENDER
(5) COXSWAIN

NOTE: The flutterboard is moved from aft to forward in the IBS to ease reeling in.

SUBMERGED RECON

GENERAL: The submerged recon was developed to meet the need of conducting surveys on enemy held beaches. In its purest form this type recon is completely covert. However, there are so many problems inherent in the operation that at the present time it should not be considered within the Teams' capabilities.

The first problem is location of the swimmers underwater at a specific point. This is not difficult with regard to depth, but is hard to do along the face of the beach. The second problem is conducting the actual recon itself, for present methods are slow and inaccurate and require many lines. The third problem is rendezvous at sea between the swimmers and their pick-up craft.

Additional problems inherent in this type recon are the lack of foreshore information, the improbability of finding obstacles, and the possibility that if swimmers simply proceed into a given depth and then reverse course they may actually be stopping at a reef or sandbar.

Attempts are being made to develop recon craft which, either with or without swimmers, can accomplish this mission satisfactorily. In addition, greater electronic sophistication would make the operation more feasible.

PERSONNEL: OIC, Flutterboard man, two swimmers for each 25 yards of beach to be reconned.

EQUIPMENT: Base line flutterboard (see picture), one stake with numbered snaffle hook for each 25 yards to be reconned, and one special flutterboard (see picture) for each swimmer pair.

PROCEDURE: Swimmers, led by OIC, swim in a predetermined compass course for a preset distance, or to a predetermined depth. ("A")

OIC surfaces, ("B") checks and notes landmarks, submerges, and, if satisfied with the location, begins the reconnaissance.

OIC and flutterboard man swim to opposite flank ("C") on a predetermined course, paying out flutterboard line and fixing it to the ground with a stake every 25 yards. (A metal ring in the line every 25 yards makes this easy to do). Flutterboard man snaps a numbered snaffle hook into each ring (#1 on first ring, #2 on second ring, etc.).

When flutterboard line is run out, the OIC and flutterboard man detach F/B and swim back to point "B" checking all stakes ("D"). Meanwhile swimmer pairs have begun the reconnaissance ("E") unsnapping the numbered snaffle hook on their lane, and keeping

it. (This way, the OIC can tell if any lanes have been missed, also, the swimmers will be sure what lane they have done).

All hands muster at the end of the line ("F"), when recon has been completed. OIC and flutterboard man have been reeling in F/B line. When this is completed, OIC takes a muster and proceeds to sea with all hands ("G"), on a predetermined course, to intercept mother craft.

KEY POINTS

Do not emerge in surf zone. (One man can stay outside the surf zone and anchor the line with his body while his buddy proceeds in further. This will give the person going through the surf zone some stability.)

When swimming along the Base Line, hold the line in the left hand and stay to the right of the line. When two swimmers meet, they can pass each other with no confusion, even in murky waters, if this simple procedure is followed.

recon PHOTOGRAPHY

During every reconnaissance, the most thorough photographic coverage possible should be obtained. The following paragraphs describe the areas to be covered:

OFFSHORE TO HINTERLAND PANORAMAS: From both the left and the right flanks of the beach, standing at the water's edge, take panoramas of 10% overlaping views beginning offshore and sweeping inshore. Show the approaches, reefs, water lines, the full length of the beach, full width of the beach and beach gradient.

BACKSHORE AND HINTERLAND PANORAMA: From the scarp at the center of the beach, take a panorama of the backshore and hinterland; ridges, escarpments, vegetation and obstacles.

BEACH EXITS: Obtain medium views and close-ups emphasizing location, surrounding features, access and trafficability. Take views from the beach facing inland and from the high ground inland facing seaward.

HINTERLAND: Show vegetation, soil and rock types, trafficability indications such as wheel tracks and swamp areas, obstacles, habitation, roads and defenses or defendable positions.

MISCELLANEOUS

Show conditions or obstacles which will assist in identifying the material composition and trafficability of the beach. Take complete coverage (including close-up) or any features encroaching on, or limiting the usefulness of the landing areas, such as hazards to approach and barriers to egress. Include personnel or familiar objects in photos whenever possible to assist interpreters in determining measurements. Whenever possible, obtain photographs of underwater obstacles by means of the "CALYPSO".

During a combat reconnaissance obtain photos from the water, by means of the "CLYPSO".

recording

As each photo is taken, make an entry on the Beach Survey Photo Data Sheet (see sample below). Be sure to include every photo taken; even the mistakes and blanks.

When a person has been included in a picture to show the relative size of beach features, be sure to include the person's height on the Photo Data Sheet.

SAMPLE

BEACH SURVEY PHOTO DATA SHEET

NOTE: ALL DATA ON TOP OF THIS SHEET IS TO BE PRINTED ON THE BEGINNING OF EACH ROLL OF FILM, IN INDIA INK.

```
BEACH_____        COUNTRY_____
PHOTOGRAPHER_____     CAMERA_____
UDT_____ DET_____     FILM SIZE_____
DATE_____      FOCAL LENGTH_____
TIME STARTED_____ TIMED FINISHED_____ ROLL#_____
```

EXPOSURE#	DATE & TIME	COUNTRY	BEACH	DESCRIPTION OF PHOTO

Submitting

There are three steps to be taken before submitting negatives of beach photographs to a command which request them:

With each set of beach photographs, submit a chart of the beach with markings indicating the locations from which the photos were taken.

Print on each negative the NIS number (or name) of the beach and the exposure number of the negative.

Submit a Photo Data Report with the negative, in the following format:

SAMPLE

PHOTO DATA REPORT

UNCLASSIFIED

PHOTOGRAPHER: FINCH, F. E., QM2, USN, UDT - 11 DET "C"

FOCAL LENGTH: 6" NEGATIVES: 4 X 5
BEACH PHOTOS OF NIS BEACH 22, UTOPIA

UTOPIA
2
NISBEACH 22
EXIT AT LEFT FLANK
031800T JUNE 1956

UTOPIA
4
NIS BEACH 22
EXIT AT RIGHT FLANK
031800T JUNE 1956

UTOPIA-
3
NIS BEACH 22
BEACH CENTER LOOKING INLAND
NOTE TANK TRAP IN FRONT
OF TREE RIGHT SIDE
031800T JUNE 1956

UTOPIA
5
NIS BEACH 22
CLOSE UP TO TANK TRAP
IN CENTER OF BEACH
031800T JUNE 1956

UNCLASSIFIED

chartmaking

SPECIFICATIONS

DIMENSIONS: The maximum dimension of original charts shall be 36" x 36". The command requesting survey information may select the specific scale to which UDT Survey charts will be drawn. If scale is not specified by the requesting command, the UDT concerned will exercise selection. If chart will not fit within 36" x 36", it shall be in two or more sections.

SCALE: The scale will normally be 1:900 (1 inch = 25 yards) or 1:1800 (1 inch = 50 yards). In circumstance where beach length is unusually long, scales of 1:2700 (1 inch = 75 yards) or 1:3600 (1 inch = 100 yards) are permissible to permit inclusion of entire beach on one chart. The scale will be indicated both numerically and by a graphic bar scale.

FORMAT: Data will be neatly and symmetrically placed on survey charts as conditions permit. Leave space in each corner and at the top and bottom of the chart for identifying data, page numbers, etc. In most cases, lettering on charts will be done with mechanical lettering guides without ink borders. However, it is permissible to draw a chart freehand whenever speed of transmission is more important than neatness of appearance (as in the case of a combat recon conducted immediately prior to H-hour). "Nautical Chart Symbols and Abbreviations" (H.O. CHART NO. 1) shall be followed whenever practicable. If non-standard symbols are used, their meaning shall be indicated.

Normally three vertical cross sections shall be on survey charts to show bottom conditions opposite beach centers and near the right and left flanks. Vertical (1" = 10 feet) and horizontal scales, 1" = 50 yards shall be indicated on the sections. The datum line and the one, two, and three fathom curves shall be drawn on the chart.

CLASSIFICATION: UDT Survey Charts will be assigned the minimum classification of CONFIDENTIAL. Higher classification shall be assigned if appropriate.

PROCEDURES

1 _____

Lay out a sheet of 10 x 10 graph paper large enough to accommodate the prospective chart. (Not to exceed 36 x 36 inches). Allow enough space for a 1" margin all around the chart (which is to be included in the 36 x 36 inches), the amount of backshore to be included, corrected soundings out to 18' (unless otherwise directed), and an additional 12" or so for the legend, scale bar, area inset, and north arrow.

NOTE: The 10 x 10 graph paper is marked off in 1" squares which are in turn sub-divided into 100 equal squares. On a horizontal scale of 1:900, each 1" square equals 25 yards of "ground distance", thus, each 1/10th" square equals 2.5 yards.

2 _____

Lightly draw in Base Line across the upper portion of the sheet of graph paper, about where the HWL will be:
  a. The base line will NOT show on the completed chart but will serve as a reference in drawing it.
  b. The base line will immediately establish the shape of the beach being drawn. Once the base line is on the chart and affixed with a bearing, everything put down after the base line becomes, in distance and bearing, relative to it.

3 _____

STEP 3: Draw in the High Water Line (HWL):
  a. Starting at the left flank (LF) draw a light dot every 25 yards along the base line, either right on or to the landward or seaward of the base line as indicated by the Cartographer's notes.
  b. Draw in a heavy black line, in a series of french curves, connecting all the dots.
  c. The HWL will terminate at the lanes marking the left and right flanks of the beach.
  d. The letters "HWL" will be printed at either end of the cut off line.

4 _____

Establish Beach Flanks - The letters LF and RF will be used to pinpoint the location of the left and right flanks of the beach being drawn. They are located between the HWL and Datum line, whenever possible.

5 _____

Correct and draw in the soundings.
  a. All soundings are corrected to area datum (e.g., MLLW on West Coast of CONUS) and are expressed in feet. (See section D of this chapter for information on determining height of tide).
  b. Individual soundings are drawn in on range, at 25 yard intervals, from the base line, seaward.
  NOTE: Combat reconnaissance soundings are drawn in, on range, at whatever distance they fall on from the HWL, seaward.
  c. Soundings are drawn in lightly, relative to the heaviness of the HWL, Datum Line, and the 1, 2 and 3 fathom curves.

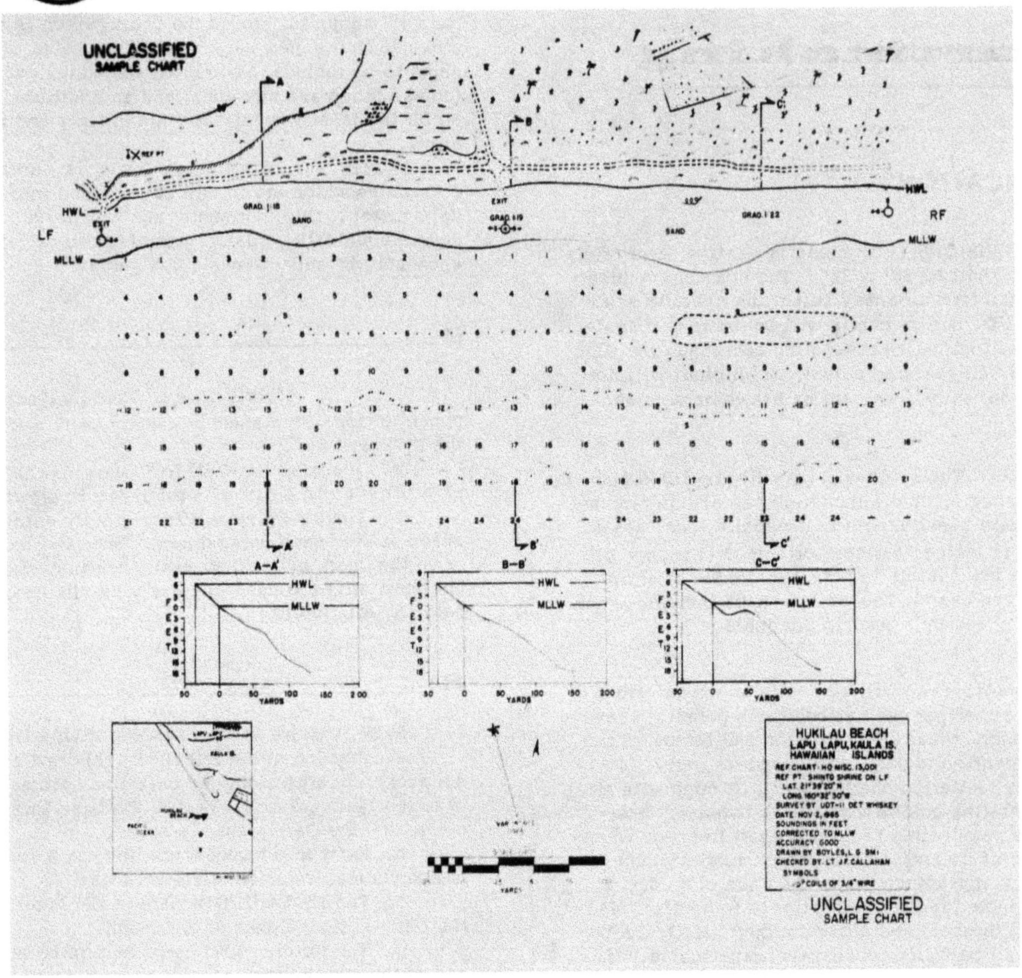

6

Draw in the Datum Line:

a. Draw a heavy black line in a series of french curves inter polating between the seaward most zeros and the first sounding. (The distance depends on the depth of the first sounding.)

b. Like the HWL, the Datum Line (e.g., MLLW) will terminate at the lanes marking the left and right flanks of the beach.

c. The letters designating the Datum (e.g., MLLW) will be printed at both ends of the cut-off line.

d. This line is often referred to as the reference or datum plane.

7

Draw in the 1, 2, and 3 fathom curves:

a. The 1 fathom curve is a dotted line, drawn in a series of french curves, connecting all the landward most (corrected) six foot soundings.

SYMBOL USED: (............................)

b. The 2 fathom curve is a line of sets of 2 dots and is drawn, in a series of french curves, connecting all the landward most (corrected) 12 foot soundings.

SYMBOL USED: (.. .. ..)

c. The 3 fathom curve is a line of sets of 3 dots and is drawn, in a series of french curves, connecting all the landward most (corrected) 18 foot soundings.

SYMBOL USED: (... ... ...)

8

Draw in Obstacles:

a. Draw in both man-made and natural obstacles. Anything that may hinder the proposed landing (e.g., cusps, submerged rocks, partially awash or submerged wrecks, scullies, berm scarps, sandbars, rails, etc.,) may be considered an obstacle.

b. Obstacles shall be drawn on the chart in proper proportion to the rest of the information as near to scale as possible.

c. Obstacles will be recorded on the swimmer's slates and in the Cartographer's notes.

9

Draw in Backshore:

a. Draw in as much backshore as is appropriate or as much as is specified in the operational order. Draw as near to scale as possible.

b. Include prominent landmarks (especially if they appear on the reference chart or map used in conjunction with the UDT charts); they are important to boat officers and coxswains who have to land boats on the beach. Include terrain features and any other information which may be helpful to the landing party. This information comes from the Cartographer's beach notes.

10

Establish Reference Point:

a. Ensure that the reference point is a prominent land feature. Indicate the location of the reference point by drawing in a small cross, with the intersection of the cross at the exact geographical point on the chart, and by printing in the symbol REF. PT.

b. The base line and reference point or points can be related to each other by taking compass cuts from known positions along the base line, or by a range and bearing to the REF. PT. from a known position on the base line.

NOTE: For a reference point try to choose some prominent natural terrain feature (mountain, river mouth, etc.), that may be found on H.O. reference chart or AMS map that was used in helping to locate and set up the beach. If this is not possible, any man made or natural feature usable to a boat coxswain or ship (such as a hill, a house, a lone tree or a wreck) may be used. The reference point will be named in the legend. If there is absolutely no feature available the LF or RF will be used for a reference point.

11

Draw in Beach Profiles:

a. A minimum of two profiles is desired. They will show bottom conditions opposite the part of the beach they are drawn.

b. They will be labeled in order from LF to RF; A-A', B-B, and C-C', etc. In selecting a lane to profile try to choose one that illustrates average bottom conditions in the beach area it represents.

c. Profiles will be drawn to a horizontal scale of 1:1800 (1" = 50 yards) with the yard scale printed under each separate profile enclosure. They will be drawn to a vertical scale of 1" = 10 feet with the foot scale printed vertically, in 3 foot increments, to the left of each separate profile enclosure (label each scale).

d. The area of the chart shown in profile will be indicated by a broken line (the break in the line will normally extend from the HWL to the 18' sounding; however, it will start below the HWL if there is more than 50 yards of foreshore) labeled at its upper end with the letters A, B, or C and at the lower end with the symbols A', B', or C'.

e. The outside dimensions of the three profile enclosures will be governed by the size of the largest one. They will be of equal length and height on the complete chart and will be drawn to the next longest 50 yards.

The length of the largest profile enclosure will be determined by the length of the longest of the three nearshore gradient lines.

If the terminate point of the nearshore gradient line falls on a mark 205 yards to the right of Datum (0 point), the profile enclosure will extend to the 250 yard mark. Profile enclosures will always be drawn to an even 50 yard mark. If the terminate point falls on the 195 or 200 yard mark, then the enclosure will be 200 yards long. PROVIDED - neither of the other two nearshore profile lines exceeds 200 yards in length.

f. Foreshore profiles will show all of the foreshore if there is 50 yards or less and at least 50 yards if the foreshore is greater than 50 yards.

g. The nearshore profile will be drawn in from the Datum (0 point) to the 18' mark as determined from the vertical scale to the left of each profile enclosure.

It will not be drawn in the profile enclosure until the corrected soundings have all been printed in on the chart.

The nearshore profile line will be drawn in a series of french curves.

h. The foreshore profiles will be drawn in from the Datum (0 point) to the HWL provided the distance between these two points is not greater than 50 yards. If the distance between them is greater than 50 yards, the foreshore profile line will terminate at the left border line of the profile enclosure.

The distance between the Datum and HWL is determined by actual measurement of the distance between the two lines already plotted on the chart. This is done in the following manner:

(a) Starting at "O" Datum, move left on a hor-

izontal plane until the actual, measured distance to the HWL is reached, even if you have to travel beyond the left border of the profile enclosure.

(b) When the HWL is reached, move upward vertically until the height of the Diurnal Tide Range (shown in the Tide Tables for the reference station used to obtain correction) is reached and make a mark.

(c) Place a straight edge connecting the mark at the tide range and the "O" point Datum inside the enclosure. If the mark is on or inside the left border of the enclosure, draw a solid line connecting the two points. If the mark is to the left of the left border of the enclosure (as in the case of a foreshore distance greater than 50 yards), draw a solid line starting at the left border and terminating at the "O" point Datum.

The HWL will be drawn in by drawing a solid, horizontal line across the profile enclosure on the Diurnal Tide Range level.

If the foreshore distance is greater than 50 yards or exactly 50 yards in length, it will terminate at both enclosure borders.

If the distance is less than 50 yards, the line will start at the mark made when plotting the foreshore gradient and be drawn to the right border of the enclosure and down to the bottom enclosure.

12

Print in Each Gradient:
The foreshore gradient figure will be printed in the foreshore area of the chart just beneath the lowest part of the upper profile indicator lines.

The correct figure is determined from the foreshore plot already made in the profile enclosures:

SAMPLE BEACH GRADIENT PROBLEM
Distance from "O" point to HWL = 40 yards
Distance up to Diurnal Tide Level = 6 feet
a. Change horizontal distance to feet. Answer: 120'.
b. Divide height of Diurnal Tide Level into horizontal distance. Answer: 20 feet.
c. Foreshore rises toward Diurnal Tide Level 1 foot every 20 feet. Foreshore Gradient = 1:20

13

Place North Arrows:
True and Magnetic north arrows are required. The True north line will be topped with a star and the Magnetic north line will be topped with a half arrow. The variation information may be printed at the apex of the north arrows (taken from reference chart). The annual increase or decrease will not be put on the chart.

The north arrows are drawn in at angles that are properly related to each other and to the base line.

The north arrows are drawn in on chart center directly above the graphic bar scale and between the legend and area inset enclosures, when space and symmetry permit.

Variation between true north and magnetic north will be brought up to date. Variation should be taken from reference chart, if it is to be put on the chart.

14

Draw in the Graphic Bar Scale:
A graphic bar scale is drawn on the chart center just above the lower margin line.

Printed above the bar scale will appear:
"Scale 1:900" (or whatever scale is used).
Printed under the bar scale will be the word "Yards" to indicate the increments.

The bar scale indicates the scale of the chart itself and not of the profiles, which have a separate scale included adjacent to the profile enclosures.

A graphic bar scale is used on UDT charts to provide an accurate scale, even if the chart has been reduced or enlarged for operational purposes.

"When working with gradients - work in like terms."

15

Draw in Area Inset:
The area inset is a 4' x 4' actual tracing of an appropriate section of the reference chart or map.

It will include some prominent features, a True north arrow (oriented due north - straight up and down), a small arrow pointing to the center of the beach where the recon took place or to a flank (label arrow LF or RF accordingly), and if practicable, the reference point shown on the chart. Outside and under the lower right hand corner will be printed the number of the reference chart from which the tracing was made. If it was drawn without the use of an H.O. chart, the words "not to scale" will be outside and under the lower right hand corner.

16

Print in Type Bottom:
In various representative areas of the chart, Nearshore, Foreshore, and Backshore print in the type bottom found at that spot, e.g., sand, rock, lava, mud, gravel, etc.

Type Bottom symbols may be abbreviated and the abbreviations will be taken only from H.O. Chart No. 1.

17

Classify the Chart:
In the upper left hand corner of the chart and in the lower right hand corner beneath the legend enclosure, print in the classification assigned to the chart in large letters (as indicated on the pen and template guide sheet for drawing charts.)

18

Draw in Legend:
The legend enclosure will be in the lower right hand corner of the chart whenever practical and will include all of the following information:

a. Beach name and general location.
b. Reference Chart.
c. Reference Point.
d. Geographic/grid coordinates of the reference point (or the coordinates of some other identifiable point if reference point is not on the chart).
e. Unit conducting survey.
f. Date
g. Datum plane and units in which soundings are expressed (preferably feet).
h. Person drawn by.
i. Person checked by.
j. An evaluation of the accuracy of the chart. (Good, Fair, or Poor).
k. Symbols (as necessary. Those taken from H.O. Chart No. 1 need not be indicated).

19

Obtain from the Photographer all information concerning the location of photos, photo numbers, and direction camera was pointing. Draw the symbols used to put photo information on the master copy of the chart.

Where symbols conflict with pertinent information on chart, arrows can be used to indicate True position.

RECOMMENDED TEMPLATES AND PEN SIZES FOR UDT CHARTS
CLASSIFICATION: 350 Pen 4
BACKSHORE, GRADIENT, SOUNDINGS, AND BOTTOM: 140 Pen 2
HWL, MLLW, A-A', HWL, AND MLLW IN PROFILES, LOCATION OF BEACH: 200 Pen 3
NUMBERS AROUND PROFILE: 140 Pen 2
RF, LF, AND BEACH NAME: 240 Pen 3
REST OF LEGEND LETTERING: 140 Pen 2
YARDS UNDER PROFILE: 140 Pen 2
FEET LEFT OF PROFILE: 175 Pen 2
VARIATION, SCALE LETTERS AND NUMBERS: 120 Pen 1
ALL LETTERING IN INSET AND H.O. CHART # UNDER INSET: 100 Pen 0
ALL LINES CAN BE DRAWN WITH BOW PEN IF PREFERED OR USE FOLLOWING PENS:
   HWL, MLLW, AND A-A' LINES: Pen 3
ALL PROFILE LINES, INSET AND LEGEND BORDERS, ARROW: Pen 2
BACKSHORE DRAWING, INSET DRAWING, AND SCALE DRAWING: Pen 1
"X" AT REF. PT., 1, 2, and 3 FATHOM CURVE DOTS: Pen 3
   NOTE: The reason for the heavy lines is that they show up better on the Ozalid machine. On special occasions you may have to use a #0 pen for lettering or drawing but you should avoid it if you can. Make sure all lines and letters are inked heavy as weak inking will not come out distinct on the Ozalid machine.

UDT CHART CHECK OFF SHEET

CHECK

_____ CLASSIFICATION (UPPER LEFT, LOWER RIGHT)
_____ LF
_____ RF
_____ HWL
_____ DATUM LINE (MLLW, MLW, MLWS, ETC.,
_____ OVERLAY MARKS
_____ REF. PT. (MARKED)
_____ SANDBARS
_____ DEPRESSIONS
_____ FORESHORE GRADIENT
_____ HINTERLAND DETAIL
_____ FORESHORE COMPOSITION
_____ OBSTACLES (IF ANY)
_____ ONE, TWO, AND THREE FATHOM CURVES
_____ BOTTOM COMPOSITION
_____ AT LEAST TWO PROFILES
_____ HWL   ON PROFILE
_____ DATUM LINE   "   "
_____ DEPTH SCALE   "   "
_____ YARD SCALE ON PROFILE
_____ PROFILE ARROWS
_____ NORTH ARROW
_____ SCALE (1:900, 1:1800, ETC.)
    AREA INSERT
_____   TOWN NAMES
_____   RIVER NAMES
_____   OCEAN, BAY, GULF
_____   ARROW INDICATING BEACH

_____ NAME OF BEACH
_____ NIS NUMBER (IF APPLICABLE)
_____ BEACH COLOR CODE
_____ REF. CHART
_____   AMS
_____   HO
_____   REF.PT. (IDENTIFY)
_____ LAT.
_____ LONG.
_____ GRID COOR.
_____ SURVEY BY:

_____ DATE
_____ SOUNDING IN FEET
_____ CORRECTED TO (MLLW, LLW, LWS, ETC.)
_____ ACCURACY: (EXC. GOOD, FAIR, POOR)
_____ DRAWN BY
_____ CHECKED BY
_____ SYMBOLS (IF NOT TAKEN FROM H.O. CHART #1)
_____ CHECK FOR NEATNESS AND SYMMETRY
_____ SYMBOLS AND PHOTO NUMBERS IN APPROPRIATE PLACES

udt survey report

COMPHIBPACINST 3820.8B
25 May 1965

UDT SURVEY REPORT FORMAT

Note: Use applicable phrases shown in parenthesis.

Survey Report of (NIS number or name assigned to beach) (UDT Team No. and Det) (Other):

Date and Time of UDT Survey: _____

Reference(s): (H.O.) (C.S.) (B.A.) Chart _____ (Scale 1: ____)
AMS Series _____ Sheet _____ (Scale 1: ____)
Special Map No. _____ (Scale 1: ____)

Photographs (ground) attached _____
(Left flank) _____ (Right flank) _____ (Center) _____ other _____

Location:
Latitude _____ Longitude _____
(UTM): _____

Reference Point:
Latitude _____ Longitude _____
(UTM) _____

1. **Introduction:** Include type of reconnaissance; i.e., UDT (combat swimmer, night, line controlled, administrative) or other. Describe appearance and location, in relation to the beach, of the reference point (an easily identifiable semi-permanent landmark). Give method used to determine location coordinates (from chart, by navigational fix, etc.) and hinterland features (from photography, chart or by eye and distance pacing). List other beach information such as: (1) location relative to landmarks such as town, rivers and reference point; (2) the facing of the beach in degrees; (3) the shape of the beach and the length surveyed; (4) prominent features which would aid ships in locating the beach from offshore.

2. **Offshore:** Include depths, navigational hazards, bottom conditions, currents and anchorages between open sea and the five fathom curve.

3. **Nearshore:** Include conditions between the five fathom curve and the sea level datum line, such as the nature of the bottom, underwater obstacles

COMPHIBPACINST 3820.8B

(natural and artificial), depths and gradients tabulated as follows from the three fathom curve to the datum line:

Average distance from datum line to 1 fathom curve: _____
Average distance from 1 fathom curve to 2 fathom curve: _____ yards
Average distance from 2 fathom curve to 3 fathom curve: _____ yards
Average gradient from datum line to 1 fathom curve: 1: _____ yards
Average gradient from 1 fathom curve to 2 fathom curve: 1: _____
Average gradient from 2 fathom curve to 3 fathom curve: 1: _____
Average nearshore gradient (datum line to 3 fathom curve): 1: _____

4. Winds, Tides, Currents and Surf: Describe the state of the tide, currents, surf, and wind force and direction at the time of the survey. The standard SUROB format (see COMPHIBPACINST P03840.3 series) may be used.

5. Foreshore: Give the length of the beach, the length of the usable portion(s), the width of the foreshore measured from the datum line to the upper limit of normal wave action, the composition of the beach and the foreshore gradient. An estimate of trafficability in terms of foot trafficability (running and walking), and the type wheeled and tracked vehicles that can be supported. Use available clues such as vehicle tracks and heel prints; state what made them and give their depths. Locate and describe obstacles on the foreshore and exits to the backshore.

6. Backshore. Give length, width and gradient. Include the height and continuity of berm scarp, sand dunes, and cliffs. Indicate the composition of the backshore and make a trafficability estimate. Describe exits from the beach and into the hinterland including information on bridge and road capacities, etc.

7. Hinterland: Give a succinct description of the terrain behind the beach, including mention of such factors as slope, vegetation, drainage, habitation, roads, obstacles, defensive installations and other significant features. Locate and describe possible helicopter landing sites.

8. Evaluation: If a complete beach study is being prepared, evaluate the types of landing ships and craft which could utilize the beach (comment on factors which reduce visability). Reports of actual landings should be included. Comment on the need for beach matting and any dozing or demolition work required. Evaluate the accuracy of the hydrographic data, the geographic location data, and the beach hinterland information in the report.

SUROB Report

GENERAL: Observe the surf for 100 breakers when making an administrative SUROB. Combat type SUROB's should be based on 50 breakers if at all possible. During an amphibious exercise, SUROB's are generally taken by UDT every other hour from H-12 to H-6 and hourly from H-6 to H-hour.

COMPOSITION
HEADING: The location and Date-time Group of observation.
ALFA: Significant Breaker. (The average of one third of the largest breakers observed). Report to the nearest half foot.
BRAVO: Maximum Breaker. (The largest breaker observed). Report to the nearest half foot.
CHARLIE: Period. (The time between breakers). Record to the nearest half second.
DELTA: Percentages of types of breaker. (Spilling, Plunging of Surging).
ECHO: Angle formed by the lines of breakers and the water's edge. Record in degrees. Also, the direction in which the wave is travelling (toward right or left flank looking landward).
NOTE: When determining breaker angle, observe the entire length of the breaker for the best perspective.
FOXTROT: Littoral current to nearest half knot. Also, the direction in which the current is heading, (left or right looking landward.)
NOTE: A one knot current moves a floating object 100 feet in one minute. When determining Littoral current, use a floating object which is not greatly affected by the wind (such as a bottle partially filled with sand).
GOLF: Minimum and maximum number of lines of breakers in the surf zone and the width of the surf zone, in feet.
HOTEL: Remarks (wind, weather, visibility, etc.)

SAMPLE SUROB
SUROB RED BEACH 181215U X ALFA 3 PT 5 X BRAVO 4 PT 0 X CHARLIE 12 PT 5 X DELTA 10 PLUNGING 75 SPILLING 15 SURGING X ECHO 10 FROM RIGHT X FOXTROT 0 PT 5 LEFT SET X GOLF 2 TO 3 LINES in 125 FOOT SURF ZONE X HOTEL VIS ONE HALF MILE OF FOG.

Beach Terminology

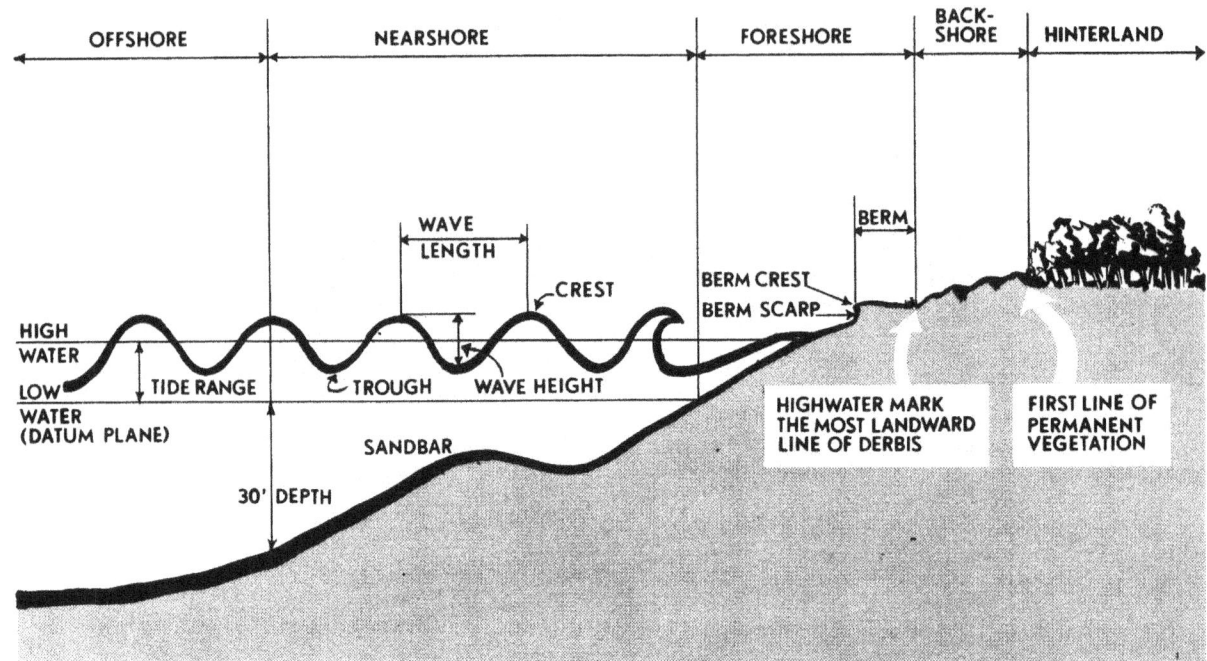

types of breakers

SPILLING: The wave becomes unstable at the crest and forms white water at the crest. The white water (foam) expands slowly down the front face of the breaker. The breaking action is mild.

PLUNGING: The wave crest advances so much faster than the base of the wave that it falls almost into the trough with a violent action. The resulting foam appears almost instantly over the complete front. At times, AIR is caught in the breaker as it tumbles forward, creating a type of explosion.

SURGING: The wave crest tends to advance faster than the base of the wave, suggesting the formation of a plunging breaker. However, just before breaking completely, the wave base advances faster than the crest, the plunging is arrested, and it is generally found at steep gradients.

AWASH	The condition of being exposed at any stage of the tide between high water and the chart datum.
BACKRUSH	The Seaward return of the water following the uprush of the waves.
BACKSHORE	The area between the HWL and the line of first permanent vegetation.
BAR	See SAND BAR
BEACH	A strip of sand, pebbles, or other unconsolidated material extending from the MLLW Line inland to the line of first permanent vegetation. Beaches are comprised of a Foreshore and a Backshore.
BEACH EXIT	Any <u>artificial</u> or <u>natural</u> feature of the terrain that may be used for the movement of troops and vehicles from the beach to the coastal terrain.
BEACH FIRMNESS	The ability of the beach to support weight trafficability; the ability of the Beach to sustain movement of military vehicles.
BEACH FLANKS	Imaginary boundaries of any beach. Every beach has a Left and Right Flank. (<u>labeled from seaward</u>)
BEACH GRADIENT	The slope of the beach expressed as a ratio. <u>When working with gradients work in like terms.</u> GRADIENT TERMS FLAT less than 1:120 MILD 1:120 to 1:60 GENTLE 1:60 to 1:30 MODERATE 1:30 to 1:15 STEEP More than 1:15
BEACH LENGTH	The length along the beach at the water's edge at high water and/or low water between the ends of the beach. Usable beach length is the overall length minus any unusable parts; that is, separated or obstructed portions.
BEACH PROFILE	A graphic representation of a cross section of a beach at right angles to the shoreline at a given point indicating the

	widths and gradients of the foreshore and backshore as well as the nearshore underwater gradients.
BEACH SWALE	An elongated depression in the foreshore or backshore or behind the beach, generally paralleling the shoreline and formed by wave action. Swales separate beach ridges.
BEACH WIDTH	The horizontal dimensions of the beach measured at right angles to the shoreline from the line of extreme low water inland to the landward limit of the beach (the coastline).
BERM	An almost horizontal portion of the beach formed by wave action (usually during higher than normal tides). It generally has a landward slope. Their composition is usually softer and more loosely packed than the rest of the backshore. Two important features are the BERM CREST and the BERM SCARP.
BERM CREST	The BERM CREST is merely the <u>peak</u> of the BERM at the top of the Scarp.
BERM SCARP	The BERM SCARP is the <u>vertical wall</u> on the seaward side of the BERM, and may vary in height from a few inches to several feet.
BOTTOM SEDIMENTS	Unconsolidated material such as clay, gravel, mud, ooze, pebbles, rock, shell, and shingle that covers the bottom of an ocean or other body of water.
BREAKER	A wave breaking on the shore, over a reef, etc. Breakers may be roughly classified into three kinds, although there is much overlapping:
BREAKER HEIGHT	The vertical distance from the tip of the wave crest at breaking to the trough line. (The trough line is essentially at the same elevation as the trough immediately preceding the breaking crest.)
CHART DATUM	The plane or level to which soundings or a chart are referred. It is usually taken to correspond to a low water stage of the tide. Also the intersection of a given parallel and meridian to which horizontal positions are referred; commonly the equator and meridian of Greenwich.
COASTLINE	The line separating the backshore part of the beach from the coastal terrain; the landward limit of ordinary storm waves. It may be marked by a change to a belt of old beach deposits and dunes more or less stabilized by permanent vegetation or by wave-cut cliffs and an immediate change to land forms and vegetation characteristic of the interior.
CURRENT	A horizontal movement of water. There are four types of currents: TIDAL: Caused by change of tide. WIND: Caused by local winds. LITTORAL: Moves parallel to the beach. Caused by quartering surf. RIP: Narrow current running seaward through surf zone. Usually an escape for LITTORAL currents.
CUSPS	A hydrographic feature usually occurring on a single beach and having the appearance of a succession of semicircles of equal size. They vary in length from about 20 to 30 feet to over 100 feet and in vertical depth from one to two feet.
DRIFT	Speed (KNOTS) with which a current moves.
DUNE	See SAND DUNE
FATHOM CURVE	An imaginary line which connects the landward most soundings of the same depth. Usually shown on a UDT chart as a series of dots.
FIRM BEACH	A beach which will support the weight of men and vehicles and allow their movements without special equipment or aids.
FLANK	The right or left side, when facing in the direction of the objective or viewed from seaward; normally identified by compass bearings.
FORESHORE	The area between HWL and MLLW.
GRADIENT	The slope or inclination of a line or surface as compared to the horizontal, usually expressed as a ratio.
HIGHWATER LINE (HWL)	The line of debris formed at the maximum height reached by each rising tide.
HINTERLAND	The area landward from the line of first permanent vegetation.
LITTORAL CURRENT	See CURRENT
NEARSHORE	The area between MLLW and the five fathom curve.
OFFSHORE	The area seaward of the five fathom curve.
RIPPLE	The ridges formed on the ocean floor by water movement.
RUNELL	An elongated shallow depression formed by waves and/or tidal action in the Foreshore and usually filled with water. Generally parallel to the shoreline.
SAND BAR	An underwater mound of sand formed by water currents.
SAND DUNE	A hill or mound of windblown sand which may or may not have vegetation on top. They are always shifting because of wind action.
SCARP	See BERM
SEA, STATE OF	Description of the sea surface with regard to wave characteristics:

CODE	DESCRIPTION	WAVE HEIGHT (FT)
0	Calm	0
1	Smooth	Less than 1
2	Slight	1 to 3
3	Moderate	3 to 5
4	Rough	5 to 8
5	Very Rough	8 to 12
6	High	12 to 20
7	Very High	20 to 40
8	Mountainous	40 and over

SHORELINE	The intersection of a specified plane of water with the shore.
SOFT BEACH	A beach which will support men and equipment, but which, because of the unconsolidated character of the

	beach materials or the presence of mud or marsh will require the use of tracked vehicles or mats for vehicular movement.
SET	Direction in which current moves.
SURF ZONE	The more or less continuous belt of breakers along a shore or over an obstruction such as a shoal or reef; the area between the outer-most breakers and the limit of wave uprush.
TROUGH	The lowest point between two waves.
TYPES OF BEACHES	There are two main types of beaches: Straight and Curved. There are two types of curved beaches: Convex and Concave.
WATER LINE	The point where the water touches the beach constantly changing with every breaker.
WAVE CREST	The highest part of a wave. Also that part of the wave above still-water level.
WAVE DIRECTION	The direction from which a wave approaches.
WAVE HEIGHT	The vertical distance between a wave crest and the preceding trough.
WAVE LENGTH	The horizontal distance between corresponding points on two sucessive waves measured perpendicularly to the crest.
WAVE PERIOD	The time for a wave crest to traverse a distance equal to one wavelength; the time for two successive wave crests to pass a fixed point.
WAVE UPRUSH	The rush of water onto the beach following the breaking of a wave.

Tide Terminology

CHARTED DEPTH	Water depth as measured from Datum. The actual water level equals CHARTED DEPTH plus heights of tide at that time.
CURRENT	A horizontal movement of water
DRIFT OF CURRENT	The velocity of a current expressed in knots.
SET OF CURRENT	Direction toward which current moves.
TYPES OF CURRENT	
EBB CURRENT	A tidal current that moves away from shore or down a tidal stream.
FLOOD CURRENT	A tidal current that moves toward the shore or up a tidal stream.
LITTORAL CURRENT	A movement of water close to and parallel to the shoreline (generally wave-induced).
OCEAN CURRENT	A movement of water which is more or less permanent in its characteristics, as the Gulf Stream.
RIP CURRENT	(Rip Surf). A narrow current of water flowing seaward through the breaker zone.
TIDAL CURRENT	The horizontal ebb and flow of water due to changes in tide.
WIND CURRENT	A movement of water produced in the open sea by local, impermanent winds.
DIURNAL TIDES	(See Tides; Types of)
DATUM	The standardized plane from which water depth is measured.
DRIFT	The velocity in knots that the current is moving.
EBB CURRENT	The horizontal motion of water away from land, during ebbing tide.
FLOOD CURRENT	Current when the rising tide causes water motion toward the land.
HALF TIDE LEVEL	The plane midway between Mean High and Mean Low Water.
HIGH WATER	(High Tide) the highest level reached by an ascending tide.
LOW WATER	(Low Tide) the minimum level reached by a descending tide.
LOWER LOW WATER	The lower of two low tides in any one day.
LUNAR DAY	Time reckoned by the passage of the moon around the earth. (Usually 24 hours and 50 minutes, as it takes this long for the moon to make one complete revolution). (See Solar Day).
MEAN HIGH WATER	(MHW) the average height of High Waters measured over a long period of time.
MEAN LOW WATER	(MLW) the average height of all low tides. (Reference: Atlantic and Gulf Coast of U. S.).
MEAN LOW WATER SPRING	The average of the low water at spring tides. (Most British admiralty charts use mean low water spring.
MEAN LOWER LOW WATER	(MLLW) the average of the lower of the two daily tides, measured over a long period of time. (Reference datum for Pacific Coast of U. S., Hawaiian Islands, Philippines and Alaska).
MEAN SEA LEVEL	Average level of the ocean.
MIXED TIDES	(See Tides, Types of)
NEAP TIDES	Tides which occur when the moon is in its first or last quarter, (moon is at quadrature). Moon and sun are opposed to each other to produce tides of reduced range. (Lower Highs and Higher Lows). (See Spring Tides).
RANGE OF TIDE	Ordinarily, the difference in height between mean high water and mean

	low water; less commonly, the difference in height between any given high water and the preceding or following low water.
REFERENCE STATION	Some principle ports and points, listed in Table One (1) of the Tide and Current Tables.
SECONDARY STATION	These are contained in Table Two (2) of the Tide and Current Table and consist of most of the ports and points that are not listed in Table One.
SEMI DIURNAL TIDES	(See Tides; Types of)
SLACK WATER	The state of a tidal current when its velocity is near zero. The term is also applied to the entire period of low velocity near the time of turning of the current when it is too weak to be of any practical importance in navigation. (See Stand)
SOLAR DAY	Time reckoned by the passage of the sun around the earth. Usually 24 hours is considered to be one solar day. (See Lunar Day)
SPRING TIDES	Tides which occur near the time of full moon and new moon, at which time the sun and moon act together to produce tides higher and lower than the average. (See Neap Tides)
STAND	A brief period at high or low water during which there is no change in the water level. (See Slack Water)
SUBORDINATE STATION	See Secondary Station.
TIDAL CURRENT	The horizontal movement of water caused indirectly by the tide-producing forces.
TIDAL PERIOD	The time interval between two consecutive like phases of the tide.
TIDE	The periodic rise and fall of sea water which results from the gravitational attraction of the moon and sun acting upon the rotating earth.
TIDE, HIGH	(1) High Water (HW), the maximum height reached by a rising tide. (2) Higher High Water (HHW), the higher of the two high waters of any semidiurnal tidal day.
TIDE, LOW	(1) Low Water (LW), the minimum height reached by a falling tide. (2) Lower Low Water (LLW), the lower of the two low waters of any semidiurnal tidal day.
TIDE, NEAP	A term applied to tides of decreased range occurring semi-monthly when the moon is in the first and last quarters, as a result of the tide-producing forces of the sun and moon acting in opposition to each other.
TIDE, SET OF	The direction towards which a tidal current flows, given in compass points, or preferably, in degrees.
TIDE, SPRING	A term applied to tides of increased range occurring semi-monthly when the moon is new and full as a result of the tide-producing forces of the sun and moon acting in conjunction with each other.
TIDES, TYPES OF	
SEMIDIURNAL	The condition wherein there are two high and two low waters each tidal day with relatively small inequalities in the high and low water heights.
DIURNAL	The condition wherein there is only a single high and a single low water each tidal day.
MIXED	The condition wherein the tides are usually semidiurnal but occasionally are diurnal. The high water and/or low water height differ greatly in an area experiencing mixed tides.

TIDE TABLES

Following is the method used to obtain the condition of the tide at a particular place and time, using the current edition of the Tide Tables published by the U. S. Department of Commerce Coast & Geodetic Survey:

(1) Enter Table #1 for the base station and obtain the predicted high and low water, one of which is before and the other after the desired time (or one hour before the desired time, if on Daylight Saving Time).

(2) Enter Table #2 for the substation, and find and apply the proper corrections to the information obtained from Table #1. Calculate:

    a. The DURATION of the rise (or fall). That is, the time difference between the high and the low tides.

    b. The RANGE of the rise (or fall). That is, the height difference between the high and the low tides.

    c. The TIME ELAPSED between the desired time and the time of the nearest high or low tide.

(3) Enter Table #3.

    a. In the section labeled "Time from the Nearest High Water or Low Water" enter the left hand colum at the number which most nearly agrees with the DURATION found above.

    b. Reading across that horizontal line, find the time which most nearly agrees with the TIME ELAPSED found in 2. c. above.

    c. Read down that column into the "Correction to Height" Section directly below. The CORRECTION sought is in that column and on a line with the RANGE of tide calculated in 2. b. above. (Found in the left hand column).

(4) Apply the correction:

    a. When the NEAREST tide (used in 2. c. above) is high water, subtract the correction.

    b. When the NEAREST tide (used in 2. c. above) is low water, ADD the CORRECTION.

    c. The result will be the height of the tide at the time desired.

CURRENT TABLES

Following is the method used to obtain the condition of the current at a particular place and time using the current edition of the Current Tables published by the US Department of Commerce Coast and Geodetic Survey.

(1) Enter Table #1 and obtain the predicted slack water and maximum current time and VELOCITY. One is before and the other after the desired time (or one hour before the desired time, if on Daylight Saving Time).

151

(2) Enter Table #2 and find and apply the proper correction to the figures obtained from Table #1. Calculate:

a. The time INTERVAL between slack and maximum current.

b. The TIME INTERVAL between slack current and the desired time.

(3) Enter Table #3.

a. Enter at the top at the figure which most nearly agrees with the INTERVAL obtained in 2. a. above.

b. Read that column down to the CORRECTION which is on a line with the TIME INTERVAL calculated in 2. b. above (found in the left hand column).

c. Multiply the maximum current VELOCITY obtained in 1. above. The result will be the velocity of the current at the time desired.

NOTE: Table #4, when used in conjunction with Tables #1 and #2, is very useful for determining periods during which swimmers will not be greatly affected by the current.

Notes

154 MAP ORIENTATION

155 COMPASS AZIMUTHS VERSUS MAP AZIMUTHS

156 DETERMING COMPASS COURSE

156 RESECTION

157 INTERSECTION

157 GRID COORDINATES

158 CONTOUR LINES

MAP-8

CHAPTER EIGHT
MAP READING

Map Orientation

A map is said to be orientated when it lies in the proper relationship to the ground which it represents.

steps

(1) Lay the straight edge of a compass along a North-South grid line.
(2) Rotate the map until the compass reading <u>DUPLICATES</u> the Declination diagram.

Compass Azimuths vs. Map Azimuths

INTRODUCTION: Direction is defined as an imaginary straight line on the map or ground and is expressed as an azimuth.

There are three types of direction printed in the declination diagram in the margin of a map:

(a) True North (The direction to the North Pole. Symbolized by a star).

(b) Magnetic North (The direction in which the magnetic arrow of your compass will point, when used in the area shown on the map. Symbolized by a half-arrow).

(c) Grid North (The direction of the north-south grid lines printed on the map. Symbolized by "GN").

When using a compass to determine the azimuth from one point to another <u>on the ground</u>, the azimuth is measured clockwise from magnetic north and is called a "Magnetic Azimuth". However, when using a protractor to determine the azimuth from one point to another <u>on the map</u>, the azimuth is measured clockwise from Grid North and is called "Grid Azimuth".

Since there is a difference (called the "G-M Angle") between Grid North and Magnetic North, it is necessary to convert one to the other before applying a Grid Azimuth to actual terrain feature, or a Magnetic Azimuth to points on a map. This conversion is done by means of a "G-M Angle Diagram".

CONSTRUCTING A G-M ANGLE DIAGRAM: To construct a G-M Angle Diagram:

(a) Refer to declination diagram, extract the G-M ANGLE, and bring it up to date. Below is a sample declination diagram, followed by explanation of how to bring it up to date.

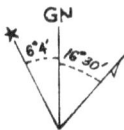

Approximate Mean Declination 1948
    For Center of Sheet
  Annual Magnetic Change 2' Westerly

Figuring for the year 1963, the G-M Angle has been changing 15 years. It has changed two minutes each year, and has changed a total of 30 minutes toward the west. According to the diagram, magnetic north has been moving toward Grid North, so the change must be subtracted from the original G-M Angle (16°30'-30' = 16°). If necessary, round off the G-M Angle to the nearest 1/2 degree. (1' to 14' = 0 degrees; 15' to 44' = 1/2 degree; 45' to 60' = 1 degree.) The current G-M Angle for the declination diagram above is 16° East.

(b) Draw this current G-M Angle.

(c) From the base of G-M Angle draw a line to the right; this line represents any azimuth.

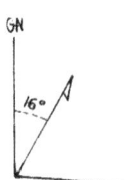

USING THE G-M ANGLE DIAGRAM: When working with a map having an east G-M Angle: To convert magnetic Azimuth to Grid Azimuth; add the G-M Angle.

MAGNETIC AZIMUTH = 200°
G-M Angle   = 16°E
Grid Azimuth   = 216°

To convert Grid Azimuth to Magnetic Azimuth; subtract the G-M Angle:

GRID AZIMUTH = 216°
G-M Angle   = 16°E
Magnetic Azimuth = 200°

When working with a map having a west G-M Angle: To convert Magnetic Azimuth to Grid Azimuth, add the G-M angle.

GRID AZIMUTH = 184°
G-M Angle   = 16°W
Magnetic Azimuth = 200°

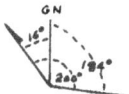

To convert Grid Azimuth to Magnetic Azimuth; subtract the G-M Angle.

MAGNETIC AZIMUTH = 200°
G-M Angle   = 16°W
Grid Azimuth   = 184°

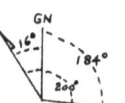

NOTE: The G-M Angle Diagram should be constructed and used each time conversion of azimuth is required.

As a time-saving procedure when working frequently with the same map, construct a G-M Angle Conversion Table on the margin. Using a map having a G-M Angle of 16°E, the following is an example of such a table:

```
FOR CONVERSION OF:
MAG AZ TO GRID AZ: ADD 16°
GRID AZ TO MAG AZ: SUBTRACT 16°
```

DETERMINING COMPASS COURSE

(1) Orientate the map.
(2) Draw a straight line between the point where you are and the point you want to reach.
(3) Lay the straight edge of a compass along this line pointed in the direction you will be traveling.
(4) Read the compass. It will read the course you will follow to reach your destination.
NOTE: This must be done in the actual area or an area with the same declination.

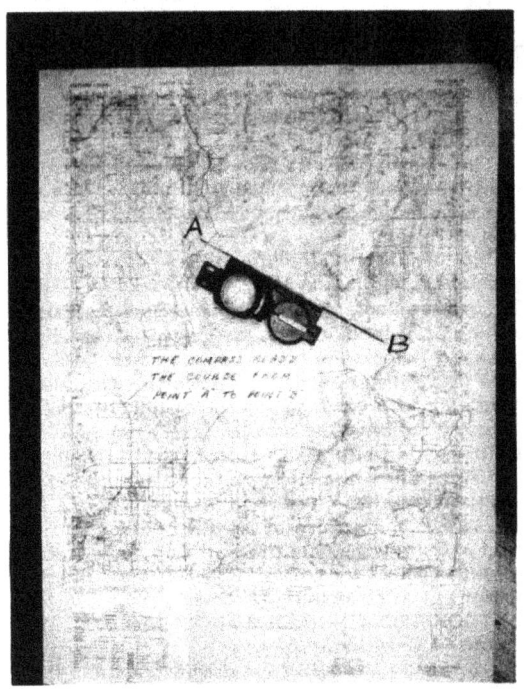

MAP ORIENTATED

RESECTION (SELF-LOCATION)

(1) Orientate the map.
(2) With a compass, get the bearing to a terrain feature that you can identify on your map.
(3) With the map still orientated, lay the straight edge of a compass across the terrain feature.
(4) Rotate the compass until it reads the same bearing as taken to the terrain feature.
(5) With the compass in place, draw a line along the straight edge and extend the line to your SUSPECTED location.
(6) Repeat steps 1 - 5 with a different prominent terrain feature.
(7) The point where the lines cross is your location.
NOTE: The more sightings taken, the more accurate your readings will be.

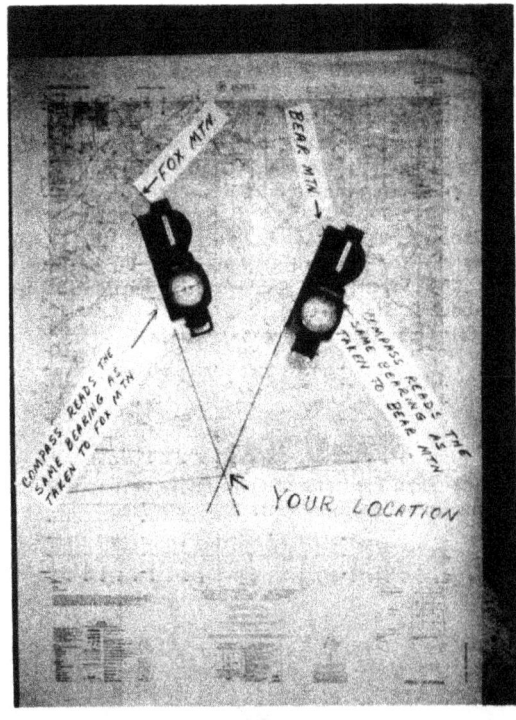

156

INTERSECTION

Intersection is determining on a map, the location of an <u>UNKNOWN</u> point, from one or more <u>KNOWN</u> points.
(1) Orientate the map.
(2) From a known point, take a compass bearing to the unknown point.
(3) Lay the straight edge of a compass across the known point and rotate the compass until it reads the same bearing as taken in step 2.
(4) Draw a straight line along the straight edge of the compass and extend it to the area of the unknown point.
(5) Repeat steps 1 - 4, (after moving to a different prominent terrain feature).
(6) The point where the lines cross is the location of the <u>UNKNOWN</u> point on the map.
NOTE: The angle formed by the crossing lines should be as close to 90 degrees as possible.

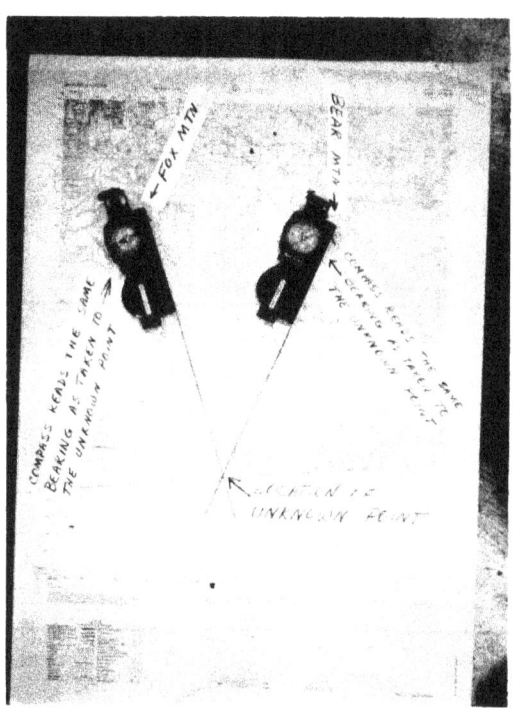

MAP ORIENTATED

GRID CO-ORDINATES

To read Grid Coordinates: Start at the lower left hand corner or the map then read right and up. A four-digit grid coordinate defines a 1000 Meter Grid Square.
EXAMPLE: 1000 meter grid square "2088"

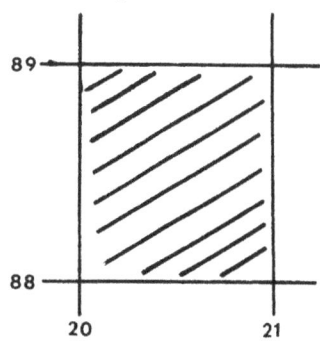

A six-digit grid coordinate defines a 100 Meter Square within a 1000 meter grid square.
EXAMPLE:
       100 meter square "208884"
       100 meter square "201881"

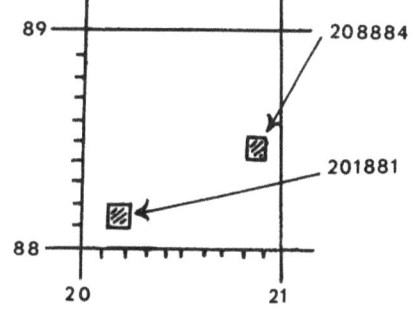

MAP-8 — COUNTOUR LINES

HILL TOP

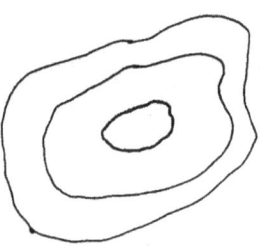

ON MAP
Last closed contour

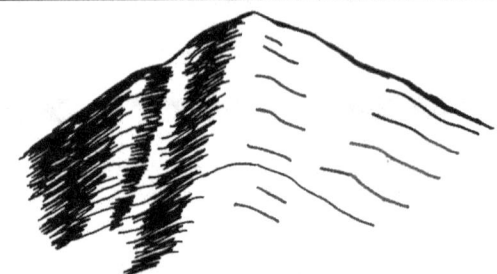

ON GROUND
When you are located on a hilltop, the ground slopes down in all directions

RIDGE

ON MAP
U or V shaped contours with the base of the U or V pointing away from higher ground

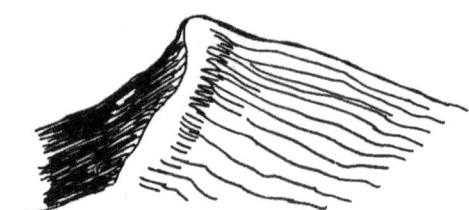

ON GROUND
When you are located on ridge, the ground slopes down in three directions and up in one direction

DEPRESSION

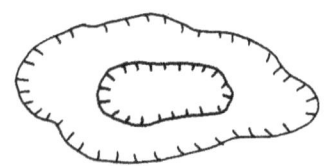

ON MAP
Indicated by depression contours

ON GROUND
When you located in a depression, there is higher ground in all directions

VALLEY

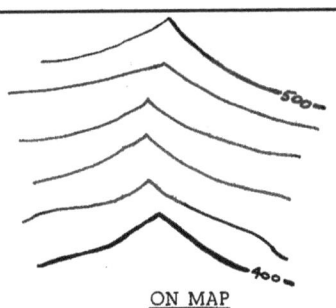

ON MAP

ON GROUND

SADDLE

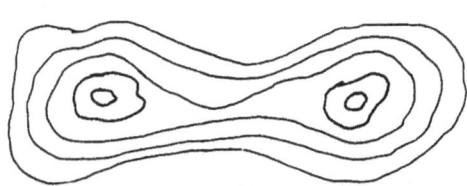

ON MAP
Hourglass or figure eight shaped contours

ON GROUND
When you are located in a saddle, there is higher ground in two directions and lower ground in two directions

160 DUTIES OF A JUMPMASTER

162 CONDUCT OF A PARACHUTE JUMP

165 EMERGENCY PROCEDURES

167 MISCELLANEOUS

CHAPTER NINE
PARACHUTE OPERATIONS

DUTIES OF A JUMPMASTER

GENERAL: There is only one jumpmaster in any one airplane. He has command authority over and responsibility for all airborne personnel in the airplane. The jumpmaster is normally responsible for an inspection of the airplane and personnel, the enplaning and jumping of personnel, and the dropping of aerial delivery containers. He is responsible that all airborne personnel aboard the airplane observe flight saftey regulations and comply with instructions from the pilot. The jumpmaster may or may not jump with planeload. The general duties of a jumpmaster include:

(1) Ensuring that the time schedule for the conduct of the operation is followed as closely as possible, primarily station time (the time at which all parachutists and other participants are in the aircraft and ready for take-off), and that a thorough Parachutists' Briefing is conducted.

(2) Conferring with the Drop Zone Officer on all air-ground procedures.

(3) Delegation of specific duties to other jumpers to assist him in the performance of those duties of jumpmaster outlined herein.

(4) Drawing and assignment of equipment to be jumped by each man and assignment of stick order.

(5) Conferring with pilot on all in-flight procedures.

(6) Briefing the pilot on Drop Zone location, and identification, drop altitude and speed, number and size of sticks, and number of support personnel riding the aircraft other than jumpers.

(7) Ensuring a loading manifest is available for the pilot with last minute corrections entered.

Pre-Jump Briefing

The assigned jumpmaster will conduct or supervise the pre-jump briefing. This briefing will be attended by all personnel listed in the Parachute Operations Schedule plus any others involved in the operation. The briefing will include discussion and explanation of all material contained in the parachute operations schedule. Any special or unusual conditions will be fully explained. The briefing will include, but is not limited to, a discussion of the following:

(1) The method of identification of the Drop Zone, assembly area, and obstacles, using maps and photographs when available.

(2) Smoke and panels for day jumps, lights for night jumps, and emergency signals.

(3) Special equipment, lights, whistles, or other assembly devices.

(4) Method of notifying the Drop Zone Officer that injuries have or have not occurred.

AIRCRAFT INSPECTION

The jumpmaster is responsible for inspection of the aircraft prior to take-off. This inspection will include:

(1) The doorway, to ensure that all sharp edges and projections are well taped.

(2) The aircraft floor, to ensure that it is free of all obstructions.

(3) Inter-communication between the jumpmaster and pilot, to ensure it is operative.

(4) Anchor line cable, to ensure that it is secured on both ends and that it has the proper amount of slack.

(5) Emergency exits, to ensure they are clear and properly marked.

(6) Ensuring that first aid kits are installed in the aircraft.

(7) Ensuring that sick cups are available.

(8) Ensuring that sufficient seats and safety belts are available for all personnel participating in the operation.

(9) Aircraft inspection for night operations will include an inspection of the lights to ensure they are of the color required and are operative.

PERSONNEL INSPECTION

PARA OPS-9

Immediately prior to take-off, a designated jumpmaster will supervise two inspections of each parachutist. One of these will be conducted by a qualified parachute rigger. The other inspection will be made by a designated jumpmaster. When only one rigger is available to conduct second checks, and he is assigned to jump, the second check of his equipment will be made by another jumpmaster or a jumpmaster trainee under the supervision of a jumpmaster. Following is the jumpmaster and rigger check for the T-10 Parachute:

FRONT

HELMET	Properly fitted and fastened.
RISERS	Free of turns from tray to canopy release assembly. Risers will be of equal length.
CANOPY RELEASE ASSEMBLIES	(1) Remove cloth cover. (2) Pull down on metal cover. (3) Check for snug fit of the lug and ensure the release assembly is free of foreign matter. (4) Replace metal cover. (5) Pull down on cloth cover and ensure cloth cover is placed under the lower lip of the release assembly.
CHEST STRAPS	Free of turns and twists and lugs properly inserted into the quick release assembly.
QUICK RELEASE ASSEMBLY	Remove safety clip and check if quick release assembly is functioning properly. Return safety clip.
WAISTBAND	Free of turns and twists. Place through reserve retaining loops. Secure to waist band adjuster with quick release.
RESERVE	(1) Snap fasteners attached to "D" ring with safety wire through the parachutists right snap fastener. (2) Six properly attached pack opening elastics. (3) Ripcord locking pins through cones with riggers seal intact. (4) Ripcord handle positioned on the parachutist's right.
LEG STRAPS	Free of turns and twists from saddle through leg strap loops and leg strap lugs properly inserted into the quick release assembly.
BOOTS	Jump type.

BACK

HELMET	Properly fitted and fastened.
BACK STRAPS	Free of turns and twists and properly adjusted to the parachutist.
SADDLE	Free of turns and twists and well down over the buttocks.
PACK TRAY	(1) Static line breaking loop properly tied with one quarter inch cotton webbing. (2) Static line first "stow" is going to the right side of the parachute pack tray. (3) Static line free of turns and twists and serviceable. (4) Static line snap fasteners will be in serviceable condition with attached safety wire.

(5) Static line placed over parachutist's (right-left) shoulder and attached to the reserve parachute carrying handle.

ADDITIONAL EQUIPMENT CHECKS

(1) Fixed blade knife, day/night flare, and life jacket as prescribed by current regulations.

(2) Static line extensions will be attached to the static line when the following aircraft are used: C-47, C-117.

Attach the static line extension to the snap fastener of the static line. Place safety wire through hole provided and bend.

Cover the snap fastener with cover provided on the extension and tie securely.

Attach the snap fastener of the extension to the carrying handle of the reserve parachute ensuring the snap fastener of the extension is of serviceable condition and the safety wire is attached.

DUTIES BEFORE TAKE OFF

Prior to take-off, the jumpmaster is responsible for ensuring that all parachutists are seated in proper stick order, that aircraft equipment is secure, and that all personnel are seated with seat belts fastened.

DUTIES DURING FLIGHT

Communications between the pilot and jumpmaster are required to relay information from pilot to the stick leader or jumpmaster. If the aircraft intercom system is inoperative, a system of hand signals will be used.

After the aircraft has reached an altitude of 500 feet actual, the jumpmaster may give the command to unfasten safety belts. He will ensure that parachutists keep safety belts fastened whenever specified by the pilot.

The jumpmaster will permit smoking only if the pilot authorizes it. He will take no emergency action unless so directed by the pilot. One of the greatest hazards during emergencies is center of gravity shift caused by personnel moving about in the aircraft.

As the aircraft approaches the Drop Zone, the jumpmaster will check the aircraft alignment with the Drop Zone. Corrections in alignment will be relayed to the pilot. When the aircraft reaches the exit point, if the area is clear, the aircraft is at drop altitude, there is no visual "NO JUMP" signal on the Drop Zone, and the surface winds are within the prescribed limits, the jumpmaster will exit the drift indicator, the wind dummy jumper, the first stick leader, or lead the stick himself, as appropriate.

After determining that it is safe to jump, the jumpmaster will give all standard jump commands to each stick. He will have the Assistant Jumpmaster ensure each man is properly "hooked up."

If, in the opinion of the jumpmaster, an unsafe condition exists, he shall abort the jump or pass, as appropriate.

The jumpmaster, at conclusion of each pass,

will notify the pilot that the parachutists have exited and cleared the aircraft. He will then, with the assistance of the Assistant Jumpmaster, pull in the static lines, unhook and stow them. In the event a decisive wind change is experienced prior to the exiting of all sticks, additional wind drift indicators or wind dummy jumpers may be dropped at the discretion of the jumpmaster. Any other arrangement of stick order as appropriate may be made by the jumpmaster.

JUMPING OF PERSONNEL

Four minutes from the drop zone, the red light goes on and the jumpmaster gives the commands:

GET-READY, STANDUP, HOOKUP, CHECK STATIC LINES, CHECK EQUIPMENT, SOUNDOFF FOR EQUIPMENT CHECK, and STNAD IN THE DOOR in sequence. The pilot notifies the jumpmaster to give the command GO by turning on the green light. The green light is the signal to jump unless one of the following conditions prevails:

(1) There is a no-jump signal (red smoke, panels, or lights) on the drop zone.

(2) There is another airplane below or dangerously close.

(3) Some condition within the airplane precludes a safe exit; fpr example, the ancho-line breaks.

If a parachutist refuses to obey a jump command, the jumpmaster has the man unhook his static line, if necessary, and move to the front of the airplane to be clear of other jumpers who are going to exit.

POST JUMP CRITIQUE

If required for training purposes, a post operation critique will be conducted by the jumpmaster. All participants listed on the parachute operation will be present. The purpose of the critique is to discuss errors and take corrective action to improve parachute operations.

PARACHUTE JUMP

SAFETY REQUIREMENTS

Training jumps are made only when weather conditions permit the pilot and jumpmaster clear visibility of a drop zone while at jump altitude.

Normally, training jumps are not made when ground winds exceed 15 knots for land jumps, and 20 knots for water jumps. The ability of a parachutist to jump and land in high winds successfully varies with his training, experience, physical condition, and the conditions of the drop zone.

Parachute drops will be executed at the airspeeds considered safe for the aircraft being used.

Training jumps are made from altitudes of 1,250 feet from fixed wing aircraft and 1500 feet from helicopters. Combat jumps may be made from as low as 400 feet during daylight hours and 500 feet during the hours of darkness.

BOARDING THE AIRCRAFT

The jumpmaster loads his men so that they are

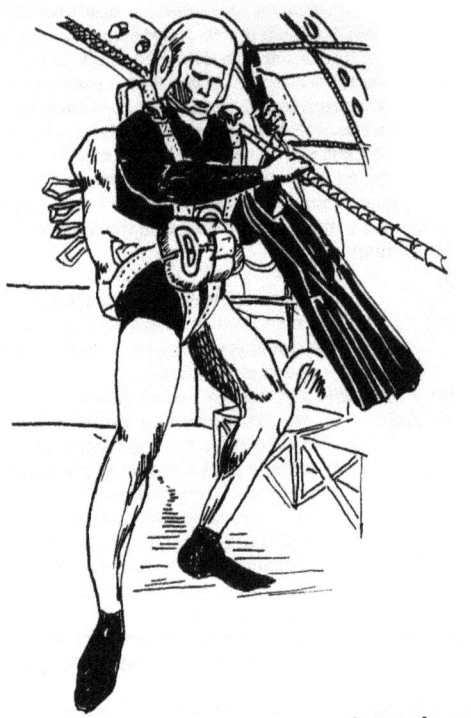

"stand up..."

seated in the desired jumping order. He checks the manifest to ensure that all parachutists are properly loaded and accounted for. When his men are properly seated, he has them fasten their seat belts and reports his readiness to the pilot.

CONUCT IN THE AIRCRAFT

Parachutists must be seated with their seat belts fastened when their airplane is taxing, and during take-off and landings. Helmets are worn during take-offs and landings. When the airplane reaches a safe jump altitude, the jumpmaster instructs the parachutists to unfasten their seat belts. Approximately 20 minutes prior to reaching the drop zone, the pilot notifies the jumpmaster who alerts his men and has them secure any equipment they may have loosened. Four minutes prior to reaching the drop zone, the pilot signals the jumpmaster by turning on the red light at the jump door. The jumpmaster starts the jump command sequence at this time to permit proper execution of the eight jump commands.

JUMP COMMANDS

Instruction in the eight jump commands is started in mockup training and continued through all parachute training. These commands are used to ensure orderly control and movement of personnel within the airplane and to provide a systematic check of equipment and jumping procedures. The command sequence is: READY, STANDUP, HOOKUP, CHECK STATIC LINES, CHECK EQUIPMENT, SOUNDOFF FOR EQUIP-

hook up...

MENT CHECK, STAND IN THE DOOR, GO. The eight jump commands are executed in the same general manner when jumping from either door of the airplane except for the necessary adjustments described below. The detailed execution of these commands is presented for parachutist jumping from the left door, with alternate instructions for the right door indicated within parentheses, thus: left (right).

Arm and hand signals are used by the jumpmaster in conjunction with the verbal commands for the first five of the eight jump commands.

GET READY

The GET READY position is one of alertness, and the GET READY command is given to ready the parachutist for the commands that follow. The parachutist is seated in the airplane with the static line over the left (right) shoulder. When GET READY is given, each man grasps his static line snap in the right (left) hand and holds it out from the body at eye level. He forms a bight near the end of the static line at its juncture with the static line snap and grasps the bight with the left (right) hand so that both the running end of the static line and the static line and the static line snap protrude above the clenched thumb and forefinger. He drops his right (left) hand and holds the static line snap with his left (right) hand so that the opening is at eye level and is pointed toward the tail of the airplane. Leaning slightly forward, he then brings his right (left) foot under the seat and places his left (right) foot to his front in the aisle.

STAND UP

The jumper executes the command STANDUP by rising quickly and turning toward the tail of the airplane in one movement. He grasps the anchor-line cable in his right (left) hand with the palm facing to his left (right) and holds the static line snap close to the anchor-line cable between his right (left) hand and his head. He holds his head on the outboard side of the anchor-line cable.

HOOK UP

At the command HOOKUP the parachutist slips the static line snap over the anchor-line cable from left to right (right to left) and jerks downward to close the static line snap. He then inserts the safety wire in its hole in the static line snap and bends it down on both sides. The parachutist does not release his hold on the static line until he enters the door to exit.

CHECK STATIC LINE

The jumper insures that the static line snap is closed and that the safety wire is properly inserted.

CHECK EQUIPMENT

The equipment check is made in three phases - personal check by each man, check of the pack body and static line of the man to his front, and check of the body and static line of the last man in the stick by the next to last man. At the command CHECK EQUIPMENT, each parachutist checks his own equipment in the following order:

(1) Static line snap, to ensure that it is locked over the anchor-line cable, that the locking button is fully seated, and that the safety pin is inserted and properly bent.

(2) Static line, to ensure that it has not slipped off the shoulder.

(3) The release assembly, to ensure that the canopy does not protrude and that the ripcord handle is in place.

(4) The reserve parachute, to ensure that the canopy does not protrude and that the ripcord handle is in place.

Next, the parachutist checks the pack body of the man to his front to ensure that the static line is not slack or through the risers, that it is over the proper shoulder, and that it has no twists or turns. Further, he ensures that the pack closing flaps are tucked in and the pack opening and closing loops are tied. Upon completing the check, he taps the thigh of the man he has inspected to indicate that the inspection is completed and that his equipment is in order.

After completing the check of the man to his front, the last man and the next to last man in each stick pivot to their left (right). The next to last man then checks the last man's pack, body, and static line.

SOUND OFF FOR EQUIPMENT

Before entering the airplane, men in each stick are numbered consecutively starting with the number 1. The lowest numbered man in each stick is placed nearest the door.

PARA OPS-9

stand in the door.....

......GO!

On the command SOUNDOFF FOR EQUIPMENT CHECK, the man numbered highest in the stick shouts his assigned number and adds, "OK". Thus, if his number is 12 he shouts TWELVE OK. At the same time he slaps No. 11 on the thigh. No. 11 then shouts ELEVEN OK and slaps No. 10. This continues until No. 1 shouts ONE OK. The No. 1 man then moves forward until he is even with the leading edge of the door and grasps the edge of the door with his free hand.

If a man finds something wrong with his own equipment or that of the man to his front, he does not soundoff, but indicates the error to the jumpmaster by raising his free hand. The jumpmaster either corrects the deficiency, or, if he cannot correct the error, removes the man from the stick.

STAND IN THE DOOR

At the command STAND IN THE DOOR, No. 1 shuffles forward with his right (left) foot advanced until the toe of his right (left) foot is one-third of the distance across the door space. He then pivots into the door on the ball of his right (left) foot. His left (right) foot is placed on the door sill, the toe extending about 2 inches over the edge of the door. The right (left) foot is approximately 2 to 4 inches in rear of and 2 to 3 inches to the right (left) of the heel of his left (right) foot, his fingers and thumbs are extended and joined, and his hands are placed on the outside of the door opening. His arms are extended downward so that his hands are on a horizontal line running midway between his hips and his knees. His knees are bent so that the top of his helmet is at least 2 inches below the top of the door. His upper body is straight; head and eyes are straight to the front. This position varies slightly to suit the conformation of the individual. The entire position is one of coiled alertness.

No. 2 shuffles toward the door, closing-up on No. 1 until the toe of his right (left) foot is against the side of the right (left) foot of No. 1, forming a T.

GO

The exit from the aircraft is made by springing up and out from the door at the command GO. This springing action is obtained by simultaneously straightening both knees and by guiding the body forward with both hands on the outside of the door opening. The parachutist springs forward bringing his right (left) foot forward alongside his left (right) foot so that both feet clear the airplane at the same time. The leap plus the pull with both hands and arms should give the parachutist enough momentum to clear the door by at least 2 feet but not more than 3 1/2 feet. As the man clears the door, his legs are straight. He drops both hands over the ends of the reserve parachute with the fingers spread and the palm of the right hand over but not grasping the ripcord handle of the reserve parachute. He holds his elbows tightly to his sides and his feet together.

At the moment he clears the airplane, he counts aloud in normal cadence, "One thousand, two thousand, three thousand, four thousand." If the parachutist does not feel his main parachute open by the time he counts "Four thousand", he activates his reserve parachute.

No. 2 starts into the door as soon as No. 1 starts to clear the airplane. He takes a short shuffle forward, pivots into the correct door position as described above, and follows the No. 1 man at a 1 second interval.

Each man in the stick assumes, in succession, the No. 2 and door positions previously described before making an exit. During qualification training, the command GO is given as each man assumes the door position and at the same time he is tapped sharply on the thigh by the jumpmaster. In unit jumps, the command GO is given only once and each man follows the No. 1 man without further command.

If the jumpmaster is a No. 1 man, he may elect not to lead the stick but stands aside while the No. 2 man assumes the proper door position. The jumpmaster then jumps at the end of the stick or elsewhere as the situation dictates.

5 POINTS OF PERFORMANCE

The five points of individual performance esential in parachute jumps are: Check body position and count, check canopy, keep a sharp lookout during descent, prepare to land, and land.

FIRST: Check body position and count. Upon leaving the door, assume the correct body position, check your body position, and count ONE THOUSAND, TWO THOUSAND, ETC.

SECOND: Check Canopy:

When you feel the parachute open, grasp the risers with your thumbs up and spread them apart. Throw back your head and inspect the canopy for malfunction, deploy your reserve parachute.

The T-10 main parachute frequently has twisted lines and this condition must be corrected. When the suspension lines are twisted, you may not be able to raise your head enough to observe the canopy properly. In this case proceed as follows:

(1) Compare your rate of descent with that of other nearby parachutists. If descending at the same rate, you need not pull the reserve but get the twists out of the suspension lines.

(2) Compare your rate with the other parachutists, activate your reserve parachute immediately.

(3) When other jumpers are not close enough for you to compare rates of descent, activate your reserve parachute immediately.

If your suspension lines are twisted and your rate of descent is not excessive, reach behing and grasp each pair of risers behind your neck, with your thumbs down and exert an outward pull on each pair of risers. Kick in the direction opposite the twist. Continue to pull outward on the risers and to kick until the twists are out of the suspension lines. When the twists are out of your lines, check your canopy and assume the normal position.

THIRD: Keep a sharp lookout during descent. Collisions and entanglements are dangerous and must be avoided. Keep a sharp lookout during descent; stay clear of other parachutists by slipping and check your landing area for obstacles.

FOURTH: Prepare to land. At treetop level or approximately 50 feet from the ground, prepare to land:

(1) Extend your hands straight up, knuckles to the front and grasp a pair of risers in each hand.

(2) Hold your head up and your eyes on the horizon.

(3) Hold your feet and knees together with your knees slightly bent and toes pointed slightly toward the ground so that the balls of your feet will contact the ground first. Maintain sufficient muscular tension in your legs to ensure that your feet and knees stay together throughout the fall and to prevent your legs from collapsing and allowing your buttocks to receive most of the impact.

FIFTH: Land. Upon contact with the ground, execute the landing fall dicated by the position of the body with respect to the line of drift. After landing, recover immediately and collapse the canopy.

PARACHUTE LANDING FALL (PLF)

Most injuries in parachute jumping result from incorrect landings. The PLF is a precise method of landing which enables the parachutist to distribute the landing shock over his entire body and reduce the chance of injury. When moderately tensed, the muscular system of the body is better able to absorb the landing shock than is the bone structure. The knee and hip joints must be unlocked by being slightly bent to prevent these joints from receiving an excessively sharp jolt on landing. Immediate recovery from the PLF is taught so that the parachutist will get to his feet unhesitatingly and collapse his parachute when moderate winds are blowing.

PLF is made in the following manner:

When the balls of your feet strike the ground, rotate your body to the right of left to expose the remaining points of contact to the ground and to avoid falling on your knees. When your feet strike the ground, drop your chin to your chest and bring your hands and elbows in front of your head and chest. Your feet, calf, thigh, buttock, and push-up muscle (muscle behind your shoulder) should make contact with the ground in that sequence. The fall is executed in a fluid, coordinated, and rhythmic manner with the five points of contact following one another rapidly.

The PLF may be made to the right, left, front or rear, depending upon which direction the parachutist is traveling across the ground at the time of impact.

Following are the key points to observe when performing a PLF:

(1) Keep your head erect, looking straight ahead until the moment of impact.

(2) Hold feet and knees together when landing.

(3) Make initial contact with the ground on the balls of the feet.

(4) Keep knees and hips unlocked while turning in the fall.

(5) Drop your chin to the chest and bring the elbows and hands in front of the chest and head upon contact with the ground.

(6) Keep your body muscles tense enough to absorb the hardest part of the landing shock.

MALFUNCTIONS

GENERAL: A malfunction is an improper deployment of the canopy. A malfunction may delay or prevent the opening of the canopy or it may turn the

PARA OPS-9

canopy completely or partially inside out. A partial malfunction is one in which some support is given by a canopy; a complete malfunction offers no support. The parachutist's technique in the use of the reserve varies, according to the type and degree of the malfunction.

When a complete malfunction occurs in the main parachute, deploy your reserve parachute immediately on completion of the 4-second count. Keep your feet and knees together, keep your elbows in to your sides, and release your reserve parachute by giving a vigorous, straight pull of the ripcord handle with your left hand. The reserve canopy will immediately deploy and inflate because of the swift rush of the air. Keep your legs together and your elbows at your sides during deployment to prevent the reserve canopy from going between your legs or under your arms.

A partial malfunction is usually discovered by checking the canopy after the opening action is felt. If your main parachute is not fully inflated when you check the canopy, activate your reserve immediately. If you have a partial malfunction, your reserve canopy may not inflate immediately. If the rush of air is not swift enough to inflate the reserve, it may drop below you. When this occurs, manipulate the reserve canopy to expose more of its surface to the rush of air and cause it to inflate as quickly as possible. Free any suspension lines remaining in the pack tray, grasp a group of them in each hand, and shake them; guide the suspension lines and canopy away from your body in the direction which the wind tends to carry them. These actions help to inflate the canopy.

When the reserve parachute has been activated for a partial malfunction, you may find that you have two inflated canopies. When descending with two inflated canopies, you have no directional control over the parachute. Since you cannot effectively control your directional movements with two inflated canopies, it is imperative that all other parachutists slip clear. Assume the proper landing attitude, reaching high on all four risers of the main parachute, and maintain this attitude until you make contact with the ground. Upon landing, make your recovery as described in section B. When descending with only the reserve parachute inflated, you will find that you can control directional movement by slipping. Assume the proper landing attitude by reaching up and grasping as many suspension lines as possible with each hand. Upon landing, make a quick recovery and collapse your reserve canopy.

TYPES OF MALFUNCTIONS

SEMI-INVERSION (MAY WEST): Characterized by a portion of the canopy and suspension lines being blown through and under the canopy and coming out the other side, giving the T-10 parachute the appearance of a large brassiere.

CIGARETTE ROLL: Characterized by one portion of the skirt having a rolled-up appearance. It may involve as much as one third of the canopy surface. This reduces the lifting surface of the canopy.

BLOWN GORE OR SECTION: Characterized by large rip or tear in the canopy. Dangerous if the hole is larger than a steel helmet. The jumper must activate his reserve parachute at once in the event of any of the above malfunctions. They may dangerously increase the rate of descent of the jumper.

TWISTED RISERS: Often the jumper will find that he is unable to check his canopy because of twisted risers behind his neck. This is an expected occurrence with a bag-packed parachute (60% of all jumps) and should not be regarded as dangerous if the following three rules are applied:

(1) If there are other jumpers nearby and he is descending at the same rate as they, then he should reach behind his neck, grasp the twisted risers, pull them apart vigorously and assist the untwisting by kicking in the opposite direction of the twist. After he gets them untwisted, he checks his canopy. He must check his canopy immediately to discover a possible partial malfunction.

(2) If there are other jumpers nearby with whom he can compare a rate of descent, and he is descending at a faster rate than they, he should activate his reserve immediately.

(3) If there are no other parachutists near the jumper with twisted risers and he cannot tilt his head back to check his canopy, he should activate his reserve immediately.

CANOPY RELEASE ASSEMBLY: The canopy release assembly is an extremely safe item of equipment. However, in the event of an irregularity resulting in premature release of one or both riser groups, either during opening or during descent, the reserve parachute should be activated.

LANDING ON ANOTHER JUMPER'S CANOPY: Should a jumper land upon another jumper's canopy during descent, he must double time or scramble off that canopy as quickly as possible.

SUMMARY: The jumper must have a cautious, alert attitude toward malfunctions and emergencies. He cannot afford to become either cocky or panicky; emergency procedures must be followed instantly and automatically should the jumper discover himself in danger. He must remember that failure of his equipment seldom causes the parachutist's injuries. Eighty per cent of all jumper injuries occur during the fifth point of performance. An alert, well-conditioned paratrooper need not worry about becoming a liability to his unit as a result of injury.

EMERGENCIES

A descending parachute causes an area of partial air compression immediately below the canopy and an area of partial vacuum and descending turbulent air above the canopy for a height of approximately 50 feet. Another parachute falling into this area of partial vacuum and descending air does not capture enough air to stay fully inflated; it may partially collapse and drop the parachutist below the other canopy until the force of unaffected air reinflates the canopy. The lower canopy "steals" the air from the canopy above it when it reinflates, causing the upper most canopy to partially collapse and drop past the lower canopy. This "leap frogging" action is repeated unless corrective action is taken. A parachutist landing

when his canopy is partially collapsed receives a harder landing fall than normal and may be injured. When necessary, vigorous slips are initiated by each parachutist to maintain a lateral interval of at least 10 yards.

When a parachutist passes through one or more suspension lines of another parachute, he firmly grasps whatever portion of the lower parachute he can secure. He then works hand-under-hand down the suspension lines of the lower parachute until each parachutist can grasp and hold the main front lift webs of the other's parachute. Upon contact with the ground, both parachutists release their grip and make a normal parachute landing fall.

Following are the standard procedures to be followed when making emergency landings in water, trees, or high-tension wires:

WATER LANDINGS: Use the same procedure as for "Determined Water Landings", leaving out steps (2) and (8).

TREE LANDINGS: The tree landing position is used to minimize the possibility of injury when forced to land in trees. To assume this position, place your feet tightly together to proctect your crotch. Place your left arm over your eyes and your left hand in your right armpit, palm outward. Place your right arm across your left arm and your right hand in the left armpit, palm outward. Turn your head slightly to the left to protect your face and throat. Maintain this position until your descent is checked. After the descent is checked, get out of your harness. If you are suspended in trees at a greater height than you can drop, release your reserve parachute and slide down the suspension lines and canopy.

HIGH-TENSION WIRE LANDINGS: When forced to make a landing in high-tension wires attempt to prevent your body from contacting two high-tension wires at one time. Place your feet together, extend your arms overhead with elbows straight, and place your hands inside and against the front risers with fingers extended and joined. Keep your head slightly down so that you may observe and at the same time avoid coming in contact with the wires.

MISCELLANEOUS

MASS JUMPING: Mass jumping is the normal technique used to clear parachutists from an airplane quickly to effect a close landing pattern in the drop zone. During mass jumps, parachutists jump from the airplane at a 1-second interval to insure proper spacing in the air and uniform landings within the drop zone. When two jump doors are used, precautions must be taken to prevent simultaneous exit of the lead jumpers in each stick. This action reduces the possibility of entanglements which can occur when two parachutes deploy simultaneously in opposite sticks. In order to have a good body position when the parachute opens, parachutists must execute all movements in a precise manner, including the exit. The parachutist's body position is determined by the correctness of his movements before the parachute opens.

DETERMINED WATER LANDINGS: When making a water jump, the following procedure will be executed in preparation for entering the water and in recovery of parachutes:

(1) After the third point of performance (get clear of other jumpers), remove waist band and loosen left side of reserve parachute.

(2) Put on swim fins.

(3) Turn quick release box to the unlocked position and remove safety clip.

(4) Remove safety covers of Capewell Releases.

(5) At approximately one hundred feet from the water, face into the wind, put fingers on Capewell Releases, BUT DO NOT APPLY PRESSURE AT THIS TIME.

(6) When feet touch water, release the left side Capewell by applying pressure and pulling down on the release. If parachute remains inflated and begins to drag you, release the remaining Capewell.

(7) Press the quick release box, free the leg straps, and remove harness.

(8) Swim to the apex of the parachute and assist boat personnel in recovering the chute by handing them the apex.

T-10

The apex vent (top center of the canopy) is 20 inches in diameter.

The canopy consists of 30 gores; a gore is the portion of the canopy bounded by the skirt, any two adjacent suspension lines, and the apex vent.

Each gore is divided into five sections; a section is that portion of a gore bounded by two adjacent suspension lines and two adjacent diagonal stitchings.

The canopy consists of 30 suspension lines; seven of these lines are attached to each of the two front risers and eight lines are attached to each of the two rear risers.

The diameter of the canopy is 24.5 feet at the bottom of the skirt of the lower lateral band; the canopy is 35 feet at the wide diameter approximately three feet above the bottom of the skirt of the lower lateral band.

The T-10 canopy is mushroom shaped; its silhouette forms a parabola when it is fully inflated.

FUNCTIONING: When the jumper exits the aircraft he falls down and to the rear of the airplane 15 feet before the deployment of suspension lines and canopy begins. The risers and suspension lines deploy first. Next the canopy, packed in the deployment bag, deploy skirt first - a characteristic of the bag-packed parachute. As the jumper continues to fall, the apex of the canopy breaks free from the static line and empty deployment bag which remain attached to the aircraft. The canopy inflates and the jumper receives the opening shock. The deployment and inflation of the T-10 parachute takes from three to four seconds. The jumper falls approximately 100-150 feet during this time interval.

jumpmaster syllabus

In order to ensure that potential jumpmasters have a thorough practical knowledge of jumpmaster techniques, candidates for jumpmaster qualification must be an E-5 or above and must execute the following syllabus for jumpmaster indoctrination:

JUMPMASTER QUALIFICATION PHASE I

HOURS	SUBJECT	METHOD OF INSTRUCTION	DESCRIPTION
ONE	Introduction & Air Department Administrative Procedures and Parachute Regulations.	Lecture	Air Officer or Loft Chief will give procedures to be followed when arranging when arranging for jump. All pertinent parachute instructions will be read by instructor.
ONE	Personnel Equipment and Equipment Containers	Lecture, demonstration, practical work.	A lecture and demonstration by qualified jumpmaster on the wearing, rigging, and packing of bags and equipment by practical application by students.
FOUR	Pre-Flight preparation.	Lecture, demonstration, practical work.	Lecture and demonstration by a jumpmaster on preparation of aircraft, seating arrangements, inter-plane communications, emergency procedure, pre-flight inspection, and personnel conduct followed by student application.
ONE	Water jump.	Lecture	Lecture and classroom demonstration on procedures for preparing to land in water.

PARA OPS-9

TWO	Jumpmaster and rigger checks.	Demonstration & practical work.	Demonstration by a jumpmaster or parachute rigger of the correct method of performing a complete pre-jump check followed by practical exercise by student jumpmaster.
ONE	Free-fall techniques.	Lecture	Lecture by a qualified free-fall parachutist on advanced parachute training, stabilization techniques, and recover from tumbles and spins.
ONEQ	Drop zone officer techniques.	Lecture	Lecture and discussion by a qualified and experiencd drop zone officer describing duties, responsibilities, and marking of DZ.

The second phase of the jumpmaster training shall not be scheduled for formal class work but shall be done under the supervision of qualified jumpmaster on an individual basis and will include:

Self-determined static line jump, day, with GP bag.

Self-determined static line jump, night, with GP bag.

Act as Drop Zone Officer under the supervision of a qualified Drop Zone Officer, day and night.

Pre-jump inspection on aircraft for static line jump on two types of aircraft.

Pre-jump pilot briefing.

Pre-jump parachutist briefing.

Jumpmaster check, static line, T-10.

Self-determined static line water jump, day.

Assist jumpmaster on static line jump.

Jumpmaster static line jump, day and night.

Formal qualification and designation of jumpmaster: Completion of the above syllabus does not automatically qualify a student. Throughout the supervised training the student must display a thorough knowledge of parachuting techniques and jumpmaster procedures and further, he must consistently demonstrate mature judgement, an ability to make responsible and competent decisions, and a confident attitude and composure in performing assigned parachute duties.

The formal designation of Jumpmaster will be made only by the Commanding Officer of the team to which the student is assigned.

NOMINATION PROCEDURE FOR AIRBORNE TRAINING CANDIDATES

To ensure that candidates for schools involving parachute jumping are thoroughly screened and meet the necessary physical requirements for entrance and participation, all candidates must successfully complete the following minimum requirements of the physical fitness test:

Six pull-ups

Twenty-two push-ups.

Twenty sit-ups

Eighty knee bends in two minutes.

One mile run within eight minutes, 45 seconds.

The physical fitness test will be administered by the UDT Air Officer or his designated representative.

Names of candidates and results of above examination will be submitted to the Executive Officer of the team concerned.

Upon recommendation to a school involving parachute jumping all candidates will complete a pre-jump training course conducted by the team to which he is assigned. The course will be designed to familiarize the candidate with the physical exercises and training procedures he can expect to encounter during the Airborne Training Course.

Notes

172 THE EIGHT ENEMIES OF SURVIVAL

173 FOOD

175 WATER

175 EMERGENCY SIGNALS

175 FINDING DIRECTION

176 TRAVEL

177 HEALTH

177 JUNGLE SURVIVAL

178 SHELTER

178 ESCAPE and EVASION

179 SURVIVAL KIT

CHAPTER TEN
SURVIVAL

In recent years many advances have been made in the development of clothing, equipment, and rations for survival, and in the development of techniques for their use. However, regardless of how good equipment is or how good the techniques for its use are, the man faced with a survival situation still has himself to deal with. Man's psychological reactions to the stresses of the survival situation often make him unable to utilize his available resources.

One of the most important psychological requirements for survival is the ability to accept immediately the reality of a new emergency situation and to react appropriately to it.

In the situation where there is more than one survivor, the group's chances of surviving will depend largely on its ability to organize activity. A tight situation does not weld a group together; rather, the more difficult and disordered the situation, the greater are the disorganized group's problems. This is true particularly in the face of common danger, when fear can result in panic rather than concentration.

Whether the survivor is alone or in a group, survival may depend more upon personality than upon the danger, weather, terrain, or the nature of the emergency. Whether fear will lead to panic or act as a spur to greater sharpness, whether fatigue will overcome the individual or leave him able to take the necessary action to survive, even whether or not he will have frostbitten feet, all are, to a large extent, dependent more on the individual than on the situation.

EIGHT ENEMIES OF SURVIVAL

Fear, pain, cold, thirst, hunger, fatigue, boredom, and loneliness. Every one has experienced these, but few have known them to the extent that they have threatened survival. The more you know about these factors and their effects on you, the better you will be able to control them, rather than letting them control you.

Fear: Fear is a very normal reaction for any man faced with an emergency situation which threatens any of his important needs. Fear influences man's behavior and thus his chances for survival; fear may ruin his chances or may actually improve them. There is no advantage in avoiding fear by denying the existence of danger. Good leadership and training will help to modify thes fears.

Pain: Is nature's way of making you pay attention to something that is wrong with you. But nature has a way of holding off pain when you are too busy doing something else to pay attention to the injury right then. In the survival situation, pain, hunger etc., may go unnoticed if the individual's mind is occupied with plans for survival. On the other hand, if once given in to, pain will weaken the drive to survive.

Cold: Is a much greater threat to survival than it sounds. It not only lowers your ability to think; it also tends to lower your will to do anything but get warm again. Cold is an insidious enemy; at the same that it numbs the mind and the body, it numbs the will to survive.

Thirst: Is another enemy of survival. Even when thirst is not extreme, it can dull your mind. It is important to remember not to deprive one-self of water unnecessarily.

Hunger: As thirst, it is dangerous in the survival situation because of the effects it can have on the mind. Both thirst and hunger increase the individual's susceptibility to the weaking effects of cold, pain, and fear.

Fatigue: Is almost impossible to avoid in a survival situation. It is therefore necessary to understand its effects and to allow for them. Fatigue can make the individual careless, and it becomes increasingly easy to adopt the feeling of just not careing. This is one of the biggest dangers in survival. Fatigue may represent an escape from a situation which has become too difficult.

Boredom and Loneliness: Are two of the toughest enemies of survival. They are dangerous mainly

SURVIVAL-10

because they are unexpected. When nothing happens, when something is expected and doesn't come off, when the individual must stay still, quiet, and alone, these feelings creep up on him.

FOOD

An endless supply of food can be found by a skilled observer in almost any survival situation. This section discusses obtaining and preparing various types of food:

Never eat large quantities of a strange food without first testing it. To test an unknown food, put a small sample in your mouth, chew it and hold it in your mouth for five minutes. If it still tastes good, you may eat a handful, then, if after 8 hours there are no ill effects consider it safe. If the taste is disagreeable, don't eat it. A burning, nauseating or bitter taste is a warning of danger. Plants with a milky substance inside should never be eaten. Whenever a good supply of food is found, eat all you can, and take as much with you as possible. You may have trouble finding more. Food can be dried by wind, sun, air, fire or any combination of these. Following are some guidelines to follow when choosing food:

AMPHIBIANS: Frogs, turtles, lizards, alligators and crocodiles are edible, but toads are not.

ANIMALS: All hair-covered animals are edible when cooked thoroughly. Always remove entrails and sex glands before cooking, and cook animals as soon as possible after killing. If an animal is disseased in any manner, the greatest amount of danger is present while you are handling the meat and preparing for cooking. Use gloves if possible. Once the animal has been well cooked there is little chance of sickness, even though the animal was diseased.

BIRDS: All birds are edible, when thoroughly cooked.

EGGS: All bird eggs are edible.

FISH: All fresh water fish and other fresh water foods are edible when properly cooked. Most fish caught at sea, out of sight of land, can be eaten raw. Several species of salt water fish are poisonous. They usually live along the shoreline, are very brightly colored and oddly shaped. Eels are edible (but not Sea Snails). Never eat fish with slimy gills, eyes, flabby flesh or skin, or unpleasant odor. Eat only freshly - caught or properly preserved fish. Do not eat eggs or intestines of any fish.

INSECTS: Many insects and their eggs are edible (grasshoppers, locusts, crickets, white grubs, termites, ants, etc.)

PLANTS: Plants eaten by birds and animals are usually safe.

DON'T EAT: Plants that taste bitter, or that taste or smell disagreeable in any way. Plants with milky juices, but don't let the milk come into contact with your skin.

Grain, cereal or grass heads having black spurs in place of normal seed grains.

Mushrooms, even if they have been cooked. Non-poisonous mushrooms are edible, but have no food value.

After having taken the above into consideration, you may eat: ferns, grasses, fruit, seeds, bark, buds, leaves, flower, sap, pods, nuts and berries.

The following are edible only when boiled thoroughly; roots, tubers, stems and shoots.

REPTILES: All snakes, except Sea Snakes (which have a bony covering on their head and body), are edible, skin all reptiles before cooking.

SHELLFISH: All crustaceans and mollusks are edible, but fresh water varieties must be cooked. Eat only shellfish that are found underwater at low tide.

HUNTING

The following areas are good for hunting: Wet or marshy areas, edges of forests, meadows, and protected mountain slopes. These areas are poor for hunting: High mountain tops or ridges, and dense continuous forest lands. The best time to catch birds, is at night, when they are roosting. When hunting animals, the neck shot is most effective.

TRAPS & SNARES

Indiscriminate placings of traps is a waste of time. Small game such as rabbits, mice, etc., travel on paths through the vegetation. Set traps in or over these trails.

A serpentine fence will guide certain birds, like pheasants and some larger animals, to your traps. Cut or collect brush for the fence and build it two feet high or more. Place traps in depth of curve.

FISHING

Fish are attracted to light. Use torches at night to attract the fish. A head net made in a circular form by threading with bamboo or strung on a crotched stick will make a dip net. Fish in ponds or at the edge of the beach can be driven into the shallows by flailing the water with hands or brush. Clean fish immediately when caught. If you are in a group, work together to drive the fish and to net them.

COOKING

Keep your fire small.
Dry fuel may be difficult to obtain. Carry dry tinder with you to assist in starting your fire. By cutting away the wet outer cover of a sound log, dry fuel can be obtained.

To start fire, shave dry wood or dead bamboo into thin slivers and stack in tent formation over tinder. Pile heavier fuel around fire, and add slowly until fire is well started. If fuel is damp, stack it close to fire to dry out.

If the ground is wet or may become so, build your fire on a hearth of stones or wet wood. If necessary, build a shelter over the fire to protect it from the rain. If the weather gets cold and you need a fire for survival, build a screen on the opposite side of the fire from you to reflect the heat toward you. A screen of leaves or branches three of four feet square tied together with fish line or vines will do the job. Tilt the screen with the top toward you. Fiber soaked in insect repellent makes good tinder.

If larger game has been killed, the stomach or

skin can be made into a cooking vessel after being cleaned. Fasten three strings into holes made in the top of the wall of the open stomach or skin pouch and tie to the apex of a tripod made of sticks. Fill with water, which can be brought to a boil by putting in fire-heated stones. If sticks are not available and if the ground is not too wet or stony, the skin or stomach pouch can be used as a liner for a hole in the ground. Then fill with water and place fire-heated stones into it.

Meat and fish can be stuck onto a sharpened green stick and roasted over a fire.

Small animals and birds can be roasted easily. Draw and skin them and wrap in leaves, clay, or mud. Bury in a pit, the bottom of which is lined with heated stones. Fill pit with dirt. In the morning when the pit is opened, you will find the meat well cooked and hot. Larger game can be prepared the same way by cutting into small pieces. To get the maximum food value, boil all foods and drink the broth.

WATER: Is the most important single factor in determining survival. Without it, the presence or absence of food is of little importance. You can survive many days without food if you have water. On

the average a man needs one quart of water per day, but can survive on less, **never drink** wine, blood or seawater, as your body must give off more liquids in expelling them than it gets from them.

WATER

In dry country, the path of flight which small birds take in the late afternoon, usually leads to water. Water can usually be found by digging near vegetation, in the outside of a bend in a river bed, or in the sand along the seashore. Water found along the seashore will be brackish, but will not contain enough salt to harm you. Most cactus and large stemmed plants contain enough water to drink. Rainwater and melted ice and snow may be drunk without purifying or boiling.

TREATING IMPURE WATER: It is often necessary to use muddy, stagnant, or polluted water which, although unpleasant, is harmless if purified either by boiling or by use of purification tablets. To be safe, such water should be boiled for a minimum of one minute plus an additional minute for every 1,000 ft. of elevation.

Water purification tablets will purify water that has not been boiled. When using tablets containing chlorine compounds, water should be allowed to stand for thirty minutes. If there is an odor of chlorine in water, it is fit to drink. If not, more tablets should be added. Five basic rules for purification of water are as follows:

BOILING: One minute plus an additional minute for every 1000 ft of elevation and shake afterward to restore oxygen and eliminate flat taste.

HALAZONE TABLETS: As directed.

IODINE: Nine drops per quart and shake for 25 minutes.

If considerable sediment is in the water, filter it through soil taken from 12 inches or more below the surface.

The flavor of safe but unpalatable water may be improved by adding charcoal from fire and allowing to stand overnight.

EMERGENCY SIGNALING

The most effective all-purpose signaling device is a mirror. A flash from a mirror can be spotted from great altitudes, even when fire or smoke would be indiscernible.

Following are the international ground-to-air signals to be used in a functional survival situation. They can be made of any material, as long as they provide a contrast with the ground on which they are placed. Whenever possible, allow a space of ten feet between elements.

International distress signal is three of anything; fires, lights, signs, sounds etc.

FINDING DIRECTION WITHOUT A COMPASS

By day: The best known method of determining direction without a compass during the day is the "W-E (West-East) Stick" method. It is done in the following manner:

(1) Drive a stake into flat unshaded ground, so that at least 3' of it is above the ground.

(2) Mark the tip of the shadow cast by the stick, and label the mark "W".

(3) Wait 10 minutes (or until the shadow has moved appreciably) and mark the tip of the new shadow labeling it "E".

(4) Draw a line connecting the "W" and "E" marks. This is a west-east line.

Near the spring and fall equinoxes (March 21 and September 21), the W-E stick method is most accurate, at any time of day. Near the summer and winter solstices (June 21 and December 21), it is least accurate, but still usable. On every day of the year except the spring and fall equinoxes, the method produces a slight error before local apparent noon, and a slight error in the opposite direction after local apparent noon. Therefore, the errors in two readings, taken an equal amount of time before and after local apparent noon, will cancel each other out.

NOTE: Any permanent object can be used in place of a stick, as long as it is 3' high or more, and casts a well-defined shadow.

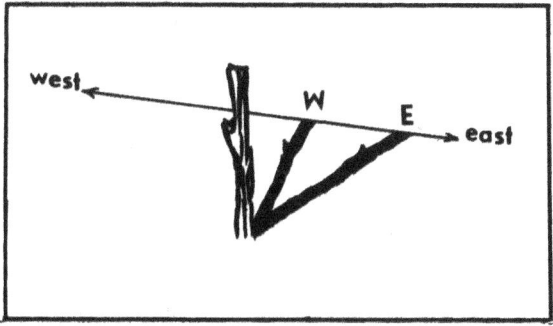

SURVIVAL-10

By night:
   Using the Big Dipper to find North:

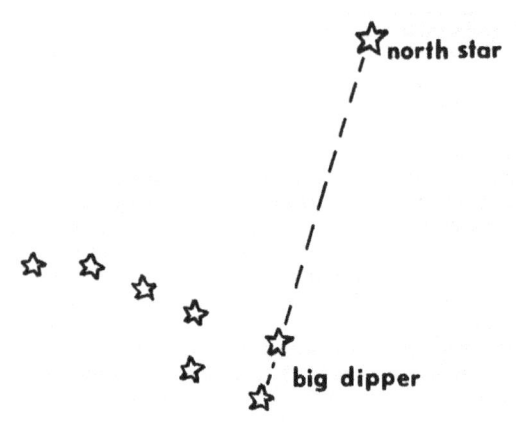

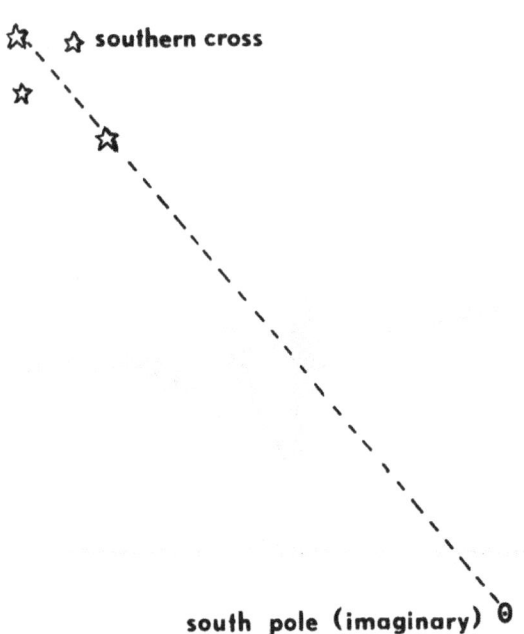

Using the Southern Cross to find South: In the Southern Hemisphere you can find south by locating the Southern Cross. Compare this group of stars to a kite. If you can figure the length of the kite from tip to tail and extend and imaginary line from the tip of the tail four and one-half times the length of the kite, you can determine the approximate direction of south.

TRAVELING

After an airplane crash, travel is not recommended except under conditions where the survivor finds himself in an area where static survival might prove difficult or dangerous. Under these circumstances, you should travel only as far as is necessary to find a good, safe, dry location for your camp.

Each survival incident, however, must be considered with regard to its own specific problems, and the decision, as to whether or not to travel, must be made by you, the survivor, and made quickly. If you do decide to travel, you must travel while you still have strength.

There are five basic requirements for travel:
   (1) Know where you are and where you are going.
   (2) Have a means of setting and maintaining direction. If you have a hand compass and know how to use it, you should be able to maintain a planned course. If you have not, then you will have to use the Big Dipper and Pole Star, or the "W-E stick" method.
   (3) Physical Stamina: Most people are inclined to over estimate their physical capabilities. Be very, very careful when trying to estimate your physical stamina.
   (4) Suitable: Clothes make the man. This is particularly true in survival where the proper clothing can mean the difference between life and death. Proper clothing is important for all seasons of the year, as it not only affords protection against the elements but also against insect bites. Adequate footwear is perhaps the most important item of clothing. Wet socks can cause grave discomfort and may completely incapacitate a man. Wind proof clothing is a must in cold weather and should be worn over an insulating type of underwear such as wool.

Food, Fuel, Shelter, and Signals: These must be considered in relation to the type of country and the season. It is advisable to carry sufficient materials to construct a basic shelter. A piece of parachute cloth or tarp is all that is required. A sleeping bag should be carried during all seasons. Signaling aids are a must for the survivor and constitute a definite requirement while traveling. A mirror and flares should be carried in your pockets or on the top of your pack, where they can be put to use at a moment's notice.

The following equipment is suggested for most survival situations: Sleeping bag, fabric for shelter, waterproof match container (full), food, candles, cooking utensils, axe, knife, gun and ammunition, fishing gear, maps, compass, extra clothing, first aid kit, sun glasses, signal mirror, and pyrotechnics.

TRAVEL HINTS

   (1) Travel on ridges or divides if possible. It is easier going, and better time can be made.
   (2) Following a stream or river has many disadvantages, but water and food are easy to obtain. Such travel is slow, but it will usually lead to civilization.

(3) Study the map. Determine the direction in which you wish to go; move in one direction, but not necessarily in a straight line. Pick a linear objective, as it is easier to locate. Avoid obstacles; don't fight them. Blundering through dense growth leads to bruises, scratches, and quick exhaustion.

(4) Check bearings often.

SHELTER

Before building a shelter, look for caves, rock overhangs, etc., which could be used as natural shelters. If it is necessary to build your own shelter, select your site during daylight hours and observe the following points:

Pick a site which is protected from natural hazards (flash floods, rockfalls animals etc.). Avoid dry river beds, dead trees and ant nests. Avoid bat caves, as bat droppings may carry rabies.

Try to pick a site with following close at hand: Water, food, building material, firewood.

To obtain some measure of freedom from insects, build your shelter in an open area, and use green wood in its construction. If practicable, burn dead leaves in your camp area, and spread the ashes in a circle around the site. This will help to prevent intrusion by ground insects.

Do not sleep on the ground if you can avoid it. Use your hammock if you have one, or make one of poncho or the multi-purpose net. If this is not possible, build a platform of branches. It will assist in avoiding insects, reptiles etc.

HEALTH

Care of your person is extremely important. If you have a survival kit, directions for the use of drugs are printed on the containers.

Treat every wound or sore as soon as possible. To stop bleeding in the absence of bandages, apply freshly made spader webs. This will assist in the coagulation of the blood.

In the absence of toilet paper, use leaves and grasses. Be careful to examine the leaves and grasses for insects. Use no leaves that have any fuzzy or hairy surfaces or are taken from a tree or plant with milky sap, or grass that has a serrated edge. Do not use material that is lying on the ground.

Leeches and ticks can be partially avoided by tying cuffs of your jacket at the wrist and the bottoms of trouser legs outside the boots and applying insect repellent to all openings. Check your clothes and body frequently. Remove leeches and ticks carefully. If pulled off quickly, they may leave their heads in the bite. Infection will result. Wet salt, fire, or lime juice will cause them to withdraw their heads and fall off. Don't hurry the process.

In cases of diarrhea when no drugs are available, a tea made from boiled guava leaves, or charcoal eaten with hot water will be beneficial.

Snakes: If bitten by a snake, take no chances. Treat all snake bites as poisonous. First aid for snake bites is covered in Chapter 13 of this book.

Most important of all, keep your head, try not to get too tired, rest frequently, be careful, and do not give up.

SURVIVAL-10

JUNGLE SURVIVAL

Survival in the jungle requires the same ability for survival demanded in other areas. However, you may have to travel thousands of miles, and spend months in the jungle before reaching civilization.

Most jungles are the same regardless of what part of the world you may find them. Oppressive heat, thick vegetation, and insects must be overcome if you are to survive.

Keep shirt buttoned, belt fastened, and pant cuffs tucked into shoes or socks. This, probably the protection you will have against ants, mosquitoes, and leeches, is a must.

If you have a compass, effort should be made to follow a compass course, rather than an easy route of travel.

If no compass is available, your best chance is to travel in rivers or streams, using a raft or boat.

FOOD

There is food in the jungle if you know where to find it. Plan one good meal each day but nibble on any food that you may have or can find. Eat strange food in small quantities and wait for a reaction. Avoid all mushrooms. There is little nutritional value in them, but much danger.

In villages, eat only food that is hot, if possible. If for fear of offending your host you have to eat native food that is not hot, take medication to avoid dysentery. All vegetables or fruit procured in a village or handled by natives should be peeled.

Possession of a knife is vital for successful foraging. If you do not have one, a serviceable blade can be made from split bamboo. Split dry bamboo with a stone, break out a piece, sharpen on a stone, fire harden and resharpen. The result will be a crude but effective tool or weapon.

Grasshoppers, ant eggs, hairless caterpillars, larvae, and termites are good when cooked. Remove heads, skin, and intestines of snakes, rats, mice, frogs, lizards, before cooking. Bats can be caught in caves by flailing the air through which they are flying with a multi-branched stick. Inasmuch as bats are carriers of hydrophobia, do not get bitten.

Cook all plants prior to eating.. To eliminate bitterness in plants boil in two or more changes of water. The jungle natives of Southeast Asia use the slash-burn method of farming and move their villages frequently, leaving many formerly cultivated areas throughout the jungle. Among the most common edible plants and fruits are coconut, banana, and papaya.

WATER

Water is more important than food. If you have no water, do not eat. Check all drinking water for leeches and other small aquatic animals.

Indiam Wells; in dry areas, water can usually

be found by digging a hole two or three feet deep in the bottom of dried up streams and river beds.

Many vines have water in them. The vine should be cut through. When a nick is cut in the vine about three feet above the original cut, a potable liquid will drip out. Do not apply vine to lips. Avoid any vine, plant, or tree with milky juice as many are poisonous. Water can be found at the base of the leaves of palm or in sections of dead bamboo (see figure). A section of bamboo placed against a tree will collect water during rain. Moisture collects under leaves in the dry season. Rub these with a cloth or other absorbent material; squeeze water out into container.

At the seashore, drinkable but brackish water can be procured by digging a hole ten feet above the high tide line.

If water is scarce, travel during coolest part of day or during the night. Rest during heat of day. This conserves the water content of the body.

Don't sleep on the ground; make yourself a bed of bamboo or small branches covered with palm leaves (see figure). A parachute hammock may serve the purpose. You can make a crude cover from tree branches or ferns; even the bark from a dead tree is better than nothing.

MISCELLANEOUS

Take time to repair your clothes. It helps to prevent insect bites and further tearing of clothes.

Examine your surroundings carefully. Many of your needs are there. Thorns broken from trees can be used for needles. Strips of vines can be made into thread. If you need rope, vines will do. Your food and shelter, in fact your life, may depend on your ability to make use of things that are all around you.

Be careful. Do not use trees and vines to pull yourself up hills, as thorns, ants, scorpions, etc., will be encountered and can make sores that may become infected. Use a walking stick to push aside vines and bushes.

Poisonous reptiles and large mammals of the jungle will cause few problems. Given a chance, they will avoid you.

Many of the jungle diseases are insect-borne. Use insect repellent freely, if available.

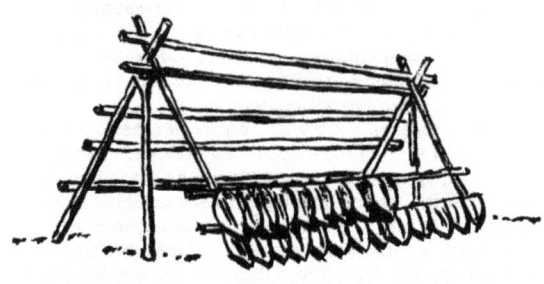

SHELTER

The thatch shelter (see figure) is made by covering an A-type framework with a good thickness of palm or other wood leaves, pieces of bark, or mats of grass. Slant the thatch shingle fashion from the bottom upward. This type of shelter is considered ideal, since it can be made completely waterproof. After you finish your shelter, dig a small drainage ditch just outside its lanes and leading downhill; it will keep the floor dry.

ESCAPE & EVASION IN JUNGLE

When evading or escaping, and before making contact with an escape net or other assistance, the evader must fend for himself.

SURVIVAL-10

The more that can be learned and applied of the general principles of survival, the greater will be the chance of reaching safety. This section deals with proper escape and evasion (E&E) conducted in the jungle.

The first rule of E&E is: Upon escape, get away from your captors as soon as possible. Sometimes this may require several miles; at other times, just a few yards. Plan your escape; do not run blindly Use your head, there is no substitute for common sense. As soon as possible, sit down, think out your problem, and recall what you learned in training.

If you have a map, study it closely. Roads and trails can be used as guides, but never travel on them. Stay alert. Natives remain on trails by preference. A few feet from the trail you are quite safe. Conceal yourself upon the approach of any other person until he passes or until you determine if he is friendly.

The easiest traveling is often on the crests of ridges. Remember, however, that crests are more exposed than hillsides, and because of ease of travel, they are apt to be traveled more frequently that other areas.

Rivers or streams can make good roads but remember that the majority of native villages and encampments are on water. Rafts attract attention. Floating on or close to a log or drifting bush may be the simplest way to travel. Keep to the middle of the stream. If using a native boat, sink it during periods when not in use.

When close to known enemy locations, move right after sunset or just before sunrise. At these times there is sufficient light to avoid enemy installations, mine fields, sentries, etc., but sufficient darkness to prevent recognition by the enemy. Arrange your clothing, weapons, etc., to present a profile as similar as possible to the natives of the area.

Be quiet. Noise carries far and natives are alert to any strange noise. Bury your refuse. Any sign of your presence may lead to your capture.

Do not sleep near your fire or your water supply. Get far enough away to be concealed.

If lost in grass that is so tall that you cannot see over it follow this procedure, as a last resort. Cut down enough grass to give you some freedom of movement and, using your machete or any other tool, dig a hole to crawl into, then set fire to the grass. Take every precaution not to get burned by fire or asphyxiated by smoke.

The jungle provides hiding places. You may have to use them. Bamboo thickets are excellent. Because of the nature of bamboo, you cannot be approached without being alerted by the noise of dry bamboo.

When approaching camp, use extra precaution, for the camp is probably being watched.

At all times when hiding or remaining in one location for a period of time, be sure to plan more than one exit.

It is difficult for a person unfamiliar with the jungle to live in it without native assistance. Conceal your weapons outside a strange village before entering. Get to a known friendly village as soon as possible.

If it is an enemy village, weapons will be taken from you.

WHEN REQUESTING NATIVE ASSISTANCE

Show yourself and let the natives approach you.
Deal with recognized headman.
Do not approach groups.
Do not display weapons.
Do not risk being discovered by children.
Treat natives well. There is much you can learn from them.
Respect local customs and manners.
Learn all you can about woodcraft.
Take their advice on local hazards.
NEVER approach a woman.

THE SURVIVAL KIT

Whenever possible, carry a survival kit with you when traveling. A small compact kit should include:
(1) A knife
(2) Flint
(3) 10 feet wire (copper or steel)
(4) Fishhooks
(5) A small mirror

You can, if you wish, carry more articles. However with the list given here, you can accomplish a great deal, if you use your head.

notes

182 TRANSPORTING A SDV

183 SAFETY PRECAUTIONS

183 SEAHORSE II

185 TRASS III

CHAPTER ELEVEN
SWIMMER DELIVERY VEHICLES

The primary advantages of Swimmer Delivery Vehicles (SDV's) are their ability to carry swimmers faster, further, and with less exertion than is possible in swimming, and their ability to carry greater loads. Disadvantages include the greater amounts of maintenance and training and the increased possibility of detection by skilled operators on finely tuned sonars. When utilizing SDV's with Closed Circuit SCUBA, an additional disadvantage is the necessity for very precise depth control, and the inability to take evasive measures into deep water.

The SDV's used by UDT frequently vary in type and modification due to rapidly improving technical developments. All, however, have the same basic characteristics and major components: some method of ballast; a propulsion unit consisting of motor, propeller, and shaft; a hull; and various gauges to indicate depth, direction, time, and status of the SDV. In addition, all presently in use are wet types, i.e., the diver is in direct contact with the water and must carry an independent life support system.

Only two types of SDV's will be discussed in this chapter: the SEAHORSE II AND
this chapter: The SEAHORSE II and the TRASS III. While a great many more exist, you should grasp the various problems and systems associated with all SDV's by studying the two here.

Note especially those steps associated with the electrical system. The dangers of severe electrical shock, acid burns, and an explosion from Hydrogen Gas are always present. These hazards can be minimized if good engineering practice and sound judgement are utilized.

TRANSPORTING A SDV

The following rules should be followed when transporting a SDV, to minimuze the possibility of damage to the vehicle:

(1) Prior to transporting by vehicle ensure the SDV is properly secured to its trailer. The use of wire straps or nylon straps and turnbuckles is recommended for this purpose.

(2) Check trailer for proper tire pressure.

(3) Ensure trailer is connected to vehicle using only approved hitches.

(4) Trailer speed will generally be governed by the type of suspension, wheel size, and road conditions. The rigged trailer must travel at LOWER speeds to avoid damage to the SDV. Generally, SDV trailers are made locally and have poor road characteristics. Center of gravity may be high due to the heavy weight of the batteries, thereby, increasing the possibility of tipover. Locally made trailers should not exceed 25 mph, converted highway types 45 mph, under good road conditions.

(5) Ensure SDV is hoisted and lowered using only approved slings, bridles, or lifting frames. Proper steadying lines should be used when applicable.

(6) Ensure the SDV is properly secured when aboard ship to those frames or padeyes which have enough strength to hold the SDV securely.

(7) Secure the SDV only to those points approved for tie down purposes.

SDV SAFETY PRECAUTIONS

(1) Do not exceed the operating depth of the SDV. Divers must be aware of decompression if the situation exists. Generally do not exceed 30' except for training purposes and for tests, and only when specifically authorized by the Diving Officer.

(2) Divers must wear an extra depth gauge and compass due to the possibility of SDV instrument failure.

(3) A safety boat is always highly desirable. It is required in congested areas and on training dives. The standby diver must be in the safety boat.

(4) Because of the speed of SDV's, tracking by bubbles may be difficult. Surface floats are always highly desirable, and are required in dirty water, reduced visibility, and during training.

(5) Always utilize a marker buoy or a pinger if the SDV is to be operated in the open sea or in areas where recovery after loss may be difficult due to poor visibility. Dives in clear, relatively shallow water need not utilize a marker buoy.

(6) Cease operation and surface if controls malfunction, amperages or voltages exceed or drop below tolerances, leaks develop in waterproof containers, or any other circumstances develop which might result in loss or damage to the SDV or injury to personnel.

SEA HORSE II

DESCRIPTION:
Length: 14.5 feet
Beam: 2-3 feet
Height: 4 feet
Surface Speed: 3.5 knots
Submerged Speed: 3.0 knots
Diving Depth: 100 feet
Operating Time: 3 Hours
Power: 1.8 HP Electric Motor
Power Source: 25 cell, 48 volt lead acid battery
Hull: Reinforced Fiberglass

The hull is completely open and contains three waterproof chambers: The forward sphere (1) (which is a permanent buoyancy tank), the battery case in the center (2), and the motor case in the stern (3). There is a removable buoyancy air chamber (5) that mounts over the battery case. Additional fittings will be discussed during preparation or operation of this unit.

PREPARATION FOR A DIVE

To prepare SEAHORSE II for operation, proceed as follows:

(1) Inspect the rudder and elevator shear pins for tightness. Check rudder cables for tightness. If slack, tighten turnbuckles until wire is just taut. Loose wires make steering a straight cours difficult.

(2) Remove buoyancy chamber.

(3) Install battery in rear half of battery case and install battery leads on terminal board. (Red to positive, Black to negative). NOTE: Battery will only fit into case one way. DO NOT FORCE. If forced, battery caps will be broken off and battery straps may be shorted out on the case. Battery cables coming from battery case must be covered with rubber protective caps.

(4) Clean mating surfaces of both battery cases, install "O" ring seal, and carefully slide forward battery case into position.

(5) Install clamp band and tighten. Be sure that mating surfaces are flush to each other.

(6) It is now necessary to check the battery case for leaks. Any of several methods can be utilized:

(a) Pressurize the case to approximately 3 pounds, using Nitrogen. Wait five minutes and note any pressure drop which would indicate a leak.

(b) Same as (a). In addition, submerge case in water and check for leaks. Keep battery leads out of water and rubber protictive caps in place. Keep battery case Horizontal at all times.

(c) If vacuum pump is available, pump about 10 inches of Mercury, and note any pressure rise which would denote a leak.

NOTE: Plastic insulation on battery leads should be inspected carefully, as an opening in the insulation will allow water to channel through the wire into the battery case or motor case.

(7) Purge battery case and pressurize to about 3 psi, using Nitrogen.

(8) Install Hydrogen vent hose on battery case. Inspect check valve for proper operation.

(9) Check motor case for leaks using the methods described above.

(10) Install battery case in position and connect electrical wires. (Caution: Motor swithc must be in neutral. Avoid touching bare ends of wires, especially if hands are wet.)

(11) Install buoyancy chamber and connect blow line to blow valve.

(12) Install HP air bottle and connect to blow valve.

TRIM PROCEDURES

Assuming the operator has never trimmed the SDV, procedd as follows:

Place the SDV in the water and add ballast weights fore and aft in the holes provided, until the SDV floats level. Generally about eight weights will be required forward and none aft. Slowly withdraw the vent hose (5A) until the SDV is barely negative,

 SDV-11

and observe the attitude the SDV takes upon sinking. Insert the vent hose, depress the blow valve (4A), and observe the position of the SDV upon rising. The SDV should keep a level attitude while sinking and rising.

Once this is accomplished, the SDV is trimmed.
NOTE: To ensure proper trim the operator and driver must also be of neutral buoyancy.

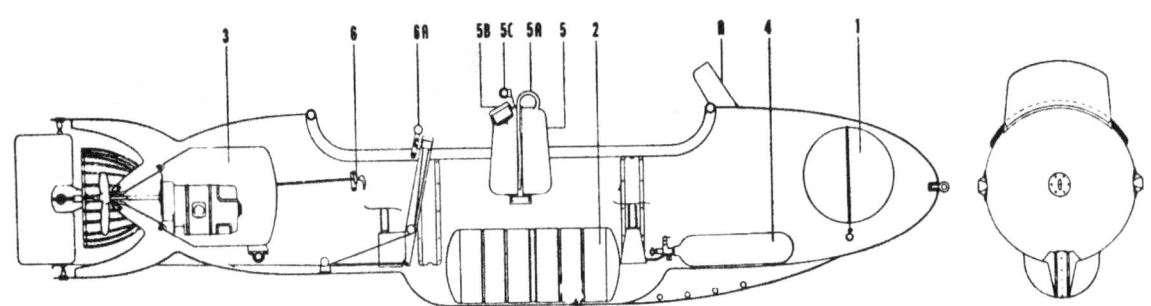

OPERATION: Operation of SEAHORSE II is very simple. Movement forward on the control stick (7) dives the SDV, and movement to the rear raises it. Turning the steering wheel (6A) right turns the SDV to the right, and vice versa. Operation is similar to that of an airplane.

The motor switch (6) has five positions: two speeds forward, two speeds reverse, and neutral. (Caution: Do not switch from forward to reverse or vice-versa until screw stops turing; otherwise you may burn out a fuse strip in the switch.)

Operation underwater will require some practice. Generally the operator should slowly withdraw the vent hose while underway, until the SDV just barely sinks. If the SDV is neutral, depth control is easily attained.

NOTE: Because the buoyancy chamber is open to the water, air in the buoyancy chamber will be compressed during descent, thereby making the SDV more negative. Upon ascending, expansion of air will vent out the vent hose, without affecting buoyancy.

The operator should manipulate the controls smoothly. Slow movements will not affect the speed of the SDV, but fast operation or a tendency of the operator to fight the controls will act as a brake upon the SDV.

Finally, the divers will find that boarding and exiting the SDV can best be accomplished while it is resting on the bottom.

MAINTENANCE

The SEAHORSE II requires very little maintenance, other than routine checks of seals on the battery and motor case. It is desirable to check the oil level in the reduction gears after about 25 hours of operation, or whenever the motor case is removed from the SDV.

After each operation, the plug on the bottom of the motor case should be removed, and the case checked for the presence of water. Should water be found, even a small amount, the motor case should be removed and thoroughly tested for leaks. Shaft seals or battery cable seals may need replacement.

Never operate SEAHORSE II if a seal is suspected of being faulty. A flooded motor or battery case will ruin the battery or motor. Furthermore, if the flooding occurs in deep water, the SDV will sink, as the buoyancy tank will not have enough positive buoyancy to counterbalance a flooded motor case.

Before each use, the battery should be washed with Baking Soda, rinsed with fresh water, and blown dry with compressed air. Do not allow soda water to get into battery cells.

Avoid quick charges on the battery. Maintain battery water approximately 1/4 inch above plates. Always charge batteries to 1300 specific gravity.

TROUBLESHOOTING

Following is a list of the more common troubles encountered with SEAHORES II, and their causes:

TROUBLES	CAUSES
SDV nose or tail heavy.	SDV Improperly trimmed.
Difficult to steer straight course.	Slack in steering cables.
Steering wheel difficult to turn.	Steering cable off pulleys, shear pins broken in elevators, control rod pin missing, or cotter pins are missing.
SDV Will not turn.	Broken shear pins in rudder.
Electric shock when speed switch is touched.	Break in insulation on battery cables. Water in motor case.
SDV will back down but not go forward, or vice-versa.	Fuse strip blown in speed switch. Faulty switch.

REFERENCES

For care of batteries: BUSHIPS Technical Manual, chapter 62.
For the craft itself: Handbook for SEAHORES II.

TRASS III

DESCRIPTION
Length: 17 to 18 feet
Beam: 2 feet 5 inches
Height: 4 feet 5 inches
Surface Speed: 3.5 knots
Submerged Speed: 3.0 knots
Diving Depth: 100 feet
Surface Endurance: 60 miles
Submerged Endurance: 50 miles
Power: 2.6 HP Electric Motor
Power Source: Four 12 cell, 24 volt lead acid batteries, connected in series for a total of 96 volts.

TRASS III may generally be thought of as a larger and more sophisticated SEAHORES II. Four waterproof chambers are contained within the open fiberglass hull: a permanent buoyancy tank forward (7), two battery cases in the center (2), and a motor case in the stern (3). Two removable buoyancy tanks (the surfacing air chamber (4) and the trim tank (5)) mount over the center of the two battery cases. Two 160 cubic feet air cylinders (9) are mounted under the SDV. The air line from one small air cylinder (8), is connected to the two large cylinders, and this entire system provides ballast air, in addition to breathing air, for the operator and three passengers.

Additional fittings, controls, and instruments will be described under Preparation and Operation.

PREPARATION FOR A DIVE

To prepare TRASS III for a dive, proceed as follows:

(1) Inspect control surfaces for broken shear pins, loose cables, and proper operations.
(2) Remove buoyancy chamber.
(3) Install batteries in battery cases, connect cable connections, and tighten battery case clamps. Be sure protective rubber caps are in place and the "O" ring is properly aligned between the battery cases.
(4) Check battery cases for leaks, using those methods described in SEAHORSE II.
(5) Purge and pressurize battery cases with about 3 psi of Nitrogen.
(6) Install Hydrogen vent hose and inspect check valve for proper operation.
(7) Check motor case for leaks, using the methods described in SEAHORSE II. Pressurize motor case with about 3 psi of Nitrogen.
(8) Install batteries and connect battery cables.
(9) Install ballast tank and connect blow lines and vent cables.
(10) Check operation of hand levers, controls, and switches.

TRASS III is now ready for operation.

As a matter of interest, the word "TRASS" stands for "Transporti Rapidi Arditi Subaequi", which is Italian for "Rapid Transport for Underwater Workers".

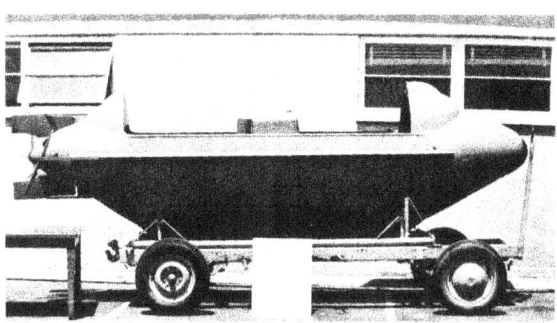

TRIM PROCEDURES

To trim TRASS III the operation of the ballast system must be understood. The ballast tank is composed of two chambers: one a small chamber called the Trim Tank (5), which can be completely sealed with two valves (5A and 5B); and a larger space surrounding the Trim Tank, open at the base, called the Surfacing Air Chamber (4). The arrangement of the ballast system may at first seem difficult to grasp, but an understanding of the purpose of the Trim Tank and of the Surfacing Air Chamber makes the arrangement seem quite logical.

THE SURFACING AIR CHAMBER

The purpose of the Surfacing Air Chamber (SAC) is to bring the craft to the surface, when desired. If TRASS III is trimmed properly, it will not sink, but will be neutrally buoyant, with the (SAC) filled with water. Therefore, when the craft is submerged and the pilot desires to ascend, filling the SAC with air will provide sufficient positive buoyancy to bring TRASS III to the surface. Used properly, the SAC is always either empty or full, depending upon whether the pilot desires his craft to be positively buoyant or neutrally buoyant. In the cockpit, the right hand lever (4B) controls the SAC. Forward movement opens the vent valve (4A), thus allowing air to escape and causing the SDV to become neutrally buoyant. Movement towards the rear causes air to be blown into the SAC thus causing the SDV to ascend.

 SDV-11

THE TRIM TANK: Prior to a dive the Trim Tank is filled with enough water to make TRASS III neutrally buoyant. It is then sealed by closing both the vent and flood valves. Once the SDV has been trimmed, the Trim Tank is not used again during the dive, except in the event that an emergency ascent becomes necessary.

In the cockpit, the two left hand levers operate the Trim Tank. Half forward movement of the inboard lever (5C) opens the bottom flood valve (5A) and full forward movement also opens the high pressure air line into the tank (thus expelling water out the bottom flood valve and causing the SDV to ascend). Forward movement of the outboard lever (5D) opens the Trim Tank vent valve (5B), thus allowing water to come into the tank and causing the SDV to descend.

TO TRIM: There are three steps involved in trimming the TRASS III: Launch, trim longitudinally, and trim:

LAUNCH: Turn the air system on and launch the SDV with due caution; be sure Surfacing Air Chamber vent valve (4A) is closed (with lever 4B). Take the SDV into about 10 feet of water. Stop the motor.

TRIM LONGITUDINALLY: Open the vent on the Surfacing Air Chamber. The SAC will fill with water, but the SDV should still float, since it is still being buoyed up by the Trim Tank. (If it does not float with the SAC fillied, surface by means of the Trim Tank and secure the operation). Longitudinal trim should now be made by rearranging passengers or trim weights onboard the SDV. The SDV should float horizontally or slightly stern-heavy.

TRIM: With the right lever locked forward (vent valve open) push both left levers forward, (but do not push inboard lever so far forward that it opens the Trim Tank blow valve). This opens the Trim Tank flood and vent valves. The air escaping from the Trim Tank will now flow out through the Surfacing Air Chamber vent valve (since it is locked open). As soon as the TRASS submerges, seal the Trim Tank by releasing the left levers. If TRASS III proceeds to the bottom and rests there, blow air into the Trim Tank until the craft becomes neutrally buoyant. You may need to blow and flood the Trim Tank several times, before the craft becomes neutral. If absolute neutral buoyancy cannot be achieved, it is best to have TRASS III slightly negative for operation.

OPERATION: TRASS III is navigated essentially in the same fashion as SEAHORSE II. Once the craft has been trimmed, the Trim Tank controls are not utilized except for an emergency ascent. Normal ascent and descent are accomplished by use of the Surfacing Air Chamber lever (forward for ascent, aft for descent). The electrical system must be watched closely on TRASS III. While underway, the voltmeter and ammeter should read as follows:

SPEED	FORWARD 1	FORWARD II	FORWARD III
VOLTS	48	96	48
AMPS	22	15	22
REVERSE			
	48		
	8		

Should any higher reading be observed, the craft should be secured until the trouble has been found. Should the amperes go beyond 30, the thermic switches

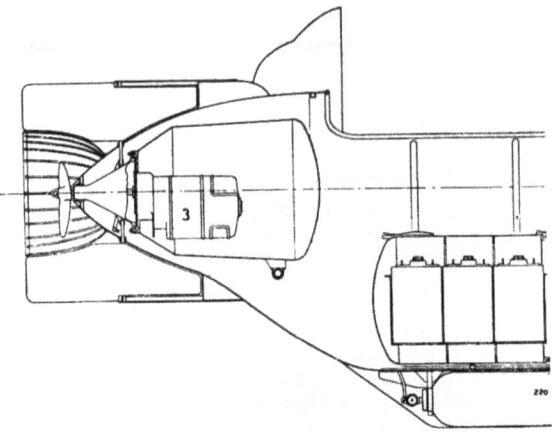

will trip, causing the craft to stop. To reset the switch, turn the handle on the right side of the forward buoyancy tank, clockwise.

MAINTENANCE

TRASS III requires about the same maintenance as SEAHORSE II insofar as the hull and control surfaces are concerned. Before each operation, battery cables should be carefully examined for breaks in the insulation, loose packing rings, and worn "O" rings. TRASS III has high voltage (96 volts) when operating. The possibility of severe electric shock should never overlooked when servicing this unit. Operators should go to great lengths to ensure that no possibility of injury to personnel from the electrical system exists. Seals on switches, motor, and battery case should be carefully examined.

Check the oil level in the transmission case every 25 hours of operation. Repair air valves, lines, and cables as needed. Service batteries as with SEAHORSE II.

TROUBLE SHOOTING: All troubles associated with SEAHORSE II apply also to TRASS III. Troubles peculiar to the TRASS, and their causes, follow:

TROUBLES	CAUSES
SDV will not dive.	Surfacing Air Chamber vent valve cable improperly adjusted.
SDV tends to sink.	Trim Tank flood valves or vent valves leaking.
SDV tends to rise.	Leak in ballest system blow valve.
SDV will not go forward or reverse.	Thermic switches tripped or solenoid switch burned out.
SDV progressively getting nose or tail heavy.	Water leak in motor case, forward buoyancy case, or battery case.

186

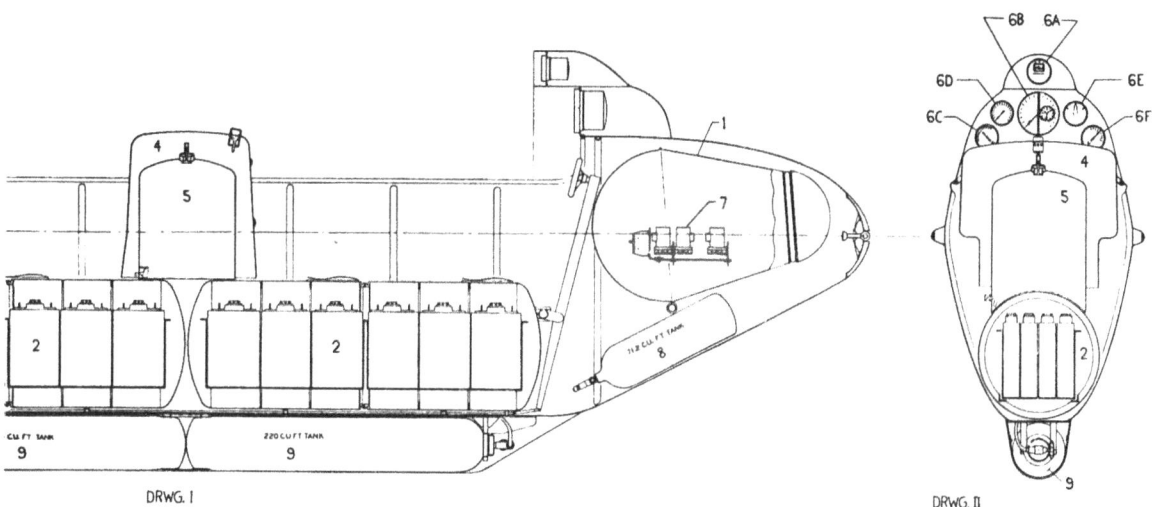

NOTE: Should a water leak occur in any waterproof case, cease operation immediately. The craft must be surfaced and recovered quickly, or else it will sink. Even with all ballast systems fully charged with air, the TRASS will not float, should any one waterproof case fill with water.

REFERENCES

    FOR CARE OF BATTERIES: BUSHIPS Technical Manual, Chapter 62.

    THE CRAFT ITSELF: Handbook for TRASS III.

---

notes

190 SMALL ARMS

192 HAND GRENADES

195 BOOBY TRAPS

CHAPTER TWELVE
WEAPONS

AR-15 (M-16)

The AR-15 (M-16 Rifle) is a .223 caliber gas operated, air cooled, semi or full automatic shoulder fired weapon, manufactured by the Colt Fire Arms Company, Inc.

* SPECIFICATIONS

Overall Length: 38-3/4"
Barrel Length with flash suppressor: 21-1/4"
Weight: 6.3 pounds
Weight Loaded (20 round magazine): 6.92 pounds
Rear Sight: Two-leg peep sight adjustable right and left for windage. Also adjustable from 0 to 300 yards at short range, and from 300 to 500 yards at long range. One click of the rear sight, whether vertically or horizontally, will move the strike of the bullet one inch for each 100 yards.
Magazine Capacity: 20 rounds
Rate of fire, sem-automatic: 45 to 65 rounds per minute.
Rate of fire, full automatic: 120 to 150 rounds per minute.
Maximum range: 2,833 yards

FIELD STRIPPING: Following are the steps to be taken to field strip the AR-15:

(1) Remove magazine and pull charging handle to the rear and inspect the chamber.
(2) Depress bolt lock and put safety in safe position.
(3) Press take down pin to the right.
(4) Lift up on carrying handle and separate the upper and lower receiver.
(5) Withdraw charging handle and remove bolt and bolt carrier, then remove handle from it's recess.
(6) Remove firing pin retaining pin.
(7) Remove firing pin.
(8) Turn bolt cam pin one half turn to the right and remove.
(9) Separate the bolt from the bolt carrier.

NOTE: Further disassembly is not necessary. Notice gas tube and where it enters the bolt carrier. Notice gear type projections on front of the bolt and where they lock into the barrel extension. Note the location of the hammer, disconnect, and automatic sear.

CARE AND CLEANING: The AR-15 is made of a metal alloy which resists rust and corrosion. DO NOT use cleaning solvent on it. The rifle needs only to be kept dry and clean and all excess carbon simply wiped off the working parts. All springs must be checked to ensure that they are not broken, weak, or bent out of

shape. Do not oil the weapon. Oiling it would cause it to function at a very slow rate of speed, and eventually malfunction. Because of its high cyclic rate of fire, (700/800 rounds per minute) all carbon should be removed as soon as possible after firing, before it hardens. The cleaning rod should be inserted from the rear of the bore, to ensure that the cleaning patch follows the same path as the projectile, thus preventing the bore from becoming pitted.

DETAIL STRIPPING: Detail stripping should be done only under the supervision of qualified armory personnel.

REFERENCES

Contractor's Operation Manual TO-11W3-5-1, Colt's Patent Fire Arms Manufacturing Company, Inc., Hartford 14, Connecticut.

Pamphlet; Colt Fire Arms Company, Inc., Dated February 1960.

M-3 SUB-MACHINE GUN

The M-3 Sub Machine Gun is a .45 caliber, blowback operated, air cooled, automatic, shoulder fired weapon.

✴ SPECIFICATIONS

Overall Length (with stock extended): 29.8"
Barrel Length: 8"

Empty Weight: Approximately 8.2 pounds.

Loaded Weight: Approximately 10.25 pounds
Rear Sight: Fixed Peep
Front: Fixed ramp. The sights are set for 100 yards.
Magazine Capacity: 30 rounds
Cyclic Rate of Fire: 450 rounds per minute

Maximum Range: 1,700 yards
Maximum Effective Range: 100 yards

FIELD STRIPPING: Following are the steps to be taken to field strip the M-3.
(1) Remove Stock
(2) Remove trigger guard
(3) Remove trigger housing assembly
(4) Remove magazine catch and spring
(5) Remove barrel
(6) Withdraw bolt group from front of receiver
(7) Press out sear pin
(8) Withdraw trigger pin from receiver
(9) Withdraw trigger assembly from opening at front of sear. Do not allow connector pin to be lost. The trigger and the connector are a permanently assembled unit; the trigger spring and the connector pin may be removed. No further disassembly is permitted.

CARE AND CLEANING: Following are the steps to be taken when cleaning the weapon:
(1) Field strip the weapon.
(2) Clean the bore and chamber. NOTE: Do not apply oil to the bore or chamber before firing. Clean all parts.
(3) Apply a light coat of lubricating preservative oil to all parts that do not come in contact with the ammunition.
(4) Reassemble weapon
(5) Wipe excess oil from the receiver.
(6) Clean and oil magazines.

DETAIL STRIPPING: Detail stripping should be done only under the supervision of qualified armory personnel.

IMMEDIATE ACTION: If the weapon fails to fire, remove the magazine, retract the bolt, and inspect the chamber to ensure that it does not contain a live cartridge or any other obstruction. If there is no obstruction, close the cover, replace the magazine, open the cover, and attempt to fire. If the gun still does not fire, check to see whether a live cartridge has chambered; if it has not, remove the magazine and insert a new magazine.

If there is a live cartridge or other obstruction lodged in the chamber, cock the gun and hold the cover down firmly; remove the barrel; then clear the chamber by using the stock to push the obstruction out of the barrel. Under combat conditions, when time is short, omit the step of removing the barrel.

REFERENCE: Army Publication FM 23-41

SMITH AND WESTON K-38

GENERAL: The S&W K-38 is a .38 caliber solid frame, six-shot, breach loading hand weapon, with a swing-out type cylinder. It can be used either single or double action.

FIELD STRIPPING: Field stripping should be done only under the supervison of qualified armory personnel.

CARE AND CLEANING: After firing, clean the bore and cylinder with an approved nitro solvent. Then brush clean the weapon, using nitro solvent to remove all deposits from breech, muzzle, extractor head, and other adjacent parts. Remove all solvent

from weapon; then cover all parts with a light oil.

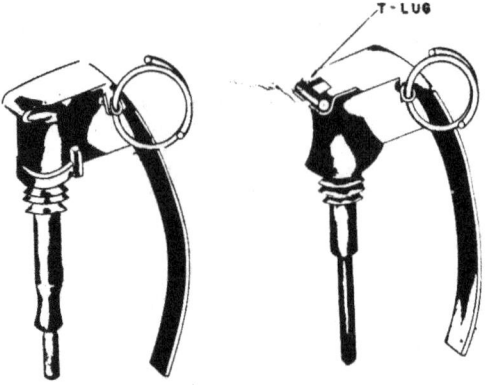

IGNITING FUZE (M200A1)   DETONATING FUZE (M204) SILENT TYPE.

sets off the fillers; these are called igniting fuses. Other fuses burn into a blasting or detonating cap; these are known as detonating fuses. Some detonating fuses are of the silent type. They do not sputter, smoke, or sparkle while delay fuse is burning. These fuses are identified by a protruding T-lug that holds the safety lever to the top of the fuse body.

FILLER: The substance with which the grenade is filled may be any explosive such as TNT or any of a number of chemical compounds.

BODY: This is a container that holds the filler; it is made of metal, glass, paper, or any other suitable material. Grenade bodies have different shapes; for example, the body of a fragmentation grenade is shaped like a lemon, while chemical grenades usually have cylindrical bodies.

* SPECIFICATIONS

Overall Length: 9-1/8"
Barrel Length: 4"

Weight loaded: 34 oz.
Rear sight: Adjustable Micrometer Click Sight
Front sight: Fixed

DETAIL STRIPPING: Detail stripping should be done only under the supervision of qualified armory personnel.

IMMEDIATE ACTION: In the event of a misfire, open cylinder, and eject and replace the faulty cartridge. Check the weapon for a broken firing pin.

REFERENCES: S&W Pamphlet dated 1 January 1960. Catalog of Naval Material, Section 9651.

Grenades

When first employed in war, grenades were chiefly weapons for defensive purposes. Today there are grenades for a wide variety of purposes: to produce casualties among enemy personnel; for screening and signaling; for illumination, incendiary action, demolition, and harassing purposes. The hand grenade is a small bomb or missile filled with explosives or chemicals; or it may be an empty container designed for practice in throwing.

COMPOSITION: Although they vary in size, shape, and weight, hand grenades are made up of three main parts:

(1) FUSE: This device automatically sets fire to a train of powder that burns at a controlled rate. The burning time is called the delay of the fuse, which prevents the grenade from exploding until several seconds after it is thrown. Some fuses burn into an igniting cap (igniter) which

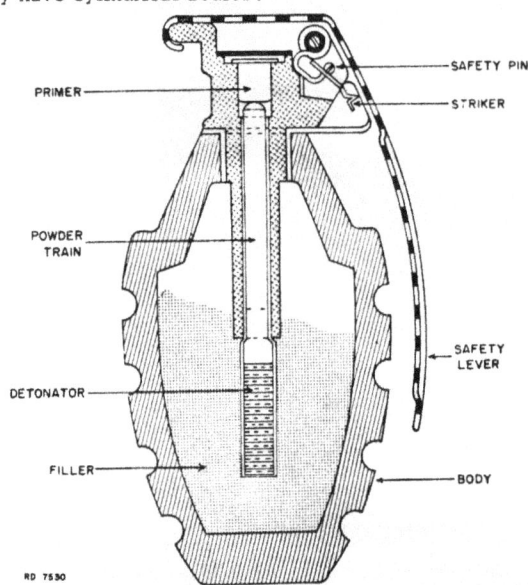

OPERATION: When the grenade is to be thrown, it is held in such a manner that the fingers of the throwing hand pass around the body of the grenade and the palm is over the safety lever, holding it in place. Before throwing the grenade, the safety pin is removed and the safety lever is held in place by the palm. When the grenade leaves the hand, the

WEAPONS-12

safety lever, which is no longer held in place is thrown clear of the grenade by the action of the striker spring, forcing the striker through its arc. The striker then continues through its arc until it strikes the primer, igniting it. The primer, in turn ignites the powder train which burns for a predetermined time down to the detonator, or igniter, which then explodes or ignites the filler.

GRENADE THROWING

The grenade should be thrown like a baseball, using the throwing motion that is most natural to the individual. To give the grenade a spinning motion in its flight, it should be allowed to roll off the tips of the fingers and released with a snapping motion of the wrist. As a rule, this method will achieve the most accuracy and distance. The individual should not change his throwing style completely, although minor corrections might be necessary to improve throwing skill.

To follow through is an important point to remember when throwing the grenade. This not only improves accuracy and distance, but relieves the strain on the arm. When throwing the grenade from the standing position, an additional step forward should be taken and the thrower should fall to the ground after releasing the grenade.

To prevent injury to the throwing arm, a beginner in his first practice should limit his throws to about twenty yards. The distance and the number of throws should then be gradually increased until accuracy up to a range of thirty-five yards has been gained.

THROWING POSITIONS: In combat, the target will probably be in builtup areas, in jungles, or in wooded areas. You may have just a fleeting glance of your target. Therefore, the grenade may have to be thrown from any position in which you may find yourself, or one from which it can be placed on the target with a degree of accuracy, depending upon the situation. You must learn to throw the grenade from a standing, kneeling, crouching, or prone position.

STANDING: Half face the target with the weight of the body balanced evenly on both feet. With the grenade held in front of you, chest high, remove the safety pin with a twisting-pulling motion. As the grenade leaves the hand, take an additional step forward to follow through. Keep your eyes on the target to observe the strike as you fall to the prone position.

KNEELING: Use the kneeling position when you are protected by a low wall or trench. Don't expect to get as much distance from this position as from the standing position. Half face the target and kneel on the knee nearest the target. Extend and slightly bend your other leg to the rear. Hold the grenade chest high, using the proper grip. Remove the safety pin with a twisting-pulling motion. Throw with a natural motion. Push off with your rear foot to give added power to your throw. When you release the grenade, fall forward to a prone position, breaking your fall with your hands and arms. Observe the probable strike and then duck your head.

CROUCHING: Use the crouch position in built-up areas, woods, or jungles where a certain amount of accuracy is required. For short throws under low-hanging tree limbs or into pillbox embrasures and other openings close to the ground, throw the grenade with an underhand motion. Use the regular grip. Let the grenade roll off the finger tips, as pitching a softball. Stand and face the target and assume crouching position. Grasp the grenade firmly and hold it chest high. Remove the pin with a twisting-pulling motion. Bring back the arm and throw the grenade with a softball pitching or bowling motion. Fall forward into a prone position. Observe the probable strike of the grenade (if possible) and duck your head.

PRONE: This position limits both accuracy and range. Use it when you are pinned down by fire and must keep a low silhouette. Lie on your back with your body perpendicular to the thrower-target line and your throwing arm away from the target. Hold the grenade chest high as in the standing position. Remove the pin with a twisting-pulling motion. Cock your right leg (left leg for left-handes thrower), bracing the foot against the ground. Try to maintain a low silhouette. Bring your throwing arm back straight to the rear, or else cock it over the rear shoulder. At the same time, grasp and hold on to any substantial object within reach of your free hand. This will improve your accuracy and distance. Throw the grenade, pushing with your rear foot. As you release the grenade, roll over on your stomach. Observe the probable strike and then duck your head.

TYPES OF GRENADES

FRAGMENTATION HAND GRENADE, M26

A typical fragmentation hand grenade is the GRENADE, Hand, Fragmentation, M26. This is an improved type that consists of a thin steel body, approximately the size and shape of a lemon, lined with a wirewound coil, and replaces the older type (MK 2) cast iron body. The M26 body is approximately 2-1/4 inches in diameter at the center and 3 inches long; 3.9 inches long including fuse. The explosive charge consists of Composition B. This grenade is shipped fused with a detonating fuse, which has a striker, primer, delay charge, and detonator. This fuse is of the "silent type", which means only that the delay charge burns silently. When the grenade is thrown, the striker under the force of the spring pushes the safety lever free of the fuse and strikes the primer. The primer ignites the delay charge which, after a 4 to 5 second delay, explodes the detonator and the bursting charge, thereby fragmenting the grenade body. The pedestal base allows the grenade to be stood on end and to be distinguished from the Mark I Illuminating Hand Grenade in the dark. The M26 grenade is painted olive drab, with a yellow band at the neck near the fuse, and yellow markings.

FRAGMENTATION HAND, GRENADE MARK 2

The Mark 2 is made of cast iron varying in thickness from one-eight to one-fourth of an inch. The body is lemon-shaped, approximately 2-1/4 inches in diameter and 3-1/2 inches in length, without the fuse. It contains an explosive charge of 2 ounces of flaked TNT which, upon detonation, breaks up the body of the grenade and fuse, and projects the fragments outward at high velocity in all directions. The horizontal and vertical grooves in the body cause the body to break up into a large number of fragments that are roughly the same size. Those fragments are large enough to cause casualties within a radius of 30 feet. The neck of the body is threaded to take a fuse or a standard firing device base. The time delay is from 4 to 5 seconds. The body of this grenade is painted olive drab with markings in yellow.

OFFENSIVE HAND GRENADE, MARK 3A2: The offensive Hand Grenade Mark 3A2 has a body of sheet metal ends and pressed fiber sides. Its filler consists of eight ounces of TNT. It uses a detonation type fuse with a delay time of from 3 to 6 seconds. The weight of the grenade complete is 14 ounces. Its color is black with an identifying band in yellow. The offensive hand grenade is used for demolitions and is effective against personnel in closed-in places because of its shock effect.

THE INCENDIARY HAND GRENADE, AN-M14 (THERMITE): This grenade consists of a body of smooth metal (sheet) with no vents, a filler of thermite, and an igniting type fuse. When the filler is ignited, it burns with a white-hot flame that develops a temperature of 4330 degrees F., for 30 to 35 seconds. Clamps of steel strapping, which fit around the grenade body, may be used to nail the grenade against an object to be burned. The grenade is placed rather than thrown. Since it creates such terrific heat, it is very useful in destroying enemy abandoned guns and machinery. Its color is blue-gray with band and markings in purple. The grenade weighs 32 ounces.

COLORED SMOKE GRENADE, M18 (See figure):

This grenade is identical with the CN-DM Grenade except that the container has emission holes in the top, and a single hole at the bottom. A tapered hole extends through the center of the grenade from the bottom emission hole to the fuse. The starter mixture lines the tapered cavity. The M18 is available in red, green, yellow, and violet. It is used for signaling purposes from ground-to-air and ground-to-ground, and frontline identification. The body is painted blue-gray with markings and band in yellow. The top of the container is painted the color of the smoke that is produced.

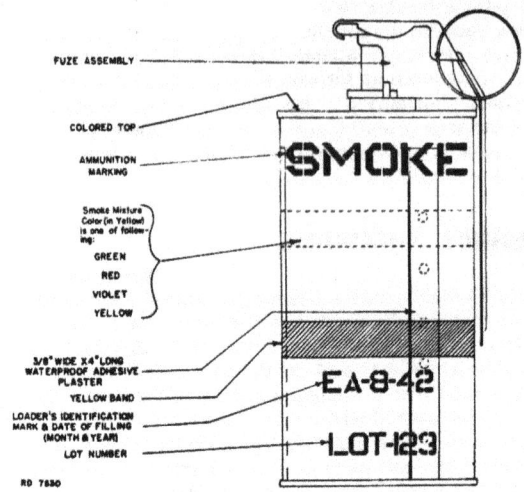

WP SMOKE GRENADE, M15 (white phosphorus): The WP Smoke Grenade, M15 has a drawn-steel cylindrical body similar in size to the burning-type chemical hand grenades. However, the body is made of a heavier sheet metal than the other smoke grenades. The sides and bottoms are pressed out of one piece of sheet steel; no ridge or fold is present where the bottom and sides meet. Its edges are rounded. Its filler is white phosphorus, and has a detonating fuse with delay of 4 to 5 seconds. The white phosphorus filler, upon coming in contact with the air, burns with a dense white smoke that blinds the enemy, giving it the dual purpose of harassing the enemy by screening and of producing casualties. White phosphorus also causes severe burns if it comes in contact with the skin. A detonating type of fuse ruptures the grenade body; this allows the filler to come in contact with the air and scatter over an area of about 15 yards. The body is painted blue-gray, with stenciling and one band of yellow.

HC SMOKE GRENADE, AN-M8: This grenade is the burning type. Its container is standard except that there are no emission holes in the side, only in the top. Its filler of HC MIXTURE, when ignited by the 1.2 to 2 second igniting fuse will burn from two to two and one-half minutes, producing a dense screening purposes.
white smoke. It is a standard white smoke grenade used for signaling and screening purposes. Its smoke is not dangerous when breathed in light doses for a short period of time. The sheet metal body is painted blue-gray with a band of yellow. The top of the container is painted the color of the smoke that is produced.

RED SMOKE GRENADE, AN-M3: This grenade is larger than the usual chemical grenades; it measures 3 inches by 5 1/2 inches. It is used for signaling, and its red smoke can be seen for great distances when used against a background of snow. Attached to the body of the grenade are three metal flaps which are bent upward to provide additional surface so that it will not sink into the snow, mud or swampy ground. Its weight is 21 ounces. Other characteristics are the same as the HC grenade.

CN TEAR GASS GRENADE, M7: The CN Tear Gas Grenade, M7, is identical to the CN-DM grenade except that it has only a tear gas filler, and its effect is to cause a painful burning sensation in the eyes. It is made of smooth sheet metal. The filler is activated with a 1.2 to 2 second igniting fuse and is released by means of holes in the grenade body that are covered with adhesive plaster. The adhesive plaster is burned off as the CN is ignited. This hand grenade is painted blue-gray with a band and markings in red. Its principal uses are to control civil disturbances and to train in the use of the gas mask.

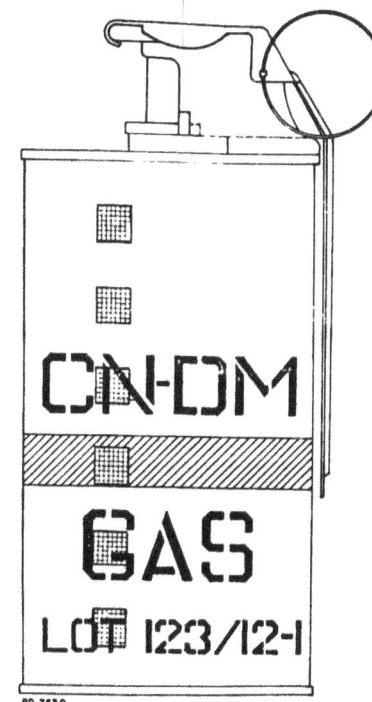

CN-DM IRRITANT GAS HAND GRENADE, M6: (See figure): This grenade is filled with a combination of tear gas and adamsite. This makes the grenade more effective when used for harrassing purposes or in controlling riots and mobs by causing choking, tears, and nausea. It has a sheet metal body. Its fuse is the igniting type because the grenade contains a burning mixture. In the body are holes or vents covered by adhesive plaster squares that are burned off when the filler is ignited. The body is blue-gray with the markings and band in red.

PRACTICE HAND GRENADE, M21: This practice grenade is similar to the Mark II Fragmentation Grenade, but it has a filler of 21 grains of black powder and an igniting fuse. The charge is normally not sufficient to cause fragmentation, but due precautions should be taken since occasional detonation occurs. It does throw out a puff of smoke. This puff of smoke not only enables the thrower to gauge his accuracy and to estimate possible damage to the target; it also adds realism to practice throwing and to field exercises. It is fused with an igniting fuse with a delay of 3 to 6 seconds. The grenade is painted blue and has no body markings.

PRACTICE HAND GRENADE, M30, w/fuse M20 5A1: This is a practice version of the M26, Fragmentation Grenade and has internal features similar to M 21 Practice Grenade. It has a spotting charge of 37.5 grains of black powder.

TRAINING HAND GRENADE, Mark IA1: This hand grenade is just what its name implies; it is used to train personnel to throw grenades accurately at a usable distance. It is an iron casting of the same general size, shape, and weight of the Mark II Fragmentation Grenade. It is completely inert and may be employed without the special precaution necessary when explosive grenades are thrown. It is painted black with no markings of any kind.

IMPROVISED GRENADES: Excellent grenades may easily be improvised from any number of explosives, containers, and shrapnel producing materials. However, it is difficult to fuse a grenade safely and also effectively. The following fuse is recommended for improvised grenades: Cut a piece of time fuse approximately 2 inches long. Divide this length into thirds, and cut a notch at the 1/3 and 2/3 mark, deep enough to expose the powder train. When ignited, the time fuse should be observed carefully. When the flame sparks through the first cut, the thrower should move the grenade to the throwing position; when the flame sparks from the second cut, throw the grenade.

NOTE: It is imperative that a trial fuse be burned for proper timing before using a fuse from the same roll on a live grenade.

Booby Traps

Booby traps are defensive weapons, used primarily to harrass and delay offensively. They may be used to hold a position while advancing.

SAFETY

(1) Be extremely careful when setting a booby trap. Many a booby trap has turned out to be a booby!

(2) In arming manufactures' booby traps, remember that the primary safety device is a positive block between the cocked striker and the cap. Always remove this positive block last. If there is any pressure on the primary pin, its removal will cause detonation.

(3) When rendering a booby trap "Safe", insert the primary safety pin first, and then the secondary safety pin. Bend the pins open to prevent them from working back out. Finally, remove the device from the explosive.

(4) On the other hand, when in an area which might have been occupied by the enemy, be suspicious of even the most innocent-looking objects. They may be booby-trapped. Also remember that they are usually set in groups of two or more.

TYPES OF BOOBY TRAPS

M1 PULL BOOBY TRAP: This device is activated by a 3.5 lb pull on the trip wire. The wire is usually

stretched across a trail or doorway, or attached to an object.

M1A1 PRESSURE BOOBY TRAP: This device is activated by applying 20 lbs pressure on its head. It is usually found under the loose board of a step, or the like. The collar is the primary safety on the M1A1.

M5 PRESSURE RELEASE (Mousetrap) BOOBY TRAP: This device is found under books, souvenirs,

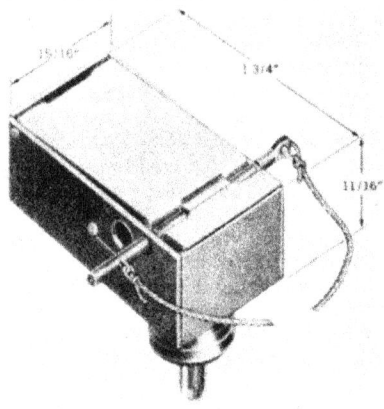

etc., or anything which weighs 3.9 lbs or more. It may be screwed into the fuse cell of a hand grenade.

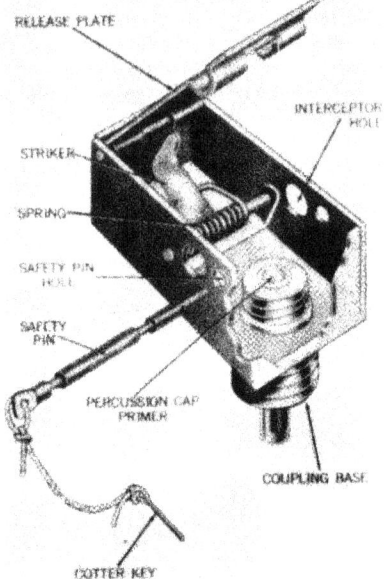

It is fired by removing the weight from it. Its one safety pin cannot be removed to arm it, unless sufficient weight is resting upon it.

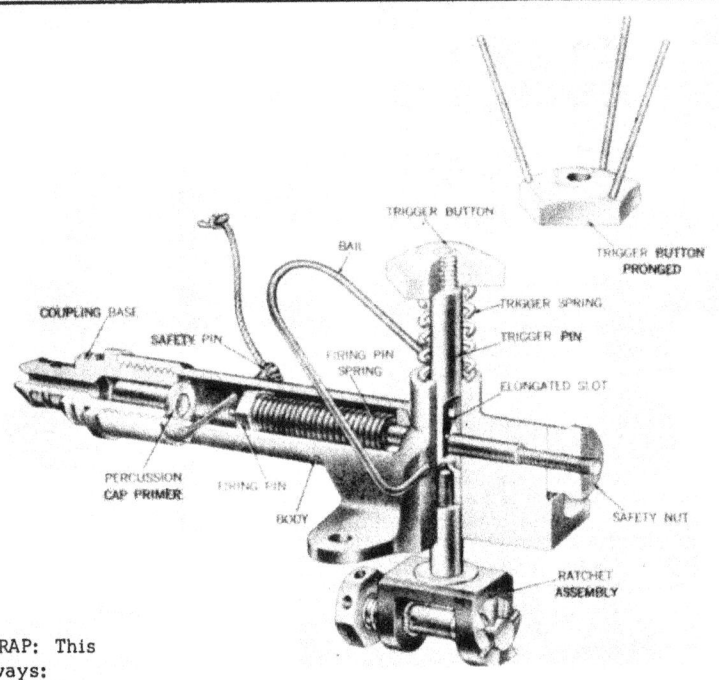

MK1 MOD 1 COMBINATION BOOBY TRAP: This type can be activated in any one of three ways:
- Pressure on head or prongs.
- Increased tension on tip wire.
- Decrease of tension on trip wire.

The primary safety on the MK1 MOD 1 is the pin between the striker and the base coupling. The secondary safety is the lock nut on the after part of the trap.

M3 PULL-PULL RELEASE BOOBY TRAP: As its name implies, this device is activated by either increasing or decreasing the tension on its trip wire. Its secondary safety is the pin between the rachet and the striker. NOTE: The rachet has been known to slip on this device, causing several accidents.

M-14 ANTIPERSONNEL MINE: This is a simple, safe, and effective device, which can be set around fox holes at night and retrieved in the morning. It can also be used along trails. It is activated by a pressure of approximately 20 to 35 lbs. To arm, remove the horeshoe on top, and turn the safe and arm button to "A". To disarm, reverse the procedure.

THE GRENADE - IN - CAN BOOBY TRAP: This is one of the most popular improvised booby traps. It is constructed in the following manner:

Remove grenade from shipping container.
Attach container to tree, post, or other object.
Attach trip wire to grenade.
Remove safety pin from grenade, and replace grenade in container, leaving the container top off. When the trip wire is pulled, the grenade will be snapped from the container and activated.

CLOTHESPIN INITIATOR: As demonstrated by the following diagram, a spring-type clothespin can easily be rigged to act as a pull-type initiator for an electrical firing circuit.

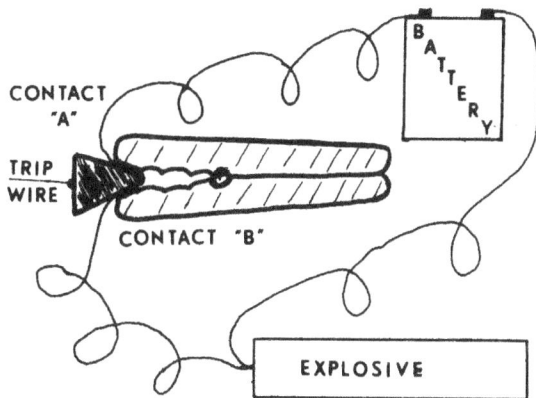

Notes

200 UDT WARNING ORDER

200 UDT BRIEF

201 DROP and PICKUP

202 IBS TOWING

203 LIMPETEER ATTACKS

205 SUBMARINE OPERATIONS

207 UNDERWATER SEARCHES

208 BEACH DEFENSE PERIMETER

209 INLAND DEMOLITION RAID

210 SENTRY STALKING

211 HAND - TO - HAND COMBAT

215 PT EXERCISES

miscellaneous OPERATIONS and TECHNIQUES

CHAPTER THIRTEEN

UDT WARNING ORDER

A warning order often precedes a standard UDT briefing. Its purpose is to provide the men with sufficient information to prepare adequately for the problem in advance. Following is the format for a UDT warning order:
(1) DEPARTURE (Date and Time)
(2) BRIEFING OF PATROL OR PATROL ORDER (Date and Time)
(3) EQUIPMENT AND PERSON RESPONSIBLE FOR EACH:
   a. Rations
   b. Ammunition
   c. Flashlights
   d. Watches
   e. Radios (include frequencies)
   f. Rubber Boats (include necessary accessories)
   g. Explosives
      (1) Packs (Type)
      (2) Trunk Line
      (3) Fuzes - time and type (waterproof)
   h. Special Equipment
(4) UNIFORM

UDT BRIEFING

Because the nature of UDT operations often makes communication between operational elements impossible, each element must thoroughly understand beforehand the procedure to be followed in a particular operation. The operating procedure can best be presented to those involved by the presentation of a comprehensive briefing before an operation. Following is the format for a UDT briefing:
(1) OBJECTIVE-includes a statement of the mission, area sketch (if one is necessary) and any general information necessary to the mission.
(2) INTELLIGENCE
   a. Contains any pertinent weather, hydrographic, or terrain information necessary for the success of the mission. (Temperature, (water and/or air) sun, moon, tide, visibility, surf, set, wind, landmarks, land peculiarities, etc.)
   b. Contains any enemy disposition necessary for the success of the mission.
(3) EQUIPMENT-list of all equipment to be used, both personal and general.
(4) UNIFORM-type of uniform required
(5) PROCEDURE
   a. A step by step outline of how the preparation, mission and clean-up is to be accomplished.
   b. It is important that specific time references by made.
   c. Emphasize necessary musters.
(6) SAFETY
   a. List of all safety precautions to be observed.
   b. Emergency procedures and equipment provided.
   c. Warning of possible danger situations, and suggested solution.
   d. Emphasize lifejacket inspection, buddy system, and UDT distress signals for all water problems.
(7) PERSONNEL-assignment of specific tasks to individuals.

(8) CHAIN OF COMMAND-the chain of command should be included in a briefing, especially before a combat operation. The presentation should be simple but effectively organized, it should include all key positions.
(9) KEY POINTS-This is a review of major points, techniques and any pertinent supplementary information. Emphasize those points which will most greatly influence the success of the mission.

DROP AND PICKUP

In order to place a line of swimmers in the water with each swimmer or swim pair 25 yards apart, and recover them rapidly, UDT has developed several drop-and-pickup systems: standard, Fulton, and helicopter:

standard

The Drop: Standard drop-and-pickup is conducted from an LCPL, LCPR, or other similar small craft, at a speed of about 15 knots. Using this method, swimmers can be dropped either singly or in pairs. The same procedure is followed in either case, but for the sake of clarity, the following paragraphs describe the procedure using swimmer pairs:

As the delivery craft approaches the drop point, all swimmers line up inside the delivery craft. They stay in a crouching position and in proper order, the first pair next to the roll off pad. At the signal from the officer in charge, the first pair enters the IBS (which is being towed alongside the delivery craft) and lays down on the outboard main tube. The next swim pair enters the IBS, and lays down on the inboard main tube. All hands watch the OIC. His job is to drop each swim pair every 25 yards. To measure this distance, he can either tow an inflated lifejacket 25 yards behind the boat, or else drop a swimmer each time the second wake of the delivery craft passes over the point where the last swim pair dropped.

When the OIC drops his arm, the after man in the first swim pair slaps his buddy's leg, and enters the water. When his buddy feels the slap, he enters the water also. When entering the water, each swimmer holds his facemask, to keep it from being torn away. He planes his body in such a manner that he is propelled down several feet under the water. He remains underwater until the boat is well away from him.

As soon as the first pair leaves the IBS, the second pair moves to the outboard main tube. The third pair enters the IBS, and all the swimmers in the boat move toward the roll off pad.

This procedure is repeated until all pairs have been dropped.

PICKUP: At the time for pickup, the swimmers spread out in a straight line, at 25 yard intervals, forming on the guide. When the guide raises his hand, all swimmers raise their hands. This is the signal to the pickup boat to commence its run.

As the boat closes on a swimmer, he kicks hard to raise himself out of the water, crooks his left arm and makes a target for the pickup man with his left fist. When he feels the sling on his arm, he grasps his left wrist with his right hand, and rolls into the IBS. Once in the IBS, he lets go of the sling, scrambles into the delivery craft, and moves all the way forward, keeping at low silhouette.

fulton

THE DROP: Since the Fulton drop is done from an LCSR at speeds of about 40 knots, proper preparation and techniques are of great importance.

During the run to the drop point, the swimmers are seated in the swimmer cabin, with the #1 man on the port side next to the after door. The #2 man sits to his left, and so on around the cabin. Each swimmer holds his fins against his chest, blades up, with his left hand through the loops. He holds his facemask in his left hand, and ensures that all of his gear is secured, with no "irish pennants" anywhere.

When the time for the drop approaches, the OIC stands in the after doorway, and gives the standard airborne hand signal for "stand up". At this command, all swimmers stand up and grasp the overhead handrail with their right hand. The #1 swimmer faces the OIC, and each swimmer faces the man ahead of him.

When the LCSR reaches the drop point, the OIC gives the standard airborne command "go". The #1 swimmer runs out the door straight aft to the stern, and jumps. He takes a good airborne position (feet and legs together and pointed towards the horizon, hands holding his gear against his chest, and head and chin tucked). If he desires, he may hold his head against his chest with his right hand, to prevent whiplash. Upon hitting the water, he maintains this position for a few seconds, until he comes to a stop. He then surfaces and dons his fins and facemask.

The #2 swimmer follows the #1 swimmer out the door, and all swimmers follow suit. With the LCSR at 80% RPM, the swimmers will land 25 yards apart in the water, if they follow each other immediately from the stern.

THE PICKUP: At the time for pickup, the swimmers split into two groups of eight men each, one group 100 yards seaward of the other. The LCSR passes by the two groups, dropping a fiberglass pod by each.

The swimmers swim the two pods apart until the slack is out of the floatable line connecting the two. They then face the bows of the pods toward each other,

and keeping at low silhouette, board the pods. The senior man in each pod then raises his hand to signal the OIC in the LCSR that his pod is ready for pickup.

When the OIC sees the pickup signal from both pods, he commences his run towards the center of the line. The swimmers in the pods grasp their handloops securely, taking care not to entangle their hands in the loop.

The LCSR probe picks up the line on contact, and LCSR, pods and swimmers head to sea. While being winched in, the swimmers must keep low, and keep arms and legs in the pod, especially when the pods come alongside each other.

HELO Drop·Pickup

While this method of drop and pickup is in many ways superior to the other two, it is also potentially more dangerous to all concerned. For this reason, the OIC must be especially concerned that all personnel involved (including the aircraft crew) are thoroughly briefed on the preparations for an techniques of the operation.

THE DROP: Prior to takeoff, a metal bar is rigged in the aircraft in such a manner that it protrudes from the aircraft door about three feet. A rope ladder is also rigged in the aircraft door. While this is being done, the OIC conducts a check of all jumpers to ensure that they have all equipment, and that it is properly stowed on their person. The minimum equipment for each jumper is:

Wet suit top	Facemask
Lifejacket	Flare
Knife	Fins
Web Belt	

Upon boarding the aircraft, the jumpers take seats and fasten their safety belts.

Once airborne, the UDT OIC converses with the aircraft pilot, over the intercom, to ensure that they both are satisfied with the aircraft's heading, speed and altitude, as well as the drop zone conditions.

As the aircraft approaches the drop zone, the OIC, using standard airborne hand signals orders the jumpers to "get ready", "stand up", "check equipment", and "stand in the door" (at which command the first jumper sits in the door). When the drop zone is reached, and if the OIC is satisfied with all conditions (among them, that the aircraft is not exceeding a height of 20 feet or a speed of 20 knots), he taps the first jumper and gives the command "go".

When he receives the command "go", the jumper reaches out and grasps the bar protruding from the doorway. He then leaves the cabin, and hangs, facing forward, from the bar. He swings his body, and, with his body angled slightly forward, releases the bar and grasps his fins and facemask (which are looped over his forearm) to his chest. As soon as he hits the water and comes back to the surface, he dons his fins and lines up with the rest of his buddies.

PICKUP: At the time for pickup, the OIC hangs the rope ladder from the helicopter door, and the helicopter proceeds down the line of swimmers at a slow speed, keeping the end of the ladder a foot or two from the water. The swimmers keep their fins on, and as the ladder reaches each swimmer he grabs the ladder and climbs up into the aircraft.

IBS Towing

This technique is used whenever it is desired to tow one or more IBS's to a target area. The procedure is as follows:

(1) The IBS approaches the delivery craft from astern, and comes along the port side.

(2) The #1 starboard paddler grasps the towline from the delivery craft, and holds the IBS alongside.

(3) The #1 port paddler hooks the pelican hook from the IBS towing bridle into the grommet at the bitter end of the towline.

(4) All paddlers back water and a crewman in the delivery craft pays out the towline until the next grommet appears.

(5) The next IBS in line repeats steps 1 through 4. This process is repeated until all IBS's have hooked up.

To drop IBS's individually (starting with the IBS farthest astern, and working forward:

(1) The OIC of the drop gives the "attention" signal from the sternsheets of the delivery craft (by day: waving semaphore flags in front of his body. By night: 10-15 short flashes).

(2) As the delivery craft nears the drop point, the OIC signals "standby" (by day: ROMEO. By night: one 5 to 10 second dash).

(3) At the time for the first drop, the OIC signals "execute" (by day: dropping ROMEO; by night: securing the long dash) and the #1 paddlers in the last IBS trips the pelican hook to release themselves from the tow line.

(4) "Standby" and "Execute" are repeated for

each IBS, until all have been dropped.

The procedure for a simultaneous drop is the same as that for an individual drop, with the following exceptions:
(1) The "attention" signal consists of waving the semaphore flags overhead by day, and a circular motion of the flashlight by night.
(2) When the "execute" signal is given, all IBS's are released.

NOTE: Should any IBS crew desire that the delivery craft stop at any time, they give the "trouble" signal (paddles raised overhead, blade up).

Limpeteer Attack

The limpeteer attack is one of the oldest tactics used by underwater combat troops. In UDT, there are innumerable variations on the procedure. The following paragraphs, therefore, do not attempt to describe the operation completely, but are designed rather to present a few general principles which apply to all limpeteer or "sneak" attacks.

(1) COMPHIBPAC INSTRUCTION 03500.17 series outlines the duties and responsibilities of the UDT OIC, as well as swimmers and CO's of participating ships, during a training limpeteer attack.

(2) It is often desirable for the swimmers to swim upstream of a target and drift down upon it, especially if highly phosphorescent water makes motion in the water visible. If the wind is not extremely strong, the current can be determined by the direction in which a ship tends on its anchor chain.

(3) Proximity to a ship is indicated to an underwater swimmer by some or all of the following phenomenon:

    a. An increase in noise level.
    b. An increase in water temperature.
    c. The "darker darkness" experienced when passing under the hull of a ship.

(4) Even during training limpeteer attacks (when participating ships take precautions to protect the

swimmers), caution must be taken to stay clear of screws, rudders and underwater suction openings (which are usually located midships at the chine of the hull). Should a swimmer discover that his buddy has been pinned to the hull by underwater suction during a training mission, he should not attempt to go to his aid, but should surface and notify the OOD immediately.

SUBOPS

The duties and responsibilities of all participants in UDT SUBOPS are outlined in COMNAVOPSUPPGRUPAC INSTRUCTION 3120.1 series.

The following paragraphs outline the procedure to be followed when locking out of and into a submarine.

THE ESCAPE TRUNK: Description: The escape trunk is a watertight extension of the submarine's pressure hull, which is equipped for flooding. Its primary components are:

- Lower hatch
- Upper hatch
- Side door
- Pressure gauges
- Blow Valve
- Vent Valve
- WRT Flood Valve
- Sea Flood Valve

31MC intercom to forward torpedo room and conn.

Water for flooding the escape trunk can be supplied

either from the boats water retaining tank, or from the sea. Usually the former is used.

LOCKOUT and LOCKIN: Following is the procedure for locking out of an escape trunk:
(1) Enter trunk.
(2) Test 31 MC, ensure that knife and mallet are present in trunk, and that all valves are shut.
(3) Shut bottom hatch.
(4) Undog side door.
(5) Open WRT
(6) Open vent
(7) Shut vent when water is 2/3 up side door.
(8) Shut WRT when water is at top lip of side door.
(9) If side door hasn't opened yet, open blow valve and blow it open-then shut blow.
(10) Leave trunk, and shut and dog side door behind you.

The lock in procedures is as follows:
(1) Enter trunk through side door.
(2) Shut and dog side door (3 1/2), turns counter clockwise.
(3) Open blow valve, keep pressure on ears equalized.
(4) Open WRT
(5) Shut blow valve when rumbling noise is heard.
(6) When rumbling noise stops, shut WRT.
(7) Open vent valve (Same conditions as in rapid free ascend).

(8) When hissing noise stops shut vent valve.
(9) Open bottom hatch.
(10) Ventilate trunk by opening blow valve for a few seconds.
(11) Secure blow valve and leave trunk through bottom hatch.

NOTES: Breathe normally throughout all phases of the operation. Remember to exhale when the vent is opened to equalize the trunk.

During lockout/lockin, keep the forward torpedo room and conn. informed of your actions via the 31 MC.

underwater searches

circle

This search is the most practical and the most simple of all the UDT searches. It can be done with a minimum amount of equipment and personnel.

Equipment: Clump, buoy (attached to clump), and a search line of the desired length. Minimum number of divers: two. Any number of divers can be placed on the search line, depending upon the objective of the search. Most of the searches made by the teams are for helicopters and two divers are adequate, as the search line would snag anything as large as a helicopter.

Procedure:

swimmer tow

This method requires more equipment and more personnel than the circle search but is an effective way to search a larger area systematically.

Equipment: One weighted 30-yard search line (size of weights dependent upon weather conditions, surf, set, etc.). This line will be in five yard sections joined by snaffle hooks and weights spaced along whole length of search line.

SWIMMER TOW SEARCH

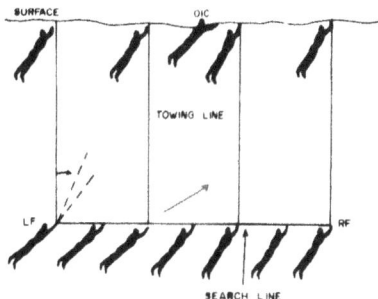

SWIMMER TOW

Four 40-foot tow lines (may be longer depending upon depth of water at 500 yards from beach).

One LCPR with IBS.

Varying amount of buoys with 4' range poles and 2' x 2' red flags.

Two 30' cod lines and floatation device per diver (floats may be: cork floats, blocks of wood, small inflation devices, lifejackets, etc.).

Procedure: The search line is tied to two buoys 30 yards apart, parallel to the beach. The surface swimmers space themselves along the line 10 yards apart, and hook their towlines into the search line. The divers space themselves along the search line five yards apart.

On command from the OIC, the divers descend, bringing the search line with them to the bottom. The OIC then ties the two buoys together with a 25 yard line, and orders the swimmers to commence the search.

The swimmers proceed towards the beach, on range with the range poles. The divers hold the line lightly, and follow it along the bottom. If they find a mine or obstacle, they give two jerks on the line. All hands pass this along, and swimmers and divers stop. The diver buoys the obstacle or mine, and when the OIC sees the buoy, he orders the search to resume.

At the end of the search pattern, the OIC may order the swimmers to shift up or down the beach, and proceed seaward, overlapping the previous pattern.

jack stay

Equipment: Two 200 yard grid lines. One 50 yard search line with a snaffle hook at each end. Four buoys with length of line equal to depth of water attached. Four weights, 100 - 200 pounds, depending upon conditions. Necessary equipment for establishing control ranges. Delivery craft(s).

Procedure: The search rig is set up as indicated by the diagram below.

The divers space themselves along the search line at such an interval that their search lanes will overlap (varies with water visibility).

On command of the OIC, the divers proceed to the bottom, attach the search line to the grid lines with snaffle hooks, and commence the first sweep.

At the end of the sweep, the divers ascend, shift to an overlapping lane, and repeat the process outlined above.

BDP

The BDP is a defensive measure to protect a UDT beach party from detection and surprise attack on an enemy beach.

There are five positions, or stations, on or within the BDP. They are Left Flank, Center, Right Flank, Cover and Command. In the basic BDP these positions are manned by 11 men; including two swimmer scouts and command and are as follows:

LEFT FLANK: Left Flank is comprised of two men equipped with automatic weapons and an AN/PRC-6 radio. Left Flank is usually positioned (with at least one man stationed on the berm line) the desired distance to the left of Strongpoint. The two men assigned to this position cover an area of approximately 36 degrees of the total 180 degrees covered by the perimeter. They should be individually positioned within audio-visual contact of one another, and should be able to cover the assigned area both visually and with a "field of fire" from their automatic weapons.

CENTER: Center is comprised of two men, automatic weapons and an AN/PRC-6 radio. Center is positioned approximately in the center of the perimeter, the desired distance landward of Strongpoint. They cover, both visually and with a "field of fire", approximately 110 degrees of the total arc of 180 degrees. Center's visual and fire fields should overlap those of the flank positions.

RIGHT FLANK: Same as Left Flank, but these personnel are positioned to the right of the Strongpoint.

COVER: Cover is comprised of two men with automatic weapons and an AN/PRC-6 radio. Cover's primary duty is to camouflage, hide, or move the beached IBSs' as directed by Command. Secondarily, they will assist the BDP personnel in holding off the enemy, in the event of an attack, until the last of the beach party has left the beach. Cover will leave the beach in the last beach party boat.

COMMAND: Command is OIC of the BDP and coxswain of the BDP boat. He is directly responsible to WHEEL who is the OIC of the entire operation. He has an AN/PRC-6 radio and may use the Swimmer Scouts as runner-messengers should the need arise. He will satation himself approximately in the center of the BDP, between Center and Cover, but may move about as he sees fit inside the perimeter. He will work closely with the OIC of the beach party. Usually the beach party OIC requests that a certain area of the beach be covered by the BDP, and Command complies with this request. In the event of an emergency, Command will take charge of all UDT personnel on the beach during the evacuation, and will be the last man off the beach.

STRONGPOINT: Strongpoint is a definite position on the beach, tentatively selected by the Swimmer Scouts. It is Command's prerogative, however, to withhold his stamp of approval and to choose another Strongpoint himself. Strongpoint is usually located just landward of the berm crest, wherever the best cover is, and "ideally" in the center of the perimeter directly seaward of Center. It is the responsibility of the men on the perimeter to keep in mind the exact location of Strongpoint at all times. Command may, on a short beach (200 - 300 yards) select a Strongpoint nearer to one of the flanks if he feels there is more cover, higher ground, or a better all around defensive position, at one of these locations. Strongpoint may have a stationary location for an entire operation, though the perimeter may move up and down the beach around it. "Cover is Strongpoint, Strongpoint is Cover, and there is where the boats are found."

commands

There are five, and only five, commands used in maneuvering the BDP. These commands are designed to give Command exact control of the perimeter, its position and movements, with an absolute minimum of radio traffic. The commands are:

EXTEND: This command applies to one designated station on the perimeter. It will always be preceded by the name of the station to be repositioned and followed by a number and a direction; in that order. The directions are: left, right, seaward and landward. All numbers used in those commands represent yards. Therefore, the word "yards" will not be transmitted.

EXPAND: This command applies to the Flanks and Center, and is given under the blanket call sign: "Perimeter." Upon reception of this command, Left Flank will move the specified distance down the beach to the left of Strongpoint. Right Flank will move the specified distance up the beach to the right of Strongpoint. Center moves the specified distance landward on a line perpendicular to the shoreline. Cover stays put, though Cover's radioman will acknowledge reception of the command.

WITHDRAW: This command by itself means that all stations on the perimeter will withdraw toward Strongpoint and take up their original positions around

Strongpoint (usually a proper perimeter of approximately 25 yards diameter).

The command "Withdraw," followed by a number, means that all stations on the perimeter will withdraw towards Strongpoint AND STOP after they have traversed the specified distance.

"SHIFT": This command refers to all points. It is followed by a number and a direction ("left" or "right"). It means to move that many yards in that direction.

This command is issued when the UDT shore party (including the BDP) has either been detected or brought under fire by the enemy. Upon reception of this command, all stations on the perimeter fall back (firing if being fired upon) in a rapid but orderly fashion. The dead and wounded will be carried and the beach party will be encompassed at all times. The perimeter stations will take up their original positions around Strongpoint and cover the departure of the beach party and the two men who had been assigned to Cover. The remaining BDP personnel, under the supervision of Command, will then leave the beach; either in the IBS or swimming, depending upon the seriousness of the situation.

Problem: Command wants the perimeter to shift 200 yards left. He will say: "PERIMETER, COMMAND, SHIFT TWO ZERO ZERO LEFT, OVER".

The station on the perimeter will reply, in order from left to right flank around to and including Cover: "COMMAND, (PROPER STATION), ON STATION, OUT."

NOTE: Center will keep radio silence until Left Flank has reported. Right Flank will keep radio silence until Left Flank and Center have reported. Cover will keep radio silence until Left Flank, Center, and Right Flank (in that order) have reported. This procedure will be strictly adhered to whenever Command requires replies from all perimeter stations.

Problem: Upon completion of the Shift maneuver, Command discovers that Center is 25 yards to far to the right, preventing good coverage of the area beyond the perimeter. To place Center in the most advantageous position he will give the following command:

"CENTER, COMMAND, EXTEND TWO FIVE LEFT, OVER" Center (and only Center, as the command EXTEND applies to only the named station) will reply: "COMMAND, CENTER, ROGER, OUT." Upon reaching the new position, Center will say: "COMMAND, CENTER, ON STATION, OUT."

Problem: After Command has "fixed" the perimeter in this manner, the beach party OINC asks him if he may have a little more of the Backshore. Command looks the situation over and decides to EXPAND the perimeter another 25 yards. He will say: "PERIMETER, COMMAND, EXPAND TWO FIVE, OVER." Left Flank, Center and Right Flank will reply, in the proper order: "COMMAND, (NAME OF STATION), ROGER, OUT." After reaching the new positions the stations, once again in order: "COMMAND, (NAME OF STATION), ON STATION, OUT." In this maneuver Cover stays put (unless expressly directed otherwise by command) and need not come up on the net. In the event of an Emergency, Command will say: "PERIMETER, COMMAND, EMERGENCY WITHDRAWAL, OUT". "OUT" at the end of the transmission precludes any reply by the perimeter stations.

NOTE: If at any time during this operation any of the radios should fail, or should the net be jammed by the enemy, Command will utilize the Swimmer Scouts to transmit all messages.

INLAND DEMOLITION RAID

This operation involves the landing of personnel on an enemy beach, movement inland to a target, loading of the target with explosives, and withdrawal to the sea. When the raid is properly executed, the shot will go after the raiders have put out to sea.

Personnel involved in an Inland Demolition Raid are: Officer in Charge, (Usually called "WHEEL"). He is in overall command of the raid, and remains in the delivery craft, offshore, throughout the operation. (Command (from the BDP) is in immediate charge of all personnel while away from the delivery craft.)

Swimmer Scouts: The two Swimmer Scouts swim in to the beach, scout the area, choose a Strongpoint (see BDP, Page   ), and signal in the rest of the raiding party. They lead the powder train to the objective, and act as runners for Command, if necessary. Once at the objective, they attach and pull the fuzes.

Powder Train: The Powder Train is composed of the "workhorses" of the operation. They load the powder in the IBS, unload it on the beach, and carry it to the objective (usually, two packs per man).

Riggers: Two men in the Powder Train are designated as riggers. They head up the powder train on the trip to the objectives. In addition to carrying their packs, they are responsible for:
(1) Supervising the stacking of powder at the objective.
(2) Tying in the packs to the trunkline.
(3) Leading the powder train back to Strongpoint.

Conducting the Raid: The IBSs' containing the raiding party stop outside the surf zone, and the Swimmer Scouts are sent in. They proceed in to the beach, scout the area, and (if all is clear) signal in the BDP boat. When the BDP boat hits the beach, Command sets up the BDP and signals in the Powder Train Boat(s).

When all hands arrive at the beach, they are informed of the location of Strongpoint, and the trip to the objective begins. The Swimmer Scouts carry the fuzes, and all hands stay at low silhouette throughout the operation.

After the riggers have tied the packs to the trunkline, they lead the Powder Train back to Strongpoint. The BDP covers the withdrawal at Strongpoint, Command conducts a muster, sends the Powder Train to sea, and radios the Swimmer Scouts (who have remained at the objective) to pull the fuzes.

The swimmer scouts radio a reply, pull the fuzes, and withdraw to Strongpoint. Upon their arrival, Command calls in the BDP, and all hands head to sea.

SENTRY STALKING

Whenever it becomes necessary to

take down a sentry, two factors are extremely important:
  (a) Get as close as possible to the sentry before attacking him.
  (b) Kill him swiftly and silently.
The following paragraphs outline some points to be kept in mind while stalking a sentry.

THE APPROACH: Bad weather or periods of reduced visibility are best for approaching a sentry undetected. All movement near man-made or natural obstacles in the presence of the enemy should be made cautiously because these areas will almost always be covered with fire. The danger of booby traps and mines on and near obstacles is a constant hazard. Utilize all available cover. Be sure to expose nothing which glitters, and attempt to blend with the background as much as possible. Move exposed parts of the body slowly; however, when changing positions, move as rapidly as possible to a previously selected position, and drop quickly. Make use of all available cover and concealment when moving by creeping and crawling. Running at night should be avoided except in an emergency. Always take advantage of natural sounds to cover up your own movements. Stop frequently (especially at night) and listen for other movement.

THE ATTACK: If possible, get to within six feet of a sentry before attacking him. Following are some effective weapons and techniques of using them:

Club or sand-filled sock - often the only weapon available. With weapon, a blow at the base of the

210

skull will render a man unconscious.

Cord, wire, rope, etc., - can be made into a noose and used to strangle victim. Approach from rear, and while placing noose over his head, kick him behind the knee to knock him off balance. Draw the noose back tightly under his chin with one hand while keeping the other hand on the back of his head, arm stiff. Lower the body to the ground gently, after unconsciousness or death.

Entrenching tools: Keep the cutting edge of entrenching tools extremely sharp. They are good silent weapons and can be used in lieu of a machete. From the rear, give powerful direct blow to small of back, kidney, or (if the sentry is not wearing a helmet) the base of the skull.

Helmet Neck Break: Grasp the front rim of sentries helmet with your right hand. At the same time, place your left forearm against the back of his neck, and place your left hand on his right shoulder. Holding firmly to the front rim of the helmet, pull his helmet up, back and down, and press your left forearm forward. Your left forearm, under the ledge of his helmet, acts as a fulcrum against which his neck is broken. This method is possible only when the sentry's helmet strap is fastened underneath his chin.

Helmet Smash: If you see that the strap is not fastened, or should you discover this when attempting the helmet neck break, silence him with a helmet smash.

Pull the sentries helmet quickly from his head. While doing this, grasp his collar with your other hand, jerking him off balance to his rear. Then smash the helmet to the back of his head or at the back of his neck.

The UDT knife is an effective and silent weapon when used on a victim's kidneys or throat.

HAND TO HAND COMBAT

Hand to hand fighting is a method of combat which utilizes various techneques to disarm, disable or kill one's opponent. It involves:
(a) Making use of any available weapon.
(b) Attacking aggressively by using your maximum strength against your enemy's weakest point.
(c) Maintaining your balance and destroying your opponents balance.
(d) Using your opponent's momentum to your advantage.

Each phase of each technique must be learned precisely before going through the technique rapidly, or using it in actual practice. There are no rules of good sportsmanship in hand to hand combat. It is a fight to the death.

Defense against an attack by an opponent who is armed with a knife.

Countering a downward knife stroke: There are two counters for this type of attack:

Stop the blow by catching his wrist in the pocket formed by bending your fist forward at your right wrist. Step through with your right foot to protect your groin area. At the same time strike him sharply in the crook of his right elbow with the thumb side of your forearm or wrist. This causes his arm to bend. Bring your left hand behind his right forearm and underneath your right wrist, and grasp your right forearm. Bring your elbows close to your body. Bend swiftly from the wrist, putting pressure on your opponents arm. This causes him to fall backward and lose his weapon.

Another defense against the downward stroke of a knife, is to stop the blow by catching your opponent's wrist in the pocket formed at your left wrist by bending your fist forward. Step through with right foot to protect groin. Keep your left forearm level with the ground. At the same time, bring your right hand underneath your opponent's knifearm, and grasp your left fist. Bend swiftly forward from the waist, and put pressure on your opponent's arm. This will cause him to fall backward and lose his weapon.

Countering an upward knife stroke: There are three counters for this type of attack:

Block an upward knife stroke: Catch your opponent's wrist or forearm in the pocket formed at your left wrist by bending your fist forward. Keep elbow low. At the same time, twist your body to the right. As soon as you stop the blow, grasp attacker's right hand with your right hand and place your thumb on back of his hand. Reinforce this hold by grasping his wrist with your left hand and placing your left thumb on back of his hand. Twist his wrist to your left and bend his hand towards his forearm, causing him to fall to the ground.

Another method of defending yourself against an upward knife stroke is to block your opponent's wrist or forearm in a "V" formed by your hands. Keep your arms extended. Take a short crowhop to the rear as you block this thrust, so that your midsection is further from the point of the knife. Grasp your opponent's wrist tightly with both hands, and pivot to your left on the ball of your left foot. At the same time, raise your opponent's knife hand and step directly beneath his arm. From this position, snap his arm forward and downward, bending at the waist and, at the same time drive him to the ground with a whipping action.

A third counter to an upward knife stroke is the same as mentioned above except that you pivot on your right foot, raise his hand and bring his arm down over your left shoulder. Apply downward pressure on his arm. This will throw him to the ground or break his arm. This method can be varied by stepping completely under his arm and behind his back, and forcing him to drop the knife by bending his arm. You must pivot quickly to prevent him from spinning out of the hold.

Countering a backhand knife slash: Defend yourself against a backhand slash with a knife, bend your knees and lower your body without ducking your head. At the same time, raise your right arm and block your opponent's thrust with your forearm or wrist. As soon as you block the blow, grasp your opponent's knife hand with your left hand, your thumb in the center of the back of the hand. Apply pressure with your right wrist against his right wrist or forearm. Start to twist the knife hand to your left, and then reinforce your left hand hold with a similar hold with your right hand. Both your thumbs are now in the center of the back of his hand, and your fingers are around his palm. A twist to your left, or pressure that bends your

opponent's hand forward and under against his wrist causes him to lose his weapon and, in many cases, to suffer a broken or dislocated wrist.

Countering a knife attack when the attacker approaches cautiously: The counter used against an opponent using a cautious approach is one of the hardest of all counters. He will attack with his left foot forward and his left hand extended, to ward off any of your possible blows. He holds his knife hand close to his right hip, ready to strike when an opening occurs. As soon as he comes within reach, spring from the ground, throwing your body at him feet first and twisting to your left. Hook your left instep around his forward ankle and kick his knee with your right foot. Break the force of your fall with your hand or arm. This motion drops him on his back. When both of you strike the ground, raise your right foot and kick his groin or midsection. This is a well trained and well prepared man, and your actions must be perfect.

Defense against a bayonet attack: In a bayonet attack, wait until your opponent has committed himself, and then parry.

Parrying a short thrust: If your opponent attacks you with a short thrust, you can parry in one of two ways:

Twist your body to the left but keep your feet in

place. At the same time, slap your right forearm or wrist against the barrel of his rifle, deflecting the bayonet from your body. As soon as the bayonet has passed your body, grasp your opponent's left hand with your right hand. At the same time, take a long step with your left foot forward toward your opponent's right, reach under the rifle with your left hand and press your left shoulder against the upper handguard. With your left hand, grasp his right hand where it holds the top of the small of the stock. Pull with your left hand and push with your right hand. Keep your weight on your left foot and kick your attacker with the calf of your right leg behind the knee joint of his right leg. Your opponent will fall to the ground and loosen his grip on his rifle.

A second parry against the short thrust is: As your opponent makes his thrust, use the heel of your left hand to parry the bayonet to your right, and sidestep to your left oblique. You are now in position, facing the side of the rifle with your groin area protected by your left leg. With your right hand, palm up, grasp the rifle anywhere on the upper handguard, and with the left hand, palm down, grasp the receiver. Keep a firm hold on the rifle with both hands and step through with your right foot, moving quickly past your right foot, moving quickly past your opponent. Jerk the rifle sharply up and backward in an arc over the attacker's shoulder, and twist it out of his hands. Whirl and smash him with the butt, or attack him with the bayonet.

Parrying a long thrust: There are three parrys to a long thrust:

Parry the bayonet to your left by slapping it with the heel of your right hand, and side step to the right oblique. You are now in a position facing the side of the rifle with your groin area protected by your right leg. With your left hand, palm up, grasp your opponent's left hand and the rifle from underneath. Twist your body to the left in front of your opponent, and place your right leg in front of his body. With the right hand, palm down, grasp your opponent's left hand and rifle from above. Twist the rifle and pull your opponent across your right leg. At the same time, exert pressure with the right elbow against the outside of his left arm and elbow. Sufficient pressure downward with your elbow, while twisting and pulling up on the rifle, can break your opponent's elbow. Continue the twisting motion, pulling your opponent completely across your leg and throwing him to the ground. Regrasp the rifle and follow through with an attack.

The second parry to a long thrust is: Parry your opponent's bayonet to your right with a sharp slapping movement of the heel of your left hand. As you parry with your left hand, move your body to the left oblique, slipping off to your left front with your left foot. You are now in position, facing the rifle from the side with your groin area protected by your left leg. Slap the open palms of both hands down on the rifle near the muzzle, driving the point of the bayonet into the ground. Do not follow the rifle all the way to the ground, but allow your opponent's momentum to imbed the bayonet into the ground. Grasp the butt of the rifle with your left hand and with the right hand grasp your opponent anywhere on his back or head. To completely disarm him, drive the stock of the rifle into your opponent's body and at the same time, pull him with your right hand, spinning him to the ground. You are now in a position to recover the rifle and attack him.

The third method of parrying a long thrust is essentially the same as the second, except that you parry left instead of right. As you parry, step to your right front with your right foot. Make the same movement as described in the second method of parry. Use the open palms of both hands and drive the bayonet into the ground. It may be difficult to reach across your opponent's body to grasp the butt of the rifle. Therefore, grasp his clothing with both hands and pull him forward, throwing him to the ground. Grasp the rifle and attack.

Disarming an opponent armed with a rifle but no bayonet: In disarming an opponent armed with a rifle and no bayonet, make each movement quickly and without hesitation. Although your opponent has the weapon, you are in a good position, because you know what you are going to do (whereas he has to react to your movement). Although his reaction time is short, it is not as short as the time it takes you to act.

Countering a challenge from the front: At your opponent's order of "hands up", bring your hands to shoulder level. Then, in one motion, twist your body to your right and strike the muzzle of the rifle away from your body with your left forearm or wrist. As you strike the muzzle, step forward with your left foot. Grasp the upper hand guard with your right hand and the small of the stock with your left hand. Pull with your left and push with your right, and step to your opponent's right with your own right foot. This knocks him off balance and at the same time, enables you to strike him on the head with the muzzle of the rifle, or to take the rifle from him by twisting it over his right shoulder.

Countering a challenge from the rear: When your opponent has his rifle in your back, start to elevate your hands as ordered. When your hands reach shoulder height, twist from the hips to your right and bring your right elbow back, striking the muzzle of the rifle. This deflects the rifle away from your body. Do not as yet move your feet from their original position. Turn to the rear by pivoting on your right foot. Face your opponent and bring your right arm under the rifle and over your opponent's left wrist. Place your left hand on your opponent's right hand where it grasps the stock. This prevents him from executing a butt stroke. Pull with your left hand and push with your right shoulder and arm, forcing your opponent to the ground and making him release his grip on the rifle.

Disarming an opponent armed with a pistol:

Countering a challenge from the front: Your opponent orders you to raise your "hand". As you do so, keep your elbows as low as possible, twist your body to the right, and strike your opponent's wrist with your left forearm. Grasp the bottom of the barrel with your right hand, making certain that your hand is not near the muzzle. At the same time, strike downward on your opponent's wrist with your left fist. When applying pressure with your left fist, bend the pistol towards your opponent's body with your right hand, causing him to release his grip. If he should retain his grip, his index finger will be broken. From

this position, you can strike your opponent on his temple with the butt of the pistol.

Countering a challenge from the rear: When your opponent is holding pistol in his right hand, against your back: This counter should be used only when you are certain that the pistol is in your opponent's right hand. As you raise your hands, keep your elbows as close to the waist as possible. Twist your body to the right, and, at the same time, bring your right elbow against your opponent's forearm. Keep your feet in place. Bring your right arm under your opponent's right forearm and place it on his elbow joint, so that his forearm rests in the crook of your right elbow. Grasp your right hand with your left hand, and bend swiftly from the waist. By doing this, you force your opponent to the ground and cause him to drop his weapon.

When your opponent is holding pistol in his right hand, against the back of your neck: In raising your arms bring your elbows shoulder high. Twist your body to the left and bring your left arm under your opponent's right elbow. Reach across with your right hand, and grasp your own left hand. Twist forward and put pressure on your opponent's elbow with your left forearm. You can now either break his arm, or force him to the ground, causing him to release his weapon.

When your opponent is holding a pistol in either hand, against your back: Twist your body to the right, striking your right elbow against your opponent's hand or wrist. Pivot to the right and place your left wrist against your opponent's pistol wrist, grasping the pistol barrel with your right hand, palm up. Apply pressure to his hand and trigger finger by pushing the barrel toward his upper arm. This releases his hold on the pistol and may break his index finger. You now have the pistol in your right hand, opposite your left shoulder. By twisting forcefully to the right, you can strike your opponent on the chin or neck with the butt of the pistol.

PT Exercises

Following is a list of PT exercises most commonly done by UDT:
GENERAL WARMUP:
Full jumping jacks
Half jumping jacks
Side twister stretcher
Trunk rotation
Trunk bending fore and aft
Trunk twister
Windmill 4 count
Windmill 2 count
Trunk side stretcher
Rocking chair
EXERCISES FOR STRENGTH
(a) Abdominal
Regulations set ups
Hand and toe sit-ups
Cherry picker
Stomach flutter kicks
Sitting flutter kicks
Back roller
Stomach Stretcher
Setting knee bends
Leg levers
Leg thrust
(b) Side and Oblique
Thigh flexing shoulders secured
Back flexing legs secured
Side flexing legs secured
Sitting back bends
Side snapper
Judo trunk rotation
(c) Legs and groin
Knee bends 4 count
Knee bends 2 count
Squat thrust
Leg stretcher
Thigh stretcher
Groin stretcher 4 count
Groin stretcher 2 count
Calf stretcher
One leg sit-ups
Bend and reach
Squat stretch
Good morning darling
(d) Arms, Chest, and Shoulders
Spread eagle
Deep breather
Eight count body builder
Neck rotation
Push-ups
Press, press fling up, back and over
(e) Endurance
Running
Swimming
(f) Agility and Coordination
Obstacle course
Sports

APPENDIX I

selected weights and measurements

3 ft = 1 yard
5,280 ft = 1 Statute mile

9 square ft = 1 square yard
43,560 square ft = 1 acre
640 acres = 1 square mile

16.387 Cubic Centimeters = 1 Cubic inch

6 ft = 1 fathom = 1.829 Meters
60 Nautical Miles = 1 degree of a great circle of the earth

60 seconds = 1 minute
60 minutes = 1 hour
90 degrees = 1 Quadrant or 1 right angle
1 circle = 4 quadrants or 360 degrees

Dry Measure: 1 pint = 33.60 cubic inch = 0.5505 liter
Liquid measure: 2 pints = 1 quart = 57.75 cubic inch = .9463 liter

16 ounces = 1 pound = 453.59 grams
2000 pounds = 1 ton = 907.18 kilograms

APPENDIX II

techniques of instructing

STAGES OF INSTRUCTION
    Preparation
        (a) Estimate the training situation
        (b) Select and organize subject matter
        (c) Make lesson plan
        (d) Rehearse the lesson
        (e) Make final check
    Presentation
        (a) Lecture
        (b) Conference
        (c) Demonstration
    Application
        (a) Individual performance
            (1) Supervised individual performance
            (2) Group performance
            (3) Coach and pupil method
        (b) Team performance
    Examination
        (a) Oral tests
        (b) Written tests
        (c) Performance
        (d) Observation
    Discussion or Critique
        (a) Sum up and clarify the lesson
        (b) Reemphasize important points
        (c) Correct errors made during application and examination stages

---

LESSON PLAN FORMAT
Title of Lesson:
Day and Date:
Hours:
Place:
Class:
Instructor:
Assistants:
Uniform and Equipment:
References:
Training Aids:
Transportation:
(1) Presentation: (state method and time required)
    (a) Introduction: (time required)
        (1) Objectives (what will be presented)
        (2) Reasons (why it is important)
        (3) Standards (minimum student will be expected to learn)
    Explanation and/or demonstration (time required)
        (1) Main Point
        (2) Outline in proper form. Do not use paragraphs.
    Second main point
        (1) Outline in proper form
        (2) Continue breaking subjects into three or four main points and as many subdivisions as necessary.
    Summary
        (1) Review main points
        (2) Stress important items that are difficult under each main point.
    Application: (state method and time required)
        (1) Outline a detail what your going to do.
            (a) Arrangement of students and equipment
            (b) Detailed instruction
        (2) Supervision and assistance which will be rendered (plan of conduct)
    Examination: (state method and time required)
        (1) If written, attach a copy
        (2) If oral, write questions in your lesson plan
        (3) If observation, describe what you

will do
(4) If performance, outline plan of examination

Review or Critique: (state method and time required)
(1) Clarify points of difficulty
(2) Summarize the lesson
(3) Reemphasize important points (safety precautions)
(4) Strong closing statement - write out in detail

APPENDIX·III

application and qualifications for UDT

GENERAL: The first step in becomming a UDT man is the easy one: Volunteer. If your are highly motivated and can meet the requirements, your acceptance will be almost automatic.

You may apply for UDT Training through your fleet commander or, if you are an officer, the Bureau of Naval Personnel. Specific requirements vary, depending upon where your request will go, but the basic prerequisites are the same regardless: Your commanding officer must feel you are motivated, and you must prove you have the strength and stamina to cut the mustard.

Here is a breakdown of requirements by fleet and, for officers according to BUPERS.

Officers: As an officer applying for the UDT program you must:
Be in code 110X or 6XXX
Be less than 31 years of age
LDOs must have significant diving, EOD, or UDT experience as offcers or enlisted men.

(For more information concerning the BUPERS requirements for officer volunteers, see Article C-7305 of the BUPERS Manual.)

If you meet the above standards, your training officer will assist you to prepare your request. Your CO will endorse your letter and recommend approval or disapproval.

Enlisted: (Atlantic Fleet): As an enlisted applicant you must:
Be between the ages of 18 and 31, in any rate or rating.
Have no history as a chronic mast offender.
Have no history of claustrophobia or motion sickness.
Have no excessive fear of water or explosives.
Have demonstrated maturity and emotional stability by past personal performance

Have the apparent ability to maintain composure under adverse circumstances.
Pass a swimming and running test. In the presence of a commissioned officer you must run one and one half miles in 15 minutes or less, and swim 300 yards, using backstroke and sidestroke in nine minutes or less, with no rest periods.
Have a GCT of 45 or higher.
Have at least 30 months' obligated service when you report for training.
State in your application that you understand the nature of UDT duty and that your immediate family has agreed to make no objection to your assignment to such a billet.

(For more information concerning the Atlantic Fleet requirements for enlisted men, see EPDOLANT INST 1510.2B)

Pacific Fleet: If you are an enlisted applicant you must:
Be at least 19 years old and of mature disposition.
Be screened to determine loyalty and integrity for access to classified papers and information.
Have no record as a chronic mast offender.
Have no history of claustrophobia or motion sickness.
Have no excessive fear of water or explosives.
Have a GCT of 45 or higher.
Have a minimum of 28 months' obligated service upon reporting for UDT Training.
Successfully complete a swimming test. Current instructions require you to swim 100 yards using the backstroke, 100 yards using the breaststroke, and 100 yards using the sidestroke. You may have rest periods between the three examinations, but you must swimm all three examinations on the same day and in a total time (disregarding rest periods) of 11 minutes or less.

(For more information concerning the Pacific Fleet requirements for enlisted men, see CINCPACFLTINST 1510.4A)

APPENDIX IV
seabag checklist

MINIMUM OUTFIT: The minimum outfit of articles of uniform and accesories prescribed for enlisted men, other than chief petty officers of the Regular Navy, is as follows:

ITEM	QUANITY
Belts:	
Black	1
White	1
Caps:	
Blue working	1
Service, blue	1
Watch	1
Clothes stops:	3 pkg.[1]
Drawers:	6 pr.
Gloves, black:	1 pr.
Hat, white:	4
Insignia:	as required
Jacket, blue working	1
Jumpers:	
Blue, dress	1
Blue, undress	2
White, undress	4
Neckerchief:	1
Peacoat:	1
Raincoat, blue:	1
Seabag:	1
Shirt, blue chambray:	3
Shoes:	
Black dress	2 pr.
Black, service	1 pr.
Gymnasium	1 pr.[2]
Socks, black:	8 pr.
Sweater, blue:	1
Towel, Bath:	
Large	2
Small	2 [2]
Trousers:	
Blue	3 pr.
Dungaree	3 pr.
White	4 pr.
Trunks, swim:	1 pr.
Undershirt:	6

[1] Optional after completion of recruit training at the discretion of local commanding officer.

[2] Will be replaced by the large towel when present stocks are exhausted.

The following articles of the uniform are optional:
  Belt, khaki
  Gloves: Blue, working
  Helmets, Tropical: Khaki, White
  Lanyard, white
  Overshoes
  Scarf, blue
  Shirt, white tropical
  Shorts, Tropical: Khaki, White

APPENDIX V
warbag checklist

The following Warbag equipment shall be in the posission of every member of UDT. It shall be "ready to go" at all times:

ITEM	QUANTITY
Bag, Duffel:	1
Belt, webb:	1
Cap, Utility:	1
Cylinder, CO_2:	3
Fins, swim, duck:	1 pr.
Jacket, Life, UDT:	1
Jacket, Olive Green:	3
Jacket, Winter N1:	1
Jersey, Athletic:	1
Knife & Sheath:	1
Lead & Line:	1
Mask, swim:	1
Shoes, field:	1 pr.
Shoes, swim coral:	1 pr.
Shirt, utility:	1
Slate, swimmers:	1
Supporter, Athletic:	1
Trousers, olive green:	3
Trunks, swim:	2
Thermo lite socks:	1 pr.
Wet suit complete:	1

APPENDIX·VI
UDT requalifications

DIVING: (REF: BUPERS MANUAL, ART. C-7408. For diving pay regulations, see NAVCOMPT MANUAL, VOL., IV, CHAPTER 4, PARA 044055). UDT divers are qualified for six month periods, by completing the below listed dives. When the dives are conducted within the period of qualification, the diver will be considered qualified for another six month period, beginning on the date his qualification would have lapsed. If a diver's qualification has lapsed, he will be considered requalified if the below listed dives are conducted within one year of the date on which his qualification has lapsed:

TYPE DIVE	MIN. DEPTH OR DIST.
DAY:	
Two	120 feet (10 min. bottom time)
Two SCUBA swims on compass course	One 1,000 yards One 1,500 yards
NIGHT:	
Two SCUBA swims on compass course	One 1,000 yards One 1,500 yards

PARACHUTING: (REF: BUPERS MAN., ART. C-7405. For parachute pay regulations, see NAVY COMPT MAN., VOL. IV, CHAP. 4, PARA 044110). A parachutist will not be considered to be on parachuting duty if he fails to perform one or more jumps during any three consecutive calendar months. If he is prevented from doing this by circumstances beyond his control, he may meet the requirements by performing four jumps during a period of 12 consecutive months, and such requirement may be met at any time during the period.

DEMOLITIONS: The NAVCOMPT Man., Vol IV, Chap. 4, paragraph 044112 outlines demolition requirements for purposes of pay. BUPERS Man (Art. A-4303) defines "duty involving the demolition of explosives" as duty involving proficiency training (involving live explosives) for the maintenance of skill in demolishing (by use of explosives) underwater objects, obstacles or explosives.

INDEX

A

Absolute pressure, 94
AE (air embolism), 102
Accessories
   compressor, 87
Advance Demolitions, 50
Airborne Training
   Qualifications, 169
Air compressors, 87
   Procedures, 88
   Safety, 87
Aircraft Inspection, 160
Air Embolism, 102
Amatol, 80120, 30
Ammonium Nitrate, 32
   Specifications, 39
Angles, G-M, 155
Anoxia, 103
AN/PQS-1B (hand held sonar), 121
   Active mode, 123
   Listen mode, 123
   Maintenance, 123
   Operating Instr. 122
   Preparation, 122
   Specifications, 124
AN/PRC-6 Radio, 112
   Maintenance, 113
   Operating Instr. 112
   Specifications, 112
AN/PRC 8, 9 and 10 Radio, 113
   Maintenance, 116
   Operating Instr. 114
   Specifications, 114
Aqua-master regulator, 65
AR-15, 190
Artifical Respriration, 127
Ascent Problems, 102
Atmospheric pressure, 94
Aximuths, 155

B

Bangalor torpedoes
   Coral blasting, 48
   Specifications, 39
Barometric pressure, 94
Barotra UMA, 99
BDP, 208
Beach Defense Perimeter, 208
Beach Gradient, 144
Beach Profiles, 143
Beach Report Format, 146
Beach Survey, Photo Data
   Reports, 140
Beach Terminology, 148
Bends, 103
Big Dipper, 175
Blackout, 104
Black Powder, Improvised, 52
Blasting Cap, 37
   Electric, 37
   Delay, 38
   Improvised, 52
Blasting, coral, 48
Block Demolition, M5A1, 41
Blood, 97
Boat Crew, Diving
   Responsibilities, 60
Booby Traps, 195, 196, 197
Boyle's Law, 95
Breaching Walls, 45
Breaker, Type of, 148
Breath holding, 98
Bridges, charge placement, 47
Bridge stringers,
   pressure charge, 45
Brief, UDT, 200
Buddy line, 78
   System, 56

C

Cable and Chain Cutter
   MK 1 MOD 0, 41
   MK 3 MOD 1, 42
C-4 use in improvised, 52
Caisson's, 103
Caculation, fuse length, 36
Calypso,
   Camera, 139
   Regulator, 64
Cap, blasting, delay, 38
   Non-electric, 37
   Specifications, 37
Carbon Dioxide
   In respiration, 98
   Poisoning, 104
Carbon Monoxide Poisoning, 104
Catographer, 137, 138
C-4 Block Demolition, M5A1, 41
C-4, 32
Chamber
   Decompression, 105
   Recompression, 105
   Locations, 58
Chain Cutter, MK 1 MOD 0, 41
Charge Assembly, MK 135, 45
Charge Assembly,
   MK 133, MOD 0 and 2, 44
Charge,
   Diamond, 51
   Ear-muff, 51
   Estimation and Placement, 45
Charge, MK 2, MOD 2 and 3, 44
Charge Placement, 45
   Bridges, 47
   Obstacles, 46
Charge ribbon, 51
Charge saddle, 50
Charle's Law, 95
Chartmaking, 141
   Steps for construction, 141
Checklist, Diving Supervisor, 60
   OIC of Diving Operation, 59
   Recompression Chamber, 107
Circle Search, 207
Circulatory System, 96
Closed Circuit, 66
Cylinder Valve Assembly, 62
   Open Circuit
Code, Morse, 27
Cold Weather Demolition, 50
Collisions, and Entanglements,
   Para. Ops., 166
Combat, hand to hand, 211
Compass Asimuths, 155
Compass Course, 156
Compass, MK 1 MOD 0, 78
Composition band B-2, 32
Composition C-4, 32
Composition C-3, 32
Compressed Gas, Safety, 91
Compressors, 87
Contours, 158
Conversion,
   Relative Effectiveness, 45
Convulsions, 105
Cooking, survival, 173
Coral blasting, 48
Coral shoes, 78
Corpsman, Diving
   Responsibilities, 59
CO^2 Inflatable Boat, 16
C-2, 32
Current Tables, 151
Cutter, Cable and Chain
   MK 1 MOD 0, 41
Cutter, Cable
   MK 3, MOD 1, 42
Cyclonite (RDX), 33

D

Daltons' Law, 95
Datum Line, 141
Day Combat Recon. 132, 134
"DEADMAN", 137
Decompression Chamber, 105
Decompression Tables, 106
Delay, Blasting Cap, 38
Demolishing Walls, 45
Demolition, Cold Weather, 50
Demolition, improvised, 52
Demolitions, 30
   Advanced, 50
   Firing, 30
   Safety Precautions, 30
   Stowage, 30
   Trucking, 30
Demo Raid, Inland, 209
Depth Gauge, 79
Depth Limits, 02, 69

219

INDEX

Depth Time, MK VI, 74
Diamond Charge, 51
Diseases
    Closed Circuit, 69
    Decompression, 103
    Diving, 99
Diving, 56
    Accessories, 78
    Barge, 58
    Department responsibilities, 57
    Diseases, 99
    Operation, 56
    Emergency Procedures, 85
    Procedures, MK VI, 73
    Responsibilities, 57
    Responsibilities, Boat Crew, 60
    Responsibilities, Corpsman, 59
    Responsibilities, Divers, 60
    Responsibilities, Diving
        Supervisor, 58
    Responsibilities, Doctor, 60
    Responsibilities, OIC, 57
    Responsibilities, Stand-by
        Diver, 59
    Responsibilities, Tender, 60
    Responsibilities, Timekeeper, 60
    Safety Precautions, 86
    Signals, 57
    Supervisor, 58
    Supervisor Checklist, 60
Division Recon, 11
Doctor, Diving Responsibilities, 60
Drop and Pickup, 201
Drop, IBS, 202
Drowning, 105

E

Ear, 100
Ear-muff Charge, 51
Ear, Squeeze, 99
80/20 Amatol, 32
Eight Enemies of Survival, 172
Electric, Blasting Cap, 37
Electronic, 112
Emergency Landings, Para Ops, 167
Emergency Procedures, Open Circuit, 62
Emergency Signalling, 175
Emergency Diving Procedures, 85
Emerson,
    Closed Circuit, 65
    Parts Breakdown, 66
    Emergency Procedures, 70
    Preparation, 69
    Preventative Maintenance, 68
    Resuscitator, 109
Emergency Withdrawl, BDP, 208
Emergency Procedure, MK VI, 74
Emphysema, 102
Equipment Check, Para Ops, 161, 163
Escape and Evasion, 178
Escape and Evasion, Jungle, 178
Escape Trunk, 205
Estimation, Charge, 45
Eustachian Tube, 100
Exercises, Physical Training, 215
Explosive Materials, 35
Explosive Packages, 39

Explosives, Types, 32
Exposure Suit, 79

F

Facemask, 79
Face Squeeze, 100
Finding Direction without Compass 175
Fins, 80
First Aid, 126
Fishing, Survival, 173
Five Points of Performance, 165
Flare, MK 13 MOD 0, 80
Flare, Very Pistol, 80
Flexible Linear Charge, 43
Float, 81
Flutterboard, 138
Flutterboard Line, 138
Force Recon., 11
Food, Jungle Survival, 177
Food, Survival, 173
Fulton Drop and Pickup, 201
Fuze, Improvised, 52
Fuse Length Caculations, 36
Fuse, Safety, 36

G

Gas Laws, 95
Gas Laws, Application, 96
Gas Splitting and Mixing, 75
Gauge, Depth, 79
Gauge, Pressure, 94
G-M Angle, 155
Grenades, 192
Grenade Throwing, 193
Grenades, Types, 193
Grid Coordinates, 157

H

Hand Grenades, 193
Hand Operated Transfer Pump, 90
Hand Operated Transfer Pump
    Operating Instructions, 90
Hand to Hand Combat, 211
HBX-3, 32
Health, Survival, 177
Heart, 97
Helo Drop & Pick-up, 202
Henry's Law, 95
History, of UDT, 11
Hook-up, IBS, 202
Hunting, Survival, 173
Hyperventilation, 98

I

IBS Towing, 202
Improvised Demolition, 52
IBS, Motor (Outboard), 17
    Maintenance, 18
    Operations, 17
    Specifications, 18
IBS, Patching, 16
IBS, 16
IBS, Specifications, 16
IBS Recon, 137
Inflatable Boat, Small, 16
Inland Demo. Raid, 209
Intelligence, 132
International Morse Code, 27

Intersection, 157
Intestinal Pains, 102

J·K

Jack Stay Search, 207
Jump Commands, 162
Jump Master, 160
Jump Master Duties, 160, 161
Jump Master Qualifications, 168
Jungle Survival, 177
Knife, 81
K-38, 191

L

Landing Craft Personnel
    Launch, MK-4, 20
Landing Craft Personnel
    Launch, MK 11, 21
Landing Craft Personnel
    Ramp, 20
Landing Craft Swimmer
    Reconnaissance, 21
Laws, Gas, 95
LCPL, MK-4, 20
    Specifications, 20
LCPL, MK-11, 21
    Specifications, 21
LCPR, 20
    Specifications, 20
LCSR, 21
    Specifications, 21
Lifejacket, 81
Lifejacket, Inspection, 82
    Repair, 82
Life-saver Steps, 126
Light, Single Cell, 83
Limpeteer Attack, 204
Liquid Pressure, 94
Lockout/Lockin, 206
Lungs, 97
Lung Capacity, 98
Lung Squeeze, 100

M

Map Asimuths, 155
Map Orientation, 154
Map Reading, 154
Maintenance, Look Under Name
    Of The Equipment
Malfunctions, Para. Ops., 166
Marines, 11
Marine, Force Recon, 11
Mask, Face, 79
Mediastinal Emphysema, 102
Metabolism, 96
Miscellaneous Operations, 200
M5A1, Block Demolition, 41
MK 1 MOD 0, Cable and Chain
    Cutter, 41
MK 1 MOD 0, Compass, 78
MK 2 MOD 2 and 3, 55 Pound
    Demolition Charge, 42
MK 3 MOD 1, Cable Cutter, 42
MK VI, Depth Time, 74
MK VI, Emergency Procedures, 74
MK VI, Semi-Closed, 71
MK VI, Semi-Closed, Description
    of, 72

INDEX

MK VI, Semi-Closed Diving Procedures, 73
MK 8 MOD 2, Flexible Linear Demolition Charge, 43
MK 13 MOD 0, Flare, 80
MK 133 MOD 0 and 2, Demolition Charge Assembly, 44
MK 135 MOD 0 and 2, Demolition Charge Assembly, 44
Morse Code, 27
Motor, IBS, 17
M-3, Shape Charge, 40
M-3, Submachine Gun, 191
M2A3, Shape Charge, 40

N·O

Narcosis, Nitrogen, 103
Native Assistance, Survival, 179
Night Combat Recon., 135
Nitrogen Narcosis, 103
Non-Electric, Blasting Cap, 37
NAVOPSUPPGRU Diving Barge, 58
North, Finding, 175
North Star, 175

O_2 Depth Limits, 69
Obstacles, Charge Placement, 46
Obstacles, Felling Trees, 45
OinC, Checklist on a Dive, 59
OinC, Diving Operations, 57
Open Circuit, 61
Open Circuit, Cylinder Valve Assembly, 62
Open Circuit, Emergency Procedures, 62
Open Circuit, Operating Procedures, 61
Operating Procedures
  See Particular Equipment
Operation, Diving, 56
Operations, Miscellaneous, 200
Outboard Motor, IBS, 17
Oxygen Poison, 103
Oxygen Transfer Pump, 89
Oxygen Transfer Pump Operating Instructions, 89

P

Parallel Admin. Recon., 133
Parachute Inspection, 161
Parachute Operations, 160
Panoramas, 139
Parachute Operations, Malfunctions,
Parts Breakdown   166
  Aqua-Master, 65
  Calypso, 64
  Emerson, 65
Patching, IBS, 16
Pen Sizes for UDT Chart, 145
Pentolite, 33
PETN, 33
Perpendicular Admin. Recon., 137
Pistol, Very, 80
Phonetic Alphabet, 24
Phonetic Numbers, 24
Photo Data Reports, 140
Photo Data Sheets, 140
Photography, 139
Physics, Underwater, 94
Physiology, Underwater, 96
Placement, Charge, 45

Placement, Charge
  Bridges, 47
  Obstacles, 46
PLF, 165
Pneumothorax, 102
Poison, Carbon Dioxide, 104
Poison, Carbon Monoxide, 104
Poison, Oxygen, 103
Post Jump Critque, 162
Post Recon, Questionnaire, 133
Pressure Charge, for Bridge Stringer, 45
PRC-6, AN, Radio, 112
PRC-8, 9, and 10, AN, Radio, 113
Pre-Jump Briefing, 160
Pressure, Various Types, 94
Primacord, Reinforced, 35
Primacord, Wirebound, 35
Prosigns, 25
Prowords, 25
PT Exercises, 215
Pump, Hand Operated Transfer, 90
Pump, Oxygen Transfer, 89

R

Radio, AN/PRC-6, 112
Radio, AN/PRC-8, 9, and 10, 113
Radiologically Hazardous Equipment, 84
Radio Voice Procedures, 24
Radio, URC-17 and 17A, 116
Radio Voice Procedure, BDP, 208
Recompression Chamber, 105
Recompression Chamber Check-List, 107
Recompression Chamber, Operating Instructions, 108
Recompression Chamber, Precautions, 107
Reference Points, 143
Recon
  Day Combat, 132, 134
  IBS, 132, 137
  Parallel Admin., 133, 136
  Perpendicular Admin., 132, 137
  Submerged, 138
Reconnaissance Techniques, 132
Regulator, Aqua-Master, 65
Regulator, Calypso, 64
Regulator, Two Hose, 63
Reinforced Primacord, 35
  Specifications, 35
Relative Effectiveness Conversion, 45
Resection, 156
Residual Volume, 98
Resuscitator, Respiration, 96
Resuscitator, 109
Resuscitator, Operating Instructions, 109
RDX (Cyclonite), 33
Ribbon Charge, 51
Rules of Open Circuit, 62

S

Saddle Charge, 50
Safety, Air Compressor, 87
Safety, Compressed Gas, 91
Safety, Diving Precautions, 86
Safety Fuse, 36
  Specifications, 36
Safety Precautions, Demolition, 30

Safety Precautions, Diving, 56
Safety Requirements Para Ops., 162
Safety, SDV, 182
Scuba, Open Circuit, 61
Scuba, Open Circuit, Operating Procedures, 61
SDV's, 182
SDV, Safety, 182
Sea Horse II, 183
Searches, Underwater, 207
Self Location, 156
Semaphore, 27
Semi-Closed Circuit, 71
Semi-Closed Dive Preparation, 73
Sentry Stalking, 209
Shelter, Jungle Survival, 178
Shoes, Coral, 78
Shape Charge, 15 Pounds, M2A3, 40
  Specifications, 40
Shape Charge, Improvised, 52
Shape Charge, M-3, 40
  Specifications, 40
Simultaneous Drop, 204
Single Cell Light, 83
Sinus, 101
Sinus Squeeze, 101
Slate, 83
Small Arms, 190
Snorkel, 83
Sonar, Hand Held, 121
Specifications of Equipment
  Look Under the Name of the Equipment
Splice, Western Union, 38
Southern Cross, 175
Squeeze (Barotra UMA), 99
Squeeze, Ear, 99
Squeeze, Face, 100
Squeeze, Lung, 100
Squeeze, Sinus, 101
Squeeze, Suit, 101
SRS, 20
Stalking Sentry, 209
Stand-by Diver, 59
Stomach Pains, 102
Stowage, Radiologically Hazardous Equipment, 84

Structural Steel, Cutting, 45
  With Explosives, 45
Subcuteaus Emphysema, 102
Submachine Gun, 191
Sub Ops, 205
Submerged Recon., 138
Suit, Exposure, 79
Suit, Squeeze, 101
SUROB Report, 147
SUROB, Sample, 147
Survival, 172
Survival, Food, 173
Survival, Jungle, 177
Survival Kit, 179
Swim Fins, 80

INDEX

Swimmer Delivery Vehicles, 182
   (See also SDV)
Swimmer Recovery Sled, 20
Swimmer's Slate, 132
S&W, K-38, 191

T

Tables Decompression, 106
Tender, 60
Tender Line, 84
Swimmer Tow Search, 207
Templates for UDT Charts, 145
Terminology, Beach, 148
Terminology, Tide, 150
Tetryl, 34
Tetrytol, 34
Thermite, Improvised, 52
Tidal Volume, 98
Tide Tables, 151
Tide, Terminology, 150
Timber, Cutting with Explosives, 145
Timekeeper, Diving Responsibilities, 60
T-10, 168
Transporting, SDV, 182
Traps and Snares, Survival, 173
TRASS III, 185
Travel Hints, Survival, 176
TNT - Half Pound Blocks, 43
TNT - One Pound Blocks, 43
Torpedo, Bangalore, 39
Torpedoes, Bangalore, Coral Blasting, 48
Transfer Pump, Oxygen, 89
Trinitrotoluene, 34
TNT, 34
Towing, IBS, 202
Tube, Eustachian, 100
Two Hose Regulator, 63

U

UDT Admin. Organization, 11
UDT Brief, 200
UDT Chart, Check-Off List, 145
UDT Demolition Raid, Inland, 209
UDT, History, 12
UDT, Warning Order, 200
Underwater Physics, 94
Underwater Physiology, 96
Underwater Search, 207
URC-17 and 17A, Radio
   Operating Instructions, 116
   Specifications, 116
   Troubleshooting, 117
   Tube Check, 118
UTEL, 118
   Maintenance, 121
   Operating Instructions, 118
   Pre-Dive Check, 120
   Specifications, 118

V-W

Vaseline, Used Improvised, 52
Very Postol, 80
Walls Breaching, 45
Walls Demolishing, 45

Warning Order, UDT, 200
Water, Jungle Survival, 175
Water, Sirvival, 175
Weapons, 190
Weather, Cold Demolitions, 50
"WEST-EAST" Stick - 175
Western Unit Splice, 38
Whistle, 84
Wirebound Primacord, 35
   Specifications, 35
Wristwatch, 84

credits

PROJECT EDITOR
   T. Dunne, LTJG., USNR

ASSISTANT PROJECT EDITORS
   W. B. Humes, PTC, USN
   N. L. Dufault, YN1, USN

LAYOUT, DESIGN, AND ILLUSTRATIONS
   G. A. Sougstad, LTJG., USNR, Director
   J. P. House, QM3, USN
   W. L. Book, DM3, USN
   J. H. Wendorf, CN, USNR

TYPIST
   N. L. Dufault, YN1, USN
   R. E. Grooms, YN3, USN
   W. F. Gould, SN, USN

CONTRIBUTING EDITORS
- BOATS — J. B. Batton, LT., USN
- ELECTRONICS/COMMUNICATIONS — B. J. Pester, LTJG., USNR
  - L. C. Burger, ETC, USN
- DEMOLITIONS/WEAPONS — P. Witter, LTJG., USNR
  - J. L. Hutchins, GMGC, USN
- DIVING — C. E. Dorman, LTJG., USNR
  - H. M. Ruth, ENC, USN
- FIRST AID — W. L. Dewey, LCDR, (MC), USNR
  - E. M. Baldassare, HMC, USN
- INTELLIGENCE — M. M. Hammond, LTJG., USNR
  - G. H. Mackin, LTJG., USNR
  - L. G. Boyles, SM1, USN
- MAP READING — E. L. Dunn, DCC, USN
  - W. E. Raschick, EA1, USN
- PARACHUTE OPERATIONS — J. H. McGee, LT., USN
- SURVIVAL — J. F. Callahan, LT., USN
- SWIMMER DELIVERY VEHICLES — D. F. Rose, ENCS, USN
- OPERATIONS AND TECHNIQUES — R. S. Bioren, LTJG., USNR

PHOTOGRAPHY
   H. L. Rautio, PH2, USN
   D. P. Maury, PH2, USN

TECHNICAL ASSISTANTS
   Mrs. Vera Del Giudice
   D. Johnson, LT., USNR
   J. R. Perkins, PH1, USN
   N. T. Spark

COLOPHON:
   Text is IBM EXECUTIVE CODE 79
        ROYAL MANIFOLD ELITE, SINGLE GOTHIC
   Headings and titles are:
        FORMATT 5182, 5183, and 5184
        DECA-DRY 1916 and 1912
   The entire reduced 33 1/3%

ALSO NOW AVAILABLE
WWW.PERISCOPEFILM.COM

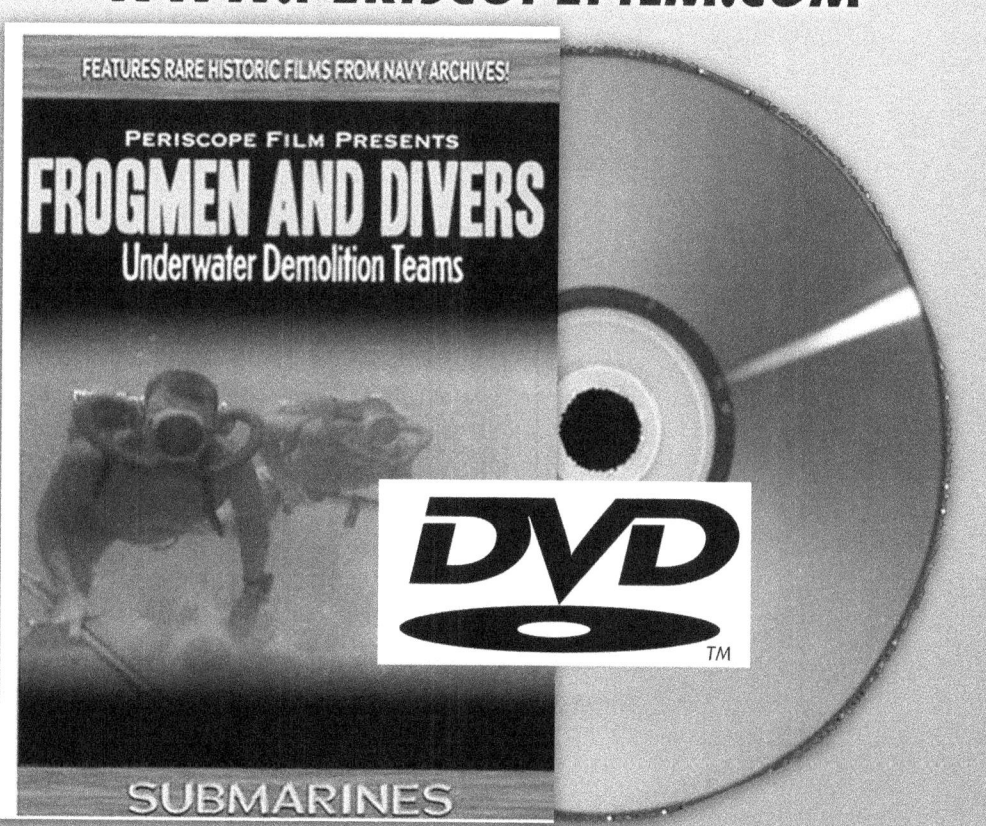

©2011 Periscope Film LLC
All rights Reserved
ISBN #978-1-937684-82-2
www.PeriscopeFilm.com

www.ingramcontent.com/pod-product-compliance
Lightning Source LLC
Chambersburg PA
CBHW080400170426
43193CB00016B/2770